Richthofen
BEYOND THE LEGEND
OF THE RED BARON

Also by Peter Kilduff:

THE RED BARON   THAT'S MY BLOODY PLANE

GERMANY'S LAST KNIGHT OF THE AIR

U.S. CARRIERS AT WAR   A-4 SKYHAWK

GERMANY'S FIRST AIR FORCE 1914–1918

Richthofen
BEYOND THE LEGEND
OF THE RED BARON

PETER KILDUFF

ARMS AND
ARMOUR

*This book is dedicated to my friend and colleague
Neal O'Connor, with appreciation for his encouragement
and help with many World War I history projects*

Arms and Armour Press
An imprint of the Cassell Group
Wellington House, 125 Strand, London WC2R 0BB

Distributed in Australia by Capricorn Link (Australia) Pty. Ltd.,
2/13 Carrington Road, Castle Hill, NSW 2154

First Published 1994
This paperback edition 1995

British Library Cataloguing-in-Publication Data: a catalogue record
for this book is available from the British Library

ISBN 1-85409-304-5

Cartography by Peter Burton

Designed and edited by DAG Publications Ltd.
Designed by David Gibbons; edited by Philip Jarrett;
printed and bound in Great Britain by Hartnolls Limited, Bodmin, Cornwall

CONTENTS

INTRODUCTION

Manfred *Freiherr* von Richthofen was a proficient hunter who transferred his skills to the most dangerous hunting ground of all: the battlefield. Like his mentor, the 40-victory German fighter ace Oswald Boelcke, Richthofen was an avid sportsman who responded to the challenge of competition. He was especially devoted to marksmanship, and gloried in the thrill of the hunt and the triumph of the kill, both in the forest and in the air. *Freiherr* von Richthofen himself noted the intertwining of his blood sport talents in describing his feelings while hunting the rare European bison on a prince's estate in Silesia in late May 1917:

> ... suddenly I saw, in the high timber, a giant black monster trundling along straight toward me. I saw this even before the forester, got ready to shoot and, I must say, I had hunting fever. It was a mighty bull. At 250 paces away, he sniffed the air for a moment. I was too far away to shoot. Perhaps I would have hit the monster, as one generally does not miss something so gigantic ... He probably noticed the drivers, for suddenly he made a sharp turn and came directly toward me at remarkable speed for such an animal. A bad angle for a shot ...
> Whether it was the unusual view of such an animal or who knows what — in any case, I had the same feeling in the moment when the bull came at me, the same hunting fever that grips me when I sit in an aeroplane, see an Englishman and must fly along for five minutes to come at him. Only with the difference that the Englishman defends himself.'[1]

Of the 80 aircraft shot down and positively confirmed as being victims of the First World War ace of aces, only 33 pilots or crewmen in 22 aircraft are known to have survived Manfred von Richthofen's deadly prowess. His dedication to the craft of aerial warfare was witnessed by Erwin Böhme, a 24-victory ace, recipient of two of Germany's highest honours and a flying companion of Richthofen's from their early days as Boelcke's students. Böhme wrote:

> Hunting is Richthofen's whole passion and for him the ultimate. And, primarily, he has to thank his hunter's eye for his incredible success. Watching like an eagle, he spots the weakness of his opponent and like a bird of prey he dives on his victim, which is inescapably in his clutches. As for flying itself, I believe he does not care very much for it. Most likely, he has never made a loop out of the sheer joy of sport, only for his own pleasure, and above all he has strictly forbidden his *Staffel* to do any "acrobatic tricks", as he calls them.'[2]

Manfred von Richthofen was not just a hunter, however; he was also a military organization man. He was the 20th-century embodiment of the Teutonic Knights who conquered eastern Europe 700 years earlier. Just as fear was inspired by the sight of those resolute figures clad in shining steel helmets and pure white cloaks bearing the black cross that became a national emblem, so Allied pilots came to dread the sight of Richthofen's blood-red aeroplane decorated with the same iron cross. Like the Knights before him, he was a daring and cool-headed leader in battle. He was also a seasoned manager who knew how to use his resources to the best advantage and how to motivate his subordinates.

Oswald Boelcke is considered to be 'the creator of the *Jagdstaffel*'[3] (literally 'hunting section,' but equivalent in function to an Allied fighter squadron). His best student, Manfred *Frhr* von Richthofen, became the first *Kommandeur* (Commander) of the first German *Jagdgeschwader* (fighter wing). Richthofen developed that fixed group of four *Jagdstaffeln*, with a total strength of about 50 aircraft,[4] into an effective large-scale fighting unit to defend German-occupied territory from American, British and French aircraft and aggressively hunt down targets of opportunity within the combat zone.

Shortly before his death in combat at the age of 25, Manfred von Richthofen wrote a short air combat operations manual, a fresh translation of which appears in its entirety as an appendix to this volume. In this treatise, Manfred von Richthofen the combat leader sets forth with calculating methodology the elements necessary to become successful in both initiating and repulsing aerial attacks. Most of these points — Richthofen's dictum, if you will — are as valid in today's jet-age, supersonic, high-technology air combat as they were when developed by the biplane and triplane fighter pilots of the First World War.

As expressed in the operations manual and other documents, and in the reminiscences of friends and foes, Manfred von Richthofen's combat 'managerial' vision bridged two eras. He was a prize-winning, highly competent horseman who began his wartime service as a cavalryman and was quite satisfied to be in the forefront of military activity, charging headlong into enemy forces. When extensive barbed-wire entanglements and trench emplacements rendered tradition-rich mounted fighting and reconnaissance obsolete, Richthofen saw military aviation as the aerial cavalry of the new century, and swiftly adapted his fighting and leadership talents. He saw the parallels in preparing missions, organizing forces, using recognition markings for various units (discarding coloured pennants for distinctive aircraft markings), maintaining order under way and in battle, attacking, regrouping and engaging the enemy in a way that depended more on raw courage than on technical ability.

The following points from the report show his transition from horse to fighter aeroplane to have been a smooth one:

... [each] *Staffel* assembles ... over a point ... previously designated ... [and then] the *Kommandeur* flies to where the collected Staffel leaders have taken up their prescribed places ...

... So that the *Staffeln* do not come together in disorder, it is advisable that each *Staffel* has its own emblem marking. The *Kommandeur*'s aircraft must be very conspicuously painted.

... In such a large formation (30 to 40 machines) the position of the *Staffel* leader must be maintained during the entire flight. It is recommended that, especially for beginners, there be an order of position within the *Staffel*.

... my favourite way [of leading a *Staffel*] is like hunting on horseback across a field, then it is of no consequence if I turn, push ahead or pull back.

... at the moment the *Kommandeur* goes into a dive to swoop down on the enemy formation, under any circumstances it must be his aim to get one, to be the first to engage the opposition.

... One does not need to be an aerobatic artist or a trick shooter; rather, [one has] to have the courage to fly right up to the opponent.

... One should never obstinately stay with an opponent which, through bad shooting or skilful turning, he has been unable to shoot down when the battle lasts until it is far on the other side ...

Failure to heed that last point was a cause of his own demise in the air over Vaux sur Somme, France, on 21 April 1918.

But this book is more than the story of *Rittmeister* (Cavalry Captain) Manfred *Frhr* von Richthofen, whose all-red aircraft earned him the sobriquets '*der rote Kampfflieger*', '*le diable rouge*' and '*the red baron*'. It is more than a recounting of the deeds of the great fallen German national hero whose family home in Silesia was once a museum filled with remnants of his victims' aircraft and equipment, as well as other aerial hunting trophies.

This story is told within the perspective of the development of German fighter aviation, from the attacks by Fokker *Eindeckers* in 1915 to the massed attacks of *Jagdgeschwader I*, the battle force that *Rittm* von Richthofen built, refined and developed into a most effective air weapon. *JG I* and the leaders trained by Richthofen carried on the *Rittmeister*'s tradition of bravery just as he had advanced the legacy of Oswald Boelcke. Of the 81 aviation officers who received Prussia's highest award for bravery, the *Orden Pour le Mérite*, 59 were fighter pilots, 14 of whom were members of or came up through *JG I*.[5]

Manfred von Richthofen has remained a model of daring and leadership in aerial combat. During the Second World War the German *Luftwaffe* named *JG 2* in his memory. *JG 2* built an enviable record, producing 39 recipients of that era's highest German award for valour, the Knight's Cross of the Iron Cross. Among those air combatants were three *JG 2* pilots who earned the further distinction of Oakleaves and Swords to the Knight's Cross: *Oberstleutnant* Egon Mayer, a 102-victory ace and *Kommodore* of *JG 2* at the time of his death; *Oberstleutnant* Kurt Bühlingen, who scored 112 victories and was *JG 2*'s last wartime *Kommodore*; and *Major* Erich Rudorffer, who, while flying with *JG 2*, attained 74 of his 222 victories.[6]

The legacy of Manfred von Richthofen as a combat leader lives on in the modern *Luftwaffe*, which maintains a *Richthofen Geschwader*. Forbidden to take an offensive rôle by the German Federal Constitution, the *Geschwader* embraces the spirit of its illustrious namesake as it fulfils its commitment to NATO and the defence of its reunited homeland.

★ ★ ★ ★ ★

To get as close as possible to the events of the First World War, the author has quoted extensively from contemporary sources. In some cases accounts are woven together, in much the same way that a documentary film enables the viewer to 'experience' events through participants' narratives. These documents, books, articles and letters provide first-hand information set down while events were fresh in mind. They also offer personal insights no longer available.

In tracing the life of Manfred von Richthofen and important events peripheral to it, the author has reviewed thousands of archival source documents to make this account more complete by determining which units were involved in the various aerial combats. That form of inquiry is often an imperfect endeavour in which the researcher studies combat reports, squadron record books and other documents in an attempt to determine when and where units and individuals encountered each other in aerial combat. One fixed point, however, is that, unless otherwise noted, all British air casualty information is from the official *RFC/RAF Western Front Casualty List* (hereinafter called the *RFC/RAF Casualty List*).

Furthermore, a variety of maps were consulted to assure that it was physically possible for potential opponents to be within the same geographical area at about the same time. As an aid to future researchers, where more than one spelling has been applied to geographic locations, the variations are noted within brackets. Any comments within brackets are the author's; quotations with comments within parentheses simply replicate the form used by the original source cited. Finally, in matters of style, the author has used spellings, abbreviations and various nomenclature the way they were used in the First World War. Other cultural elements also appear, such as omission of the prefix 'von' where only the family name is used, which is commonly done in German.

Some pilots, such as Manfred von Richthofen — who covered the walls of his trophy room with the serial numbers of many of the aircraft he shot down — can be credited with great accuracy for certain victories. The reader should bear in mind, however, that other such match-ups or contentions are not perfect, and often depend on what is best described as informed speculation. Opinions which disagree with long-held beliefs are generally clarified in footnotes, and the evidence is presented to enable readers to draw their own conclusions.

The author wishes to point out that the use of the word aerial 'victory' is not intended to heap glory on the 'victor' or to diminish the fate of the victim(s). The French and Germans use the same word: *victoire* and *Luftsieg*, respectively. In humanistic terms, a new word needs to be coined — 'vict(im)ory', perhaps —but in this historical account the language of the time is used.

While on the subject of language, the author does not entirely agree with most existing English-language translations of German texts pertaining to Richthofen, *JG I* flight operations and related matters. That includes his own translation of the 1933 edition of *Der rote Kampfflieger*, published in 1969 under the title *The Red Baron*. Consequently, all translated passages in this work have been rendered anew, to ensure that they remain as faithful as possible to the style and substance of the original texts.

Manfred von Richthofen and his era have long been popular subjects of study and the author gratefully acknowledges the help provided by the works of many researchers whose articles and books were necessary resources in preparing this volume. Thus, corrections suggested in this book to replace earlier contentions are *not* criticisms of preceding writers and researchers; rather, they are merely refinements of the work of those pathfinders.

The author has high regard for the late Floyd Gibbons, the colourful American journalist whose book *The Red Knight of Germany* (1927) has served as a primer to many First World War aviation history dévotees; the late H.A. Jones, CMG, MC, principal researcher and writer of the monumental nine-volume Royal Air Force official history *The War in The Air* (1922-1937); and Claud W. Sykes, author and translator of a number of important early books, of which *Richthofen - The Red Knight of the Air* (n.d.) is one of the best known.

The author remains grateful for the friendship and personal information provided by a number of men who flew during the First World War and who, in various ways, have helped to shape this book. Now all gone to their final reward, they are: W/Cdr Ronald Adam, OBE, who survived an encounter with the *Richthofen-Geschwader*; Major John Blanford, DFC; Douglas Campbell; *Major der Reserve a.D.* Carl Degelow; *Generaloberst a.D.* Alfred Keller, Major Clayton Knight, OBE; Major Cecil Montgomery-Moore, DFC; *Oberstleutnant der Reserve a.D.* Hanns-Gerd Rabe; and *Oberst der Reserve a.D.* Paul Strähle.

Other writers and researchers whose works have been helpful in the creation of this book include: F.W. Bailey, William T. Evans, A.E. Ferko, the late Col Brian P. Flanagan, Peter M. Grosz, Suzanne Hayes, Philip Markham, the late Heinz J. Nowarra, Neal W. O'Connor and his extensive studies of German honours and awards, the late William R. Puglisi, Karl S. Schneide of the US National Air and Space Museum, Marvin S. Skelton, and Stewart K. Taylor with his encyclopaedic knowledge of Canadian aviators. The author is grateful to long-time Richthofen researcher Charles H. Donald, who provided unique materials from his extensive archives, and to the Imperial War Museum for certain photographic resources.

Other assistance has come from friends and colleagues, including: Dagmar Blaha, Alan Chaniewski, Richard Duiven, Beate Sandra Götz, Dena Harwin, Georg Hermann, *Oberstleutnant* Manfred Kampa, Patrick Kennedy, *Dr* Volker Koos, *Dr* Zdzislaw Kremens, *Dr-Ing* Albert Niedermeyer, Judith Robinson, *Ministerialrat Dr* Ulrich Rosenow, *Frau* Christa Rothenbiller, *Oberbürgermeister a.D. Prof Dr* Franz J. Rothenbiller, *Dr* Hans-Jörg Ruge, Michael Schmeelke, David E. Smith, Lothair Vanoverbeke, Greg VanWyngarden, Prof Dr H-G. Peter Wallach, Prof Dr Martha Kaarsberg Wallach, George H. Williams, H. Hugh Wynne and *Dr* Erdmann Zimmer-Vorhaus.

Worthy of praise is a cadre of otherwise unsung loyalists who have performed silent but vital services to this endeavour. In an age when the word processor has become an important means to create written works, a writer needs to know a computer wizard; I have been fortunate in having Gary Warner to help me through the computer battles that became part of the struggle to bring this book to completion. Another long-time friend, Karl Eckert, has been helpful in ways too numerous to mention, but deserves to be acknowledged as reflecting great credit on his Bavarian ancestors. Thanks are also due to Dr S. Martin Harwin, whose skills as a physician are equalled by his talent in the darkroom, squeezing out precious details from the copy negatives of many of the photos that appear in this book.

Last, but by no means least, sincere thanks go to John Toland, who urged me (too long ago) to write this book, and to Roderick Dymott, Director of Arms and Armour Press, who encouraged me further to undertake this work and was most understanding of tribulations along the way. And special gratitude goes to my wife, Judy, who endured what must have seemed like endless hours of my babbling in English and in German as I worked to separate the facts from the legends surrounding Manfred von Richthofen.

Peter Kilduff, New Britain, Connecticut, February 1993

NOTES

1   von Richthofen, *Der rote Kampfflieger*, (1917), pp.177-178.
2   Böhme, *Briefe eines deutschen Kampffliegers an ein junges Mädchen*, (1930), p.112.
3   Zuerl, *Pour-le-Mérite-Flieger*, (1938), p.82.
4   Imrie, *Pictorial History of the German Army Air Service*, (1971), p.66.
5   O'Connor, *Aviation Awards of Imperial Germany in World War I and the Men Who Earned Them*, vol II, (1990), pp.219-224.
6   Obermaier. *Die Ritterkreuzträger der Luftwaffe*, vol I, (1966), pp.43, 45, 46.

CHAPTER 1
ARENA IN THE SKY

With the bright morning sun behind them and scattered low clouds beneath them, the four flights of angular, mean-looking Fokker triplanes and sleek, sharklike Albatros and Pfalz biplanes were hard to see as they headed for the invading bombers and their escorts. Squinting into the eastern horizon, even the best-trained British aircrews could make out little more than strings of dots, drifting in and out of the sun like gnats on a hot day.

On that Wednesday, 27 March 1918, the large formation of two-seaters, de Havilland D.H.4 bombers of No.25 Squadron, RFC, and their Bristol F.2B Fighter escorts of No.48 Squadron, were intent on their targets in the vicinity of the manufacturing centre of Albert. The straight, chalky-white road and the winding muddy ribbon of the Ancre River guided them from the important railway centre at Amiens to the shattered ruins of Albert. A week earlier, III Brigade Headquarters had been in Albert. Now the German *2. Armee* was rushing westward into Flanders in the spring offensive. To help hold the line at Albert, heavy concentrations of British aircraft came in at low levels to bomb and strafe the hordes of field-grey soldiers swarming over the shell-pocked landscape.

As if the old city had not suffered enough — changing hands four times during the First World War — two aerial forces were now about to turn its skies into a gladiators' arena. Flying ahead of and just below his multicoloured fighters, German air group commander *Rittmeister* Manfred von Richthofen noted the hour; 0745. Time to begin the day's work. He had shot down his 69th and 70th victims in this area the previous afternoon and the new day ahead offered even greater opportunities.

Nearby, *Leutnant der Reserve* Heinrich Bongartz, leader of *Jagdstaffel 36* and, like Richthofen, a recipient of Prussia's highest bravery award, the *Orden Pour le Mérite*, watched for his cue. Bongartz recognized *der rote Kampfflieger*, Richthofen, by the red colouring of the top wing and most of the fuselage of his Fokker triplane. When the red hawk began his descent, Bongartz led his pilots in a dive on to the British two-seaters. The five flights came down in an orderly manner; then, as they closed in on the bombers, the fighters split off in pursuit of individual targets.

FIRST KILL OF THE DAY

The first *Jagdgeschwader I* pilot to inflict tangible damage was *Jasta 6*'s *Vizefeldwebel* (Sergeant Major) Franz Hemer in a dirty-green triplane. Singling out a Bristol Fighter, Hemer benefited from the combination of surprise and adherence to Richthofen's tactical dictum in attacking a two-seater as low as possible from behind. The F.2B dropped out of the formation and headed for home with Hemer in hot pursuit, trying to stay in the Bristol gunner's blind spot behind the tailplanes. He fired short, effective bursts to finish off the aircraft, which became his fifth aerial victory. Hemer, a well-disciplined enlisted pilot and a hard-driving air-fighter, was well aware that such triumphs were the key to awards and promotion in a German *Jagdstaffel*. Those incentives, as much as the sense of purpose in stopping the enemy, motivated many a German fighter pilot to use his flying and shooting skills in relentless pursuit of the khaki-coloured aircraft of Britain's Royal Flying Corps and France's *Armée de l'Air*.

At about the same time, *Ltn* Erich Loewenhardt of *Jasta 10* closed in on D.H.4 A7664 and poured short bursts of machine-gun fire into it. Each spray of bullets tore into the wood and fabric. Then incendiary rounds hit the fuel tank. The cumbersome bomber was not quick enough to evade the more manoeuvrable triplane and the D.H.4 went down in flames and crashed just west of Miraumont. A subsequent German note reported that the observer, Lieutenant Alex Rentoul, was wounded and taken prisoner; no mention was made of the pilot, 2/Lt C.G. Pentecost.[1] German ground forces located the D.H.4 wreckage and confirmed *Ltn* Loewenhardt's 15th victory.

Bongartz brought down a Bristol Fighter and a Sopwith F.1 Camel, his 32nd and 33rd victories, and *Unteroffizier* (Corporal) Alfred Hübner of his *Staffel* outfought a Bristol Fighter for his first confirmed aerial victory. The rest of the fight offered inconclusive results and, to make best use of his resources, Richthofen climbed above the mêlée. He expected that most of his comrades would see him and form up with him to attack another large British formation dropping bombs on German troop concentrations northeast of Albert.

RICHTHOFEN'S 71ST AERIAL VICTORY

Just before 0900, Richthofen spotted a flight of Sopwith F.1 Camels covering the bombers at 4,000m. The red triplane immediately led the group toward them. Richthofen targeted Capt Thomas S. Sharpe, DFC, a six-victory ace with No.73 Squadron, and opened fire at close range. Sharpe was a skilful fighter pilot, but no match for the German he and his comrades called 'the bloody red baron'. Within minutes, Sharpe's aircraft, C6733, caught fire and went down near Aveluy in a recently-flooded bank of the Ancre River.[2] Sharpe was captured by German troops and the victory was recorded as Manfred von Richthofen's 71st.

There was a certain irony in this event, as exactly two weeks earlier *Rittm* von Richthofen's younger brother had been shot down in a fight with Camels from No.73 Squadron and F.2Bs of No.62 Squadron. Wounded in that fight, *Ltn* Lothar *Frhr* von Richthofen had been sent back to Germany for medical treatment.

Twenty minutes after Capt Sharpe went down, *Ltn.d.Res* Johann Max Janzen of *Jasta 6* in the dark-coloured Fokker Dr.I 403/17 shot down an R.E.8 two-seater which was making a low-level reconnaissance south of Aveluy Wood to determine what troops and equipment were concealed in the forest. The R.E.8 was credited as Janzen's fourth victory.

Richthofen regrouped his aircraft again and headed northeast. Just beyond Pozières *JG I* intercepted a flight of No.40 Squadron's square-nosed S.E.5a fighters, heading for the main road from Arras to Cambrai to shoot up German traffic moving between the two cities. One of the British fighters never made it. During a short fight, at about 1030 *Ltn.d.Res* Friedrich (Fritz) Friedrichs of *Jasta 10* shot down 2/Lt F.C.B. Wedgwood in S.E.5a D4507. Wedgwood was wounded and came down within German lines, where he was captured. He was listed as Friedrichs' third victory. Unable to keep up with the fast S.E.5as, the German formation swung southward. *Oberleutnant* (First Lieutenant) Wilhelm Reinhard pounced on an R.E.8 patrolling between the Somme Canal and the Ancre River. He scored his tenth victory at 1140, sending the two-seater down over Morlancourt.

Ten minutes later, victory No.21 was achieved by *Ltn.d.Res* Ernst Udet, a new arrival who had been invited to join *Jasta 11* by Manfred von Richthofen. With 20 confirmed kills to his credit, Udet had already qualified for (but not yet received) the *Pour le Mérite* and was recruited as part of Richthofen's plan to have goal-oriented, high-scoring, high-visibility commanders for each of his four *Jagdstaffeln*. Udet passed his first test of combat with *Jasta 11*, Richthofen's first squadron command, by quickly dispatching an R.E.8 south of Albert.

In the same area, at 1205, *Vzfw* Edgar Scholz of *Jasta 11* shot down a Bristol Fighter for his sixth victory.

A GOOD MORNING'S WORK

Eight enemy aircraft down and no losses of their own was a good morning's work for *JG I. Rittm* von Richthofen orbited Albert once more, to pick up any stragglers, and then headed northeast, back to his airfield at Lechelle.

The airfield had been abandoned with such haste six days earlier by No.15 Squadron, an R.E.8 unit, that fully intact hangars and other buildings offered immediate accommodation to Richthofen. In addition to taking over No.15 Squadron's installations on 26 March, Richthofen shot down and killed one of that unit's aircrews not far from their old 'drome. That R.E.8 marked the 70th aerial victory of Germany's undisputed master fighter pilot and aerial tactician.

Lechelle aerodrome's amenities enabled the groundcrews to refuel and rearm the aircraft while the pilots had a comfortable midday meal. Aircraft to be repaired were replaced by fresh machines; some of the pilots were relieved by men who had not flown the morning patrol.

Geschwader-Kommandeur von Richthofen led the second mission. The triplane he had used in the morning, Fokker Dr.I 127/17, was replaced for the afternoon patrol by Dr.I 477/17, an aircraft which bore his brick-red colour on all upper surfaces and was all the more conspicuous from most of the other triplanes, which were painted in a standard brown and green streaked finish with a few individual adornments barely visible from a distance. The whole point was for everyone — friend and foe — to be able to recognize Germany's now legendary air combat leader.

Once *JG I* returned to the Albert area, however, it was one of Manfred von Richthofen's newer hawks who scored the afternoon's first triumph. Southwest of the city the Richthofen group saw a triplane from another unit in a heated battle with an Armstrong Whitworth F.K.8, a slow but steady two-seat general-purpose aircraft known as the 'Big Ack'. The two-seater had just sent the lone triplane into a spin, apparently out of control, when *JG I*'s fighters dived on it. One after another they roared past the F.K.8 and fired into it. The 'Big Ack's' observer hit one of the triplanes, which appeared to catch fire and fall away.

Ltn Hans Kirschstein of *Jasta 10* came down firing and then pulled up, turned and raked the two-seater's underside with machine-gun fire. The British observer, although wounded, shot at another triplane and reported that it exploded. Meanwhile, Kirschstein climbed above what now proved to be a formidable opponent and shot up the F.K.8 from front to back, again wounding the observer and this time setting the fuel tank afire. One other triplane opened fire, wounding the pilot and adding to the observer's injuries. The remaining triplanes milled about, not interfering to avoid hitting Kirschstein, as he jinked back and forth, deciding whether to deliver a fatal shot to the flaming Armstrong Whitworth.

Kirschstein had an opportunity to kill the observer, who struggled out of his burning cockpit and climbed on to the F.K.8's bottom wing, grasping the Scarff ring gun mounting to keep from falling to his death. But the German did not fire; his mission was to destroy enemy aeroplanes and he knew that in this instance he had succeeded. Then the F.K.8's pilot climbed out on the wing and held on to the control column in the hope, somehow, of landing the burning two-seater.

Hans Kirschstein, a 21-year-old Rhinelander who had fought in the ground campaigns in Poland and Galicia, and had survived a two-seater crash on the Western Front,[3] did not need to administer a *coup de grâce* to the Armstrong Whitworth. It was finished and would be recorded as his second victory.[4] He pulled away and let some of the newer pilots — called *Häschen* (young hares) — follow the crippled aircraft down.

Moments later, Kirschstein shot down a Sopwith Camel, his third victory.[5] At the same time, another (but unidentified) *Jasta 6* pilot was credited with shooting down an R.E.8 about eight kilometres east of Albert, marking the *Staffel*'s 96th aerial victory since its establishment on 26 August 1916.[6]

As the Armstrong Whitworth headed down, a pursuing Fokker triplane got too close and was hit by a burst of fire from the observer. Finally free of its pursuers, the F.K.8 made a crash landing between the trenches. 2/Lt Alan A. McLeod, the pilot, scrambled out and pulled his observer, Lt A.W. Hammond, MC, from the flaming wreckage. McLeod was wounded again as he crawled with Hammond on his back toward the safety of British lines. Both men survived the ordeal. On 4 September 1918 Alan McLeod went to Buckingham Palace, where King George V presented him with Britain's highest award for bravery, the Victoria Cross. The 19-year-old Canadian was the First World War's youngest air VC recipient.[7]

TWO MORE FOR THE *RITTMEISTER*

An hour after the F.K.8 went down, another flight of Bristol Fighters approached Albert and Manfred von Richthofen led the group to them. In classic style, Richthofen engaged the first aircraft and sent it down over Foucaucourt at 1630.[8]

Five minutes later he shot down another Bristol Fighter, northeast of Chuignolles. Richthofen later wrote: 'Shortly after I shot down in flames my 72nd opponent, again I set upon gentlemen of the same squadron, saw a Bristol Fighter attack one of my gentlemen, got behind him [the F.2B] and, from 50 metres, shot him down in flames. At the same time I noted that only one crewman was present. The observer's compartment was closed and I presume filled with bombs. I [had] just shot the pilot dead and the aeroplane remained hanging on its propeller [in a stall]. I fired a few more shots, then the aeroplane caught fire, broke up in the air [and] the fuselage fell into a woods and continued to burn.'[9]

Despite *Rittm* von Richthofen's contention that the two-seat Bristol Fighter had been converted into a single-seat bomber, it is most likely that his 73rd victory was the crew of Capt H.R. Child and Lt A. Reeve in F.2B B1332 of No.11 Squadron, who were reconnoitring the area from Albert to the Somme River[10] and were subsequently listed as missing in action.[11]

The British air effort continued into the night, but for Manfred von Richthofen 27 March had been a most successful day. His *Geschwader* had flown 118 sorties and engaged in 13 successful air fights, as well as 39 combats without conclusive results.[12] In its official weekly report the *Luftstreitkräfte* (Air Force) claimed the day's total of 33 enemy aircraft down,' of which 26 were in aerial combat, seven by anti-aircraft [and] one by a railway sentry post', and its own modest losses of 'three aircraft, of which one was in aerial combat, one is missing in action and one [hit] by anti-aircraft fire, crew uninjured'.[13]

The Royal Flying Corps claimed 16 confirmed 'kills' in which crashes were witnessed and four enemy aircraft were driven down out of control, as well as casualties of seven RFC airmen dead (two in non-combat accidents), 23 wounded and 32 missing in action.[14] It is unlikely that these statistics are completely accurate; at best, they indicate the high level of activity on 27 March.

JG I's successes that day were impressive enough to merit a special telegram to the unit from *Generalleutnant* Ernst von Hoeppner, *Kommandierende General der Luftstreitkräfte* (Commanding General of the Air Force):

> To the father of *Rittmeister* Freiherr von Richthofen I have expressed my and the *Luftstreitkräfte*'s best wishes on [the occasion of] the 100th aerial victory of both brothers. To the *Leutnants* Udet and Loewenhardt, who, in quick succession and exemplary fashion, have raised the number of their victories continuously, I express my most sincere appreciation. The 27th of March was again a proud day for *Jagdgeschwader* I.[15]

Manfred von Richthofen's only disappointment was that, owing to the heavy fighting on the ground near where his victims went down, he was unable to retrieve any souvenirs of his victories. His customary hunting trophy was the strip of fabric that bore the downed aircraft's serial number. This day there were no trophies, but the spring offensive was only a week old and he knew there were other days and other air fights yet to come.

NOTES

1   *RFC Western Front Casualty List* entry, 27 March 1918.
2   Ibid; Other sources have identified this pilot as 2/Lt H.W. Ransom of No.70 Squadron, who, according to the *RFC Casualty List*, did not take off until 0900 hours, making it impossible for him to have been shot down by *Frhr* von Richthofen at exactly the same moment.
3   Zuerl, *Pour-le-Mérite-Flieger*, (1938), pp.259-260.
4   Bodenschatz, *Jagd In Flanderns Himmel*, (1935), pp.76, 174; the German casualties claimed by the crew of Armstrong Whitworth B5773 are not noted in available German records. Very likely, those Fokker triplanes were forced to withdraw, as there is no evidence that they exploded or crashed.
5   Considered by some researchers to be Capt Thomas S. Sharpe, DFC, in Sopwith Camel C6733 of No.73 Squadron. According to the *RFC Casualty List*, however, Sharpe left his aerodrome at 0700 hours, making it more likely that he became Manfred von Richthofen's 71st victory at 0900, rather than falling seven hours later, at 1525, when Kirschstein claimed a Camel northeast of Albert.
6   Bodenschatz, op.cit, p.174.
7   Bowyer, *For Valour - the Air V.C.s*, (1978), pp.108-113.
8   Long considered to be crewed by Capt Robert K. Kirkman, an eight-victory two-seater ace, and Capt J.H. Hedley in F.2B B1156 of No 20 Squadron. They were shot down at midday, however, making it more likely they were the ninth victory of *Ltn.d.Res* Karl Gallwitz of *Jasta Boelcke* (ref: Shores, et al., *Above the Trenches* (1990), p.226).
9   Quoted in Bodenschatz, op.cit., p.77.
10   *RFC Casualty List*, op.cit.
11   *RFC War Diary* entry of 27 March 1918, p.244.
12   Bodenschatz, op.cit.

13   *Nachrichtenblatt der Luftstreitkräfte, 2. Jahrgang, Nr 6,* 4 April 1918, p.76.
14   *RFC War Diary,* op.cit., pp.242-244.
15   Bodenschatz, op.cit., pp.77-78.

CHAPTER 2

A NATURAL HUNTER

Manfred von Richthofen's first hunting trophy was a small piece of brown pasteboard with three duck feathers fastened to it by a dab of red sealing wax. The result of a boy's misadventures, that trophy was a portent of things to come, when as a young man in a red aeroplane he would hunt other creatures of the air.

His mother, Kunigunde *Freifrau* von Richthofen, recalled those days in the late 19th century: 'We passed our vacations in the country with Grandmother. One day Manfred could not suppress his fast-developing passion for hunting. He had his first air rifle and with it killed three or four of Grandmother's tame ducks that he found swimming in a little pond near the house. He proudly related his exploit to his grandmother, and I started to reprimand him. His good old grandmother stopped me from scolding him because, as she said, he had been right in confessing his misdeed.'[1]

So it was that Manfred von Richthofen grew up in a hunting, sports-minded environment, encouraged in physical rather than intellectual pursuits. He was the product of several prominent bloodlines, filled with honours and achievements in statecraft, the arts and sciences, and military exploits. Yet, the refinement of his particular talents, combined with the families' inherent drive to excel, made Manfred the most recognizable member of the Richthofen lineage.

CENTURIES OF TRADITION

The family traces its origin to Bernau, a small Prussian town in Brandenburg that was once bigger than its famous neighbour, Berlin. Sebastian Schmidt, a young theologian from Koblenz in the Rhineland, served as pastor in Bernau from 1543 to 1553. Having studied under Martin Luther in Wittenberg, Pastor Schmidt was warmly welcomed in this bastion of the Reformation. Schmidt latinized his surname to Faber, in the custom of the time, and also made a good match when he married Barbara Below, daughter of a Berlin city councillor. Favour smiled on him further when Faber Schmidt gained as a friend and patron Paulus Schultze (or Schultheiss).

Schultze's father and grandfather had been mayors of Bernau, and Paulus himself was a learned man with an enviable reputation as a judge. Indeed, as the final symbol of his devotion to the law, he latinized his family name to Praetorius. Paulus Praetorius amassed considerable wealth and held many prestigious posts; he was Counsellor to the Elector of Brandenburg, and Privy Counsellor to the Archbishopric of Magdeburg and Halberstadt, as well as being hereditary feudal lord and supreme legal authority in various dominions. Old engravings of him bear the Latin inscription: '*Vir prudens et orator gravissimus*' (a smart man and a distinguished speaker).

Paulus Praetorius had no male heirs, but his proposal to adopt Pastor Schmidt's son Samuel was warmly received. Upon Paulus' death at age 44 in 1565, 22-year-old Samuel Praetorius inherited his namesake's vast wealth, many responsibilities and the coat of arms granted in 1561 by Holy Roman Emperor Ferdinand I. The principal figure in the heraldic device is a black-robed judge seated on a *Richterstuhl* (tribunal chair) and, after completing his education, Samuel Praetorius (1543-1605) lived up to the image. He moved east and became a city councillor, city judge and Mayor of Frankfurt an der Oder. His son Tobias Praetorius (1576-1644) was more interested in land, and enlarged the family's holdings. Tobias acquired the family's first property in Silesia through his marriage to a daughter of a local nobleman.

Tobias' son Johann Praetorius (1611-1664) emigrated entirely to Silesia and, in 1661, Holy Roman Emperor Leopold I elevated him into the hereditary Bohemian Knighthood under the name Johann Praetorius von Richthofen. Richt-Hofen means 'court of judgment', a germanization of Praetorius. Current members of the Richthofen family are all descendants of Johann Praetorius von Richthofen.

By the mid-17th century the family had grown and settled predominantly in the Silesian districts of Striegau, Jauer, Schweidnitz and Liegnitz (Strzegom, Jawor, Swidnica and Legnica in modern-day Poland). But the family never relinquished its historic and Protestant links with Brandenburg; despite other favours granted by the Holy Roman Empire, the Richthofens supported King Friedrich II of Prussia (Frederick the Great) in wresting Silesia from the Habsburg dynasty that succeeded the Holy Roman Emperor in Vienna. As a reward, on 6 November 1741 the Prussian monarch elevated the family to the baronial ranks and male members were granted the hereditary title *Freiherr*; their spouses used the title *Freifrau*.

The family members were brought up to live well, to be active in social affairs and, of course, to marry well. The accent was on leadership, and generations of Richthofens occupied key posts in civic and educational endeavours. Perhaps the leading family member of the 19th century was *Prof* Ferdinand *Frhr* von Richthofen, a world traveller and geographer who published an impressive body of work related to his explorations in both hemispheres.

The military strain seems to have come from the maternal side of the family tree. Manfred von Richthofen's paternal great-grandmother, Thecla von Berenhorst, was a granddaughter of the Prussian Field Marshal *Fürst* (Prince) Leopold of Anhalt-Dessau, who so ably served King William III of England (1650-1702) and then the Duke of Marlborough. Prince Leopold was 'a daring, dashing commander, who, like Manfred, loved to swoop down on the unsuspecting foe. He helped to lay the foundations of Prussia's military reputation and the German nation still remembers him today by his nickname of "the old Dessauer".'[2]

To balance the military side, Manfred von Richthofen's beloved paternal grandmother, whose maiden name was Marie Seip, came from Mecklenburg landed gentry of Hessian origin and related to the family of the great German poet Johann Wolfgang von Goethe.

THE MILITARY HERITAGE BEGINS

The first member of the famed flyer's line to become a career military officer was his father, Albrecht Phillip Karl Julius, who was born on 13 November 1859 in Romburg (now Samotwór, Poland), about 15km west of Breslau (now Wroclaw). In those days a soldier could spend his career at one duty station, and Albrecht *Frhr* von Richthofen served many years in the saddle, wearing the distinctive polished cuirass of *Leibkürassieren-Regiment Nr 1* in Breslau. His first three children were born in that city: daughter Elisabeth Therese Luise Marie (always called Ilse) on 8 August 1890, eldest son Manfred Albrecht on 2 May 1892 and second son Lothar Siegfried on 27 September 1894.

After reaching the rank of *Major*, Albrecht von Richthofen had to retire on a medical disability owing to the deafness he suffered in one ear after rescuing one of his men who had fallen into the chilly Oder River. He retired to a pleasant villa in the Silesian industrial town of Schweidnitz (Swidnica, Poland) in the Weistritz (Bystrzyca) Valley, which stretches to the border with Czechoslovakia. His third son, Karl Bolko, was born in Schweidnitz on 16 April 1903.

There, *Maj* von Richthofen encouraged his sons' activities in horsemanship and athletics; Manfred's favourite sports being swimming and shooting. The woods in the Weistritz Valley offered an abundance of game and, at an early age, Manfred combined his interests and then experienced the thrill of the chase and the triumph of the kill on horseback. He was further inspired by the tales of a frequent guest in the Schweidnitz manor, his mother's brother, Alexander von Schickfuss und Neudorff, who had hunted in Europe, Asia and Africa.

Manfred's mother's family also had notable connections. His maternal grandmother was from the distinguished Falkenhausen military family, whose progenitor, *Markgraf* (Margrave) Karl Wilhelm Friedrich von Ansbach, descended from a Frankish line of the House of Hohenzollern that has since died out and married a sister of Silesia's 'liberator', Frederick the Great.[3]

No doubt, Albrecht *Frhr* von Richthofen saw in his eldest son the right blood line, the equestrian and athletic ability, and the natural leadership talent to make the successful Prussian officer that he would like to have become. With luck and perseverance, the young man would turn out like his great-uncle, godfather and namesake, who became *General der*

Kavallerie Manfred *Frhr* von Richthofen. A peacetime aide-de-camp to the *Kaiser* and *Kommandeur* of the Prussian Army's élite formation, the *Garde du Corps, Gen* von Richthofen commanded an army corps in the First World War.[4]

In August 1903, at an age when other well-born Silesian boys were packed off to private schools to prepare for their future careers in land management or commerce, Manfred von Richthofen entered the military training school at Wahlstatt (now Legnicke Pole, Poland), a suburb of nearby Liegnitz. The prestigious *Kadettenanstalt* (Cadet Academy) at Wahlstatt counted among its alumni such outstanding Prussian generals as Paul von Beneckendorff und von Hindenburg,[5] who, at the age of 66, would be called out of retirement and go on to become Germany's great *Generalfeldmarschall* and Chief of the General Staff in the First World War.

The Cadet Academy offered these boy would-be warriors only a Spartan existence, long hours of study and rigid discipline. 'Learn to obey that you may learn to command' was the credo, and it was harshly enforced. Manfred's typically brisk prose reveals how his inherent discipline mastered his true feelings: 'I entered the Cadet Corps as a boy of eleven. I was not particularly eager to become a cadet, but my father wished it, and I was not consulted.'[6]

Manfred was not a particularly good student. He was a bright boy, but reacted to the harshness of Wahlstatt by doing the bare minimum of classroom work, thereby receiving only passing grades. His athletic interests were quite a different matter, however, and they earned him prizes from the school's commandant. His slight build concealed the wiriness and agility that enabled him to master nearly any physical task upon which he set his icy blue eyes. Manfred's physical abilities and a certain bearing — a presence —kept him safe from the older boys, who were prone to pick on their juniors. He learned to follow orders, function with the group at all levels and find recognition in acceptable ways that were part of his training.

Manfred's inner strength and total self-control enabled him to withstand the most withering upbraiding on the parade ground; thus he survived and advanced during the six years at Wahlstatt. The combination of circumstances moulded him into a tough, resilient fighter — a modern Germanic hero, awaiting only the crucible of combat to prove himself.

He became a much happier young man in 1909, when he was graduated to the *Hauptkadettenanstalt* (Senior Cadet Academy) at Gross-Lichterfelde,[7] on the outskirts of Berlin. There, he wrote, "I did not feel so isolated from the world, and I began to live more like a human being. My happiest memories of Lichterfelde are those of the great sporting events when my opponent was *Prinz* Friedrich Karl of Prussia. The Prince won many first prizes and other awards beyond mine, as I had not trained as carefully as he had.'[8]

The two young men had other parallels, as well. Prince Friedrich Karl, a distant cousin[9] of *Kaiser* Wilhelm II, also became a pilot during the war. Almost a year younger than Manfred, the Prince died a year earlier than his schoolmate.

A CHOICE CAVALRY ASSIGNMENT

But those grim days were far ahead of them when Manfred von Richthofen and Prince Friedrich Karl graduated from Gross-Lichterfelde in 1911. Both men were posted as *Fahnenjunkers* (Officer Candidates) to their first choices of light cavalry units — the Prince in *Leibhusaren-Regiment Nr 1* and Richthofen in *Ulanen-Reg 'Kaiser Alexander III. von Russland (westpreussisches)' Nr 1*, named in honour of the *Kaiser*'s uncle, who was the father of the (then) Russian monarch, Czar Nikolai II.

After completing his course at the *Kriegsschule* in Berlin, Manfred was commissioned as *Leutnant* in 1912. He returned to his unit, based in Militsch (today Milicz, Poland), north-northeast of Breslau, not far from his home. To celebrate the end of Manfred's formal military training, his father presented him with a beautiful mare, which he named Santuzza. The horse was a good jumper and he entered her in a hurdle race in Breslau. The day before the event, however, Santuzza hit a high fence and suffered a shoulder injury; Manfred went flying and broke his collarbone. Undaunted, Manfred continued to ride in the great Uhlan tradition; further spills from the saddle served to toughen him for rough landings in aeroplanes. Indeed, his courage was tested to the limit in the spring of 1913 in the *Kaiserpreis-Ritt* (Emperor's Prize Race), a cross-country event. He rode a charger named Blume (Flower) which had not been trained for competition. The animal promptly stepped into a rabbit-hole, and threw Manfred to break another collarbone. Manfred remounted Blume, rode the remaining 70km and won the race before seeking medical attention.

The following summer Manfred was patrolling the outskirts of Ostrovo (now Ostrów, Poland), a small town 10km from the border with the Russian portion of Poland. Rumours of war were heard everywhere, but the border units — 'the eyes of the army'[10] —had packed and unpacked their kits so many times in preparation for mobilization that they no longer believed the news stories and the after-hours discussions provoked by them.

Events in the Bosnian capital of Sarajevo on 27 June 1914 changed that. The assassination of the heir to the throne of the Austro-Hungarian Empire, *Erzherzog* (Archduke) Franz Ferdinand, and his wife brought into focus many of the underlying conflicts between the Triple Entente of Great Britain, France and Russia, and the Triple Alliance of Germany, Austria-Hungary and Italy. Reinforced by the Hohenzollerns it had once cursed for the 'theft' of Silesia, the Hapsburg Dual Monarchy set forth harsh demands on Serbia that led to a series of events resulting in battle lines being drawn throughout Europe.

THE WAR BEGINS

On 28 July 1914 Austria-Hungary declared war on Serbia. When the attendant Russian mobilization was not recalled, Germany supported its Teutonic ally by declaring war on Russia on 1 August. Germany declared war on France on 3 August, the same day that Italy proclaimed its neutrality. The German violation of Belgian neutrality led to Britain's declaration of war on 4 August. Europe's century of peace following the Napoleonic Wars was over.

In the Silesian outpost of Ostrovo, on the evening of 1 August, *Leutnant* von Richthofen and some friends were having a small party in the mess. The young officers were trying to allay the fears of *Frau* von Wedel, the mother of Manfred's best friend in the regiment, who had come to the frontier to see her son before the anticipated war broke out. The festivities were interrupted by the arrival of *Graf* (Count) Kospoth, magistrate of the Öls district. Grimly, he informed the officers and their guests that all Silesian bridges had been placed under guard and important locations were being fortified.[11]

At midnight on the following day, Manfred led his first combat patrol, across the Prosna River into Russian Poland. This was the mission the 22-year-old officer had spent half of his life preparing for, and it turned out to be as peaceful as a ride in the country. All the nervous energy, mustered at the prospect of armed conflict, drifted away as he and his men rode through the village of Kieltze (Kalisz). As a precautionary measure, Richthofen had the village Orthdox priest confined to the church belfry, to keep him from alerting Russian forces to the presence of the German patrol.

Five days later, with his force diminished daily by the loss of a man taking dispatches back to Headquarters, the patrol leader and his remaining Uhlans were nearly captured when a troop of Cossacks entered the village. *Ltn* von Richthofen and his men managed to slip away, but the lesson in careful deployment was not lost on him. He vowed not to be caught short and cut off again.

The main battle on the Eastern Front was taking place far to the north, where the German *8. Armee* prepared to resist a major Russian fighting force moving into position for a massive pincer movement against East Prussia. At the same time, German forces were making a swift drive through France and needed fast-moving cavalry forces there. Consequently, *Ulanen-Reg Nr 1* was soon on a train heading west.

BROTHERLY COMPETITION

Meanwhile, Manfred's younger brother Lothar was about to enter the war. Lothar had remained in the public school system in Breslau and, after matriculating at the local *Gymnasium* (high school), he was enrolled in compulsory military training at the *Kriegsschule* in Danzig (Gdansk, Poland) when war began. On his own initiative Lothar returned to his unit, *Dragoner-Reg 'von Bredow (1. schlessisches)' Nr 4* then being mobilized at Lüben (Lubin, Poland), north of Liegnitz, and about to be sent west for the assault on Belgium.

The sibling rivalry between Manfred and Lothar continued in their military endeavours. After travelling a day and a night through Germany, Manfred's unit disembarked at Busendorf, north of Metz, and Manfred noted with regret that Lothar had got into the real excitement before he had. In his first letter from France, on 19 August 1914, Manfred wrote to his mother:

> We Uhlans are unfortunately attached to the infantry; I say unfortunately, for surely Lothar has already taken part in great battles on horseback, as we would hardly be assigned to do. I am often sent out on patrol and try very hard to come back with the *Eisernes Kreuz* (Iron Cross). I believe that it will take eight to fourteen days before we are in a great battle.[12]

As *Ulanen-Reg Nr 1* continued northward through Luxembourg, Manfred's grand dreams of fighting in epic battles on horseback —man against man in brief and brutal encounters to the death — were dulled by the reality of new forms of warfare that were evolving. He learned that, on 12 August, his first cousin and former playmate Wolfram von Richthofen had died ignominiously in a village near Arlon — shot dead in the doorway of the home in which he had been billeted. It was apparently the work of a vengeful villager, who was not caught. In retaliation Wolfram's unit, *Dragoner-Reg 'König Friedrich III. (2. schlesisches)' Nr 8*, burned to the ground every house that might possibly conceal the *franc-tireurs* (sharpshooters) said to be roaming the area, looking for targets of opportunity such as a young officer stepping out for a breath of fresh morning air.[13]

Manfred's first meeting with his French counterparts was just as disappointing and nearly as fatal. He and fifteen of his Uhlans were reconnoitring an area some 20km west of Arlon on 21 August when, at the edge of the forest south of Etalle, they saw a troop of French dragoons. *'Ran auf den Feind!'* After the enemy! The Uhlans charged into the forest at top speed, only to find that their opponents seemed to have vanished. At the other end of the forest they came out between a rock wall and a stream, with a broad meadow beyond the water. He later wrote:

> Just as I put the field glasses to my eye, a volley of fire cracked from the edge of the forest about 50 metres away. There were about 200 to 250 French riflemen over there. We couldn't move to the left or forward because the enemy was there, and to the right was the wall of rock; therefore we had to go back. Yes, but it wasn't so simple. The way was quite narrow and it led right by the enemy-fortified forest's edge. To

take cover was also useless; therefore I had to go back. I was the last one. In spite of my orders, all the others had bunched together and offered the Frenchmen a good target. Perhaps that was the reason why I escaped. I brought only four men back. This baptism of fire was not as much fun as I thought. That evening some of the others came back, although they had to come by foot, as their horses were dead.[14]

A TASTE OF GLORY

That defeat was soon followed by a brilliant victory that gave the young Uhlan a taste of the glory yet to come. While the lucky stragglers from his patrol returned, *Ltn* von Richthofen and other members of his regiment were mobilizing into divisional strength that evening for an assault on Virton. With great precision, the various German units of *General* Otto von Below's *9. Infanterie-Division* moved into place. Near Manfred's horsemen were rank upon rank of *Grenadier-Reg 'König Wilhelm I. (2. westpreussisches)' Nr 7* commanded by *Prinz* Oskar of Prussia, the 26-year-old fifth son of *Kaiser* Wilhelm II. Manfred looked on in awe as Prince Oskar 'stood on a pile of rocks and urged his regiment ... onward, looking each grenadier in the eye. A splendid moment before the battle.'[15]

After two days of hard fighting against a vastly superior French force, von Below's *9. Division* won a decisive victory. During the fighting, Manfred von Richthofen drew great inspiration from the *Kaiser*'s son. 'In this battle Prince Oskar fought at the head of his regiment and remained unscathed,' Manfred wrote home, adding with great pride: 'I spoke with him right after the battle, as he was presented with the Iron Cross [2nd Class]'.[16]

Clearly, Manfred von Richthofen felt a warrior's kinship with the son of Germany's Supreme War Lord. He observed how the young Prince's determined gaze into each man's face steeled the grenadiers for the grim task ahead. Then, having achieved his object, the Prince received so high an honour as the Iron Cross, even in its 2nd Class award a mighty symbol of German battlefield success.

Established on 13 March 1813 by Prince Oskar's great-great-grandfather, King Friedrich Wilhelm III, the Iron Cross initially replaced other Prussian bravery awards. Going to the roots of German military tradition, the award was designed after the cross *patée* worn in battle by the Teutonic Knights of old, and was cast in iron, with a silver edge to make it stand out against any dark uniform colour as a dramatic symbol of the Prussian monarch's recognition of valour. Although the Iron Cross eventually lost its high value, with over five million presentations of the 2nd Class award made during the First World War, it was still an important honour in 1914, and significant in being the first award by an old-line European monarchy to be presented both to officers and enlisted men.[17] Small wonder, therefore, that Manfred von Richthofen and millions of other German soldiers were willing to fight to the death for this coveted award.

While Manfred struggled to prove himself worthy of the Iron Cross, the rest of his household went off to war. The war was a week old when his sister Ilse joined the Red Cross as a nurse. Shortly thereafter, the faithful family servant Gustav Mohaupt answered the call to the colours and was happy to be accepted into the *Hirschberger Jäger (Jäger-Bataillon 'von Neumann (5. schlesisches)' Nr 5)*, a crack rifle unit that suffered huge losses in the first fighting near Metz.[18] Even 55-year-old *Maj* Albrecht von Richthofen applied for return to active duty in some capacity. On 24 September 1914 *Maj* von Richthofen's hope was realized and he was assigned as an administrator to the Silesian Reserve Hopsital in Kattowitz (Katowice), near Krakow.

On the preceding day *Ltn* Manfred *Frhr* von Richthofen was awarded the *Eisernes Kreuz II. Klasse* — popularly abbreviated *EK II*. A month after he had seen the award pinned to the breast of a lineal heir to the Hohenzollern soldier kings, the young Silesian nobleman had attained the same distinction. It made him understand the necessary hardships of Wahlstatt and the Prussian military system, moulding boys and young men into modern Germanic heroes, each a young Siegfried, but without the weak spot where the oakleaf kept the legendary hero from being immune from all harm. Now young Richthofen was ready to perform even greater deeds in battle.

NOTES

1   Quoted in Gibbons, *The Red Knight of Germany*, (1927), p.10.

2   'Vigilant', *Richthofen - The Red Knight of the Air*, (no date), p.17.

3   von Richthofen, *Der rote Kampfflieger*, (1933), pp.9-17.

4   von Richthofen, *Der rote Kampfflieger*, (1917), p.10.

5   von Hindenburg, *Out of My Life*, (1921), p.3.

6   von Richthofen, *The Red Baron*, (1969), p.1.

7   Italiaander, *Manfred Freiherr von Richthofen - der beste Jagdflieger des grossen Krieges*, (1938), p.56.

8   *Der rote Kampfflieger*, (1917) op.cit., p.13.

9   *Prinz* Friedrich Karl's father, *Prinz* Friedrich Leopold of Prussia (1865-1931), and *Kaiser* Wilhelm II (1859-1941) were great-grandsons of King Friedrich Wilhelm III of Prussia. (Ref: Louda, *Heraldry of the Royal Families of Europe*, (1981), p.186).

10   *Der rote Kampfflieger*, (1917), op.cit., p.19.

11   Ibid, p.21.

12   Quoted in von Richthofen, *Mein Kriegstagebuch*, (1937), p.14.

13   Ibid, pp.15-16.

14   *The Red Baron*, op.cit., p.13.

15   Ibid.

16   Ibid., p.14.

17   O'Connor, *Aviation Awards of Imperial Germany in World War I and the Men Who Earned Them*, vol. II, (1990), pp.7-9.

18   *Mein Kriegstagebuch*, op.cit., pp.13-14.

CHAPTER 3
OVER THE TRENCHES

As his unit marched toward Belgium, Manfred von Richthofen saw an occasional aeroplane overhead, but gave little thought to it. 'At the time I hadn't the slightest idea what our flyers did,' he wrote. 'I considered every flyer an enormous fraud. I could not tell whether he was friend or foe. I had no idea that German machines bore [black] crosses and the enemy's had [tricolor] cockades. As a result, every flyer came under our fire. Even today the old pilots tell how painful it was to be fired at by friend and foe alike.'[1]

At the time the cavalry units were able to perform their traditional reconnaissance role, dashing along and even behind the enemy lines to gather situational information. Such intelligence was used by local area commanders and passed up to higher levels so that overall strategy and tactics could benefit from the best available information. But when *Ulanen-Reg Nr 1* was transferred from Belgium to Verdun, Richthofen saw the dissolution of one old order of battle and the emergence of a new one.

The German *5. Armee*, commanded by 33-year-old *Kronprinz* (Crown Prince) Wilhelm of Prussia, stood opposite Verdun, the ancient fortress city straddling the Meuse River. The city was only 50km from the border with the Lorraine province ceded by France to the newly-created German Empire after the War of 1870. Occupied for three years during that war, Verdun and the surrounding hills were later heavily fortified to offset the German stronghold of Metz, only 64km to the east. Verdun was one of the main barriers to Paris; hence, a decisive German victory at this location would augur well for the future *Kaiser*. His forces were gathered for a major engagement, but, as they dug in, the advance began to grind to a halt. The intricate network of trenches and fortifications soon eliminated the need for fast-charging uhlans, dragoons and hussars. A dulling boredom set in, punctuated by deadly shrapnel from unseen artillery batteries far behind enemy lines.

Manfred wrote that, during a rare patrol in October, he had just dismounted from his horse when a grenade struck his saddlebag and destroyed it.[2] A short time later Lothar was nearly cut down by sniper fire while on patrol. Where was the glorious 19th-century war for which Manfred and Lothar had trained? Lothar's only consolation was that in mid-October he was awarded the *EK II* and then transferred to the Eastern Front, where there was more activity on the ground.

'We are now in and out of the trenches, like the infantry; 2,000 metres in front of us are the French,' Manfred wrote on 2 November. 'It is no fun to lie quietly for the duration of 24 boring hours. Some shells come back

31

and forth in singular exchange; that is all I have experienced in the last four weeks. It is too bad we are not employed in the major battle. For weeks the position before Verdun has not shifted 50 metres ... I would like very much to have the Iron Cross, 1st Class, but there is no opportunity here. I must go [in] to Verdun dressed as a Frenchman and blow up a gun turret.'[3]

ACTION ON THE RUSSIAN FRONT

While Manfred endured the boredom of settling in on the Western Front, Lothar von Richthofen's unit was deployed to the Russian Front, where there was still a great danger to eastern Germany. En route to his new duty station, Lothar stopped briefly to visit his mother in Schweidnitz, where the impact of the war was felt in a strange way.

On the morning of 3 November *Freifrau* von Richthofen journeyed by train to Ostrovo to retrieve Manfred's dress uniforms and other portions of his kit that he had not taken to France. Normally a two-and-a-half-hour ride, the journey took six hours because the rail lines were full of military traffic, headed for the Front. Once in Ostrovo, she found the old garrison city filled with Poles and Germans fleeing the advancing Russian Army. *Freifrau* von Richthofen could hear the distant thunder of cannon fire from the battlefront. When she returned to the railway station it was totally jammed and she had to spend the night at a small inn. She was quite happy to be back in Schweidnitz the following afternoon, but was concerned that her second son was heading for the confrontation she had left behind.[4]

Germany's situation on the Eastern Front was saved by the brilliant leadership of a graduate of the Wahlstatt military training school, (then) *General* Paul von Beneckendorff und von Hindenburg. First, Hindenburg successfully concluded the Battle of Tannenberg in August, after which he was promoted to *Generaloberst* (Colonel-General). Second, his victory at the Battle of the Masurian Lakes in September routed the Russians. Third, his victory at Lodz in November halted the Russian advance toward Silesia, after which he was promoted to *Generalfeldmarschall*. *Ltn* Lothar von Richthofen came under fire during the latter campaign; his less fortunate 17-year-old cousin, Siegfried von Richthofen, was killed not far from Lothar's position.[5]

With the coming of winter, Manfred became more uncomfortable and frustrated in his dugout in France; Lothar continued to write home of his exploits on the move in Poland and then in Hungary, as German success on the Eastern Front mounted. Manfred's big news in January 1915 was his appointment as *Ordonnanzoffizier* (Assistant Adjutant) of the *18. Infanterie-Brigade*.

Spring brought rain to the battlefields and made the mud more difficult to walk in. At home in Silesia, 11-year-old Bolko von Richthofen entered the military training school at Wahlstatt. Great battles raged in Flanders and along the Marne, but the situation at Verdun was little changed and produced only an endless litany of minor events that got on Manfred's nerves. He spent his 23rd birthday — 2 May 1915 — in his dugout, counting the days until he could go on leave. He returned home three weeks later, a bit fatter and softer than before from lack of activity.

Manfred had gained a depressed view of the war, seeing no chance for victory on the Western Front. 'Have you not heard anything about the withdrawal from the Marne?', he asked his mother. She replied that people at home knew nothing about it. Manfred did not elaborate; he retreated into frustrated silence.[6]

LIBERATED BY THE *FLIEGERTRUPPE*

Within a week Manfred had returned to the Front and had been given more administrative chores. This was the final indignity for a cavalry officer who had been prepared since boyhood for greater things. In a curious form of denial, he was later quoted as saying: 'I wrote a request to my commanding general in which it was falsely reported I had said: "Dear Excellency, I did not go to war to gather cheese and eggs, but for another purpose". At first people took offence at [the brashness of] my request, but then it was granted, and so at the end of May 1915 I joined the *Fliegertruppe* (Air Service). Thus, my greatest wish was fulfilled.'[7]

The young *Leutnant* was one of 30 officers assigned to the aviation training unit *Flieger-Ersatz-Abteilung 7* in Cologne for assessment of their suitability as aviation observers. Only the best were chosen, and Manfred wrote home with pride: 'It is under these extremely difficult and doubtful circumstances that I, fortunately, find myself one of these selectees'.[8]

Being out of the trenches and in the company of normal human beings — eating in a regular officers' mess, sleeping between clean sheets, putting on clean clothes — was itself an exhilarating experience. But the prospect of getting back into the war in a more meaningful way struck the loudest chord within Manfred von Richthofen.

The night before his first orientation flight he went to bed early, to be completely fresh for the great event. He was so excited, however, that it is doubtful whether he got a full night's rest. A car picked him up in the morning and, promptly at 0700, he was at the airfield, seeing for the first time the big, ungainly B-type two-seat biplane trainer that would take him up to test his mettle.

The observer or student sat in the front seat of a B-type aeroplane, which gave an element of shock to his first flight, even before take-off. 'The blast of wind from the propeller disturbed me enormously,' he wrote. 'It was impossible to communicate with the pilot. Everything flew away from me. If I took out a piece of paper, it disappeared. My crash helmet kept slipping, my scarf loosened, my jacket was not buttoned securely — in short, it was miserable. Before I could tell what was happening, the pilot opened the throttle and the machine began to roll. Ever faster, ever faster. I held on frantically. Suddenly the shaking stopped and the machine was in the air. The ground slipped away beneath us.'[9]

Manfred had no idea where the pilot was steering the aeroplane, nor did he care. He was in the air and the ride was as challenging as if it were on a new horse. Ever so carefully he peered over the side and saw the mighty Rhine river shrink into a blue ribbon, glistening in the morning sunlight. The *Kölner Dom*, the landmark twin-spired cathedral, looked like a toy. As the pilot banked and turned, Manfred saw the Rhenish landscape as it could scarcely be imagined from horseback.

The importance of the air weapon was obvious. The network of trenches and barbed wire barriers being set up by the belligerents from the Swiss border near the Vosges Mountains to the North Sea near Holland effectively deprived the cavalry of its traditional reconnoitring rôle. New tethered observation balloons offered some advantages, but were limited in scope. The aeroplane, however, could range far and wide to gather information and to harass rear areas. Small wonder, therefore, that some military visionaries referred to air units as 'the cavalry of the clouds'.

On 10 June Manfred and the other aviation observer candidates reported for training to *FEA 6* at Grossenhain in the Kingdom of Saxony. Manfred could have applied for pilot instruction, but stayed with the two-week observer training programme because it promised a faster return to active duty. 'Of course I wanted to go to the Front quickly,' he wrote, 'for I was afraid that [otherwise] I would be too late for the World War. Three months were required to become a pilot. By then peace could have come; therefore, that [longer course] was out of the question.'[10]

Manfred von Richthofen completed his course so quickly that, on 21 June, he was assigned to the field aviation unit *Feldflieger-Abteilung 69*, which was then being formed on the Eastern Front. Germany's first mobile combat squadron, given the cover name *Brieftauben-Abteilung Ostende* (Carrier Pigeon Section at Ostende), had been deployed to the Eastern Front in March 1915 and had been quite successful in supporting *Gen* August von Mackensen's *11. Armee* operations in Poland and Galicia. So successful, in fact, that the unit's commander, *Hptmn* Hermann Gustav Kastner-Kirdorf, had to accommodate demands for air support from many commands by splitting off two *BAO* sections which became *Feldflieger-Abteilungen 66* and *69*.[11]

Manfred arrived at the Front right after Mackensen's forces had smashed through the Russian lines at Gorlice and were attacking Rawa Ruska in the south, in concert with Austro-Hungarian forces. He had been at the Front hardly a week when he received bad news from home. On 27 June his adventurous favourite uncle, Alexander von Schickfuss und Neudorff, had been injured in a crash while making a test flight over St. Quentin, France, to qualify for observer training. The 50-year-old *Rittm der Reserve* suffered a skull fracture and brain concussion, and had to be sent to a hospital in Berlin for treatment. His pilot, *Flieger* (Private) Hermann

Meise, 23, was killed in the crash. From his hospital bed Schickfuss voiced only one complaint to his sister, *Freifrau* von Richthofen: '[That] he would never be allowed to fight with the enemy in the air. That must have been hard for him to take, for it was his dream.'[12]

IN THE AIR OVER RUSSIA

Onkel Alexander's dream would be realized by Manfred von Richthofen. He flew with *Feldfl.-Abt. 69* through June, July and August, performing extensive reconnaissance work for the Austro-Hungarian *kuk 6. Armeekorps* in the drive toward Brest-Litovsk. Manfred and his first pilot, *Obltn* Georg Zeumer, flew morning and afternoon patrols nearly every day in a big Albatros B.II three-bay biplane. The B.II was a sturdy aircraft, but not well suited to reconnaissance work, as the observer sat in the front cockpit and had to make his observations by peering between the wings and over the engine cowling. Usually armed with a rifle, the observer had limited defensive capability.

Georg Zeumer, an original *BAO* member, shared Richthofen's thirst for adventure and made sure his observer gained the close look at important ground installations that a former cavalryman needed in order to gather intelligence information. Zeumer hailed from *Infanterie-Reg 'König Wilhelm II. von Württemberg (6. elsässisches)' Nr 105* in Strassburg. Despite its nomenclature, the regiment was a Royal Saxon Army unit. Zeumer had been nicknamed 'the black cat' because his recklessness was sure to lead to disaster; in fact, he had tuberculosis and knew he would not live long. His devil-may-care attitude made him an ideal combat pilot.[13]

Manfred wrote home on 20 July 1915: 'Now we are again right into completely mobile warfare. I fly over the enemy almost daily and bring back reports. I reported the retreat of the Russians three days ago. It is so much more fun for me, in any case more than playing Assistant Adjutant. We live only in tents. Almost all of the houses have been burned to the ground and those that still stand are of the kind that no human wants to enter. I am especially happy to be right here, in the most important theatre of operations, and to be able to participate in it.'[14]

'*Glück muss man haben*' (One has to be lucky) is an old German saying. By the summer of 1915 Manfred had become the luckiest Richthofen. Manfred was at the Front and in action, while Lothar was back in Lüben, where his regiment trained replacements for the men lost in the earlier fighting. At the same time, Lothar's schoolmate and cousin Gottfried was killed in action. Gottfried's brother, Siegfried, had been killed earlier and, in the interim, death claimed their father, Hermann von Richthofen, *Landeshauptmann* (County Commissioner) of Silesia.

In a move typical of the times, there was a quick shift of personnel at the Front and *Obltn* Georg Zeumer was transferred back to Flanders with the *BAO*. Manfred von Richthofen's immediate concern was to be paired with another pilot as skilful and bold as Zeumer. He soon found the ideal replacement in *Rittm* Erich *Graf* (Count) von Holck, a veteran of *Dragoner-Reg 'König Carl I. von Rumänien (1. hannoverisches)' Nr 9* and, at 29, a 'mature old man' in the unit.

'*Graf* Holck was not merely a sportsman on the green grass,' wrote Manfred, 'to all appearances the sport of flying gave him more than a little pleasure. He was a pilot of rare ability and, most especially and importantly, he was in a class far above the enemy. We made many splendid reconnaissance flights — who knows how far — into Russia. I never had [any] feeling of insecurity with this young pilot; on the contrary, at the critical moment he gave me support. When I looked into his determined face, I had even more courage than before.'[15]

Their last flight together was nearly the end of Manfred von Richthofen and *Graf* von Holck. To determine the size of the force, they followed retreating Russian troops who were burning everything in their wake. As the Albatros approached the city of Wicznice, a column of choking black smoke rose up some 2,000m in its path. As they were at only 1,500m, Richthofen turned around and motioned the pilot to fly around the obstacle. This was not for *Graf* von Holck, who had been a successful racing-car driver before the war.

Richthofen later wrote:

> ... the greater the danger, the more attractive it was to him. Therefore, right into it! It was fun to be with such a plucky fellow. But our carelessness soon cost us dearly, for barely had the tail of the aircraft disappeared into the cloud than I noticed a swaying in the aeroplane. I could see nothing more, the smoke stung my eyes, the air was significantly warmer and beneath me I saw only an enormous sea of fire. Suddenly the aeroplane stalled and plunged spiralling downward. I could only grab a strut to brace myself; otherwise I would have been tossed out. The first thing I did was look [back] into Holck's face. I regained my courage, for his bearing was of iron confidence. The only thought I had was: it is so stupid to die a heroic death in such a needless way.[16]

Suddenly the Albatros dropped out of the cloud and Holck regained control. He pulled up at barely 500m altitude and headed straight for German lines, while the columns of Russian soldiers opened fire at the easy target. Ultimately, the machine was hit and forced to land near what had been a fortified Russian position. The airmen had an immediate fright when soldiers ran toward their aircraft, but fear changed to joy when the men turned out to be from *Grenadier-Reg 'König Friedrich Wilhelm IV. (1. pommerisches)' Nr 2*.

Soon the main force appeared, along with its commander, *Prinz* Eitel Friedrich of Prussia, the 32-year-old second son of *Kaiser* Wilhelm II. The Prince ordered Holck and Richthofen provided with horses so that the two flyers could return to their unit.

Their aeroplane was a total loss, but it was of little consequence. The old Albatros B.II types were to be replaced by the C.I, which was very similar in appearance but had the observer in the rear cockpit, where he was better able to perform his duties and help defend the aircraft. Aircraft were always less important than aircrews, many of whom could now be sent to the Western Front, thanks to the positive developments in Russia.

Among the crews lost by *Feldfl.-Abt. 69* were *Rittm* von Holck and *Ltn* von Richthofen, as each man was transferred to a different unit. Manfred was ordered to the *Brieftauben-Abteilung Ostende* on the *4. Armee* Front in Flanders. On 21 August, in transit to his new posting, he managed to stop off at Schweidnitz, where his parents greeted him. His mother recalled: 'We fetched him from the train station at about midnight; he was accompanied by his orderly, the ever faithful Menzke, who had been with him in the [uhlan] squadron since peacetime. Manfred looked splendid in appearance, he beamed and related his experiences at the Front, each one more interesting than the other.'[17]

Manfred's spirits were lifted higher when he and Menzke arrived at Ostende and were met by the frail, yet ever-enthusiastic 'black cat' himself, *Obltn* Georg Zeumer. They had a rousing reunion at the train station, where Zeumer told Richthofen about the French and British aviation units operating in the area and the British naval squadrons that had the temerity to come in close to their splendid oceanside beach and fire at them.

The *BAO* promised the exciting military life that Manfred von Richthofen craved. Since its return from Russia the unit had sent its old B-type aircraft to training schools and received new single-engined C-type machines, as well as twin-engined AEG G-type '*Grosskampfflugzeug*' (Big Combat Aircraft, hence the appellation G-type) bombing aircraft. In the AEG G.II the observer/bomb-aimer sat in a protruding forward cockpit which the flyers called the '*Kanzel*' (pulpit). In this position, unobstructed and ahead of the pilot, the observer had the same offensive capability as enemy rear-engined 'pushers' and the new German E-type fighters, which were then the only aircraft with forward-firing machine guns synchronised to fire through the propeller arc. Manfred saw immediately that 'the cavalry of the clouds' also had a lance, and he was eager to use it.

ENCOUNTERING THE ENEMY

Richthofen and Zeumer flew five to six hours every day, dropping their bombs first and then patrolling in the hope of finding an enemy in the air. On 1 September they were put to their first test. Up for a morning flight, Manfred suddenly saw in the distance a British Farman, an ungainly biplane in which the crew's nacelle seemed to be laced between the wings and twin booms that carried the tail; the Germans called the type '*Gitter-schwanz*' (lattice-tail). Zeumer headed straight for it.

'My heart was pounding as Zeumer approached him,' Richthofen later wrote. 'I was excited about what was about to happen. I had never seen an aerial combat and had only a very vague conception of it ... All of a sudden both of us, the Englishman and I, were rushing toward each other. I got off at most four shots, while the Englishman suddenly got behind us and shot the whole works at us. I must say that I did not have the feeling of danger because I could not imagine at all how the final result of such a battle would turn out. Time and time again we circled each other until finally, to our great astonishment, the Englishman, quite satisfied, turned away and flew off. I was greatly disappointed, as was my pilot.'[18]

Back at Ostende there were recriminations. Richthofen blamed Zeumer for not putting him in a good position to fire; Zeumer faulted Richthofen for being a bad shot. On reflection, they both understood that a successful combat flyer must control both the aircraft and the firepower.

They also knew that a divided team could not function effectively, and did not discuss the Farman incident further. Indeed, a few days later Manfred had quite another concern. While on a bombing mission in the AEG G.II, he leaned over the side to watch a bomb hit and imprudently stretched his arm to point out the success to Zeumer. The stretch was just far enough to bring him close to the arc of the propeller alongside his cockpit, and a blade nicked a fingertip. Except for this first drop of blood shed for his Fatherland, Manfred was otherwise uninjured; later versions of the AEG G-series were fitted with screens on the right and left of the fuselage to protect the observer against the hazard.

In mid-September *BAO* crews were sent to the *3. Armee* Front, to provide aerial security for other air units operating over the Champagne Front. Initially, four *BAO* C-types, augmented by two Fokker *Eindeckers* (monoplane offensive aircraft), were assigned to *Feldfl-Abt 22*'s airfield at Vouziers to cover the *VIII. Reserve-Korps*; two other *BAO* two-seaters were provided to the *X. Armee-Korps* and the *XII. Reserve-Korps* to escort *3. Armee* aircraft.[19]

The deployment offered Manfred von Richthofen opportunities to fly in the smaller, more manoeuvrable C-type aircraft on a Front covered by greater numbers of potential adversaries. Georg Zeumer was delighted to find the two Fokker monoplanes at Vouziers; news was spreading of the successes attained by *Leutnants* Oswald Boelcke and Max Immelmann, the emerging master airfighters of *Feldfl-Abt 62*, and he wanted to join their ranks. Zeumer devoted so much time to becoming proficient with the Fokker *Eindecker* that Richthofen had to seek a new flying partner.

At length, Richthofen was assigned to fly with 27-year-old *Obltn* Paul Henning von Osterroht, an alumnus of Wahlstatt and Gross-Lichterfelde who had become one of the original *BAO* fliers. Osterroht had no cavalry tradition but, as a prewar military flyer,[20] he had looked for opportunities to use the aeroplane as a weapon. When they went up in their Aviatik C.I, Osterroht scouted for targets and Richthofen stood by his Parabellum

7.9mm machine-gun, ready to move it from one mounting to another on either side of his cockpit as the occasion required.

One day they were lucky and spotted a Farman two-seater some 5km within its own lines. 'He let us calmly approach him and for the first time I saw an opponent at quite close range in the air,' Richthofen later wrote. 'Osterroht flew very skilfully so close to him that I could easily bring him under fire. The opponent had not noticed us at all, for he did not fire back until I had my first gun jam. After I had fired off my entire cartridge case of a hundred rounds, I could not believe my eyes, as all of a sudden the opponent went down in a peculiar spiral. I followed him with my eyes and tapped Osterroht on the head [to take note of it]. He fell and fell and in fact went into big shell crater; we saw it, standing on its nose, with the tail up.'[21]

Manfred carefully noted on his map the site of his first aerial victory, but, as he had no independent confirmation and the wreckage lay within enemy lines, his claim for credit was denied. Trying to be philsophical about the loss of this recognition, he later stated '... besides, the main point is that the fellow is brought down, not that one is credited with an aerial victory.'[22] On many subsequent occasions, however, Manfred von Richthofen obtained or had someone else obtain physical proof of his aerial prowess. The highly-prized duck feathers at the family home in Schweidnitz were to be joined by so many trophies of war — patches of fabric bearing the serial numbers of downed enemy aircraft, captured machine-guns, flare pistols and other souvenirs — that the house would become a Richthofen museum.

On 23 September French artillery units initiated a massive barrage all along the Champagne Front, part of a three-day offensive intended to break the German lines. The German *3. Armee* held fast, but reinforcements were brought in and certain units were redeployed to assure adequate coverage on other Fronts. Initially, Manfred was shifted back to Ostende and then, on 1 October, quickly redeployed to Rethel, some 30km northeast of Vouziers.

RICHTHOFEN MEETS OSWALD BOELCKE

The *BAO* was an early rapid deployment force. It had its own train to carry aircrews, ground personnel and aircraft to augment the aircraft and crews that flew directly to a new Front. Manfred von Richthofen was in the *BAO* train dining car when he recognized a *Leutnant* of about his own age at a nearby table. There was nothing special about his uniform, which was the ubiquitous field grey worn by so many ground units. But his face, with its strong, rugged features, had already appeared in newspapers and periodicals: he was Oswald Boelcke, a victor of four aerial combats. He was one of the most successful pilots of the Fokker *Eindeckers* that were achieving stunning victories over British and French aircraft.

Unable to contain his enthusiastic curiosity, Richthofen approached Boelcke and simply asked: 'Tell me honestly, how do you really do it?'. Boelcke laughed, even though he knew the question was serious, and then replied: 'Yes, good God, it is quite simple. I fly right up to [the enemy], take good aim [and open fire], then he falls down.'[23]

Manfred was perplexed. He had done just what Boelcke had said and yet had achieved little success. Richthofen made it a point to get to know Boelcke better; they whiled away many hours, playing cards on the train. At length they grew close enough to use the familiar form of address and, in the spirit of such a comradeship, Boelcke advised: '*Du musst selber einen Fokker fliegen lernen, dann wird es vielleicht besser gehen*' (You must learn to fly a Fokker yourself, then perhaps it will be better).[24]

Manfred von Richthofen's first order of business at Rethel was to persuade Georg Zeumer to give him flying lessons. In-between and after their regular missions, Manfred poured his energy into flying. Displaying his usual impatience, he wanted to learn everything immediately. On 10 October he made his first solo flight and, except for a rough landing, he performed well.

Gradually, German ground units recovered lost territory and inflicted such heavy losses on their opponents that the French had to halt their attack in the Champagne region. The attendant reduction in air activity made it easier for Manfred von Richthofen's *BAO* superiors to grant his request to complete his pilot's training at *FEA 2* at Döberitz, located at a military exercise ground east of Berlin. Very likely, they thought that he would return to the *BAO* as a pilot for its C- or G-type aircraft.

COMBAT PILOT TRAINING AT DÖBERITZ

At *FEA 2*, however, Richthofen made a new friend in *Obltn* Bodo *Frhr* von Lyncker, a 21-year-old native Berliner with the same passion for adventure and devotion to Fokker *Eindeckers*. They were instructed to use two-seaters for so-called *Sperreflüge* (barrier flights)[25] for local air defence to keep enemy aircraft from penetrating German lines. In spite of the current strategy, Richthofen and Lyncker were passionately interested in aerial *offence*, in hunting in the air.

Manfred's mother recorded in her diary: 'He had the phenomenal eye and steady hand of my husband. Often — when Manfred was just a boy — they both went into the thickets. Manfred was always with him; the word "hunt" fascinated him; one could wake him in the middle of the night with it. Only once, when my husband got him out of bed in the dewy morning darkness, he muttered a bit: "Well, just wait until my kids are this big, [and] then I will throw them out the hatch so early." But then he jumped out of bed with both feet and the two hunters were off.

'This marksmanship was the mutual heritage of both my husband's and my own family. I was not surprised when Manfred wrote that he wanted to be a *Jagdflieger*.'[26]

On Christmas Day Manfred completed his third examination. As part of the test he flew with his orderly, Menzke, to the Fokker factory in Schwerin. After a visit long enough to say he had been there, the neophyte pilot was off to Breslau and thence by train to Schweidnitz. The newest weapon of warfare had brought him home to Silesia to celebrate Christmas with his entire family for the last time in his life.

Freifrau von Richthofen, realizing how fortunate she was to have her husband and all of her children at home in wartime, prepared as extensive a holiday feast as she could. She played the piano after dinner, as they all gathered around the Christmas tree aglow with lighted candles. As they sang carols, she recalled, 'Manfred and Ilse sang splendidly, with their beautiful clear voices. Lothar (completely unmusical and with no voice) held his lips closed, but his eyes beamed all the brighter. All three, even Bolko, were in uniform; Ilse wore her nurse's outfit.'[27]

After a brief holiday at home, Manfred von Richthofen and his orderly returned to Berlin for further duty. On 1 February he returned with Lothar as his passenger to Schweidnitz; Manfred had 'rescued' his brother from the boredom of training new troops in Lüben and took this opportunity to gain another recruit for the *Fliegertruppe*.

This time Manfred had called ahead so that proper arrangements could be made. Local officials granted permission for him to land in the parade ground across the road from the family home, and the aircraft's arrival caused a great commotion. For most of the townspeople it was their first close look at an aeroplane and they were full of admiration for the brothers who flew it. And only 15 minutes by air from Breslau to Schweidnitz, at that! The admiration, the questions and the attention were all quite new to Manfred and Lothar, but they were phenomena to which the brothers would become accustomed. Lothar needed no further convincing, and soon applied for training as an observer.

A few weeks later Manfred was again at the Front, about to begin his career as a fighter pilot.

NOTES

1   von Richthofen, *The Red Baron*, (1969), p.11.
2   Ibid., p.22.
3   Ibid., p.23.
4   von Richthofen, *Mein Kriegstagebuch*, (1937), pp.28-29.
5   Ibid., pp.33-34.
6   Ibid., p.56.
7   von Richthofen, *Der rote Kampfflieger*, (1933), p.61.
8   Ibid., p.64.
9   Ibid., p.62.
10   Zuerl, *Pour-le-Mérite-Flieger*, (1938), p.373.
11   Ferko, *Fliegertruppe 1914-1918*, (1980), p.4.
12   *Mein Kriegstagebuch*, op.cit., pp.57-58.

41

13   Supf, *Das Buch der deutschen Fluggeschichte*, vol II, (1958), p.437.

14   *Der rote Kampfflieger*, op.cit., p.59.

15   Ibid., p.66.

16   Ibid., p.67.

17   *Mein Kriegstagebuch*, op.cit., p.63.

18   *Der rote Kampfflieger*, op.cit., pp.76-77.

19   *AOK 3. Armee Bericht Nr Ia 5515*, 12 September 1915.

20   On 9 October 1912 Osterroht qualified for *Deutscher Luftfahrer-Verband* (German Air Travellers' Association) licence No.305 (Ref: Supf, op.cit., vol I, p.570).

21   *Der rote Kampfflieger*, op.cit., p.78.

22   Ibid., p.79.

23   Ibid., p.80.

24   Ibid..

25   Many sources translate *Sperreflüge* to mean 'barrage flights,' presumably because the gunnery term *Sperrefeuer* is used to describe massive artillery fire; the author feels that 'barrier' or 'blockade' captures more of the sense of *Sperre* as applied to aviation.

26   *Mein Kriegstagebuch*, op.cit., p.68.

27   Ibid., p.69.

CHAPTER 4

THE BOELCKE ERA

Manfred von Richthofen's desire to become a combat pilot was fuelled by reports and discussions within the *Fliegertruppe* of the rising number of aerial victories achieved by the pilot he had met on the train to Rethel, *Ltn* Oswald Boelcke. Month by month, victory after victory, Boelcke and his squadron companion *Ltn* Max Immelmann were becoming the most successful practitioners of aerial combat with the single-seat Fokker *Eindecker*.

The uniqueness of their achievements led to a quick succession of high awards and growing recognition that encouraged like-minded combat pilots. One special honour came at Christmas 1915 from *Maj* Hermann von der Lieth-Thomsen, the *Chef der Feldflugwesens* (Chief of Field Aviation). He sent Boelcke and Immelmann each a one-litre silver goblet inscribed '*Dem Sieger im Luftkampf*' (To the Victor in Aerial Combat), and showing one eagle defeating another in the air. Named the *Ehrenbecher* (Goblet of Honour), this distinction was eventually awarded to every pilot, observer and aerial gunner on the occasion of attaining his first confirmed aerial victory. The *Ehrenbecher* became one more incentive to German airmen, encouraging them to seek out and destroy enemy aircraft.

After Boelcke and Immelmann had each attained eight confirmed aerial victories, on 12 January 1916 both were presented with the Kingdom of Prussia's highest award for bravery, the *Orden Pour le Mérite*.[1] The Order's handsome badge, a Maltese Cross of deep blue enamel with gold trim, worn at the neck, became the German Empire's *de facto* highest bravery decoration for commissioned officers. Other German states awarded high bravery honours in the grade of Commander's Cross, worn as a necklet, but the *Pour le Mérite* was generally considered to be *the* premier German bravery award.

THE WINDS OF CHANGE

While Manfred von Richthofen was undergoing his training in Döberitz, significant organizational changes were made in the combat aviation units. On 1 December 1915 the *Feldflugchef* ordered the establishment of two *Kampfgeschwader der Obersten Heeresleitung* (Combat Wings of the Supreme High Command), generally referred to by the acronym '*Kagohl*.' On 20 December the *BAO* was redesignated *Kagohl 1* and the *Brieftauben-Abreilung Metz* became *Kagohl 2*. *Kagohls 3, 4* and *5* were created at the same time. Each *Kagohl* had six *Kampfstaffeln* (Battle Squadrons) of six aircraft each, which could be deployed as units, responsible to the *Geschwader-Kommandeur,* who reported through Thomsen to the Supreme High Command.

Thus, when Richthofen returned to Metz on 16 March 1916, he reported to *Kasta 8* of *Kagohl 2,* commanded by prewar military pilot and *BAO* veteran *Hptmn* Victor Carganico. A neighbouring unit, *Kasta 10,* was led by *Hptmn* Wilhelm Boelcke, brother of the *Eindecker* pilot, which meant that Richthofen might have further contact with the celebrated combat flyer. Indeed, Oswald Boelcke had arrived in Metz only a few days earlier.

So that Manfred von Richthofen would have air combat matters to discuss with his new idol, he had his mechanics fasten a machine-gun to the top wing of his Albatros two-seater. In the same way that the French fixed machine-guns to the top wings of their Nieuport scouts, Manfred's gun was operated by a cable from the pilot's cockpit and aimed to fire *over* the propeller arc. 'People laughed at it because it looked so primitive,' Richthofen later wrote. 'I had absolute confidence in it, of course, and soon had the oppportunity to put it into practical use.'[2]

RICHTHOFEN'S FIRST SUCCESSFUL AIR FIGHT

During a 'barrier flight' near the Douaumont fortifications on 26 April, Richthofen spotted a Nieuport scout and dived on it before it could endanger German aircraft. In the Albatros' rear cockpit, his observer prepared to shoot at the target once he was properly aligned with it. He was surprised when Richthofen pursued the French aircraft and opened fire on it. Both men were startled when the Nieuport reared up and then fell over and went spiralling down into the ground. As there was no independent confirmation, Manfred was not credited with the victory. His and another anonymous victory were acknowledged only in an official communiqué, which was quoted in the foreign press: 'Apart from other aerial enterprises [on 26 April], one of our flying squadrons dropped a large number of bombs on the French flying ground of Brocourt, east of Clermont, and on the strongly held village of Jubécourt. Two enemy aeroplanes were shot down in an aerial fight above Fleury (south of Douaumont) and west thereof.'[3]

The prospect of aerial combat occurred again on 1 May, when, off in the distance near Verdun, Richthofen saw a Fokker *Eindecker* boldly attack a flight of twin-engined Caudron bombers. He was hampered by a headwind and, as he struggled to come to his countryman's aid, he witnessed the Fokker pilot's valiant efforts: 'First, he shot down a Frenchman in the midst of a hostile squadron. Then he evidently had a jam in his machine-gun and wanted to return to the air above our lines. A whole swarm of Frenchmen were on him. With a bullet through his head, he fell from an altitude of 3,000 metres — a beautiful death.'[4]

Subsequently, Richthofen learned that the Fokker pilot had been his old friend *Rittm* Erich *Graf* von Holck, whom he had visited a few days earlier. Richthofen flew to Sivry for the funeral, just one of many such events, both modest and elaborate, that he would attend within the next two years.

The grim reality of aerial combat had also been brought home to Lothar von Richthofen, who, at Manfred's suggestion, had joined the *Fliegertruppe* in the summer of 1915. By the year's end Lothar had become an observer with the newly-constituted *Kagohl 4*'s *Kasta 23*, operating on the Verdun and Somme Fronts.

Lothar's letter of 8 May recounts: 'Manfred visited me for an hour [recently]. It was very nice to see him again, here in the field. A few days later [26 April] he shot down a Frenchie. Unfortunately, I have not yet succeeded at that, although I already have a few aerial combats behind me. Once [on 28 April] I saved one of our aircraft from the clutches of two Frenchmen. The observer, a *Ltn* von Schwerin of my *Staffel*, was mortally wounded[5] and could no longer defend himself. Unfortunately, he later died. The pilot was only lightly wounded.'[6]

DANGEROUS FLIGHTS AND CRASHES

A few days later Manfred von Richthofen had a close encounter with another enemy in the air: bad weather. He had flown his Albatros C.III from *Kasta 8*'s airfield at Mont, near Landres, to the main field at Metz to attend to administrative duties. As it was a routine, behind-the-lines flight, he flew without an observer; a 100kg ballast sack was secured in the rear compartment to balance the aircraft. Thus, with no observer to order him not to fly when a storm was obviously impending, Richthofen disregarded other pilots' advice against such a move and was soon on his way for the short hop of some 35km.

Within minutes he flew into blinding rain and fierce winds that tossed the Albatros about like a piece of paper. Only luck kept him from smashing into the Moselle Mountains. The would-be Germanic hero was forcefully reminded by deafening claps of thunder and precariously close flashes of lightning that, like Siegfried, even the bravest of warriors cannot defy the powers of the heavens.

Wotan's point having been made, Manfred von Richthofen was allowed to thread his way through the rain and back to his own airfield, where reports were already circulating that he had been last seen disappearing into a thundercloud. Chastened by the experience, but losing none of his plucky spirit, Manfred later wrote: 'Never again, unless required by my Fatherland, would I fly through a thunderstorm. In recollection [however], everything was beautiful, [and] there were some beautiful moments that I would not have wanted to miss in my life as a flyer.'[7]

Manfred sensed within himself that he was an airfighter and, potentially, a leader of other airfighters. But he knew that the fulfilment of his destiny lay in single-seaters, not in the reconnaissance and bombing aircraft he flew with *Kasta 8*. His *Staffel* leader, Victor Carganico, recalled: 'At the time he came to my *Staffel* as a two-seater pilot, he was already urging that I send him for two or three days to the *"Heldenvater"* [father of heroes], the head of the Air Park in Montmédy, [Alfred] Keller,[8] for single-seat fighter instruction. After his return, I placed my own single-seater at his disposal, as, due to engine failure [and] through no fault of his own, he had had to "set down" [his own aircraft] near Verdun.'[9]

Richthofen eagerly sought to become *Kasta 8*'s resident fighter pilot. But *Hptmn* Carganico assigned two pilots to provide the air defence role: *Ltn* Manfred von Richthofen to make the morning flights and 24-year-old *Ltn.d.Res* Hans Reimann to fly afternoon patrols.

The first day's operations were uneventful. Richthofen and Reimann were each afraid that the other would crash the *Eindecker* and end their dreams of glory. On the second day Reimann encountered a French Nieuport over the lines and was badly shot up. He made a forced landing between the lines and had to set fire to the aeroplane. It was several weeks before another *Eindecker* arrived, and then it was Manfred von Richthofen's misfortune to have the engine quit on take-off, sending the fast little Fokker into a heap at the end of the runway.

BLACK JUNE

Obltn Max Immelmann was flying an *Eindecker* when he was killed during an air combat with an F.E.2b of No.25 Squadron, RFC, on 18 June. That event was ominous for other *Eindecker* pilots to whom Immelmann and Boelcke had become larger-than-life heroes. Moreover, the unexplained loss of a top fighter pilot in one of his aeroplanes was bad for Anthony Fokker. The other leading combat flyer, Oswald Boelcke, was then testing the 120hp Mercedes-powered Fokker D.I biplane, one of several proposed successors to the E-series.

To prevent German combat pilot morale from eroding further with another loss, Oswald Boelcke was removed from flight status on the direct orders of *Kaiser* Wilhelm II. He was sent to the Balkans on an 'inspection tour' of German units and their local allies.

Great air battles eluded Manfred von Richthofen. Even with his machine-gun-equipped two-seater he was unable to attract a worthy opponent. Richthofen, *Obltn* Georg Zeumer and *Ltn.d.Res* Hans Reimann continued to gain experience with the *Eindecker* —undaunted by Immelmann's sad fate — but with nothing to show for their efforts.

Frustrated and impatient again, Richthofen wrote home:

> A few days ago I nose-dived into the ground with my Fokker. Witnesses were more than a little astonished when, after quite some time, I crawled out of the heap of rubble totally unhurt. My good friend Zeumer has already gone one better. First he was shot down by the French and received only light grazing shots, [and then] three days later he broke his thigh under quite stupid circumstances.

I am entertaining the thought of going to Boelcke and [asking about] becoming his student. I always need a change. That would be something new again and would not hurt me.[10]

Before Richthofen could apply for a transfer to *Kampfgruppe Boelcke*, the famous ace was en route to Turkey and the men and aircraft of *KG 2* were on a train heading to the Eastern Front.

BACK TO THE EASTERN FRONT

The opening of the Russian offensive in June provided the opportunity — and the need — to shift some Western Front air units away from the area of such significant losses. *Feldfl.-Abt. 62* had already been sent in response to the offensive launched by Russian General Aleksei Alekseievich Brusilov's South-West Army Group; his objective was to draw German forces away from France and Austro-Hungarian forces away from the Italian Front. The desired effect was achieved, but the crack German units sent east inflicted a series of stinging defeats on the Russian forces.

In early July *Kagohl 2* arrived at an airfield outside the Ukrainian city of Kovel, an important railhead that was threatened by Brusilov's forces. In the absence of barracks and other amenities, the unit lived aboard a special train put at their disposal. Richthofen and two other comrades — *Leutnants* Alfred Gerstenberg and Franz Christian von Scheele from *Kasta 11* — found the train hot and stuffy, parked under the beating summer sun. They set up a tent in a nearby forest, to ensure that they were rested when they undertook long flights over the Russian lines.

A frequent target was the railway station at Manjewicze, and Richthofen flew numerous successful missions there. When writing his memoirs, while on leave the following summer, Richthofen recalled wistfully:

> Many times I hauled 150kg bombs with an ordinary C-type aeroplane. Moreover, I even had with me a heavy observer, who had apparently not suffered at all from the meat shortage and, "just in case", I had two machine-guns. I was never able to try them out in Russia. It is too bad that not a single Russian is in my collection [of airfighting souvenirs at home]. His cockade would have looked very colourful on the wall. In any case, a flight with clumsy, heavily-laden machines is not easy, especially in the Russian noonday heat. The big barges sway very unpleasantly, [and] they don't falter, of course, [as] the 150 "horses" see to that, but it is still not a pleasant feeling to have so much munitions and fuel along. Finally one is in a sea of calm air and gradually comes to enjoy the bombing flight. It is nice to fly straight ahead, to have a definite target and firm orders. After a bombing flight one has the feeling: you have accomplished something. Many times during a fighter patrol when no one has shot down anything, one says to oneself: you could have done better.[11]

Once, on the way back from Manjewicze, Richthofen and his observer flew near a Russian airfield just as an aeroplane was taking off. 'Did he have in mind to attack us?', Richthofen mused. 'I believe not. More likely he sought security in the air, for most certainly that is the comfortable place to avoid personal mortal danger during bombing attacks on an airfield.'[12]

Undisturbed by the Russian aeroplane, Richthofen and his observer chose a tethered observation balloon as a suitable target for their last bomb. They dropped it on the base, hoping to sever the tethering cable or destroy the winch that controlled the balloon's ascent. It was not clear what damage they had done, so they headed back to Kovel.

As the summer wore on, *Kagohl 2* aircraft made further attacks against Russian forces and helped to drive them off to the north and east so that German and Austro-Hungarian army units could move on to victory under *Generalfeldmarschall* von Hindenburg, who had become commander of all German forces in the east.

Hindenburg's brilliant successes on the Eastern Front were offset by a lack of any meaningful progress on the stalemated Western Front. The British offensive on the Somme and greater efforts by French forces at Verdun and along the Meuse River were becoming two powerful pressure points to the German war effort. Furthermore, Allied air forces were gaining superiority in numbers and quality.

BOELCKE RECALLED TO DUTY

Clearly changes were needed. Boelcke's admirer and patron, *Feldflugchef* Thomsen, was developing plans for the reorganization of the *Fliegertruppe*. Part of that plan called for the creation of *Jagdstaffeln* that would tactically support each *Armee* in a co-ordinated manner. Thomsen, now an *Oberstleutnant* (Lieutenant Colonel), made one obvious and one unlikely choice for commanding officers of the first two fighter units: *Hptmn* Oswald Boelcke, the highest-scoring ace at the time, to lead *Jasta 2*, and *Hptmn* Martin Zander, a prewar flyer who had also shot down one enemy aircraft, to command *Jasta 1*.[13] When he received his orders on 11 August,[14] Boelcke used part of his 'tour' to identify some of the first-class pilots he would need.

By then, Boelcke had gone from Turkey to Macedonia and on to Bulgaria. After visiting a variety of Austro-Hungarian dignitaries, *Hptmn* Boelcke relaxed for a short time with his brother Wilhelm, discussing the merits of various pilots they knew.Before departing on 15 August, Oswald Boelcke made two selections. The first was *Ltn.d.Res* Erwin Böhme, who at 37 was an 'old man' in *Kasta 10*; twelve years Boelcke's senior. The second was Manfred von Richthofen, who later claimed that he did not expect to be asked to join the new *Jagdstaffel*, but he certainly hinted at his objective when recounting that golden moment:

Suddenly in the early morning there was a knock at the door and before me stood the great man with the *Pour le Mérite*. I really did not know what he wanted of me. To be sure, I knew him ... but it did not occur to me that he had sought me out to invite me to become a pupil of his. I could have hugged him when he asked whether I wanted to go to the Somme with him.

Three days later I sat on a train and travelled across Germany to my new field of action. Finally my fondest wish was fulfilled and now the most beautiful time of my life began for me.

I dared not hope at the time that it would turn out so successfully. On parting, a good friend called out to me: "Don't come back without the *Pour le Mérite*!".[15]

In fact, Manfred von Richthofen did not report directly to his new unit, the formal title of which was *königliche preussische Jagdstaffel 2* (Royal Prussian Fighter Squadron 2); the Prussian distinction is important, as the Kingdoms of Bavaria, Saxony and Württemberg also had their 'own' units, staffed largely (but not exclusively) by subjects of the respective monarchs,[16] and placed at the disposal of the overall German war effort.

Manfred arrived in Schweidnitz on 25 August and spent a quiet few days at home. One day he and his father went hunting and, between them, they bagged fifteen partridges.[17] Within a month Richthofen and his new comrades were 'bagging' aerial prey in the skies over France.

As Manfred von Richthofen headed for the Western Front, a major change occurred within the German military structure. On 29 August *General der Infanterie* Erich von Falkenhayn, Chief of the General Staff and architect of the unsuccessful Verdun offensive, 'requested' to be relieved of command at the relatively young age of 55. Falkenhayn was succeeded by an officer fourteen years his senior, *Generalfeldmarschall* Paul von Beneckendorff und von Hindenburg, the renowned overall commander of the Eastern Front. This shift at the top echelon was good for the *Fliegertruppe*, as 49-year-old *Feldflugchef* Thomsen was a protégé of Hindenburg's chief of staff, Erich Ludendorff, who at 51 had just been promoted from *Generalleutnant* to *General der Infanterie* and appointed *Generalquartiermeister* (Quartermaster General), as well.

As the winds of change blew through the German military establishment and area commanders sought new solutions to their problems, the death knell was sounded for the free-ranging but tactically ineffective *Kampfeinsitzer* units then in service on the Western Front. The *Einsitzer* units had to be made more effective. Even the name *Kampfeinsitzerstaffel* had to be changed[18] to reflect the offensive capabilities of the new D-Type aircraft being built for front-line service.

Thus, *Jagdstaffel 2* was formally established on 10 August 1916.[19] Over the next few weeks, pilots from other units arrived to fill the *Staffel* roster. On 1 September *Ltn* Manfred von Richthofen and his one-time

Fokker *Eindecker* 'co-owner' from *Kasta 8*, *Ltn* Hans Reimann, arrived at Bertincourt on the Somme Front.

LEARNING FROM THE MASTER

Hptmn Oswald Boelcke had little time to train his new unit, as Entente ground and air forces were gaining strength daily. While he waited for more and better aircraft to arrive, Boelcke simply gathered his men around and told them everything he had learned about air combat. He was most familiar with the Fokker series, having flown all models of the *Eindecker* and having helped to develop the D-Type single-seat biplanes; hence, he could comment on the strengths and weaknesses of each, compared with many Entente aircraft. All of his warriors were fully qualified *Feldpiloten* (Military Pilots), so it was quite sufficient for him to explain what he expected and then to watch the men perform.

Of course, they expected the *Staffelführer* to perform as well, and Boelcke did not disappoint them. During an afternoon patrol on 2 September he spotted anti-aircraft shellbursts in the distance, over Bapaume, a sure sign of enemy air activity. His aircraft, Fokker D.III 352/16, was equipped with the powerful 160hp Oberursel U.III rotary engine and quickly brought him to the scene of the action. Even though Boelcke had not flown in combat for three months, he was ready to fight. It was like old times; he was in a fast, powerful fighter with two machine-guns, and below him was a B.E.2c, apparently on an artillery-spotting mission, escorted by three Vickers-type single-seat pusher biplanes.

Using the advantage of height, Boelcke made the classic hawk-like dive on to the B.E. with guns firing, hoping for a fast kill. He did not hit the two-seater; instead, he sparked the interest of the escorts, one of which pursued him, but without success.

Within the next two weeks *Hptmn* Oswald Boelcke used his Fokker D.III to shoot down six more British aircraft. But he was not merely demonstrating his own prowess in the air; in his exercises behind the lines Boelcke had to retrain his pilots. They had become accustomed to individual flying or the ineffective two-aircraft 'barrier flights' to keep enemy aircraft from penetrating German lines. Boelcke drilled them in the close formation flying needed to pierce the the Entente formations that flew over German positions. As his fledglings proved themselves in the skies of Bertincourt, Boelcke began to bring them along on his 'hunting flights'.

Hptmn Boelcke had achieved his 23rd, 24th, 25th and 26th victories by the time he led the patrol in which *Ltn* Manfred von Richthofen became a true *Jagdflieger*. The steel-tube-framed and fabric-covered Fokker D-Types never lived up to their expectations as successors to the once formidable E-Types that had given the *Fliegertruppe* its first reign of aerial superiority; something more than moderate generational progress was needed to regain mastery of the air. The answer lay in the new single-seat biplane series developed by the Albatros Flugzeugwerke in Schneidemühl, best known for its sturdy and reliable two-seat B- and C-Type biplane reconnaissance aircraft.

On Saturday 16 September *Jasta 2*'s first batch of six Albatros D.I fighters arrived, and they were taken to the firing range to check the alignment of their twin fixed 'Spandau' LMG 08/15 machine-guns. The Albatros D.I was slightly heavier than the Fokker and 120hp-engined Halberstadt D-types then in service, but it was faster[20] and more manoeuvrable. Instead of the troublesome air-cooled Oberursel rotary engine with its built-in torque problem, the Albatros D.I was powered by the 'eminently reliable six-cylinder, water-cooled Mercedes D-III'[21] 160hp stationary engine.

From its rounded propeller spinner to the end of its streamlined, plywood-covered semi-monocoque fuselage, the Albatros D.I was sleek. Its appearance and success in aerial combat led to the Albatros D-Types being nicknamed '*Haifisch*' (shark).

RICHTHOFEN'S FIRST KILL

On 17 September at about 1100 (German time), Boelcke led five of his pilots in close formation toward the British lines. It was the moment of truth for Manfred von Richthofen. Before him lay the opportunity to combine his enthusiasm and long-cultivated skills for the hunt, his ability as a pilot and his iron-hard discipline as a professional military man.

'We were all beginners, [and] none of us had until now been credited with a success,' Richthofen later wrote. 'Whatever Boelcke told us was taken as gospel ... Before we took off Boelcke [had] imparted precise instructions to us and for the first time we flew as a squadron under the leadership of the famous man in whom we had blind confidence.

'... each one of us struggled to stay close behind Boelcke. It was clear to all of us that we had to pass our first test under the eyes of our revered leader.'[22]

Boelcke led his pupils into the fray, but did not fire at first. He was there to observe and perhaps protect any newcomer so intent on the prospective victory before him that he would not spot the Angel of Death, the enemy aircraft that might get above and behind him in the classic 'kill' position.

Richthofen closed on F.E.2b 7018, piloted by 2/Lt L.B.F. Morris of No.11 Squadron. 'But he appeared to be no beginner, for he knew precisely that the moment I succeeded in getting behind him, his last hour was being chimed,' Richthofen wrote. 'At the time I did not have conviction that "he must fall", as I now have competely; rather, I was much more anxious about *whether* he would indeed fall and that is a substantial difference. After the first or even the second or third try, it dawns on one: "That's how you must do it."'[23]

Morris did his utmost to evade Richthofen. His observer, Lt T. Rees, clung to the rearward-firing machine-gun and fired at the Albatros constantly. For a moment, the two young Britons thought they had eluded the tenacious Albatros pilot; Morris headed for home. In that instant of non-evasive flying, Richthofen suddenly popped up behind the 'Fee' and opened fire.

> I was so close to him that I was afraid I would ram into him. Then, suddenly, the opponent's propeller turned no more. Hit! The engine was shot up and the enemy had to land on our side, as it was out of the question for him to reach his own lines. I noticed the machine making swaying movements that [indicated] something was not quite right with the pilot. Also the observer was no longer to be seen, his machine-gun pointed unattended up in the air. Therefore, I had hit him and he was lying on the floor of the fuselage.[24]

The pilot managed to land the stricken aircraft at a nearby German airfield at Flesquières, used by *Feldfl.-Abt. 22* and *41* at the time. Richthofen was so exhilarated by the thrill of the hunt that he followed close behind and made a rough landing that almost wiped out his new Albatros. As his propeller windmilled to a stop, Richthofen leapt out of his aeroplane and joined the group of soldiers running toward the F.E.2b. He watched as its dying pilot and dead observer were removed.[25]

Richthofen flew back to Bertincourt, 10km away, where Boelcke and his comrades were enjoying a late breakfast and reviewing the morning's work. When asked where he had been for so long, Richthofen proudly replied: 'One Englishman shot down!'.[26]

There was much cause to rejoice at *Jasta 2* that day. In addition to Richthofen's first confirmed victory, *Ltn* Erwin Böhme had scored his first, a Sopwith two-seater,[27] and *Ltn.d.Res* Hans Reimann had achieved his second, an F.E.2b[28] from the same flight that Richthofen had attacked. Assured that his pupils were in successful situations, the *Staffelführer* had attacked and shot down an F.E.2b,[29] recorded as his 27th aerial victory.

RAF Historian H.A. Jones put *Jasta 2*'s achievements that day in this perspective: 'Their success, against seasoned opponents, achieved on aeroplanes which had arrived only the previous evening, constituted a remarkable performance. It gave Boelcke's new fighting squadron immediate prestige.'[30]

That evening *Hptmn* Boelcke hosted a celebration for everyone in *Jasta 2*. As *Fliegertruppe* officers and enlisted pilots were indistinguishable in the 'battlefield' of the air, they had a closer bond with each other. Likewise, there was a greater dependency on the enlisted ground crews who maintained the aircraft. Hence it was in everyone's best interests to be more open and less rank-conscious.

The highlight of the evening came when *Hptmn* Boelcke awarded the Iron Cross 1st Class to *Ltn* Böhme and personally pinned the medal to his new fellow pilot's tunic. By that time, the *EK I* had lost much of its lustre as a decoration — but, when personally presented by an officer of high rank or prestige, the time-honoured Teutonic battle symbol gained a special significance.

Manfred von Richthofen may not have received an award from the hand of his *Staffelführer*, and his *Ehrenbecher* had not yet arrived, but he ensured that this achievement did not go unmarked. Later that evening he wrote to a Berlin jeweller he knew and ordered as a special memento a small plain, silver cup, about an inch across and two inches tall, with the lip sloping slightly toward the base. It was to be inscribed '1. Vickers 2. 17.9.16' to indicate his first victory, scored over a 'Vickers-type' two-seat aircraft on 17 September 1916. This cup was the first of 60 to be ordered to mark the ace's victories before the jeweller was no longer able to produce them owing to the acute shortage of silver by the time Richthofen had scored his 60th victory in September 1917.[31]

The following day Richthofen wrote to his mother, recounting his own success and betraying his envy of Boelcke's special talent: 'Boelcke is a mystery to each of us, [as] he shoots one down on almost every flight. I was in the air and took part in the fights [in which he shot down] his 24th, 25th, 26th and 27th.'[32]

Despite a ground mist on the morning of 23 September,[33] Boelcke led five comrades on a hunt over the road from Bapaume and Cambrai. Near Bapaume they intercepted six Martinsyde G.100 'Elephant' single-seaters of No.27 Squadron, the only RFC unit completely equipped with the ungainly two-bay biplanes that were more suited to bomb-carrying than aerial combat.[34]

Richthofen pursued 'Elephant' 7481 and shot it down over Beugny, killing the pilot, Sgt Herbert Bellerby, and scoring his second victory. In the next instant, *Ltn* Reimann engaged and shot down a Martinsyde, which was credited as his fourth victory. Reimann then went after Lt L.F. Forbes in A1565. His ammunition spent, Forbes deliberately rammed Reimann, sending him down out of control over Noreuil; Reimann crashed fatally just north of Beugny. Forbes managed to fly his badly damaged Martinsyde to No.24 Squadron's aerodrome at Bertangles. There, Lt (later Air Marshal Sir Leslie F.) Forbes was injured when he purposely hit a tree to stop his uncontrollable aircraft on the ground.[35]

That evening, Richthofen wrote to his jeweller in Berlin and ordered a second silver cup, inscribed: 2. Martinsyde 1. 23.9.16.

Amidst a dense morning haze on Sunday 24 September, *Jasta 2* began relocating to Lagnicourt, about 9km north of Bertincourt, to improve the dispersal of the aviation units around Bapaume. Manfred von Richthofen achieved his third victory on 30 September, a bright autumn day. Capitalizing on bad weather the previous day, British ground forces had made significant progress in recovering the Pozières Ridge and the Ancre Valley. On the 30th the Royal Flying Corps reinforced the offensive.

Escorted by the Nieuport and Morane fighters of No.60 Squadron and the F.E.s of No.11 Squadron, aircraft of Nos.12 and 13 Squadrons bombed *Jasta 2*'s airfield at Lagnicourt. The one acknowledged RFC loss, an F.E.,[36] was no doubt Richthofen's work.

Richthofen was following the route from Bapaume to Cambrai that he had come to know so well. On that road, over the town of Frémicourt, he surprised F.E.2b 6973 of No.11 Squadron and sent it down in flames, killing its crew, Lt Ernest C. Lansdale and Sgt Albert Clarkson. He described that victory and his further ambitions in a letter home:

> The heart beats a little faster when the opponent, whose face one has just seen, goes roaring down from 4,000 metres. When I arrived down below, of course nothing remained of the men or the machine.
>
> I removed a small [national] insignia as a souvenir. From my second [victory] I took the machine-gun as a souvenir. It has a bullet of mine in the bolt and is useless. My Frenchman from Verdun does not count, unfortunately; at the time it was claimed he was forgotten.
>
> Earlier, one received the *Pour le Mérite* after the eighth [victory], but no longer, even though it is becoming ever more difficult to shoot down [an enemy aircraft]. In the last four weeks since the establishment of *Jagdstaffel Boelcke* we have lost five of our ten aircraft.[37]

On 1 October *Hptmn* Boelcke scored his 30th victory. He executed the classic 'hit-and-run' manoeuvre against a B.E.2c, sending it down over Eaucourt l'Abbaye, southwest of Bapaume.

After nearly a week of bad weather, the *Staffel*'s fortunes improved on 7 October, when Boelcke and Richthofen scored. Once again, Boelcke managed to creep up on his opponent and open fire, after which 'the aeroplane, a Nieuport two-seater, exploded in the air' east of Morval, for his 31st victory.[38]

Richthofen's fourth victory was described in an official report: 'The biplane single-seater (Lt Fenwick) shot down by *Ltn Frhr* von Richthofen near Equancourt belonged to the 21st Squadron and, indeed, according to the papers [found in it] to a B.E. Flight. The aeroplane is apparently one of new construction.'[39]

THE NEW *LUFTSTREITKRÄFTE* EMERGES

While the weather again hampered flight operations on the Somme Front, the general reorganization of German forces continued. As a consequence, on 8 October the *Fliegertruppe* itself changed. *Gen-Ltn* Ernst von Hoeppner, an old cavalryman commanding the *75. Infanterie-Division*,[40] became *Kommandierende General der Luftstreitkräfte* (Commanding General of the Air Force). The loose command structure of the old *Fliegertruppe* gave way to a unified command: 'the scope of what had been under the *Feldflugchef* (Thomsen) for aviation, captive balloons, Army airships and the Army

Weather Service, as well as the anti-aircraft and home defence units.'[41]

The *Kogenluft*, as the office was known in its abbreviated form, expanded some units and reassigned or consolidated others. The *Jagdstaffeln*, which had grown to 15 at this point, were to be expanded to 37 in time for the spring 1917 offensive.[42] While there would continue to be patrols by lone aircraft seeking targets of opportunity, increasing emphasis was placed on developing strategies and tactics for massed air strength.

Hptmn Oswald Boelcke proved the value of co-ordinated attacks during a break in the bad weather on 10 October. He led repeated attacks against RFC aircraft intent on bombing German airfields and other targets from Longueval to right over his own airfield at Lagnicourt. During one of these forays *Ltn* Manfred von Richthofen claimed as his fifth victory a 'Vickers' over Roeux, but it was disallowed.[43]

Richthofen's confirmed fifth victory was achieved six days later, when he attacked B.E.12 6580 of No.19 Squadron over the village of Ytres (a few kilometres east of Lechelle on the Somme Front and *not*, as other sources contend, the city of Ypres, more than 80km to the north, in Flanders); the pilot, 2/Lt John Thompson, was killed.

At 0935 on 25 October *Ltn* von Richthofen shot down another B.E.12, north of Bapaume. This aircraft was 6629 of No.21 Squadron; again, the pilot, 2/Lt A.J. Fisher, was killed.[44] Richthofen was credited with his sixth victory.

BOELCKE FALLS

Low clouds, rain and heavy wind all day curtailed flight operations on Friday 27 October. It was a welcome respite for both sides. The following day the weather was little better. Low clouds and strong wind all day with occasional showers.

It started out as another day of rest for *Jasta 2*, as described by *Ltn* Erwin Böhme in a letter:

> On Saturday afternoon we sat around in a state of readiness inside our little cottage at the airfield. I had just begun a game of chess with Boelcke — when shortly after 4:00 [1600] we were called up to the Front during an infantry attack. Boelcke himself led us, as usual. Very soon we were over Flers and attacking several British aeroplanes, fast single-seaters, which ably defended themselves.
>
> In the fierce aerial combat that followed, during which we had only a brief time to fire, we sought to drive them down by alternately cutting them off, as we had already done so often with success ...
>
> ... Boelcke and I had an Englishman right between us, when another opponent pursued by friend Richthofen cut in front of us. During the simultaneous lightning-quick evasive manoeuvre, Boelcke and I, obstructed by our wings, did not see each other for an instant and that is when it happened.

How can I describe for you my feelings at that instant when Boelcke suddenly appeared a few metres to my right, dived down, [while] I pulled up , [and] yet we grazed each other and had to go back to the ground! It was only a gentle touch, but at such a furious speed it also meant a collision.[45]

The other participant in the action, Manfred von Richthofen, described the final scene and what followed in a letter to his mother dated 3 November 1916:

... Nothing happened to the other poor fellow [Böhme]. At first Boelcke went down normally. I followed him immediately. Later one of the wings broke away and he went rushing down. His skull was crushed on impact; therefore he died instantly. It affected all of us very deeply — as if a favourite brother had been taken from us.

During the funeral, I carried the *Ordenskissen*. The service was like that of a reigning prince. In six weeks, we have had six killed and one wounded; two are washed up because of their nerves.

Yesterday I shot down my seventh, after I had shortly before dispatched my sixth.[46] My nerves have not yet suffered as a result of the others' bad luck.[47]

A special RFC mission was detailed to fly over the German lines with a token of condolence. Ground troops near the airfield at Lagnicourt found a parachuted wreath with the inscription: 'To the memory of Captain Boelcke, our brave and chivalrous foe. From the British Royal Flying Corps.'[48]

The mortal remains of *Hptmn* Oswald Boelcke, then Germany's highest-scoring fighter ace, were sent to his adopted home town of Dessau for a hero's burial. *Ltn* Manfred von Richthofen was accorded the honour of being named the *Staffel*'s representative to the official funeral cortège. Unfortunately he missed the train to Dessau and had to return to his flying duties at Lagnicourt.

NOTES

1   O'Connor, *Aviation Awards of Imperial Germany in World War I and the Men Who Earned Them*, vol II, (1990), p.62.
2   von Richthofen, *Der rote Kampfflieger*, (1933), p.86.
3   *Aeronautics*, 3 May 1916, p.294.
4   Quoted in Gibbons, *The Red Knight of Germany*, (1927), p.59.
5   According to the official German aviation casualty list, *Ltn* Wilhelm Schwerin, 18 years old, formerly of the *Garde du Corps*, was shot down over Rethel on 28 April 1916 and died of his wounds on 2 May.
6   Quoted in von Richthofen, *Mein Kriegstagebuch*, (1937), p.76.
7   *Der rote Kampfflieger*, op.cit., p.91.
8   Alfred Keller, a prewar *Feldpilot* (Military Pilot), commanded *Feldfl.-Abt. 27* at the beginning of the war and subsequently headed *Armeeflugpark 5* at Montmédy. A pioneer in night-time bombing operations, *Hptmn* Keller was awarded the *Orden Pour le Mérite* as *Kommandeur* of *Kagohl 1* on 4 December 1917.
9   Quoted in Supf, *Das Buch der deutschen Fluggeschichte*, vol II (1958).

10   *Der rote Kampfflieger*, op.cit., p.95; *Mein Kriegstagebuch*, op.cit., pp.75-76 notes that
      Zeumer was shot down over Fort Vaux and was subsequently injured in an automobile
      accident.
11   *Der rote Kampfflieger*, op.cit., pp.97-98.
12   Ibid., p.99.
13   Ferko, *Fliegertruppe 1914-1918*, (1980), p.6.
14   Miller and Puglisi, *Jasta B*, (1968), p.314.
15   *Der rote Kampfflieger*, op.cit., pp.102-103.
16   Ritter, *Der Luftkrieg*, (1926), pp.166-167.
17   *Mein Kriegstagebuch*, op.cit., p.79.
18   While the name *Kampfeinsitzerstaffel* was withdrawn from use at the battlefronts, it was
      not retired. To meet the threat of increased Entente air raids on German cities, six new
      home defence units were created and named *Kampfeinsitzerstaffeln*, abbreviated *Kest*.
      Initially, *Kests 1* and *2* were assigned to Mannheim, *Kest 3* to Karlsruhe, *Kest 4* to
      Böblingen, *Kest 5* to Freiburg and *Kest 6* to Köln. (Ref: Kriegsministerium *Bericht Nr
      941/16.g.A7L*, 5 September 1916.)
19   Kriegsministerium (organization manual), *Teil 10 Abschnitt B, Flieger-Formationen*,
      p.234.
20   Lamberton, *Fighter Aircraft of the 1914-1918 War*, (1960), pp.218-219.
21   Gray, *The Albatros D.I-D.III*, (1966), p.3.
22   *Der rote Kampfflieger*, op.cit., pp.103-104.
23   Ibid., p.105.
24   Ibid., pp.105-106.
25   *RFC Casualty List* information for this crew and aircraft reports: 'Left aerodrome at
      9.10 a.m. Two F.E.s seen to go down under control west of Marcoing. Information
      received from 2/Lt Pinkerton that both Morris and Rees were killed. Information from a
      private source that 2/Lt Morris died at Cambrai hospital on Sept. 17th." If F.E.2b 7018
      went down *west* of Marcoing, as stated, and on to a German airfield, as Richthofen
      reported, the likely site would have been at Flesquières, which is closer to Cambrai than
      Villers Plouich, which other sources identify as the landing site.
26   *Der rote Kampfflieger*, op.cit., p.107.
27   Sopwith 1½ Strutter A1913 of No.70 Squadron, 2/Lt O. Nixon and Lt R. Wood (both
      KiA).
28   F.E.2b 4844 of No.11 Squadron, 2/Lt T.P.L. Molloy (PoW) and Sgt G.J. Morton
      (KiA).
29   F.E.2b 7019 of No.11 Squadron, Capt D. Gray and Lt L.B. Helder (both PoW).
30   Jones, *The War in the Air*, vol II, (1928), p.283ff.
31   Gibbons, *op. cit.*, (1927), p.80.
32   Quoted in *Mein Kriegstagebuch*, op.cit., p.82.
33   *RFC War Diary* entry, 23 September 1916.
34   Lamberton, op.cit., p.50.
35   Bowyer, *The Flying Elephants*, (1972), pp.40-41.
36   Jones, op.cit., pp.295-296.
37   *Der rote Kampfflieger*, op.cit., pp.108-109.
38   *Stofl 1. Armee Wochenbericht, Teil 3* 9 November 1916; while there were no RFC Nieu-
      port losses that day, the aircraft could have been French, as the Morval area came
      under French control at the end of September 1916 (Ref: Jones, op.cit. p.300ff).
39   Ibid, *Teil 6*; B.E.12 6618 of No.21 Squadron, piloted by 2/Lt William C. Fenwick
      (KiA).
40   Neumann, *Die Deutschen Luftstreitkräfte im Weltkriege*, (1920), p.5; Zuerl, op.cit., p.227
      lists *75. Reserve-Division*.
41   von Hoeppner, *Deutschlands Krieg in der Luft*, (1921), p.82.
42   Kriegsministerium (organization manual), op. cit., pp.234-239.
43   Evans, *Manfred Freiherr von Richthofen Victory List*, (1992), p.131; the aircraft claimed
      was probably F.E.2b 4292 of No.25 Squadron, 2/Lt Moreton Hayne (KiA) and Lt
      Arthur H.M. Copeland (PoW), which was awarded to *Vzfw* Fritz Kosmahl and *Obltn*
      Neubürger of *Feldfl-Abt 22*, which operated within the *1. Armee* area.

44 The *RFC Casualty List* reported: 'Left aerodrome at 7.45 a.m. A B.E.12 was reported by 11th A.A. Battery to be seen diving down 15,000 yards N.E. of Maricourt, apparently under control pursued by a German biplane. Letter from 5th Aus.Divn. ... states the grave of 2/Lt. A.J. Fisher has been located ... [and] is marked with the regulation German wooden cross giving particulars.'

45 Böhme, *Briefe eines deutschen Kampffliegers an ein junges Mädchen*, (1930), pp.69-70.

46 Richthofen's count does not match the record, which shows his sixth victory to have been attained on 25 October 1916, as previously noted. Richthofen's seventh victory was attained the day he wrote this letter, as noted in the following chapter.

47 Quoted in *Mein Kriegstagebuch*, op.cit., p.86.

48 Jones, op.cit., p.312ff.

CHAPTER 5
COMMAND IN THE AIR

*O*bltn Stephan Kirmaier was the logical choice to succeed *Hptmn* Oswald Boelcke as commanding officer of *Jagdstaffel 2*. After Boelcke, Kirmaier was both the senior officer and, coincidentally, the *Staffel*'s highest-scoring fighter pilot at the time. The weather had just begun to clear when *Obltn* Kirmaier assumed command on 30 October. He reaffirmed Boelcke's tactical dictum: no fancy flying, just approach the enemy carefully and keep after him until he is hit. According to Manfred von Richthofen, Kirmaier 'maintained that he could fly only straight ahead,'[1] yet he was a successful fighter and an aggressive successor to Boelcke.[2]

On the afternoon of 1 November *Obltn* Kirmaier shot down a B.E.2d of No.9 Squadron over Le Sars. It was his eighth confirmed victory and, although little was said, his *Staffel* comrades anticipated that Kirmaier would receive the *Pour le Mérite*. Hence he became more and more the man to emulate.

Two days later, *Jastas* 2 and 5 were directed against F.E.2b photographic reconnaissance aircraft from Nos.18 and 22 Squadrons bound for Bapaume. *Obltn* Hans Berr led *Jasta* 5 south of Bapaume, while Kirmaier's pilots headed west. *Jasta* 2 intercepted the 'Fees' over Grévillers and, at 1410, the first opponent of the day fell into the nearby woods under the fire of *Ltn* von Richthofen as his seventh victory;[3] the two crewmen were killed.[4]

In a combat unrelated to the extended fight with the 'Fees', *Ltn.d.Res* Hans Imelmann shot down Nieuport 11 A125 of No.60 Squadron at 1645. The Nieuport, with its gun on the top wing, was no match for the Albatros and crashed at Douchy, northwest of Bapaume, mortally wounding its pilot, Lt J.M.J. Spencer. It was the fourth of six victories scored by the 19-year-old Hannover-born ace, who, despite a similar spelling of the family name, was not related to the great Saxon ace *Obltn* Max Immelmann.

A DUKE REWARDS RICHTHOFEN

News despatches in early November held great portent. On the 5th, eight-victory ace *Ltn.d.Res* Gustav Leffers of *Jasta* 1 was awarded the *Pour le Mérite*. On the 9th, *Jastas* 1 and 2 intercepted a large raiding force of sixteen single-seat B.E.2 bombers escorted by fourteen Nieuport Scouts of No.60 Squadron and F.E.2s of No.11 Squadron en route to the German ammunition dump at Vraucourt, northeast of Bapaume.[5] The B.E.2s, from Nos.12 and 13 Squadrons, attacked from the south and west. *Obltn* Kirmaier drove down one of them, credited as his ninth victory, and thus should have qualified to receive the *Pour le Mérite*.

Ltn Imelmann's fifth victory, a B.E.2, was recorded as a 'Vickers'(*sic*) brought down near Haplincourt at 1030.[6] At the same time, *Ltn* von Richthofen went after a B.E.2 that was to be his eighth. 'Just short of the target, I caught up with the last of the opponents,' Richthofen wrote. 'Right away my first shots put the gunner in the enemy aeroplane out of action and probably tickled the pilot a bit also; in any case he decided to land with his bombs. I burned him a little around the edges, and because of that the speed with which he sought to reach the ground became somewhat greater, to wit he tumbled down and fell [at Beugny] right near our airfield at Lagnicourt.'[7]

Richthofen and Imelmann landed immediately to confirm their kills. For Richthofen it was *the* important victory, and he wanted to secure his claim. He and Imelmann drove close to the crash site and then raced across acres of mud to seize souvenirs from the B.E.2cs.

Soon, other troops and officers arrived to see the fallen warbirds and their German victors. *Rittm* von Schack, a staff officer with *38. Infanterie-Division*, approached Richthofen and asked him to speak briefly with his superior. Richthofen later wrote:

> That was not very pleasant for me, for I had ... messed up my clothes. And the gentlemen I was now to be with were all fastidiously dressed. I was presented to a personage who had a strange appearance to me. A general's trousers, a high award [hanging] at his neck, but for all that a relatively youthful face, [and] indefinable epaulettes — in short, I sensed something exceptional [about him] and in the course of the conversation straightened out my shirt and trousers and took on a more military bearing. I did not know who he was. I took my leave of him and went home.
>
> That evening the telephone rang and I learned that he was His Royal Highness, Duke [Carl Eduard] of Saxe-Coburg-Gotha. I was ordered to report to him. It was known that the British had intended to drop bombs on his headquarters.[8] To that end I had helped keep the assailants away. For that I received the *Ovale Silberne Herzog Carl Eduard-Medaille* [Oval Silver Duke Carl Eduard Bravery Medal].[9]

The 32-year-old head of one of Europe's most prominent royal houses — linked to the House of Windsor and many other dynasties[10] — was the first in a long line of crowned heads and titled dignitaries to bestow honours upon Manfred von Richthofen. More than that, Duke Carl Eduard was also the first member of German royalty to take a personal interest in Richthofen. His fascination with flying dated back to the prewar years, when he supported aviation activities and was the principal sponsor of the Duke Carl Eduard Flying School in Gotha. One of the school's first instructors had been Richthofen's old comrade, Paul Henning von Osterroht. At the outbreak of war the flying school became *Flieger-Ersatz-Abt 3*, a primary military aviation training centre.[11] Given his high station, the Duke was not allowed to fly, but he could enjoy the company of aviators and subsequently hosted Manfred von Richthofen at his ducal residence and hunting lodge.

Richthofen was flattered to receive the medal from Duke Carl Eduard, but he was waiting for a higher award. He had every expectation that *Kaiser* Wilhelm II was about to authorize his highest award for bravery, the *Pour le Mérite*. The criteria were changing, however, and certain steps had to be followed. On 11 November *Ltn.d.Res* Albert Dossenbach of *Feldfl-Abt 22* was awarded the *Pour le Mérite* following his ninth aerial victory,[12] which had occurred on 3 November. The same army report that announced the highest awards for *Ltns.d.Res* Leffers and Dossenbach also noted that *Ltn Frhr* von Richthofen of *Jasta 2* and *Obltn* Berr of *Jasta 5* had each been awarded the Knight's Cross of the Royal Order of the House of Hohenzollern with Swords.[13] *Obltn* Berr gained his ninth victory on the same day as Dossenbach's — but Dossenbach had received the Hohenzollern award on 21 October and neither Berr nor Richthofen, or even Kirmaier, had yet received this high award from the *Kaiser*'s own royal house. With few exceptions, the Hohenzollern House Order became a required intermediate award between the *EK I* and the *Pour le Mérite* — and the aerial victory requirement for the latter honour was raised several times.[14]

Manfred von Richthofen was granted a short leave after receiving the Hohenzollern award. He 'borrowed' one of the general-purpose aeroplanes used to fetch people and parts, and headed for home. At the crack of dawn on 14 November *Freifrau* von Richthofen was surprised to find her oldest son at her doorstep.

Even though he was far from the Western Front, Richthofen spoke only about events in *Jasta 2*. He talked about Boelcke's tragic accident, Böhme's struggle to cope with the loss of their great leader, and the new type of warfare that pitted individual enemies against each other. *Du oder ich*. You or me.

The following morning Manfred accompanied his mother to the wedding of one of her nieces. The wedding festivities took him, mind and body, to happier times he once knew. Before the young couple were off on their honeymoon, however, Manfred was in his borrowed aeroplane, heading to the Front. He was back in time to help celebrate *Obltn* Stephan Kirmaier's tenth victory, a Sopwith 1½ Strutter of No.70 Squadron on 16 November.[15]

The epic Battle of the Somme came to an end on 18 November 1916, amidst a mixture of rain, snow and a thaw that turned the landscape into a sea of mud. The Entente actions succeeded in relieving the German Army's pressure on Verdun and, to a large extent, in keeping the *Luftstreitkräfte* on the defensive.[16]

Jasta 2, however, remained on the offensive. On the first day of good weather, Monday 20 November, Manfred von Richthofen had his best day so far. During the morning patrol, he claimed a B.E. single-seater south of Grandcourt.[17] At 1615 he brought down F.E.2b 4848 of No.18 Squadron south of Bapaume.[18] In his haste to order two more commemorative cups from his jeweller in Berlin, Richthofen reversed the order of the victories. The cup for the morning triumph was inscribed: 9. Vickers 2. 20.11.16. The second cup, of the same design but twice the size, recorded: 10. B.E. 1. 20.11.16. From then on, every tenth cup was of the larger size,[19] to help him keep score in what he anticipated would become a large collection.

Staffel leader *Obltn* Stephan Kirmaier was credited with his eleventh victory on 20 November, and was out to raise the score two days later. Again, he led the *Staffel* to the west of Bapaume, challenging the RFC over the lines.

Obltn Kirmaier was last seen going after a 'Vikkers' two-seater. Four *Jasta 2* Albatroses returned to Lagnicourt that afternoon. Missing was Kirmaier, who had been killed in combat over British-held territory.[20]

Until a new commanding officer was appointed, the unit was nominally led for a week by *Obltn* Karl Bodenschatz, the *Offizier zur besonderen Verwendung* (Officer Assigned for Special Duty) and the *Staffel*'s chief administrative officer.

In the absence of a formal *Staffelführer*, Manfred von Richthofen became the tacit leader in the air. He was, after all, the highest-scoring, highest-decorated junior officer in the unit. Apart from his junior status, Richthofen was the *Jagdflieger* who the other pilots looked up to. He proved his value the following afternoon.

RICHTHOFEN VS. HAWKER

Thursday 23 November was a splendid day for flying. After *Jasta 2*'s morning patrol took off from Lagnicourt, they headed southwest for Bapaume. They followed the main road toward Albert and, over Le Sars at about 1100, the Albatroses encountered de Havilland D.H.2s of No.24 Squadron escorting a flight of bombers. A general fight ensued, one of nineteen reported in the area around Bapaume that day.[21]

The fight dissolved with no further results, and *Jasta 2* returned to Lagnicourt to refuel and rearm. While Richthofen and his comrades prepared for their afternoon patrol, three D.H.2s of No.24 Squadron were warming up at Bertangles airfield, west of Albert. The squadron's commanding officer, Maj Lanoe G. Hawker, VC, DSO, led Capt J.O. Andrews and Lt (later Air Marshal Sir Robert) Saundby to Bapaume for a defensive patrol.

According to the official British account: '... The [D.H.2s] were at once attacked by the two strong hostile patrols, one of the enemy's machines diving on to the tail of Major Hawker's de Havilland. This machine was driven off by Capt Andrews, who was then attacked in the rear and, having his engine damaged, was forced to break off the combat. Lieut. Saundby drove off one hostile machine which was attacking Capt. Andrews and then engaged a second and drove it down out of control. Major Hawker was last seen engaging a hostile machine at about 3,000 feet.'[22]

Maj Lanoe G. Hawker, a nine-victory ace, master air tactician and the first recipient of the Victoria Cross 'for air *fighting*',[23] was locked in mortal combat with *Ltn* Manfred von Richthofen. Their encounter was nearly a battle of equals; both men were tenacious, aggressive fighters, neither asking nor giving any quarter. The critical difference was the superiority of Richthofen's Albatros D.II, 491/16, over Hawker's D.H.2, 5864.

'I was soon keenly aware that I was not dealing with a beginner, for [it was clear] he did not even dream of breaking off the fight,' Richthofen wrote later. 'To be sure, he had a very manoeuvrable crate, but mine climbed better and so I succeeded in getting above and behind the Englishman.'[24]

As they circled each other, looking for an advantage, the two opponents were carried ever eastward by the wind, over German-held territory. At what seemed to be a propitious moment, Maj Hawker made a break southward for his own lines. Richthofen was right after him. Hawker zigzagged to present a more difficult target, but, in so doing, lost airspeed. As Richthofen closed in for the kill, however, both of his Spandau machine-guns jammed. He pressed on after the D.H.2 with one hand on the control column and the other wielding a small hammer and banging away at the machine-gun breeches to dislodge the jammed cartridges.

The two aeroplanes went lower and lower as Richthofen fought 'the most difficult battle ... that I experienced thus far...'[25] Then one of Richthofen's guns cleared and he fired right into the back of his opponent. The D.H.2 dropped into the mud about 250m east of Luisenhof Ferme, a devastated farm along the road to Flers, just south of Bapaume. A nearby German grenadier unit pulled Hawker's body from the wreckage and determined he had been killed by one shot in the back of the head. Hawker was buried on the spot, with the broken D.H.2 serving as a final monument.[26] Ever the hunter, Richthofen removed the patches of fabric bearing the aircraft's serial number from the rudder, as well as taking Hawker's machine-gun. All went to his growing trophy collection at home in Schweidnitz.

According to Erwin Böhme, the officers of *Jasta 2* requested that Bavarian *Obltn* Franz Josef Walz be appointed to succeed the fallen *Obltn* Kirmaier as commanding officer of *Jasta 2*.[27] They wanted someone more like Boelcke and, at the time, Walz seemed to be ideally suited. A prewar military pilot, he had broad flying and command experience. Almost a year earlier he had been named leader of *Kasta 2* of *Kagohl 1* and, while still a two-seater pilot, had scored six victories within three months. After recovering from wounds received in combat on 30 July 1916, *Obltn* Walz had trained new pilots at the Bavarian *FEA 1* at Schleissheim and had then been assigned to oversee the formation of *Jagdstaffel 19* at Ronssoy in the *1. Armee* area.[28]

Just five days short of his 31st birthday when he arrived at Lagnicourt on 29 November, Walz was senior in age to every pilot except Böhme. In addition to his splendid combat record, Walz possessed the maturity of age to make him truly 'the old man' (and Germans use the same term: *'der Alte'*). Unfortunately, Walz turned out to be less of an airfighter than his pilots had hoped for; indeed, his final victory score was seven enemy aircraft shot down. When he finally received the *Pour le Mérite*, on 9 August 1918, it was principally in recognition of his long service and outstanding leadership of *Fl.-Abt 304b* in Palestine.[29]

WERNER VOSS ARRIVES

Despite *Staffel* leader Walz's shortcomings in that one area, several excellent pilots emerged from *Jasta 2* while it was under his command. One of the most outstanding was *Ltn.d.Res* Werner Voss, who had arrived from *Kasta 20* of *KG 4* the day before Stephan Kirmaier was killed.

Nineteen-year-old Voss, who also hailed from the cavalry —*Husaren-Regiment (2. westfälisches) Nr 11* — became a good friend and air combat rival of Manfred von Richthofen. At 0940 on 27 November Voss gained his first victory, a Nieuport over Miraumont.[30] That afternoon he scored his second victory, F.E.2b 4915 of No.18 Squadron, south of Bapaume.[31]

On 5 December *Jasta 2* moved 5km, from Lagnicourt to Pronville. Six days later the new hunting ground proved fruitful to *Ltn* Manfred *Frhr* von Richthofen. At 1155 on 11 December Richthofen was farther north than usual when he came upon another 'Vickers single-seater'. He shot it down near Mercatel, south of Arras, and was credited with his twelfth victory.[32]

At the time, *Gen* von Hoeppner was making a tour of air units in the *1. Armee* area. He arrived at *Jasta 2*'s new airfield just as the unit's 77th victory was being recorded officially. At dinner that evening the general assured the restive young Uhlan and his *Staffel* comrades that the new *Luft-streitkräfte* then being created had special plans for its brave fighter pilots.

The unit had a new commander, the eager young *Jagdflieger* added to their victory scores, and their mentor was not forgotten. Six days after *Gen* von Hoeppner's visit, *Jagdstaffel 2* was renamed *Jagdstaffel Boelcke* by Imperial decree.[33]

Bad weather in mid-December led to the curtailment of most flight operations on both sides of the lines, except during brief breaks. Continuous good weather on 20 December resulted in numerous RFC reconnaissance patrols and bombing attacks within *Jasta B*'s operational area. The German response, however, was vigorous and extended behind the British lines. During the morning patrol, five Albatros D.IIs led by *Ltn* Manfred von Richthofen attacked six D.H.2s of No.29 Squadron. One fell within German lines and four others were forced down, three at the squadron's own aerodrome and one in the trenches.[34]

Flying the same aircraft in which he had defeated Maj Hawker, Richthofen went after D.H.2 7927 and, at 1130, shot it down between Monchy le Preux and Adinfer Wood. Like Hawker, this D.H.2 pilot was an experienced fighter of Richthofen's calibre, but was hindered by his aircraft's inferiority to the new Albatros. Capt Arthur G. Knight, DSO, MC, was an eight-victory ace[35] and a former squadron companion of Hawker's. The 21-year-old Toronto University graduate had been the D.H.2 pilot being pursued by *Hptmn* Boelcke and *Ltn* Böhme when the fatal collision occurred on 27 October. This time 'Jerry' Knight's luck ran out and he was killed. He was credited as Richthofen's thirteenth victory.

That afternoon *Jasta 2* attacked an offensive patrol of 'Fees' from No.18 Squadron northeast of Bapaume. Richthofen shot one down over Noreuil at 1345 (German time) and was credited with his fourteenth victory. His victims are generally considered to have been 2/Lt Lionel G. D'Arcy and Sub/Lt Reginald C. Whiteside, whose deaths that day were reported by the German Red Cross. They were flying in F.E.2b A5446, and a fabric swatch bearing that serial number was displayed at the Richthofen Museum in Schweidnitz.

However, information in the *RFC Casualty List* notes that A5446 was 'last seen recrossing to our side of the lines over Le Transloy at about 1.15pm [1415 German time], apparently OK, though going southwards' — half an hour *after* Richthofen's claim. While it does not explain the presence of the fabric, a more logical time match for Richthofen's claim would be F.E.2b 4884 of the same squadron, which was 'last seen at 12.55pm [British time] going down in flames ... after firing [a] green light'. The crew, Lt R. Smith and 2/Lt H. Fiske, were reported killed.

As the fight moved southward, *Ltn.d.Res* Hans Imelmann scored his sixth and last victory, sending a 'Fee' down over Sapignies. *Ltn.d.Res* Hans Wortmann's second victory was an F.E.2b downed over Le Sars, southwest of Bapaume, as it attempted to cross the lines back to friendly territory.[36]

CHRISTMAS AT THE FRONT

Ltn Lothar *Frhr* von Richthofen eagerly followed in his brother's footsteps. Like Manfred, he grew impatient flying as an observer; he felt that the real action was to be found at the controls of a single-seat fighter. In the summer of 1916 he applied the same perseverance as Manfred and was finally transferred out of *Kasta 23* and into pilot training school.

Through a combination of manoeuvring and luck, the Richthofen family had its own Christmas party on the airfield at Pronville. *Maj* von Richthofen took Christmas leave from the small garrison he commanded outside Lille, and Lothar was able to join him in linking up with Manfred at *Jasta B*.

The three Richthofens had another occasion to celebrate the day after Christmas, when Lothar made his first solo flight. It was a rite of passage which Manfred emphasized in a letter to his mother: 'Now the next big event will be [his] first aerial victory'.[37]

To prove the point, on the day after Lothar's solo, Manfred claimed an F.E.2b over Ficheux, southwest of Arras. Victory number fifteen is difficult to confirm, however, as the aircraft apparently made its way back within British lines. It may well have been F.E.2b 6937 of No.11 Squadron, flown by Capt John B. Quested with 2/Lt Harold J.H. Dicksee (WiA) as his observer.[38]

In any event, no German victory that day could compensate for the loss of Gustav Leffers of *Jasta 1*. He was shot down over Chérisy, southeast of Arras, only some 11km west of the Richthofen victory claim site.

Word of Leffers' death circulated, as did talk of the possibility that he had been brought down by improved Entente aircraft. The new and even more advanced Albatros D.III fighters were already in production, but had not reached the front-line *Staffeln* by the year's end. Thus, *Ltn* Manfred von Richthofen was still flying Albatros D.II 491/16, the victor of the best of the D.H.2 squadrons, when he encountered a superior British aircraft — the Sopwith 'Pup'.

One of the first 'Pup' units, No.8 Squadron, Royal Naval Air Service, was attached to the RFC's 22nd Wing at Vert Galant aerodrome, less than 30km west of Bapaume. Looking like a scaled-down version of the Sopwith 1½ Strutter fighter-reconnaissance and bomber aircraft, the new Sopwith Scout was considered to be the 'pup' of its predecessor, and was always referred to by that sobriquet, which became its recognised name.[39] The new scouts were sent to the Somme Front to counter the Albatros fighters and stop German reconnaissance aircraft before they could penetrate the forward lines.

Tuesday 4 January 1917 was the best day for flying in a week. The previous days' high winds had died down, and darkness in the morning gave way to bright skies in the afternoon. At about 1430 (British time), a flight of Pups took off from Vert Galant and headed east.

The arrival of *Jasta B* at about 1600 (German time) brought an aggressive response from the RNAS aircraft. One of the Pups attacked Manfred von Richthofen and became his sixteenth victory. As Richthofen later described it, Flt Lt Allan S. Todd in Sopwith Scout N5193 'attacked us and we saw immediately that the enemy 'plane was superior to ours. Only because we were three against one, we detected the enemy's weak points. I managed to get behind him and shoot him down.'[40]

The Pup came down at Metz-en-Couture, 13km south-southeast of *Jasta B*'s airfield at Pronville, where Lothar von Richthofen was observing most of the action. Just as Manfred had learned from Boelcke, Lothar learned from Manfred.

Three days later, *Jasta Boelcke* received its first batch of Albatros D.IIIs. They had semi-monocoque fuselages, like their predecessors, and were powered by the same 160hp Mercedes engine used in the D.IIs. The instantly noticeable difference between the D.III and earlier Albatros fighters was its narrower-chord lower wings, constructed around a single main spar, as opposed to the two-spar wings used in the D.I and D.II types. This feature was adopted from the captured French Nieuport sesquiplanes which had greatly impressed engineers at the Inspectorate of Military Aviation (*Idflieg*). Albatros designers made the changes to the wing and other modifications in an attempt to give the D.III greater speed and a faster rate of climb, while retaining the manoeuvrability of its forebears.[41]

Manfred von Richthofen received one of the first Albatros D.IIIs; its precise serial number is not known, but it was probably one of the early production batch beginning with D.1910/16.[42] Most visibly under Richthofen's leadership, the new fighter became one of Germany's most important air weapons.

The same day, 7 January 1917, Germany approved another weapons decision: unrestricted submarine warfare. In a meeting at *Schloss* Pless (Pszczyna, Poland) in Silesia, the Crown Council sanctioned attacks against any and all shipping within the war zone previously defined. The *Reichstag* (Parliament) approved the measure, fully aware that it would lead to the ending of America's neutrality and bring her involvement in the war closer.[43]

Following Manfred von Richthofen's sixteenth aerial victory, *Jagdstaffel Boelcke* went into a quiet and unproductive period. On 14 January, before he could score again, Richthofen was appointed commanding officer of *Jagdstaffel 11* at an airfield just outside Douai and northeast of Arras, on the 6. *Armee* Front.[44] This was an important career move for the young officer and, although he publicly protested at having to leave *Jasta B*, he understood the opportunities that his new command offered.

RICHTHOFEN RECEIVES THE *POUR LE MÉRITE*

Two days after receiving orders to *Jasta 11*, a celebration at *Jasta B* was interrupted by another telegram from Headquarters. It read simply: 'His Majesty, the *Kaiser*, has awarded the *Orden Pour le Mérite* to *Leutnant* von Richthofen'. The *Staffel* sent the same message to his mother in Schweidnitz.[45]

The award date of Manfred von Richthofen's *Pour le Mérite* was 12 January 1917, one year to the day after the same high honour had been authorized for Oswald Boelcke and Max Immelmann.[46] Much had changed during that year. If there was any question about fighter pilot 'qualifications' for Prussia's highest bravery award, the notice distributed to

6. Armee air units plainly stated that Richthofen's *Pour le Mérite* was 'bestowed for the successful confirmed downing of 16 enemy aeroplanes'.[47]

According to one source, the reason Richthofen had to wait so long for his *Pour le Mérite* was that he had not yet shot down an enemy observation balloon. He is supposed to have been queried by telegram: 'Where is the captive balloon? /s/ Supreme Headquarters'. The *Jagdflieger's* reply, sent by normal mail, is said to have been: 'Captive balloon is in the sky. /s/ Richthofen'.

When telephoned from Supreme Headquarters by a concerned supporter of his nomination for the award, Richthofen supposedly responded: 'At the moment I am having fun shooting down aeroplanes even without your *Pour le Mérite* and the balloon is still in the sky'.[48]

It is hard to imagine such a well-disciplined, achievement-oriented, career-minded junior officer being so cavalier about an award that was so important to him. More likely, Richthofen sensed that the criteria were shifting, and it was just luck and timing that made him the first pilot to have to reach a higher level of achievement. His victory list does *not* include a single enemy captive balloon, but that is no reflection on Richthofen's ability. He applied his talents to what he did best: destroying enemy aircraft.

During their training days at *FEA 2* in Döberitz, Richthofen's friend Bodo von Lyncker once asked him to name his goal. 'Well, it must be quite nice to fly as the leading fighter pilot,' Richthofen responded.[49] Despite attempts at self-deprecation when relating that anecdote, Richthofen's ambitions were obvious from his actions.

THE RED BARON IS CREATED

Ltn Manfred *Frhr* von Richthofen arrived at *Jasta 11*'s airfield at La Brayelle, just northwest of Douai, as Germany's premier living airfighter, with the highest victory score and wearing the highest awards. As a new leader in a totally new environment, he could set the psychological distance needed between him and his subordinates so that he could command and instruct with absolute, unquestioned authority. He became the living embodiment of his mentor, Boelcke, whose tactics he refined even further and whose aura of command he assumed.

The official RAF historian, H.A. Jones, summarized Richthofen's air combat leadership and tactics as:

> ... perfectly suited to the conditions under which the German armies fought on the Western Front. Those armies were, for the greater part of the war, on the defensive and the German air service was numerically weaker than the combined air services of the Allies. Richthofen's task was to inflict the greatest damage with the minimum of loss to his own service, and he knew that on any day suitable for flying great numbers of aeroplanes of the Royal Flying Corps would be over the German

lines. He seldom had to seek combat. It was offered to him and he could make his choice, and if it was ... to avoid or to break off a fight, Richthofen would never hesitate [to do so].

... [Richthofen's unit] was, therefore, not only extremely active, but also extremely elusive. The German leader showed great acumen in his choice of [pilots] and was stern but patient in his schooling of them, inspiring them with his own high courage, confidence and sense of proportion, so that they became one of the most efficient fighting forces of the war.[50]

The Albatros D.III he brought with him from *Jasta B* was decorated in the standard colour scheme of the time: natural wood finish on the fuselage and olive green and brown (or lilac mauve) on the upper wing surfaces. Richthofen made a dramatic departure from those nondescript markings. 'For whatever reasons, one fine day I came upon the idea of having my crate painted glaring red. The result was that absolutely everyone could not help but notice my red bird. In fact, my opponents also seemed to be not entirely unaware [of it],' he wrote.[51]

Such notoriety could have the disadvantage of making the *Staffelführer* a singular target. As *Jasta 11* gained swift success under Manfred von Richthofen, the pilots expressed their concern, described by Lothar von Richthofen:

It had become known that the British had put a price on my brother's head. Every flyer on the other side knew him, for at the time he alone flew a red-painted aeroplane. For that reason it had long been our wish to have all aeroplanes of our *Staffel* painted red and we implored my brother to allow it so he would not be so especially conspicuous. The request was granted; for we had shown ourselves to be worthy of the red colour by our many aerial victories. The red colour signified a certain insolence. Everyone knew that. It attracted attention. Consequently, one had to really perform. Proudly we finally looked at our red birds. My brother's crate was glaring red. Each of the rest of us had some additional markings in other colours. As we could not see each other's faces in the air, we chose these colours as recognition symbols. Schäfer, for example, had his elevator, rudder and most of the back part of the fuselage [painted] black; Allmenröder used white [on the nose and spinner], Wolff used green and I had yellow. Each one of us was different. In the air and from the ground, as well as from the enemy's view, we all looked to be red, as only small other parts were painted in another colour.[52]

Leading the pack, on Tuesday 23 January, Richthofen took six of his pilots up to an area over the trenches near Lens to introduce them to air combat. They arrived at the end of a successful attack against German reconnaissance aircraft by the single-seat pusher fighters of No.40 Squadron, RFC. To the north, at La Bassée, 2/Lt John Hay in F.E.8 6388 had engaged an Albatros two-seater and sent it down. A British report noted: 'The wings were seen to break away from the German machine before it crashed', and Hay then 'attacked and destroyed the leading machine of a formation of eight'.[53] As the fight moved southward, Hay was finishing off the second German reconnaissance aircraft when Manfred von Richthofen led his Albatroses into the fray.

First, Richthofen made a pass at F.E.8 7627 flown by Lt Edwin L. Benbow, who misidentified the new Albatroses as Rolands in his combat report, but gained a lasting impression of his adversary. Benbow stated that his single forward-firing Lewis gun had stopped, apparently owing to the cold. He was working on the gun when he 'was attacked by a red machine from the front'.[54] Benbow dived away and finally got the gun working, only to find his adversary gone.

In fact, Richthofen had pursued Hay and set fire to his aeroplane. Just as the D.H.2 was no match for the Albatros D.II, the similarly-configured F.E.8 did not stand a chance against the new Albatros D.III. At about 500m altitude Hay jumped or fell from his burning F.E.8, which then crashed and burned.[55] The event was recorded as Richthofen's seventeenth aerial victory and his first in the impressive new Albatros.

Richthofen's triumphant day was marred by news from *Jasta B*. Two of his former comrades, *Ltn.d.Res* Hans Imelmann and *Vzfw* Paul Ostrop, were killed when their Albatros D.IIIs suffered wing failures and crashed near Miraumont.[56]

TRIUMPH AND NEAR TRAGEDY

The following day, F.E.2bs of No.25 Squadron, a respected foe of long standing, were assigned to make a photographic reconnaissance of the area west of Vimy Ridge, less than 20km west of Douai. At high noon, with the sun directly overhead, the 'Fees' swept back and forth, following a precise pattern to produce a photo-mosaic of the German lines.

Then, from out of the sun, *Ltn* Manfred von Richthofen and *Sergeant* Hans Howe disrupted the two-seaters' work by diving on the lead aircraft. After a protracted fight, the fuel tank of F.E.2b 6997[57] was punctured and the pilot, Capt Oscar Greig, was wounded in the legs. While the pilot tried to land, the observer, 2/Lt John E. MacLenan, continued to fire at the red Albatros following closely behind. Finally, the big pusher came down near German trenches. MacLenan pulled Greig from the wreckage and managed to set fire to the aircraft before nearby German soldiers arrived to secure it for its intelligence value.

With characteristic pride, Richthofen noted in his combat report: 'According to the British crew, my red-painted aeroplane was not unknown to them, as on being asked who brought them down, they answered "*le petit rouge*" (the little red).'[58]

The same report requesting credit for his eighteenth victory also mentioned that Richthofen had been obliged to land quickly after the fight, as one of his lower wings had cracked when he was at about 300m altitude. The weakened wing could have been caused by MacLenan's defensive machine-gun fire, but the previous day's loss of two Albatros D.IIIs owing to wing failure made the latest occurrence look more than coincidental.

Consequently, Richthofen's machine and other Albatros D.IIIs were withdrawn briefly to the *Armee-Flugparks* for modifications, which were also being made on the factory assembly line. The landing gear was strengthened, auxiliary braces were added to the bottom portion of the interplane vee-struts, and changes were made to the radiator to alleviate recurrent cooling problems.[59] While the Albatroses were being modified, Richthofen flew a Halberstadt D.II, an early single-seat biplane successor to the Fokker *Eindecker* series.

DEVELOPING *JASTA 11*

German military aviation forces in the First World War suffered from a chronic shortage of aggressive fighter pilots. Training facilities could not produce them fast enough to meet the needs of the growing number of fighter units requested and authorized.

To focus attention on the need for bold aerial warriors, the German government encouraged a massive propaganda campaign to promote the achievements of successful flyers and give due honour to those heroes who died for their Fatherland. Stories and photographs of outstanding military airmen were fed to the popular press by the government, and postcard companies issued series after series of collectable portrait pictures of '*grosse Kanonen*' (great flying aces), air commanders and aircraft, in addition to likenesses of other army and navy celebrities.

At the Front, squadron commanders sought honours and awards for their aircrews to recognize their achievements (and, hopefully, to retain their services). They also scanned the *Armee* weekly activity reports to read about the exploits of men worth attracting to their units. Given his success and renown, Manfred von Richthofen could request — and would be given — the services of people who caught his eye.

Among the talented airmen who attracted Richthofen's attention were three top performers: *Ltn* Karl Allmenröder, formerly of *Fl-Abt (A) 227*, who went on to become a *Pour le Mérite* recipient and *Staffel* leader; *Vzfw* Sebastian Festner, a pilot unseasoned in combat who came directly from *FEA 1b*, but who went on to become a twelve-victory ace; and *Ltn* Kurt Wolff, a veteran of *Kagohl 2* and the Verdun Front, who later earned the *Pour le Mérite* and command of a *Jasta*.

Also, *Frhr* von Richthofen became aware of the exploits of another bold *KG 2* pilot, *Ltn* Karl-Emil Schäfer, victor over a Caudron near Pont à Mousson on 22 January 1917. Not content to await the whim of fate, *Ltn*

Schäfer sent Richthofen a telegram: 'Can you use me?'. Richthofen recognized the name and sent back this terse response: 'You have already been requested.'[60]

VICTORY AND THEN HOMEWARD

Richthofen proved that he was a superior fighter pilot, even with an older, less capable aircraft. On the afternoon of 1 February he was mentoring *Ltn* Karl Allmenröder, one of his more promising students, when they saw a British two-seater directing artillery fire against German troops near Vimy. Richthofen led the way through the bitter cold winter sky to his nineteenth victory and got to within 50m of the target before he opened fire. Abruptly, B.E.2d 6742 of No.16 Squadron veered off to the right and went down out of control. It crashed within the German forward lines, just southwest of Thelus. The wounded crew, Lt Percival W. Murray and Lt Duncan J. McRae, are reported to have got clear of the wreckage before a Canadian artillery battery destroyed it. They died the following day in a field hospital.[61]

On Sunday 4 February, 1917, the United States of America severed diplomatic relations with the German *Reich* and America's entry into the war became a certainty.

Early that same morning in Schweidnitz, Germany, *Freifrau* Kunigunde von Richthofen was awakened by the sound of the doorbell. She turned on a light, but, before she could leave the comfort of a warm bed, her bedroom door swung open to reveal the splendidly uniformed figure of her eldest son. First she noticed his big smile, and then the sparkling blue enamel Maltese cross of the *Pour le Mérite* at his collar.

Snatching his hand, and speaking to him as she did when he was a boy, *Freifrau* von Richthofen said: '*Bravo*, you have done well, Manfred. But how did you get in? Was the garden gate open?'[62]

No, she was told, this knight of the *Orden Pour le Mérite* had climbed over the fence. Kunigunde von Richthofen loved her children in equal measure when they were together, but she enjoyed showering special attention on them individually. Manfred's unexpected arrival was a special occasion. Her autobiography, *Mein Kriegstagebuch* (1937), offers numerous indications that *Freifrau* von Richthofen was painfully aware of the precariousness of life in wartime and the need to enjoy such special moments to the full.

She and her daughter Ilse prepared breakfast, grinding a handful of specially-saved coffee beans to make a rich, flavourful beverage, as opposed to the weakened drink that was so typical of wartime life, with its severe shortages of imported products. Over breakfast Manfred related his discussions with officials at the Inspectorate of Military Aviation in Berlin, looking for solutions to the Albatros wing-failure problem. The focus was on workmanship and quality of materials. The science of aerodynamics was young, and subspecialties such as aeroelasticity too far beyond the technical knowledge of the time for *Idflieg* and Albatros engineers to understand the effect of flutter on the D.III's single-spar bottom wing. It was an inherent design flaw that was retained in the succeeding Albatros D.V and D.Va.[63]

But that problem was far away, and Manfred's all-red Albatros was being repaired, so he did not dwell on the subject. Indeed, he enjoyed telling of the recognition accorded his aeroplane. When his mother asked whether it was reckless to draw attention to himself in that way, Manfred replied: 'One cannot make oneself invisible in the air and so at least our people recognize me.'[64]

Freifrau von Richthofen recalled from her own interest in German history, no doubt imparted to her children, that in medieval times Dietrich von Bern had gone into battle bearing a fire-red shield. 'And did that not communicate the image of courage and force?', she mused.[65] That further reinforced Manfred's choice.

It was bitterly cold outside, so the three of them carried on an extended conversation around the hearth for hours. At one point Manfred produced a Berlin newspaper of the previous day. It contained an article about his nineteenth aerial victory, which he had neglected to mention.

The article prompted *Freifrau* von Richthofen to ask the most obvious of maternal questions: 'Why do you risk your life like this every day? Why do you do it, Manfred?'

He paused to reflect on the question, and then answered simply: 'For the man in the trenches. I want to ease his hard lot in life by keeping the enemy flyers away from him.' Manfred had gained perspective on the situation of the ordinary soldier, having endured the morass of the trench network where death was often just a step away for untold thousands who were never singled out for praise in the battle reports or had high honours conferred by royal personages. He now understood that war was more than glory and the perverse exhilaration of cheating death one more time.

He did not share this inner secret with the outside world.[66] As far as the public were concerned, Manfred *Freiherr* von Richthofen was the 20th-century incarnation of the medieval knight; the son of a noble house, extraordinarily skilful in battle in the clean skies over the Front, a model of courage and discipline for other Germans to emulate — a hero in every sense of the word. He did what a good soldier was expected to do: he kept his inner concerns, potential vulnerability and pain to himself.

The comfort of his family was all too brief. After but a few days in Schweidnitz the *Staffelführer* returned to Douai.

KARL-EMIL SCHÄFER JOINS *JASTA 11*

While Manfred von Richthofen was away, his *Staffel* ensured that he would come back to good news. On 5 February *Ltn* Karl-Emil Schäfer reported for duty with *Jasta 11*. Schäfer, a native of the Rhineland city of Krefeld (as was Werner Voss), displayed in abundance the fighting spirit that Richthofen required of his pilots. During close fighting near Maubeuge, on 26 September 1914, Schäfer was badly wounded in the left thigh. Six months later and with his left leg slightly shorter than his right,[67] he was back in action.

In May 1915 he was promoted to *Leutnant der Reserve* and, by the year's end, he had orders to the *Fliegertruppe*. Defensive two-seater flying was too tame for a former rifleman who had become good at drawing a bead on his adversary and dispatching him. His first aerial victory with *Kampfstaffel 11* convinced the 25-year-old Rhinelander that he should be flying with *Jagdstaffel 11* and, with characteristic boldness, he sent the telegram that opened the door to a highly successful, albeit short-lived, air-fighting career.

Richthofen spent part of the morning of 14 February at Pronville, visiting his old friends in *Jasta B*. On the way back, at noon, he saw B.E.2d 6231[68] of No.2 Squadron flying an artillery-spotting mission 2,000m above the road from Lens to Hulluch. This was his first encounter in his repaired Albatros D.III, so Richthofen was cautious. He approached within 50m of the B.E. without being seen, then opened fire. The two-seater crashed into German trenches in a forward fire zone. The event was recorded as Richthofen's twentieth victory.[69]

That afternoon, Richthofen and his men attacked a flight of artillery-spotters not far from the morning's action. Richthofen went after a B.E.2 and claimed to have sent it down on to a snow-covered field southwest of Mazingarbe, within British lines, at 1645 (German time). Despite a lack of corroborative statements and any physical proof of the aircraft's destruction, Richthofen was credited with his 21st victory.[70]

One person who claimed to have been Richthofen's victim that day was Harold E. Hartney, an American pilot who served with No.20 Squadron, RFC, before becoming commanding officer of the US Air Service's First Pursuit Group. Hartney and his observer, Lt W.T. Jourdan, were in F.E.2d A1960, accompanying another 'Fee' over Ypres in the *4. Armee* area, when they were attacked by 'seven brilliantly painted Albatrosses'.[71] The F.E.s were brought down within British lines near Poperinghe.

It is more likely that Richthofen's opponents were Capt G.C. Bailey, DSO, and 2/Lt G.W.B. Hampton, who were in B.E.2c 2543 of No.2 Squadron just north of Loos when they were attacked at 1550 (British time). Hampton's combat report notes that their aeroplane and B.E.2c 6250 engaged three enemy aircraft, but managed to get away. Capt Bailey was wounded in the knee, but succeeded in landing his machine.

By the criteria then existing, this claim should have been disallowed. The weather was turning bad and visibility was decreasing, however, and so it must be assumed that 'allowances' were made for Richthofen's claim.

NOTES

1   von Richthofen, *Ein Heldenleben*, (1920), p.171.
2   Bolle, *Jagdstaffel Boelcke*, (1923), p.41.
3   *Stofl 1. Armee Wochenbericht, Teil 3*, 6 November 1916.
4   Sgt Cuthbert G. Baldwin, pilot, and 2/Lt G. Andrew Bentham, observer, in F.E.2b 7010 of No.18 Squadron.
5   *RFC Communiqué No 61*, 12 November 1916, p.2.
6   RFC records show two B.E.2c aircraft put out of action in this engagement: 4589, 2/Lt T. Hayes, wounded east of Adinfer, over 13km east of the target, but able to return to his own lines, was Kirmaier's likely opponent; the other B.E.2c, 2502, Lt G.F. Knight (PoW), 'seen to descend out of control near Sapagnies', 9km from Haplincourt, was most likely Hans Imelmann's victim. In any case, Lt G.F. Knight was not 2/Lt I.G. Cameron's pilot, as noted in Gibbons, *The Red Knight of Germany*, (1927), p.95.
7   von Richthofen, *Der rote Kampfflieger*, (1933), pp.112-113; *Stofl 1. Armee Wochenbericht, Teil 4*, 21 November 1916; B.E.2c 2506, 2/Lt Ian G. Cameron (PoW/DoW), who flew alone, despite Richthofen's contention of having hit a back-seat crewman.
8   At the time, the Duke of Saxe-Coburg-Gotha was on the staff of the *38. Infanterie-Division*, headquartered at Vaux-Vraulcourt (Ref: *Thüringen im Weltkrieg*, (1921), p.282).
9   *Der rote Kampfflieger*, op.cit., pp.113-114; Richthofen neglected to mention, however, that *Ltn* Hans Imelmann received the same award at the same time (Ref: Saxe-Coburg-Gotha Archiv, fol. 107-108).
10   Louda, *Heraldry of the Royal Families of Europe*, (1981), p.85.
11   Winter, *Gotha als Fliegerstadt in der Vergangenheit*, (ca.1935). pp.37, 39, 53.
12   Kilduff, *Albert Dossenbach: Baden's Pour le Mérite Ace*, (1989), pp.293-294.
13   *Stofl 1. Armee Wochenbericht, Teil 8*, 14 November 1916.
14   O'Connor, *Aviation Awards of Imperial Germany in World War I and the Men Who Earned Them*, vol II, (1990), pp.132, 140, 142.
15   Miller and Puglisi, *Jasta B*, (1968), p.330.
16   Jones, *The War in the Air*, vol II, (1928), pp.323-324.
17   *Stofl 1. Armee Wochenbericht, Teil 4*, 5 December 1916; claimed at 0940 and possibly B.E.2c 2767 of No.15 Squadron, 2/Lt J.C. Lees and Lt T.H. Clarke (both PoW); 40 minutes earlier, however, *Obltn* Kirmaier claimed a B.E. near Miraumont, 3km north-east of Grandcourt, and he may well have been the victor over this B.E.2c two-seater.
18   Ibid.; 2/Lt G.S. Hall (DoW) and 2/Lt George Doughty (KiA).
19   Gibbons, op. cit., (1927), p.99.
20   Shores, et al, *Above the Trenches*, (1990), p.125, credit *Obltn* Kirmaier's demise to 2/Lt K. Crawford and Capt J.O. Andrews of No.24 Squadron; *RFC War Diary* and *RFC Communiqué* No.63, 26 November 1916, p.1, both mention only Capt Andrews as having 'destroyed a hostile machine, which crashed on our side of the lines near Les Boeufs (*sic*).' The village of Lesboeufs is just northwest of Morval.
21   *RFC Communiqué No.63*, 26 November 1916, p.2.
22   *RFC Communiqué No.64*, 2 December 1916, p.1; *RFC Combat Casualty List* entry for that day states: 'Left aerodrome 1.0 p.m. With two other de Havillands engaged 8 hostile machines over Achiet. Not seen after this encounter.'
23   Bowyer, *For Valour - the Air V.C.s*, (1978), p.40.
24   *Der rote Kampfflieger*, op.cit., p.115.
25   *Ein Heldenleben*, op.cit., p.193.
26   Bowyer, op.cit., p.44.
27   Böhme, *Briefe eines deutschen Kampffleigers an ein junges Mädchen*, (1930), p.82.
28   Zuerl, *Pour-le-Mérite-Flieger*, (1938), pp.467-468.
29   O'Connor, op.cit., p.66.
30   *Kofl 1. Armee Wochenbericht, Teil 4*, 12 December 1916.
31   Ibid; Lt F.A. George (WiA) and 1/AM O. Watts (KiA), attacked near Ginchy, between Longueval and Morval, and brought down in flames.
32   D.H.2 5986 of No.32 Squadron, piloted by Lt P.B.G. Hunt; *RFC Casualty List* reports: 'Left aerodrome 9.20 a.m. A newspaper cutting from "The Times" forwarded by 5th

Brigade states "Captain Philip Hunt, Yeomanry, attached R.F.C., who was previously reported missing, is now reported to be wounded and a prisoner of war in Germany.'

33 *Kofl 1. Armee Wochenbericht, Teil 8*, 26 December 1916.

34 Jones, *The War in the Air*, vol III, (1931), p.320.

35 Shores, et al.op.cit., pp.226-227.

36 *RFC Casualty List* reports that F.E.2b A5452 of No.18 Squadron, Lts C.H. Windrum and J.A. Hollis (both PoW), was 'last seen planing down over Sapignies towards Gommecourt', the likely victim of Hans Imelmann. It is possible that Hans Wortmann brought down F.E.2b A5446 and that Richthofen was given the wrong souvenir of his afternoon's work.

37 von Richthofen, *Mein Kriegstagebuch*, (1937), p.94.

38 Shores, et al, op.cit., p.309.

39 Bruce, *British Aeroplanes 1914-1918*, (1969), p.552.

40 Quoted in Jones, op.cit., p.321.

41 Grosz, *The Agile and Aggressive Albatros*, (1976), pp.40-41.

42 Ibid., p.41.

43 Esposito, *A Concise History of World War I*, (1964), p.293.

44 *Kofl 6. Armee Wochenbericht Nr 22400, Teil 1*, 23 January 1917.

45 According to von Richthofen, op. cit., (1937), p.95, *Freifrau* von Richthofen received her telegram early on the morning of 16 January 1917.

46 O'Connor, op. cit. p.219.

47 *Kofl 6. Armee Wochenbericht Nr 22400, Teil 10*, 23 January 1917.

48 Zuerl, *Pour-le-Mérite-Flieger*, (1938), p.375.

49 von Richthofen, *Der rote Kampfflieger*, (1933), p.118.

50 Jones, *The War in the Air*, vol IV, (1934), pp.396-397.

51 *Der rote Kampfflieger*, op.cit., p.120.

52 Quoted in *Ein Heldenleben*, op.cit., pp.205-206.

53 *RFC Communiqué No. 72*, 28 January 1917, p.1; the first two-seater shot down by 2/Lt Hay was most likely from *Fl-Abt (A) 240*, which lost the crew of *Offstlvtr* Wilhelm Mohs and *Ltn.d.Res* Wilhelm Riehl over La Bassée; the second aircraft was very likely from *Fl-Abt 13*, which reported the loss of *Offstlvtr* Eduard Wesselewski and *Ltn* Wilhelm Schwarz at Avion, just south of Lens (Ref: *Kofl 6. Armee Wochenbericht Nr 22639, Teil 12*, 30 January 1917).

54 No. 40 Squadron Combat Report.

55 Gibbons, op.cit., (1927), pp.111-112.

56 Miller and Puglisi, *Jasta B*, (1968), p.324.

57 Richthofen's combat report lists the serial number as '6937', but the *RFC Casualty List* has it as '6997'.

58 Quoted in Gibbons, op.cit., p.117.

59 Grosz, op.cit., pp.41-42.

60 Ibid., p.80.

61 Gibbons, op.cit., pp.119-120.

62 *Mein Kriegstagebuch*, op.cit., p.97.

63 Chionchio, *Defeat by Design*, (1989), p.69. (Author's note: This article is a thoroughly excellent and lucid examination of events that, previously, had not been well understood.)

64 *Mein Kriegstagebuch*, op.cit., p.97.

65 Ibid.

66 Ibid., pp.98-99.

67 Zuerl, op.cit., p.406.

68 *Nachrichtenblatt der Luftstreitkräfte Nr. 2*, 15 March 1917, p.11.

69 2/Lt Cyril D. Bennett (WiA/PoW) and 2/Lt H.A. Croft (KiA).

70 Gibbons, op.cit., p.125.

71 Hartney, *Up And At 'Em*, (1940), p.92.

CHAPTER 6
THE NEW MASTER BEGINS

On good-weather days in February 1917, the level of air activity rose. Entente ground and air forces prepared for the spring offensive by probing the German lines at every opportunity. Manfred von Richthofen and *Jasta 11* tried to disrupt enemy flights in their sector, to keep air units of the British First and Third Armies from observing German preparations for the spring campaign. Owing to the lack of experience among *Jasta 11* pilots, however, those initial interdiction flights contributed more to the education of the neophyte *Jagdflieger* than to the war effort. Lothar von Richthofen recalled his brother's early combat missions with Karl Allmenröder and Kurt Wolff:

> At the time both had no experience at all and in aerial combat beginners have more fear than love of the Fatherland. In the first days, my brother flew out with them, attacked numerous British [aircraft], and his machine received an enormous number of hits, without successes to make up for it, and both of them did not help. Of course my brother came back somewhat annoyed, but did not reproach them; on the contrary, he did not say a word about it. As Wolff and Allmenröder ... told me, that influenced them more than the harshest dressing-down.[1]

In preparing his pilots for battle, Richthofen set an example of personal conduct that also contributed to their future success as fighters and leaders in their own right. He had a good sense of awareness of his role as *Staffelführer*; he did not attempt to be 'one of the boys', indulging in much singing and carousing in off-duty hours, but he enjoyed a good joke and some moderate drinking. He smoked an occasional cigarette, but otherwise looked after his personal health. As there were no night-fighter operations at that time, Manfred von Richthofen went to bed early — usually before 2200 — to ensure that he was rested and in top form the following morning. He was cordial to officers and enlisted men alike; indeed, he urged his pilots to remain on good terms with the mechanics who maintained their aircraft.[2]

THE VICTORY SCORE RISES

Unfavourable weather during the rest of February and into March hampered flight operations on both sides of the lines. Consequently, good weather on Sunday 4 March brought the RFC out in force, performing the full range of missions: artillery co-operation, photographic and visual reconnaissance, bombing, and interception of German aircraft.

Manfred von Richthofen was listed as having brought down an 'enemy B.E. biplane north of Loos'.[3] Given the circumstances, it is most likely that this listing was Richthofen's 22nd victory and that his opponents were Lt James B.E. Crosbee and Fl/Sgt J.E. Prance in B.E.2d 5785 of No.2 Squadron, RFC. In his combat report, Prance noted he had been on a photo-reconnaissance mission north of Lens at 1145 (British time) when he was attacked 'from right out of the glare of the sun' by what he identified as a very fast 'Halberstadter' single-seater. The German attacker fired a burst that hit Fl/Sgt Prance on the first pass, then swung up and dived down again and shot away one of the B.E.'s ammunition boxes. On the third pass the German's machine-gun fire hit the two-seater's rear fuel tank. The aeroplane went into a slow spiral and headed for the ground.

The entire episode has the signs of a classic Richthofen attack, except for the ending, when the German pilot in this case failed to close in for the kill. Rather, Crosbee reported, the attacker was 800ft above the stricken B.E.2d when the observer fired another burst, 'after which [the] hostile machine made off low toward Hénin-Liétard, and was lost in the mist'.[4] Crosbee made it back to British lines, where Prance was hospitalized for leg wounds received during the fight.

During *Jasta 11*'s afternoon sortie, they encountered a flight of No.43 Squadron's Sopwith 1½ Strutters, this time over Acheville, east of Vimy, the scene of intense ground fighting. At 1620 Richthofen went after 2/Lts Herbert J. Green and Alexander W. Reid in Sopwith A1108. The two Britons put up a fierce fight, but they did not get off as easily as the morning victims. Richthofen followed the two-seater and eventually poured 400 rounds into it; the aircraft lost a wing and plunged down to the ground, where the wreckage was widely scattered. The bodies of the two crewmen were buried by local troops. The Sopwith's two machine-guns were taken to *Jasta 11* as souvenirs of Richthofen's 23rd aerial victory.[5]

Some sources (e.g., Gibbons) list Richthofen's 23rd victory as B.E.2d 6252 of No.8 Squadron, RFC. That aircraft was reported last seen at 1030 (British time), under attack by hostile aircraft and finally brought down in flames near Berneville, within British lines. The pilot and observer, Fl/Sgt Reginald J. Moody and 2/Lt Edmund E. Horn, were killed and their aircraft was a total wreck. That incident took place well over an hour before the Richthofen claim, and the site was south-west of Arras, in a different operational area.[6]

Nonetheless, *Ltn* Manfred von Richthofen was credited with —and most likely achieved — two aerial victories that day.

It snowed on 5 March, and all flight operations were suspended. The following day Richthofen and Allmenröder encountered two aircraft from No.16 Squadron on a low-level artillery-spotting mission near Souchez. Richthofen dived on B.E.2e A2785 and opened fire. The two-seater's wings came off and the aeroplane plunged to the ground,[7] killing both crewmen, 2/Lt C.M.G. Bibbey and Lt G.J.O. Brichta. The incident was acknowledged as Richthofen's 24th aerial victory.

RICHTHOFEN SHOT DOWN

Bad weather on 7 and 8 March made any flying nearly impossible. One of the few units to fly on 8 March was No.48 Squadron, the first recipients of the new Bristol F.2A two-seat fighter, which arrived in France that day. Often mistaken for a slower, less agile two-seat reconnaissance aircraft, the 'Brisfit' eventually proved to be a formidable opponent, possessing great manoeuvrability and structural strength.[8]

The following day, Manfred von Richthofen also received new equipment — a factory-fresh Albatros D.III — which he was eager to test in the air. Despite low clouds and snow storms along the Front,[9] he alerted the *Armee* area commander that he would lead the morning flight on a north-westerly course toward Lens, where there was always good hunting.

Jasta 11 encountered nine F.E.8s of No.40 Squadron, patrolling over Oppy, west of Douai. At first it seemed that Richthofen would gain an easy victory as he closed in on one of the lattice-tailed single-seaters. Suddenly, he was forced out of the fight. He had been so intent on his target that his new Albatros had been hit in the early moments of the battle. For the first time Richthofen was struck by the chilling reality often faced by his victims:

> Now I am 50 metres away, a few good shots and then success is inevitable. So I thought. But all of a sudden there is a big bang; I have barely got off ten shots when again there is a smack on my machine. It is clear I have been hit. At least my machine has been, [although] I personally have not. At the same moment it stinks something terrible of gasoline, also the engine slows down. The Englishman notices it, for now he shoots even more. I must break off immediately.
>
> I go straight down. Instinctively, I have switched off the engine. Just in time. If the fuel tank is punctured and the stuff squirts around the legs, the danger of fire is indeed great. Up front there is an internal combustion engine over 150 "horses" strong, [and it is] glowing hot. One drop of fuel [on it] and the whole machine will burn. I am leaving behind me a trail of white mist. I know it very well from [having seen it in] opponents. It happens just before an explosion.[10]

Richthofen was lucky. His engine quit altogether, minimizing the risk of fire, and his opponent withdrew. But he was still vulnerable, and checked constantly to be sure that he was not followed. Suddenly, a flaming object came towards him.

> Is it an enemy signal flare? No. It is too big for that. It is getting bigger and bigger. One of the aircraft is burning. But what kind? The

machine looks exactly like [one of] ours. Thank God, it is an opponent. Who could have shot it down? Right after that, a second aeroplane falls from the fight, [and] like mine, it goes straight down, spinning, continuously spinning — and then — it recovers. It flies right toward me. It is also an Albatros. Undoubtedly the same thing happened to him as [happened] to me.[11]

The pilot of the other Albatros must have determined that the *Staffelführer* was safe and then proceeded back to his airfield. Moments later, Richthofen set down in a small meadow along the road to Hénin-Liétard. An officer driving by witnessed the landing and offered him a ride to the city, about 5km away. From there, Richthofen called *Jasta 11* and was fetched in short order by Schäfer, the pilot of the other stricken Albatros. They sped back to La Brayelle and, in little over an hour, Richthofen was taking off and heading toward the Front.

Back in the air, Richthofen calculated that the F.E.8s would try to escape south, so he flew toward Arras to head them off. Just north of that city, over Roclincourt, he pounced on a single-seat pusher that went down in flames, killing its pilot, 2/Lt Arthur J. Pearson, MC. The aircraft, a badly outclassed D.H.2 (A2571), was listed as Richthofen's 25th victory.

LOTHAR JOINS *JASTA 11*

After completing his first solo flight, *Ltn* Lothar *Freiherr* von Richthofen worked so hard to perfect his piloting skills that he wore himself down. In February 1917, tired, pale and suffering from a bad cold, he was sent home on recuperative leave. Lothar was very conscious of the sibling whose trail he followed, and he wanted to prove his own worth.

'He spoke little of his own plans,' his mother wrote. 'But I know him: when the conversation turned to aerial combat, then there was a curious sparkle in his eyes ... He saw himself already in a fighter aeroplane, eye to eye with the opponent. I thought back on what Manfred wrote: "Lothar has developed splendidly as a pilot ...". And I know his boldness, he is not like Manfred; perhaps he is more impulsive, more unpredictable.'[12]

At the end of his leave, in the normal course of events, Lothar von Richthofen would have returned to his *Kampfgeschwader*. It is unlikely that Manfred would have requested such a new and unproven pilot for *Jasta 11*. But higher powers in Berlin — always looking for heroes — could appreciate the propaganda value of *two* Richthofens fighting together to defeat the enemy in the air.[13]

On a blustery Saturday 10 March, 1917, Lothar von Richthofen arrived at La Brayelle airfield and reported to his new commanding officer. The day was entirely unsuitable for flying and, therefore, a good day for a new pilot to become acquainted with his new *Staffel* comrades. There was no question that Lothar would be treated like any other new arrival; he received the same welcome and words of instruction as *Ltn.d.Res* Erich Just, a week earlier, and as *Ltn* Georg Simon a week later.

Lothar received only the slight concession of a certain talisman, which the other pilots understood very well. From his cavalry days, Lothar had always carried a riding crop that he had considered to be a lucky. There was no place for the riding crop within the tight confines of an aeroplane cockpit, so he had to fly without his talisman. To his great amazement, all of his qualifying flights had taken place without incident.

'After I had given up the riding crop,' Lothar von Richthofen recalled, 'soon I got my hand on another talisman. When I arrived as a complete beginner at my brother's *Staffel*, Manfred gave me one of his old machines, with which he had attained ten aerial victories [his 19th to 29th]. Likewise, he gave me a pair of old leather gloves, with which at just the right moment he had so often pressed the machine-gun triggers. As luck would have it, I shot down my first ten Englishmen armed with these gloves and this machine. After these ten victories, our old crate, which had a red band around the fuselage, was so riddled with bullet holes that the trusty steed had to be transported home.'[14]

Lothar also noted that other well-known flyers observed certain almost superstitious practices. For example, his brother Manfred achieved all of his aerial victories wearing the same old leather jacket, and Kurt Wolff never flew without his lucky nightcap. As proof that these rituals had to be followed, Lothar von Richthofen stated that Kurt Wintgens always flew with a riding crop (even though he had no cavalry background), and the one time he left it in his quarters was the day he was killed. Lothar reported that Oswald Boelcke forbade having his picture taken just before starting out on a flight, and the one time the rule was violated was on the day he collided with Erwin Böhme. Likewise, Karl-Emil Schäfer followed the same rule, which, when violated, had the same deadly result.[15]

Luck and skill were evident on 11 March, when *Jasta 11* came upon B.E.s of No.2 Squadron and F.E.s of No.18 Squadron working the line from Loos to Vimy. Richthofen became separated from his men as they went after the B.E.s and F.E.s. Just before noon he spotted B.E.2d 6232 of No.2 Squadron, which had taken off only 15 minutes earlier, and caught the crew unawares. Richthofen poured some 200 rounds into the two-seater, so much ammunition that the aeroplane's fuselage broke into two pieces,[16] which fell into La Folie Forest, west of Vimy, just within German lines. The crew of the 26th aircraft claimed by Richthofen, 2/Lts John Smyth and Edward Byrne, were found dead at the site.

Once again using the cover of generally bad weather, between 16 and 20 March, German ground forces made an orderly strategic withdrawal to more fortified positions from Arras south to St. Quentin. The *Siegfriedstellung* (Siegfried Position), which the British called the Hindenburg Line, offered the advantage of prepared defensive systems, from which the Germans could advance again at will. In the interim, pursuing British ground and air forces were stretched further and had to adjust to ever-changing scenarios beyond their control.

The German advantage was clear on 17 March, when *Jasta 11* attacked sixteen aircraft drawn to the area over Oppy. Sopwith 1½ Strutters of No.43 Squadron were escorting F.E.2s of No.25 Squadron on a photo-reconnaissance of the changing front lines when ten Albatroses struck just before noon. Manfred von Richthofen got behind F.E.2b A5439, a presentation aircraft with the words 'Zanzibar No.10' painted on the fuselage,[17] symbolic of the far-flung points of the British Empire that contributed to the war effort. To Richthofen it was just another *Gitterschwanz* (lattice-tail) enemy aircraft. He aimed at the two-seat pusher and fired 800 rounds into it, severing a tail boom. The aircraft broke up in the air and tumbled to the ground. The bodies of the crew, Lt Arthur E. Boultbee and 2/AM Frederick King, were buried by the local commander at Oppy.[18]

A short time later Richthofen received a grisly souvenir of his 27th victory when a witness to the crash, *Oberst* von Riezenstein, commander of the *87. Reserve-Infanterie-Regiment*, sent him a postcard photograph of the fallen pilot's body at the crash site. Ordinarily, Richthofen did not like to contemplate the fate of his victims, but, for whatever reason, he sent the photo home, where it was displayed with his other trophies.

That afternoon Richthofen scored his 28th victory when, at about 1700, he shot down a B.E. artillery-spotter above the trenches west of Vimy. It was well protected by fighters, but Richthofen slipped by the escorts and went after the more important target. After a spirited chase and exchange of fire, the two-seater's wings suddenly collapsed. The wind carried the crumpled aircraft over the German lines, where B.E.2c 2814 was confirmed as Richthofen's 28th victory. Once again, the crew, 2/Lt George M. Watt and Sgt Ernest A. Howlett of No.16 Squadron, were killed.

DEATH OF A PRINCE

On 21 March 1917 *Jagdstaffel 3* was transferred from the *2. Armee* to the *6. Armee* and assigned to the airfield at Guesmain near Douai.[19] The Richthofen brothers' cousin, *Ltn* Oskar von Schickfuss und Neudorff, was a member of that unit, and this development offered the prospect that the three relatives might fly and fight together in the air.

Despite bad weather that afternoon, Richthofen authorized lone patrols to look for targets of opportunity. There were extensive RFC air operations, including many probing flights, which had to be stopped to keep British field commanders from determining the Germans' final fall-back positions and strength. For all of the German air activity, only two victories were recorded that day: Karl Allmenröder's fourth and Manfred von Richthofen's 29th.[20]

The identity of Allmenröder's opponent is unclear, but it seems most likely that Richthofen's lone attack north of Neuville at 1730 resulted in the downing of B.E.2f A3154 of No.16 Squadron. He had sighted several two-seat artillery spotters within German lines, and caught one of them by surprise. The aircraft came down within British lines, and area troops hurried to the site only to find that the pilot, Fl/Sgt Sidney H. Quicke, was dead. According to the *RFC Casualty List*, the observer, 2/Lt William J. Lidsey, was wounded in the stomach by machine-gun fire and died two days later.

Any exuberance over the two victories was tempered by news of the loss that day of Manfred von Richthofen's classmate from Gross Lichterfelde, *Prinz* Friedrich Karl of Prussia, a cousin of *Kaiser* Wilhelm. The Prince had a meteoric career, from cavalry service to the *Fliegertruppe*, with rapid promotion to the rank of *Rittmeister* (Cavalry Captain) and command of the reconnaissance unit *Fl.-Abt. (A) 258*.

Looking for excitement beyond his two-seater unit, Prince Friedrich Karl often flew fighter patrols with *Jasta 2* in Albatros D.I 410/16. During such a patrol on the afternoon of 21 March, the Prince was brought down over Vaux Wood by Lt Charles E. M. Pickthorn in a D.H.5 (7938),[21] the tractor biplane successor to the D.H.2 pusher that had found little success against the new Albatroses. His old Albatros was no match for the faster, more manoeuvrable D.H.5, and the Prince was forced to land and taken prisoner. During an escape attempt, Prince Friedrich Karl was shot and wounded, and died of his wounds in a POW camp in St Etienne on 6 April 1917, his 24th birthday.[22]

Manfred von Richthofen admired his classmate's bravery and envied the perquisites of royal birth. The late Prince had been two ranks higher than he and, as a son of the Hohenzollern dynasty, had received high orders as a youth; the latter included the *Grosskreuz mit Krone des Roten Adler-Ordens* (Grand Cross with Crown of the Order of the Red Eagle), the second highest order of the Prussian Kingdom.[23] But Manfred also had the satisfaction of knowing that he had *qualified* for the *Pour le Mérite* and, as he learned the following day, he had earned an early promotion.

His letter of 26 March 1917 to his mother recounts the swirl of events in the days before the big battle to come:

> Yesterday I shot down the 31st, the day before the 30th.[24] Three days ago I was promoted by order of the *Kabinett* [Royal Cabinet of Ministers] to *Oberleutnant*. I have therefore gained a good half-year's seniority. My *Staffel* is doing well. I am very happy with it. Yesterday, Lothar had his first aerial combat. He was very satisfied because his opponent was hit. We say that "he stank", because he left behind him a black ribbon of smoke. Of course he did not fall, as that would have been too much luck for the first time. Lothar is very conscientious and will do well.[25]

Manfred did not score again in March, but Lothar achieved his first confirmed victory on the 28th. He forced F.E.2b 7715 of No.25 Squadron to land south of Lens. The pilot, 2/Lt N.L. Knight, was killed in the combat, and the observer, 2/Lt A.G. Severs, was wounded and taken prisoner. Their 'Fee,' the presentation aircraft 'Zanzibar No.8', was salvaged for evaluation.[26]

TIGHTENING THE ORGANIZATION

Back in his small office at La Brayelle, *Obltn* Manfred von Richthofen attended to some important paperwork. His old friend from *FEA 2* at Döberitz, *Obltn* Bodo *Freiherr* von Lyncker, who had been assigned to *Jasta 25* on the Macedonian Front, had written to Richthofen seeking transfers to the Western Front for himself and his *Staffel-Kamerad*, *Ltn.d.Res* Otto Brauneck. Then came word that Bodo von Lyncker had been killed in a collision with an enemy aircraft on 18 February. Richthofen's fallen comrade had done him a great service in recommending Brauneck, who had shot down three enemy aircraft and four balloons and had already received the Hohenzollern House Order. He was just the kind of pilot Richthofen wanted for his *Staffel*, and for whom he was willing to use his influence. He wrote to Brauneck:

> I recall that Lynker [sic] had already written me about you and a recommendation from this fine man is good enough for me. Therefore I am ready to request you immediately. Today a telegram is going to your *Kofl*, followed by a telegram to *Kogen* [Office of the Commanding General of the Air Force]. It is up to you to pressure your superior, so that he will release you from there, for without consent on his part, nothing can be done at the *Kogen*.
>
> There is plenty going on here. We shoot down at least one a day during good flying weather.
>
> Also you will find here a very nice circle of comrades. I await your answer as soon as possible.[27]

NOTES

1   Quoted in von Richthofen, *Ein Heldenleben*, (1920), p.229.
2   Ibid, pp.298, 312, 313, 324.
3   *Kofl 6. Armee Wochenbericht Nr 24030, Teil 9*, 8 March 1917.
4   No.2 Squadron Combat Report.
5   Gibbons, *The Red Knight of Germany*, (1927), pp.127-128.
6   Wright, *Richthofen's 23rd or Was It?*, (1983), pp.122-125.
7   Gibbons, op.cit., p.130.
8   Bruce, *British Aeroplanes 1914-1918*, (1969), pp.128-129.
9   *RFC War Diary*, 9 March 1917.
10   von Richthofen, *Der rote Kampfflieger*, (1933), p.127.
11   Ibid., p.128.
12   von Richthofen, *Mein Kriegstagebuch*, (1937), p.101.
13   'Vigilant,' *Richthofen - The Red Knight of the Air*, (n.d.), pp.164-165.
14   Quoted in von Richthofen, *Ein Heldenleben*, (1920), pp.221-222.
15   Ibid.
16   Gibbons, op.cit., p.140.

17   Vann and Waugh, *Overseas and United Kingdom Presentation Aircraft 1914-18*, (1983), p.93.
18   Ibid., p.142.
19   *Kofl 6. Armee Wochenbericht Nr 24620, Teil 1*, 23 March 1917.
20   *Nachrichtenblatt der Luftstreitkräfte Nr. 7*, 12 April 1917, p.15.
21   Puglisi, *German Aircraft Down in British Lines*, Part 1, (1969), p.155.
22   Zickerick, *Verlustliste der deutschen Luftstreitkräfte im Weltkriege*, (1930), p.63.
23   O'Connor, *Aviation Awards of Imperial Germany in World War I and the Men Who Earned Them*, vol II, (1990), pp.17, 23.
24   Victory No.30 was SPAD S.7 A6706 of No.19 Squadron, pilot 2/Lt Richard P. Baker (WiA/PoW); victory No.31 was Nieuport 17 A6689 of No.29 Squadron, pilot 2/Lt Christopher G. Gilbert (PoW).
25   *Ein Heldenleben*, op.cit., p.195.
26   Vann and Waugh, op.cit.
27   Quoted in Schmeelke, *Leutnant der Reserve Otto Brauneck*, (1983), p.163.

CHAPTER 7
BLOODY APRIL

It was the best of times for Manfred von Richthofen, who added 21 enemy aeroplanes to his personal victory list, exceeded the record set by his mentor, Oswald Boelcke, and became the undisputed ace of aces. It was the worst of times for Britain's air forces, which lost one-third of their airmen then at the Front, 912 pilots and observers in 50 Squadrons.[1] It was the month that has become known in aviation history as 'Bloody April'.

The Germans enjoyed the advantage of a pull-back behind strong defensive positions to reorganize their forces in the face of the impending British offensive. They also had superior aircraft with which they could fight or withdraw at will, generally over their own lines. Conversely, Maj-Gen Hugh M. Trenchard, General Officer Commanding the Royal Flying Corps in France and Belgium, faced the dual challenge of conserving his forces for the offensive and continuously and effectively countering the *Luftstreitkräfte* while trying to disrupt German communications.[2] All of this in a month that was unusually stormy, with many snowfalls.[3]

In spite of wind, rain and low clouds on the morning of 2 April, *Jasta 11* was ready to attack at a moment's notice. The *Staffel* had been divided into two *Ketten* ('chains' or Flights), and four pilots of one *Kette* were suited up and on the flight line by 0500. Three hours later, the call came: 'Six Bristols [heading] from Arras to Douai'. *Ltn* Karl-Emil Schäfer led the *Kette* consisting of *Ltns* Karl Allmenröder, Lothar von Richthofen and Kurt Wolff. As they took off they passed Manfred von Richthofen's all-red Albatros in front of its hangar, attended by his mechanics. The *Kette* climbed to 3,000m and spent over an hour trying to engage the RFC two-seaters, but without success. Upon their return to La Brayelle, the red Albatros was still in front of the hangar.

Later they learned that their leader had been awakened by the sound of their preparations, but had reached the flight line too late to join them. He had taken off and, in trying to catch up with his men, had been jumped by a two-seater. With iron nerve and cool clarity, Richthofen sized up the situation: 'During a pause in the fighting, I made sure that we opposed each other alone. Therefore, he who shot better, remained the calmest and had the best perspective at the moment of danger would win.'[4]

Soon, Richthofen manoeuvred into a superior position above and behind his bold adversaries in B.E.2d 5841 of No.13 Squadron.[5] At first it looked as though the British crew would land and surrender, which offered Richthofen both a victory claim and the opportunity to provide the intelligence officers with another captured aircraft to examine. But then the two-seater tried to make a run for it, and Richthofen opened fire and followed along at treetop height. Even though he felt his own engine take a hit, Richthofen pursued the B.E. until it flew into a block of houses in the village of Farbus, northeast of Arras. The crew, Lt Patrick J.G. Powell and 1/AM Percy Bonner, perished.

Richthofen's assessment of his adversary (which was omitted from the 1933 edition of his memoir) was: 'It was again a case of splendid daring. He defended himself to the last. But in my view it was, in the end, just more stupidity on his part. It was once again just at the point where I draw the line between daring and stupidity. He had to go down. So he had to pay for his stupidity with his life.'[6]

A VISIT FROM VOSS

Richthofen returned to his airfield, where he was greeted by his old *Jasta 2* comrade *Ltn* Werner Voss, who had flown over from Lagnicourt. They had a long conversation over breakfast, and were just finishing up when Schäfer's flight returned. Richthofen informed them of his 32nd victory. Richthofen liked Voss, but did not allow his own accomplishments to be outshone in any way. As he later wrote: 'Voss had dispatched his 23rd the day before. He was, therefore, right behind me and was at the time my strongest competitor.'[7]

As Voss was not entirely familiar with the area, Richthofen invited him to accompany the next flight, toward Arras, where he would find orientation points. Voss welcomed the opportunity to fly with — and learn from — Germany's leading fighter pilot.

Thus, Manfred von Richthofen concluded his morning's work about 1120, when he, his brother Lothar and *Ltn* Voss attacked eight Sopwith 1½ Strutters of No.43 Squadron on their way back from photographing Vimy Ridge. Manfred drove down Sopwith A2401 about 300m east of Givenchy, where, according to his combat report, the observer continued the fight: '... even as his machine was on the ground, he kept shooting at me, thereby hitting my machine very severely when I was only five metres above the ground. Consequently, I once more attacked [the aeroplane] on the ground and killed one of the occupants.'[8] The pilot, 2/Lt A. Peter Warren, survived the encounter. He later maintained that his observer, Sgt Renel Dunn, died shortly after the aeroplane landed, not from further hostile action but from a fatal abdomen wound he had received in the early moments of Richthofen's attack.[9]

On Tuesday 3 April Manfred von Richthofen led the scoring when he, Lothar and Karl-Emil Schäfer attacked three 'Fees' from No.25 Squadron assigned to make a photo-reconnaissance of the area near Méricourt, southeast of Lens. Manfred von Richthofen brought down his 34th victim, F.E.2d A6382, which landed near Liéven, southwest of Lens.[10]

Five days before the Entente infantry assault began, a British air offensive was started. The purpose of the 4 April air action along the entire British front was to draw German aircraft away from the immediate battle area, leaving reconnaissance and bombing aircraft free to perform their missions.[11]

This initial effort proved to be disastrous. During the period 4 to 8 April, 75 British aircraft were shot down in combat with an attendant loss of 19 dead, 13 wounded and 73 missing airmen; the situation was exacerbated by 'an abnormally high number of flying accidents', resulting in the loss of another 56 aircraft.[12] Only two British combat losses on 4 April occurred on the 6. *Armee* Front. Both were scored by *Jasta 4*, with no German losses indicated.[13]

The low clouds and rain on the opening day of the British air offensive were not promising signs to *Staffelführer* von Richthofen, so *Jasta 11* enjoyed a brief respite that day. But he made up for that rest period the following morning, 5 April. Despite fog and bad weather, Richthofen and four comrades encountered six of the new Bristol F.2A two-seat fighters of No.48 Squadron on their first offensive patrol.

The Brisfit flight was led by Capt William Leefe Robinson, VC, who had become the first airman to earn Britain's highest award for valour, the Victoria Cross, within United Kingdom territory, by shooting down the Schütte-Lanz airship *SL 11* on the night of 2/3 September 1916.[14] Although the Bristol Fighters' newly-issued machine-guns failed to work properly,[15] No.48 Squadron was credited with driving down out of control three of 'twelve hostile aircraft [encountered] near Douai'.[16] No corresponding German losses were recorded; indeed, German documents show this engagement to have been a great success for *Jasta 11*.

Beginning at about 1100, *Obltn* Manfred von Richthofen shot down two F.2As in rapid succession southeast of Douai, one over Lewarde and one over Cuincy,[17] while *Ltn* Georg Simon claimed one over Auchy.[18]

During the same fight, *Vzfw* Sebastian Festner brought down F.2A A3337 near Méricourt, which was credited as his fourth victory. The uninjured occupants, Capt W.L. Robinson, VC, and 2/Lt E.D. Warburton, were taken prisoner. Robinson's death on 31 December 1918 is generally considered to be an indirect result of the harsh treatment he received as a prisoner of war.[19]

NIGHTTIME RAIDS ON *JASTA 11*

Such a successful day for *Jasta 11* called for a grand celebration at La Brayelle airfield that evening. While the festivities were going on, a different sort of 'party' had been organized at the Headquarters of 13th (Army) Wing at Izel le Hameau aerodrome, barely 40km southwest of La Brayelle. Eighteen F.E.2b night-bombers of No.100 Squadron were taking off for their first raid on Douai airfield,[20] where, the unit later reported, 'Four hangars were completely destroyed, and other damage was done'.[21]

Jasta 11 had been alerted that the enemy bombers were en route. Ever the tactician, Manfred von Richthofen had his fellow pilots and other *Staffel* members take up defensive positions around their airfield. He described the encounter with the leading F.E.2b with the same zest he had for air combat:

> The Englishman seemed to fly very high. First once around the entire airfield. We thought he was looking for another target. Then all of a sudden he switched off his engine and dived down. "Now it is getting serious," Wolff ventured. We had each fetched a carbine and began to fire at the Englishman. Then we could not see him. But just the noise [of the shooting] calmed our nerves.
>
> Then he came into the searchlight beam. From everywhere on the airfield there was a great hullabaloo. It was quite an old crate. We recognized the type precisely. He was at most a kilometre away from us. He flew right toward our airfield. He came lower and lower. Then he switched the engine back on and came flying right at us. Wolff opined: "Thank God, he is looking for the other side of the airfield". But it was not long before the first and then other bombs rained down. It was a wonderful fireworks display that the "brother" put on for us. Only a frightened rabbit would have been impressed by it. I find that, in general, bombing at night has significance only on morale. If one fills his pants, then it is very embarrassing for him, but not for the others.[22]

The following evening, Good Friday, Richthofen expected retaliation and tightened his defensive perimeter. He had *Staffel* enlisted men drive poles into the ground at strategic locations and on these captured British machine-guns were mounted and ranged to hit incoming aircraft.

Right after dinner,[23] he later wrote, the marauders returned:

> The first one came over, just as on the previous evening, at very high altitude, then came down to 50 metres and, to our greatest joy, this time he aimed right for the side of our barracks. He was right in the searchlight beam. He was at most 300 metres away from us. The first [of our number] began to fire at him and then at the same time everyone opened fire. A massive assault could not have been better warded off than the attack of this cheeky fellow at 50 metres. A raging burst of fire greeted him. He could not hear the machine-gun fire over the sound of his own engine, but he saw all of the muzzle flashes and I think he was very daring in not veering off, but, rather, staying on course for his mission. He flew right over us and then off. At the moment that he flew over us, of course we all quickly jumped into the shelter, for to be hit by a stupid bomb would be a foolish hero's death for a fighter pilot. Scarcely had he gone over us when we were again at our guns, firing away at him.[24]

PROMOTED TO *RITTMEISTER*

Holy Saturday, 7 April 1917, brought news both good and bad. The good news for Manfred von Richthofen was the arrival of a brand-new aircraft, Albatros D.III 789/17, and official word of his promotion to *Rittmeister* (Cavalry Captain). Even though he no longer served on horseback, Richthofen received his captaincy through the cavalry, in keeping with Army tradition.

The bad news was that on Good Friday *Obltn* Hans Berr, leader of *Jasta 5* and the thirteenth aviation recipient of the *Pour le Mérite*, had suffered the same fate as Oswald Boelcke. While attacking an F.E.2d of No.57 Squadron over Noyelles, east of Lens, Berr and *Vzfw* Paul Hoppe collided; both aircraft broke up at 2,400m,[25] eliminating any possibility of survival.

The other Good Friday bad news, which would be fully comprehended only with the passage of time, was that President Woodrow Wilson had announced a formal declaration of war between the United States of America and the Central Powers.

Richthofen did not allow himself to ruminate about the fall of his immediate predecessor in the knighthood of *Pour le Mérite* flyers. Rather, he was off in his new Albatros, joined by four of his comrades, and heading for the abundant hunting grounds south of Arras. At about 1745 the quintet engaged a flight of six Nieuport 17s of No.60 Squadron within their own lines. The Albatroses, each equipped with two synchronized machine-guns, made short work of three of the single-gun, less manoeuvrable Nieuports. Richthofen's victim, his 37th, went down in flames near Mercatel.[26] Wolff's seventh victory and Schäfer's twelfth went down in the same area. *Vzfw* Festner was credited with his sixth victory, a Sopwith single-seater shot down at 1910 between Mont St. Eloi and Maroeuil, northwest of Arras.

Improved weather on 8 April, Easter Sunday, brought the RFC out in force in the final preparations for the beginning of the Battle of Arras. The combined aircraft of *Jastas 4* and *11* awaited and attacked British aircraft around Arras with great success.

Capt Alan J.L. Scott, Commanding No.60 Squadron, went after the Germans with five Nieuports, including one flown by Lt William A. Bishop, the future second-ranking RAF ace. The British patrol became separated, however, and *Vzfw* Festner opened the day's scoring by shooting down Nieuport 17 A311, his seventh victory.[27] During the fight, however, the lower port wing broke on Festner's aircraft, Albatros D.III 223/16. It was a recurrence of the problem that was supposed to have been fixed. In this case Festner withdrew and made a safe landing. 'The machine is being sent home as useless for combat', Richthofen wrote with disgust in his report to the Inspectorate of Military Aviation.[28]

Richthofen's own aircraft, Albatros D.III 789/17, performed perfectly and enabled him to achieve his 38th victory. At about 1140 he and three comrades pounced on three Sopwith 1½ Strutters of No.43 Squadron. The *Staffel* leader got behind Sopwith A2406, and in one long burst of fire killed the observer and shot away the aircraft's controls.[29] The two-seater crashed near Farbus.

Also that day, *Jasta Boelcke*'s Werner Voss was awarded the *Pour le Mérite*. His immediate predecessor in that high honour was Manfred von Richthofen. Voss, who had received the House Order of Hohenzollern on 17 March, had attained 24 victories (vs. Richthofen's sixteen) by the time he received the coveted blue enamel and gold Maltese cross.[30] Again, the price of glory had risen.

As the *Pour le Mérite* was Prussia's highest military honour for *merit* and bravery in wartime, it was awarded to senior officers in recognition of exemplary performance in positions of high responsibility. Hence, among the 8 April 1917 recipients of this distinction were the *Luftstreitkräfte*'s two top officers: *Gen-Ltn* Ernst von Hoeppner, the Commanding General, and *Oberstltn* Hermann von der Lieth-Thomsen, his Chief of Staff.[31]

Despite his aerial combat achievements, Werner Voss had a long way to go to match the victory list of Manfred von Richthofen. Later that day Richthofen achieved his 39th air combat success, over B.E.2e A2815 of No.16 Squadron, which broke up in the air over Vimy at 1640.[32]

THE BATTLE OF ARRAS BEGINS

An extensive British assault against the German *6.* and *17. Armee* Fronts began at 0530 on Easter Monday, 9 April. This action was to be a single massive diversion, preceding a French offensive on the Aisne Front a week later. British Army units were supported by considerable RFC air cover, but their efforts were hampered by snow and drizzle at low altitudes and strong winds at greater heights during most of the day. German air opposition was very light; indeed, the only *6. Armee* air success that day occurred at 1910, when *Ltn* Karl-Emil Schäfer shot down a B.E. two-seater which had penetrated German airspace at Aix Noulette, west of Lens.

Despite strong wind and snow on 10 April, RFC units were over the lines in support of the ground advance. Again, there was virtually no German air resistence. On 11 April, however, *Jasta 11* made up for the previous days' lack of activity; operating with *Jasta 4* they recorded seven victories and no losses.

During heavy fighting over the British-held village of Fampoux, Manfred von Richthofen attacked a low-flying two-seat infantry support aircraft over Willerval. Wolff deferred to his leader and Richthofen sent the two-seater into a shell hole.[33] In that short fight *Rittm* Manfred *Frhr* von Richthofen equalled the achievement of his mentor, Oswald Boelcke, 40 aerial victories, and became Germany's greatest living fighter pilot.

During the afternoon patrol *Jasta 11*'s score climbed higher. Schäfer and Lothar von Richthofen attacked two-seaters east of Arras, resulting in Schäfer's sixteenth and Lothar's third victories.

TRIPLE VICTORIES

On the evening of 11 April, *Prof.Dr* Georg Wegener, a correspondent for *Die Kölnische Zeitung*, had arrived at La Brayelle. To impress this guest, Richthofen had a telescope set up so that Wegener could watch the *Staffel* head out for its first mission of the following day. As it transpired, the journalist had a front-row seat for one of *Jasta 11*'s great triumphs.

Initially, *Prof.Dr* Wegener observed with great fascination the line-up of colourful aircraft and the young aerial warriors who flew them into battle:

> From a distance they looked like iridescent giant insects, like a swarm of gaily-coloured butterflies with their wings spread out, sunning themselves on the ground. The principle of looking as much as possible like the colour of the sky was entirely abandoned. "Invisibility cannot be achieved," it was explained to me, "but one does indeed run the risk of a mix-up [between] enemy and friendly aeroplanes. These different markings on the fuselages are clearly visible in the air, [and] one recognizes them during combat and can assist [a comrade]."
>
> For this reason every pilot has his personal machine, in which he always flies and to which he is so closely attached as if with a living creature, giving it a special marking that enables his comrades to keep him in sight during combat and to know at all times who controls the machine. One machine has white or red or some other coloured stripes, another carries them diagonally or longitudinally, etc. From Richthofen's eyes shine the pride of the warrior knight, whose shield and helmet ornament are known and feared by the opponent. "I make sure that my flight sees me wherever I am."
>
> In fact, we perceive very strongly how much the old knightly gallantry has come alive again in the conduct of modern aerial combat; here the personal markings of the armaments by emblems visible from a distance heighten the impression. These young combatants have a bearing quite like that of the medieval lords, of whom the fourteenth-century chronicler Froissart so colourfully recounted, with their shimmering banners, coats of arms and battle flags, which they displayed with pride and closed helmet visors.
>
> One after the other until the take-off [time] was determined they climbed into their flight clothing, which looked like a combination of a diver's suit and a Dutch fisherman's outfit, and, with their hands in their deep pockets, laughing and joking, [they] sauntered amongst their groundcrews preparing their machines for take-off or over to the big telescope to carefully observe the sky. Even Richthofen had already put on his gear and carefully scrutinized the heavens with his naked eye.
>
> All of a sudden — I myself saw not the slightest movement up in the clear blue — quickly he turned to a bell hanging nearby and

sounded the alarm. In an instant all of the mechanics ran to their machines; each pilot hurried to his own [aircraft], climbed into the seat, [as] the propellers thundered, [and] one after the other the small fast aeroplanes ran along a stretch of the ground, lifted up and quickly climbed up into the blue. The last one was Richthofen's machine.

The flyers remaining behind, the groundcrewmen, the orderlies and sentries — all followed with the greatest excitement the events in the sky. Now I recognized, first through the telescope and then without it, a squadron of British aircraft; at least six, perhaps more. I had to watch them very closely, otherwise I would lose them in the glimmering brightness.

The flyers [on the ground] saw other things. They recognized and named the various types and they shouted indignantly: "What nerve! They come over here at barely 2,000 metres! What do they think they are doing?"[34]

The object of attention was a flight of six of the new R.E.8 aircraft of No.59 Squadron en route to the Drocourt-Quéant switch line. Two were photo-reconnaissance aircraft, the other four were escorts. Just over Vitry, 8km southwest of the German airfield, fighters from *Jastas 4* and *11* attacked the two-seaters. In a brief encounter, all six went down and were recorded as *Rittm* Manfred von Richthofen's 41st aerial victory,[35] *Ltn* Kurt Wolff's tenth, *Vzfw* Sebastian Festner's ninth, *Ltn* Lothar von Richthofen's fourth and fifth, and the sixth victory of *Ltn.d.Res* Hans Klein of *Jasta 4*.

'The good friend down on the ground was more than a little astonished,' Richthofen later wrote. 'He had imagined the event [would be] quite different, much more dramatic. He thought it all looked quite harmless until suddenly some of the aeroplanes, one of them burning like a rocket, came crashing down. I have gradually become accustomed to the sight, but I must say that the first Englishman I saw go roaring down made a frightful impression on me and I dreamed about it for a long time.'[36]

Prof.Dr Wegener joined the *Staffel* members as they welcomed their returning comrades. He reported:

Scarcely half an hour had passed and they were all there again. The combatants climbed out of their seats and — laughing, proud, happy, recounting [events] animatedly — stood amidst their well-wishing comrades and enlisted men who shared the enthusiasm of their officers.

No one was injured. It all looked like it could have been a successful sporting event. But Richthofen's machine showed how little it was really like that. An enemy machine-gun burst hit the left lower wing and the fabric for about a metre and a half looked like it had been slashed open by the swipe of a big knife. And on the outer wooden covering close to the pilot's seat ran a second scar showing that another shot came close to taking his life.[37]

After a late breakfast Richthofen was off again, this time over British lines to catch RFC aircraft returning from missions over German emplacements. *Ltn* Georg Simon, an original member of *Jasta 11* who had been wounded in a fight in January and recently returned to the *Staffel*, was the Richthofen pupil/wingman for this flight. He accompanied the leader in his dive on a 'Vickers two-seater' crossing the lines. Richthofen recorded his 42nd victim's end in his combat report: 'After rather a long fight, during which I manoeuvred [in such a way] that my adversary could not fire a single shot at me, the enemy 'plane plunged to the ground between Monchy and Feuchy [just east of Arras]'.[38]

Over the German detraining station at Hénin-Liétard that evening, *Jasta 11* shot down three 'Fees' from No.25 Squadron. The two-seaters were confirmed as Richthofen's 43rd,[39] Schäfer's seventeenth, and Festner's tenth victories.

First World War aviation has been glamorized by accounts of 'noble and honourable' treatment of downed adversaries — if they survived the aerial combats that led to their capture. Following the events of what Richthofen called 'my most successful day thus far', he wrote of one such instance:

> One of the Englishmen we had shot down was captured and we had a conversation with him. Of course, he enquired about the red aircraft. It is known even to the troops down in the trenches and it is called "*le diable rouge*". In his squadron the rumour had been spread that a girl sat in the red machine, somewhat similar to Joan of Arc. He was very surprised when I assured him that the alleged girl stood before him right then. He was not trying to be funny; rather, he was convinced that only a *Jungfrau* [maiden] could sit in the perversely painted crate.[40]

On 14 April *Jasta 11* accounted for eight enemy aircraft shot down. Manfred von Richthofen led the way against five Nieuports of No.60 Squadron which were attacking two German two-seaters west of Douai, within German lines. Richthofen hit the first one at 0915 and forced it to land near Fresnoy.[41] The event was recorded as his 44th victory. During the next ten minutes three of the other RFC fighters were brought down by Kurt Wolff, Lothar von Richthofen and Sebastian Festner, and only Lt Graham Young's Nieuport returned to the squadron's aerodrome at Izel le Hameau.[42]

ACE OF ACES

Now with 44 enemy aircraft to his credit and standing as the Ace of Aces of all the belligerents, *Rittm* Manfred *Frhr* von Richthofen was a cause of great concern to his superiors. His continuing string of victories was a source of immense pride and inspiration, of course, but his loss would be devastating. No one doubted Richthofen's prowess, but those in authority knew that RFC bombers had too good a fix on *Jasta 11*'s airfield, and one lucky bomb could achieve what 44 enemy pilots had not.

Richthofen gently deflected offers of leave or other absences from the Front. Hence, one short-term means of offering him some protection was a new airfield assignment. Amidst low clouds and day-long rain on 15 April, *Jasta 11* moved from La Brayelle to a new airfield at the town of Roucourt, 6km southeast of Douai and a little further out of harm's way.

Given Richthofen's hunting nature, one important challenge at Roucourt would be to replicate the comfortable quarters of the previous airfield. *Prof.Dr* Georg Wegener described Richthofen's room at La Brayelle as being 'decorated with the trophies of his career, the colourful national insignias and other parts of the aircraft he shot down. From the ceiling hung an enemy Gnôme rotary engine sent back [and] modified into a multi-armed chandelier, [and] over the door is the machine-gun of his most dangerous opponent, the British Major Hawker, who [was] ... one of the most successful British combat pilots.'[43]

While the groundcrew settled into the new location, on 16 April the pilots achieved four more victories, bringing *Jasta 11*'s total score to 92 aircraft downed since the beginning of flight operations in January.[44]

Manfred von Richthofen was on a late afternoon patrol northeast of Arras when he surprised a B.E.2. A steady stream of fire sent the two-seater down between Bailleul and Gavrelle, northwest of Arras, at 1730 (German time). Most sources consider Richthofen's 45th victim to have been from No.7 Squadron; however, RFC records show that that aircraft took off at 1305 (1405 German time) from Matigny aerodrome, southwest of St Quentin. It was observed brought down by anti-aircraft fire at Savy, 14km away, over 55km southeast of the Richthofen claim site. Indeed, the pilot of B.E.2d 5869 told American journalist Floyd Gibbons that he thought the aeroplane had been hit by an artillery shell.[45]

The evidence suggests that Richthofen shot down B.E.2e 3156 of No.13 Squadron, which departed Izel le Hameau at 1450 (1550 German time) for an artillery patrol within Richthofen's operational area. That aircraft was reportedly attacked by a 'hostile aircraft' and fell about 25km from its own aerodrome. The crew, 2/Lts Alphonso Pascoe and F.S. Andrews, were wounded.

As further testimony to his unique national standing, Manfred von Richthofen began receiving high awards from the rulers of the German states. On 16 April he was honoured by the Kingdom of Saxony, which bestowed its Knight's Cross of the Military Order of St Henry. The award recognized his 30th aerial victory and put him in the same class as the first flyer to receive this high honour: Max Immelmann. Even the great Boelcke, a Saxon native, had not been so highly decorated. Eventually, Richthofen received high awards from the Kingdoms of Bavaria and Württemberg, as well as from most of the German duchies and other allies.

Right: Manfred von Richthofen (left) and his younger brother, Lothar, wear two different types of flight clothing in this postcard photo. They pose by one of *Jagdstaffel 11*'s Fokker Dr.I triplanes.

Below right: Trophies of war at the family home in Schweidnitz, in Lower Silesia, included serial number patches of fabric from aircraft brought down by Manfred von Richthofen. Seen in this pre-Second World War view are (from left): 4997 – victory 43, F.E.2b, No. 25 Squadron, RFC; A1108 – victory 23, Sopwith 1½ Strutter, No. 43 Squadron, RFC; 5986 – victory 12, D.H.2, No. 32 Squadron, RFC; A2401 – victory 33, Sopwith 1½ Strutter, No. 43 Squadron, RFC; 6580 – victory 5, B.E.12, No. 19 Squadron, RFC; A6382 – victory 34, F.E.2d, No. 25 Squadron, RFC; 6232 – victory 26, B.E.2d, No. 2. Squadron, RFC; 5841 – victory 32, B.E.2d, No. 13. Squadron, RFC; 5986 – victory 12; 5841 – victory 32; 2506 – victory 8, B.E.2c, No. 12 Squadron, RFC; 6997 – victory 18, F.E.2b, No. 25 Squadron, RFC; 6618 – victory 4, B.E.12, No. 21 Squadron, RFC; A3340 – victory 36, Bristol F.2A, No. 48 Squadron, RFC; 6580 – victory 5; 2506 – victory 8; N5193 – victory 16, Sopwith Pup, No. 8 Squadron, RNAS; A2401 – victory 33; A6382 – victory 34; A5446 – victory 14, F.E.2b, No. 18 Squadron, RFC. At the end of the Second World War, members of the Richthofen family living in the house fled before the Soviet Army occupied Silesia. Since that time, none of this memorabilia has been seen.

Above: Single-seat Fokker D.II biplanes succeeded the *Eindeckers*, but were replaced by the superior Albatros D-series.

Below: Albatros D.Is of *Jasta 2* arrived in September 1916. They were succeeded by the D.II, which offered improvements including a better view forward and upward, achieved by bringing the top wing closer to the fuselage.

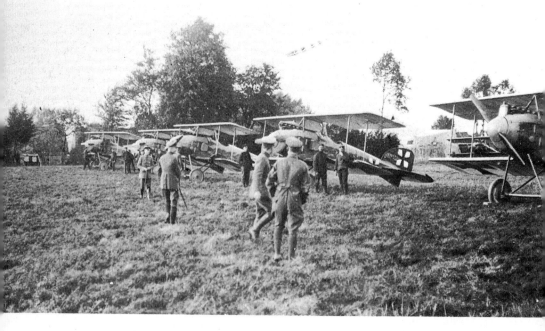

Above: The de Havilland D.H.2's forward-firing gun allowed it to match the Fokkers' and Albatros' airfighting capabilities. The prototype, 4732, was sent to France with No. 5 Squadron, RFC, in August 1915 and was captured shortly thereafter.

Below: After Boelcke's death, the new *Jasta 2* line-up was (from left): *Ltn* Jürgen Sandel, *Offzstlvtr* Max Müller (a future ace and *Pour le Mérite* recipient), *Ltn* Manfred von Richthofen, *Ltn* Wolfgang Günther, *Obltn* Stephan Kirmaier, *Ltn* Hans Imelmann, *Ltn* Erich König, *Ltn* Otto Höhne, *Ltn* Hans Wortmann and *Ltn* Diether Collin.

Opposite page, top left: Manfred von Richthofen was sent to *FEA 6* at Grossenhain to become an aviation observer. As he never completed the formal training, the Observer's Badge is one of the few military awards he did not receive.

Opposite page, top right: After 'informal' flight training, Richthofen qualified for the Military Pilot's Badge.

Left: The AEG G.I, seen here, was the predecessor of the G.II in which Richthofen flew on the Russian Front. In both aircraft the observer was precariously close to the propellers, as Richthofen learned when he was 'wounded' in the finger by a propeller blade. Later models of the AEG G-series machines had fuselage side-screens to protect the crew.

Above: Fokker *Eindecker* single-seaters were used by Oswald Boelcke, Max

Immelmann and other early German airfighters to attain superiority over Entente aircraft.

Below: *Hptmn* Oswald Boelcke, the airfighter who became Richthofen's mentor and idol.

Above: Richthofen's Fokker Dr.I 127/17, seen here in original factory finish, had his personal red colouring on the upper wing, cowling, tail and wheel covers when he flew it on 27 March 1918. He achieved his 68th and 76th aerial victories flying this aircraft.

Left: *Vzfw* Franz Hemer's Fokker Dr.I bore the standard *Jasta 6* 'wavy-line' marking along the fuselage for easier in-flight identification.

Top right: Lt A.W. Hammond, MC, and 2/Lt A.A. McLeod by the 'elephant iron' Nissen Huts of No. 2 Squadron, RFC, at Hesdigneul before their encounter with *Ltn* Hans Kirschstein of *Jasta 10* on 27 March 1918.

Right: Manfred von Richthofen spent half his life in uniform. He is seen here aged about 15, while home from the Cadet Academy for Christmas leave. Lothar von Richthofen holds the family dog, while youngest brother Bolko enjoys the ride.

Above: Nieuport 13 A135 of No. 60 Squadron, shot down on 3 November 1916, was credited as *Ltn* Hans Imelmann's fourth victory. However, an original print of this photograph was sent to Manfred von Richthofen, who added it to his souvenir collection. This print was obtained from the collection by Charles Donald.

Left: Carl Eduard, Duke of Saxe-Coburg-Gotha, wearing the uniform and indefinable epaulettes that made it difficult for Richthofen to determine his rank. The two men became friends and Richthofen was invited to the Duke's hunting lodge on several occasions.

Above: *Hptmn* Otto Zimmer-Vorhaus (right) commanded *Feldfl.-Abt. 18* when B.E.2c 1744 of No. 12 Squadron, RFC, was brought down by rifle fire nearby on 26 September 1915. Later, as Officer in Charge of Aviation on the *6. Armee* staff, Zimmer-Vorhaus was an early proponent of *Jagdstaffel* development.

Below: Early arrivals and some applicants at *Jasta 11* (obviously not concerned about the danger of smoking near the aircraft) pose before an old Albatros D.I inherited by the unit. From left: unknown, *Ltn* Konstantin Krefft (Technical Officer), *Obltn* Hans Helmut von Boddien (who joined the unit in June 1917), *Ltn* Kurt Wolff, *Ltn.d.Res* Kurt Küppers (later accepted into *Jasta 6*) and *Ltn* Karl Allmenröder.

Above: *Ltn* Karl Allmenröder's Albatros D.III after *Jasta 11*'s move to Roucourt. The aircraft appears to be mostly red-coloured, with a white nose and spinner.

Below: At Bad Homburg, Richthofen (centre) meets *Generalfeldmarschal* von Hindenburg and other high-ranking officers, including *Oberstltn* Thomsen and *Gen-Ltn* von Hoeppner (right).

Above: While at Roucourt, *Jasta 11* officers resided in a local castle. Seen here with a visitor on the castle's southern staircase are, from left (top row): *Ltn* Karl Allmenröder, *Ltn* Lothar von Richthofen, *Ltn* Wolfgang Plüschow and *Ltn* von Hartmann. (Bottom row) *Ltn* Georg Simon (PoW 4 June 1917), *Ltn* Kurt Wolff, Manfred von Richthofen, *Maj* von Richthofen, *Ltn* Konstantin Krefft and *Ltn.d.Res* Hans Hintsch (KiA 25 May

Below: Problems with the Albatros D.III led to consideration of a potentially 'promising' line of biplane fighters being developed by the Luftfahrzeug-Gesellschaft in Berlin. On 16 May 1917 Richthofen test-flew the LFG Roland D.III second test machine at Adlershof. Although the D.III's open centre-section allowed the pilot a better view than that from the D.II in the background, Richthofen was disappointed with the aircraft's performance and did not recommend it to replace the Albatros D-series.

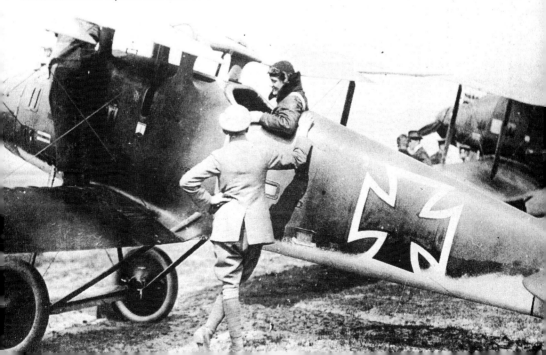

Left: This snapshot of Manfred von Richthofen walking toward Rumpler C.I 633/15 contains an interesting detail. The Albatros in the background bears the skull and crossbones personal marking of Prince Friedrich Karl of Prussia. Standing between the two crosses of the undecorated Albatros D.III in the middle is the Prince, who often flew Albatros D.I 410/16 with *Jasta 2*. The Rumpler was most likely also flown by the Prince, who commanded *Fl.-Abt (A) 258*.

Below left: Manfred von Richthofen has reason to smile, being surrounded by successful airfighting comrades who made impressive gains during 'Bloody April'. From left: *Vzfw* Sebastian Festner (ten victories that month), *Ltn* Karl-Emil Schäfer (fifteen victories), *Ltn* Lothar von Richthofen (fifteen victories) and *Ltn* Kurt Wolff (20 victories). Festner was shot down and killed on 23 April 1917.

Above: *Jasta 11* aircraft prepare for take-off on 13 April 1917. *Fwb-Ltn* Nahr, who took the photo, noted that the Albatroses attacked a British formation and sent down six aircraft, four of them in flames. Non-flying personnel, such as the men at the right, used the telescope to view the fight.

Below: Accompanying the R.E.8s on 13 April was Bristol F.2A A3322 of No 48 Squadron. It was forced to land by *Ltn* Lothar von Richthofen and was recorded as his fourth victory. The crew, 2/Lts H.D. Davies and R.S. Worsley, were taken prisoner.

Above: *Jasta 11* leader Manfred von Richthofen's first Albatros D.III was so thoroughly decorated in red that the national insignia was almost obliterated and only the small manufacturer's patch on the rudder was left untouched. In this view the national marking has been crudely 'enhanced' to make its German identity obvious.

Left: This early postcard hails Manfred von Richthofen as 'our most successful combat flyer' and shows him wearing the *Pour le Mérite*, Iron Cross 1st Class, Knight's Cross with Swords of the Royal House Order of Hohenzollern, Duke Carl Eduard Medal with Date Clasp and Swords of Saxe-Coburg-Gotha, and the Austro-Hungarian Military Merit Cross 3rd Class with War Decoration.

Above: *Ltn* Kurt Wolff achieved his second aerial victory when he shot down F.E.8 6456 of No. 40 Squadron, RFC, on 9 March 1917. The British pilot, 2/Lt T. Shepard, was taken prisoner.

Below: Kurt Wolff's lucky nightcap was the source of some amusement, as demonstrated here by *Ltn* Konstantin Krefft (left) and *Ltn* Karl Allmenröder.

Above: Richthofen's day of rest, 19 May 1917, was devoted to receiving a variety of admirers, including various youth groups.

Left: *Ltn* Otto Brauneck poses by his Albatros D.III before a flight over the battlefront.

DEUTSCHLAND ÜBER ALLES

By 16 April Field-Marshal Sir Douglas Haig's offensive at Arras became bogged down — quite literally, in view of worsening weather — and *Général* Robert Georges Nivelle's offensive against the German *7.* and *1. Armees* at Chemin des Dames was doomed from the start. Having lost sensitive battle documents, and having ignored the Germans' strategic pullback, Nivelle failed and his forces suffered devastating consequences that led to widespread mutinies among French forces and hobbled the Entente spring offensive.[46]

When the ground mist lifted late on the afternoon of 21 April 1917, *Jasta 11* was in the air west of Douai. Working like an aerial killing machine, they fell on a flight of Nieuport 17s of No.29 Squadron escorting B.E.2s of No.16 Squadron, and within 20 minutes claimed five of their adversaries.

The 22nd, while producing fewer overall results, became an important day for *Jasta 11*. Southwest of Arras at 1710 the *Staffel* attacked six 'Fees' from No.11 Squadron which were reconnoitring and photographing the Drocourt-Quéant switch line. One of the two-seat pushers went down over German lines and 'four [others], damaged in the fight or with wounded personnel, were wrecked on landing'.[47] *Rittm* von Richthofen reported that one of the latter 'dashed down and crashed to splinters on the ground'. It was recorded as his 46th victory.[48]

Matching Richthofen's description with RFC casualties, it is likely that his victim was F.E.2b A820, piloted by Lt C.A. Parker, who displayed great courage under the most arduous conditions. Parker's observer, Lt James C.B. Hesketh (KiA), had been hit at the beginning of the fight. Parker had to hold on to him while trying to land the badly shot-up F.E.2b. Just clear of the forward trenches, the aircraft burst into flames as it touched the ground. Parker pulled Hesketh clear of the wreckage moments before the F.E.2b took a direct hit from an artillery shell.[49]

Three hours later, *Ltn* Kurt Wolff shot down Morane Parasol A6727 of No.3 Squadron over Havrincourt,[50] thereby scoring his 20th and *Jasta 11*'s 100th aerial victory.[51]

A special recognition notice was published in the weekly information report of the Commanding General of the Air Force. It stated:

> In the time from 23 January until 22 April 1917 *Jagdstaffel 11* has shot down 100 enemy aeroplanes. I am pleased to be able to announce this singularly unrivalled success to the aviation forces. Here a small band of brave pilots has been trained and led into battle by an outstanding leader, *Rittmeister Freiherr* von Richthofen, who alone has contributed 39 of these 100 aircraft, for the benefit of the hard-fighting troops on the ground, [and] accomplished feats which redound to the highest honour of the German air service.

May such a spirit, the spirit of Boelcke, remain always and in all respects with the German air service.

/s/ von Hoeppner[52]

Manfred and Lothar von Richthofen scored *Jasta 11*'s only victories on 23 April, when they attacked a pair of B.E.s from No.16 Squadron over Méricourt, northeast of Arras. Although both aircraft came down within British lines, Manfred was credited with his 47th and Lothar with his tenth.[53]

That evening Manfred von Richthofen wrote home and promised his mother he would take leave at the beginning of May. He enjoyed the great distinction of an invitation to visit *Kaiser* Wilhelm at the Supreme Headquarters, then located in the palatinate spa city of Bad Kreuznach. First, he wanted to achieve his 50th victory.

JAGDSTAFFEL RICHTHOFEN

On Thursday 26 April *Jasta 11*'s daily message traffic brought news that, on orders of *Kaiser* Wilhelm, the unit would henceforth bear the name *Jagdstaffel Richthofen*.[54] *Jasta 11* was only the second aviation unit to have such a distinction, but it was used for only a brief period. Three weeks' worth of *Kofl 6. Armee* reports, 4 through 18 May, ascribe aerial victories to *Jagdstaffel Richthofen*; after that the *Kofl* and all other reports used the simple *Jasta 11* nomenclature.

Existing documentation offers no insight into the non-use of this signal honour. One would think that, given Manfred von Richthofen's great admiration for his mentor, Oswald Boelcke, he would have embraced such an accolade, which was normally reserved for very senior officers. The *6. Armee*, for example, was also known as the *Heeresgruppe Kronprinz Rupprecht* in honour of its nominal commander, the heir to the Bavarian throne. Perhaps even Richthofen, with his supremely high degree of self-confidence, was not yet ready for such a comparison with his hero.

THE TRIPLANE COUNTER-EFFECT

While April was a disastrous month for British airmen, British industry made great strides to reverse the situation. One mark of progress was the appearance of the Sopwith Triplane, used by two of the four Royal Naval Air Service squadrons attached to the RFC in response to a request by Maj-Gen Trenchard.[55]

Fitted with the 130hp Clerget rotary engine, the Sopwith Triplane helped to staunch 'Bloody April', as recorded in this contemporary account: 'An indecisive combat took place [on 23 April] between Fl/Cdr Arnold, Naval Squadron No.8, and a single-seater Albatros Scout. The flight lasted about 20 minutes and the German pilot showed great skill in manoeuvring his machine, but was at a disadvantage, as the Triplane could out-manoeuvre and out-climb the hostile machine.'[56]

German airmen were informed of the new danger. The *Kommandeur der Flieger der 6. Armee* weekly report for 28 April published this advisory: 'The number of enemy triplanes sighted has increased. They are said to surpass the Albatros D.III in manoeuvrability and above all in climbing ability.'[57]

That hazard was of little concern to Manfred von Richthofen. On 28 April he brought down another two-seater by hitting the pilot and pursuing the aircraft diligently. 'From the beginning of the engagement to the end, my adversary was never able to get out of the range of my gun,' Richthofen wrote in the combat report requesting confirmation of his 48th victory.[58]

FOUR KILLS IN ONE DAY

Like a Teutonic warrior of old, bearing grisly souvenirs of combat to gain the favour of his tribal chieftain, Manfred von Richthofen was bent on attaining 50 victories before his meeting with *Kaiser* Wilhelm just a few days hence. On 29 April, 1917, he exceeded even his own expectations and brought down four aeroplanes that day. The event had further lustre, as much of this great performance was witnessed by his father, *Maj* Albrecht *Frhr* von Richthofen, who commanded a garrison near Lille. As his post was only 30km from *Jasta 11*'s airfield, *der alte Herr* (The Old Gentleman) paid his first visit to Roucourt.

Manfred wrote that his father's train arrived at Douai at 0900 and the honoured guest was at the airfield half an hour later, just in time to see the morning patrol return. According to Manfred's account, Lothar von Richthofen was the first to jump out of his aeroplane and report proudly: 'Hello, Papa, I have just shot down an Englishman'.

Manfred reportedly gave his father an identical report and added: 'The old gentleman was happy; one could see that he was amused [by this report]. He is not one of those fathers who is worried about his sons; on the contrary, he would just as soon have got into the machine and shot one down — at least I believe that. We had breakfast with him and then flew again.'[59]

It had been rumoured amongst German forces that the RFC had formed a special 'Anti-Richthofen Squadron' solely dedicated to eliminating the Silesian nobleman. An exhaustive search of British First World War aviation records has failed to produce any evidence to confirm this notion. No doubt many British aviators wanted the honour of bringing down Germany's most successful living fighter pilot, and *all* fighter squadrons were on the look-out for red Albatroses. As Richthofen himself noted: 'Now we were all [painted] red and the Englishmen's eyes really widened when they saw, instead of one, a dozen such crates. But that did not keep them from attempting to attack us. I much prefer to have the clientele come to me than to go after them.'[60]

German records show that the *Staffel*'s successes that day began at 1215 when their flight of six Albatroses was attacked by three SPAD S.VII fighters from No.19 Squadron. That attack was typical of the actual method employed to 'get' Manfred von Richthofen. 2/Lt W.N. Hamilton, the only survivor of that fight, later recalled that the squadron commander, Maj Hubert D. Harvey-Kelly, DSO, said to him 'that the wing commander was "hot-airing" about Richthofen's circus having been seen over Douai and he wanted three SPADs to go up and deal with them'.[61]

Although the SPADs were capable of dealing with Albatroses, the trio from No.19 Squadron were outgunned and were brought down. 'Mine was the first to crash,' Manfred von Richthofen wrote. 'I had shot the engine to pieces ... I no longer know any mercy, [and] for that reason I attacked him a second time, whereupon the aeroplane fell apart in my stream of bullets. The wings each fell away like pieces of paper and the fuselage went roaring down like a stone on fire. He fell into a swamp. He could not be dug out. I have never learned with whom I had fought. He disappeared. The rest of the [aircraft's] tail simply burned up and showed the place where he had dug his own grave.'[62]

Manfred's 49th victim, 2/Lt Richard Applin (KiA) in SPAD S.VII A1573, went down near Lecluse; Wolff's 25th, Maj Harvey-Kelly in A6681, crashed near Izel, just west of Douai (not to be confused with the RFC aerodrome at Izel le Hameau, over 30km further west); and Lothar's 13th, Lt Hamilton (PoW) in A6753, was forced to land near Sailly. Maj Harvey-Kelly, who had been one of the first wartime RFC pilots to land in France in 1914, was badly wounded in the fight and died a few days later.[63]

During an afternoon patrol Manfred von Richthofen reached the magic number, 50 aerial victories, when he shot down F.E.2b 4898 of No.18 Squadron southwest of Inchy. Richthofen noted in his combat report: 'The aeroplane burned to pieces in the air and the occupants fell out'.[64] Sgt George Stead and 1/AM (Cpl) Alfred Beebee were killed. Five minutes later, at 1700, Kurt Wolff scored his 26th victory.

Not satisfied with attaining his goal, Manfred von Richthofen went out on an evening patrol and scored victories Nos.51 and 52. He and Lothar attacked two B.E.s of No.12 Squadron which were ranging artillery, 'one of which fell in flames [within German lines] and the other, with a dying pilot and a wounded observer, crashed within the British lines'.[65] Manfred claimed a B.E. that 'hit the ground near the trenches near Roeux, [where] it caught fire'[66] at 1925 and was credited as his 51st victory.[67] The other two-seater was credited to Lothar as his fourteenth victory.

Ever the teacher, Manfred watched with pride from 500m away as Lothar dispatched his victim. Manfred later wrote:

I had time to witness this scene in detail and I must say that I could not have done better myself. He had caught the opponent unawares and both circled each other. Then suddenly the enemy aeroplane reared up — a sure sign of being hit, surely the pilot had been shot in the head or something similar — the aeroplane dived and the wings of the enemy machine folded up one after the other. The wreckage fell in the vicinity of my victim. I flew over to my brother and congratulated him, i.e., we waved at each other. We were satisfied and flew on. It is nice when one can fly together with his brother.[68]

Jasta 11 re-formed and headed northward towards Lens. But they were not alone, as Richthofen observed:

We flew on, climbing to higher altitude, for above us some [members] of the Anti-Richthofen Club had gathered together. Again, we were easy to recognize, [as] the sun from the west illuminated the aircraft and let their beautiful red colour be seen from far away. We closed up [the formation] tightly, for each of us knew that we were dealing with "brothers" who pursued the same trade we did. Unfortunately, they were higher than we were, so we had to wait for their attack. The famous Triplanes and SPADs [were] completely new machines, but it is not a matter of the crate as much as who sits in it; the "brothers" were wary and had no spunk.[69]

Richthofen's bravado notwithstanding, eleven Sopwith Triplanes of No.8 Squadron, RNAS, and a Nieuport 17 of No.60 Squadron[70] attacked the Albatroses. During the course of this encounter, which lasted for 20 minutes or so, Richthofen shot down one of the attackers and thereby gained yet another victory.

As part of the Richthofen legend, victory No.52 has long been identified as Nieuport 17 A6745 of No.40 Squadron, flown by Capt Frederick L. Barwell (KiA). Records indicate that Barwell went down in the general area, having left his aerodrome at 1820 (British time). Richthofen's combat report and other German sources,[71] however, identify victory No.52 as one of the new and much-to-be-respected triplanes. Richthofen would have found the triplane much more challenging than a Nieuport. Given all the other circumstances, it is more likely that he shot down Sopwith Triplane N5463 and killed the pilot, Flt-Sub-Lt A.E. Cuzner of 'Naval 8'. Coincidentally, the only two naval fighters shot down by Manfred von Richthofen were both from No.8 Squadron, RNAS.

No.8 Squadron's history offers this further evidence: 'On the 29th we had the misfortune to lose Cuzner. The Canadians reported having seen a triplane brought down near Courrières and, as the air seemed stiff with Huns that evening, it seemed probable that he had got separated from his formation and been attacked by superior numbers.'[72]

With Manfred having passed the half-century mark, and with six victories between the Richthofen brothers in one day, the *Staffel* had a grand celebration that evening. 'It seemed we had invited The Old Gentleman just for this [celebration]. The joy was just tremendous,'[73] Manfred later wrote.

THE BLOODY END

Manfred von Richthofen did not fly on the last day of April 1917, but his brother made sure that the month came to an appropriately bloody close. In the morning mist of 30 April *Ltn* Lothar von Richthofen led *Jasta 11*'s first patrol of the day. He was being prepared to lead the *Staffel* as soon as the dates of Manfred's leave were confirmed. The high-scoring pilot *Ltn* Kurt Wolff would have been the logical choice to assume temporary command of *Jasta 11* during Manfred's absence, but there was more propaganda value to be gained by keeping a Richthofen at the head of this important *Staffel*. For Lothar it was an opportunity to show what he could do outside his brother's pervasive shadow.

In a change of German air fighting tactics, Lothar's flight joined up with aircraft from *Jastas 3*, *4* and *33* as part of a twenty-aircraft formation[74] to sweep the skies west of Douai.

Lothar von Richthofen made the day's first kill at about 0715, when he attacked B.E.2g A2742 of No.16 Squadron between Vimy and Willerval. He sent the aircraft down in flames at Méricourt; it was counted as his fifteenth victory.

Barely half an hour later the massive German formation attacked a line patrol of seven 'Fees' of No.57 Squadron, RFC, escorted by three Sopwith Triplanes of No.8 Squadron, RNAS. Again, Lothar von Richthofen led the attack, and shot down his sixteenth adversary, F.E.2d A6402 of No.57 Squadron. By the day's end *Jastas 3*, *4* and *33* had each recorded one victory. The massive fighter sweep had been much less successful than anticipated. Indeed, Lothar's two victories exemplified the operational effectiveness of small, well-trained and cohesive fighter units. It would be left to Manfred von Richthofen to apply his successful tactics to a command made up of several *Jagdstaffeln*.

Lothar's success was cause for another celebration. Amidst the revelry, at about 2100, there was an important telephone call for Manfred. After an anxious moment, the call turned out to be the news he had been waiting for, as he later recalled: '... it was nothing less than [someone at] the Supreme Headquarters who wished to speak to me. It was quite a lot of fun to be so connected with the "Great Shack". Among other things I received the pleasant news that His Majesty expressed the wish to speak with me personally and indeed the date was already set for the 2nd of May.'[75]

Meanwhile, perhaps during that telephone conversation, the *Rittmeister* did one more personal favour before going on leave. His old friend and informal flight instructor *Obltn* Georg Zeumer, the devil-may-care 'black cat' of the *Brieftauben-Abteilung Ostende,* had suffered a run of bad luck and needed help. In June 1916 Zeumer had been shot down and slightly injured near Fort Vaux. Then the car transporting him to the medical aid station was involved in an accident which caused Zeumer to break a thigh bone. The bone had not healed properly, and he was left with one leg nine centimetres shorter than the other, and had to use a cane.[76]

Already diagnosed as being tubercular and diabetic, Zeumer did not want to die at a desk job. The 27-year-old pilot wanted to be back in the air, where his recklessness offered at least a hero's end. Zeumer's motivation did not fit Richthofen's methodology, so a posting to *Jasta 11* was out of the question, even for an old friend. Instead, Richthofen arranged for Zeumer to fulfil his ominous destiny with another very active unit, *Jagdstaffel Boelcke.*

NOTES

1   Morris, *Bloody April,* (1967), p.15.
2   Jones, *The War in the Air,* vol III, (1931), p.323.
3   *RFC War Diary* daily weather reports, April 1917; 'Vigilant', *Richthofen - The Red Knight of the Air,* (n.d.), p.134ff.
4   von Richthofen, *Der rote Kampfflieger,* (1917), p.123.
5   *Nachrichtenblatt der Luftstreitkräfte Nr 11,* 10 May 1917, p.12.
6   *Der rote Kampfflieger,* op.cit., pp.123-124.
7   Ibid., p.124.
8   Quoted in Gibbons, *The Red Knight of Germany,* (1927), p.168.
9   Ibid., pp.168-169.
10   *Nachrichtenblatt,* op.cit.; 2/Lt Donald P. MacDonald (WiA/PoW) and 2/Lt John I.M. O'Bierne (KiA).
11   Jones, op.cit., p.334.
12   Jones, Ibid., pp.334-335.
13   *Kofl 6. Armee Wochenbericht Nr 25500, Teile 10, 11,* 7 April 1917.
14   Bowyer, *For Valour - the Air V.C.s,* (1978), pp.69, 75-77.
15   Ibid., p.77.
16   *RFC Communiqué No. 82,* 8 April 1917, p.2.
17   *Nachrichtenblatt,* op.cit.; F.2A A3340, 2/Lt Arthur N. Lechler (WiA/PoW) and Lt Herbert D.K. George (KiA), and F.2A A3343, Lts H.T. Adams (PoW) and D.J. Stewart (WiA/PoW).
18   *Nachrichtenblatt,* op.cit.; F.2A A3320, Lt A.H. Cooper and 2/Lt A. Boldison (both WiA/PoW).
19   Bowyer, op.cit, pp.78-79.
20   Burge, *The Annals of 100 Squadron,* (ca.1919), p.51.
21   *RFC Communiqué,* op.cit., p.4; no corresponding German damage was reported.
22   *Der rote Kampfflieger,* op.cit., pp.134-135.
23   RFC records show that No.100 Squadron and other bombing units attacked Douai on numerous occasions, but, despite the contention of Burge, op.cit., and Richthofen's own sequencing of these occurrences, there is no official record of a raid carried out by No.100 Squadron on the evening of 6/7 April 1917. Hence, while it is interesting anecdotal history, this account no doubt pertains to another evening's activities.
24   *Der rote Kampfflieger,* op.cit., pp.136-137.
25   Zuerl, *Pour-le-Mérite-Flieger,* (1938), p.55.
26   Gibbons, op.cit., p.196; Nieuport 17 A6645, 2/Lt George O. Smart (KiA).
27   *Nachrichtenblatt,* op.cit., p.13; 2/Lt H.E. Hervey (PoW).
28   Quoted in Gibbons, op.cit., p.206.
29   2/Lt John S. Heagerty (WiA/PoW) and Lt Leonard Heath Cantle (KiA).

30   O'Connor, *Aviation Awards of Imperial Germany in World War I and the Men Who Earned Them*, vol II, (1990), pp.141, 219.

31   Ibid., pp.62, 106, 109.

32   *Nachrichtenblatt*, op.cit., lists the serial number as 'A2895,' which does not match the RFC casualty list. The latter source records the loss of A2815 under circumstances that fit Richthofen's claim perfectly: '... reported to have been shot down by H.A. at 4-40pm, falling and crashing about 1,000 yards west of Vimy'. Crew of 2/Lt Keith I. Mackenzie and 2/Lt Guy Everingham (both KiA).

33   Very likely B.E.2c 2501 of No.13 Squadron, Lt Edward C.E. Derwin and 2/AM H. Pierson (both WiA).

34   Quoted in von Richthofen, *Ein Heldenleben*, (1920), pp.301-303.

35   R.E.8 A3190, which fell in flames between Vitry and Brebières, Capt James M. Stuart and Lt Maurice H. Wood (both KiA).

36   *Der rote Kampfflieger*, op.cit., pp.127-128.

37   *Ein Heldenleben*, op.cit., pp.306-307.

38   Quoted in Gibbons, op.cit., p.214; Evans, *Manfred Freiherr von Richthofen Victory List*, (1992), p.135. The aircraft claimed was probably F.E.2b A827 of No.11 Squadron, Lt C.E. Robertson and 2/Lt H.D. Duncan (both KiA); F.E.2b A831 of No.11 Squadron, also brought down at this time, crashed 1km southwest of Bailleul, about 8km from the crash site reported by Richthofen, in the area where *Ltn* Kurt Wolff claimed his eleventh victory.

39   F.E.2b 4997, 2/Lt Allan H. Bates and Sgt William A. Barnes (both KiA).

40   *Der rote Kampfflieger*, op.cit., p.129.

41   Nieuport A6796, Lt William O. Russell (PoW).

42   Warne, *60 Squadron: A Detailed History*, (1980), p.57.

43   Quoted in *Ein Heldenleben*, op.cit., p.294.

44   Duiven & Sands, *The Original Flying Circus*, (1987), p.31.

45   Gibbons, op. cit., (1927), p.222.

46   Esposito, *A Concise History of World War I*, (1964), pp.92-94.

47   Jones, op. cit., p.357.

48   Quoted in Gibbons, op.cit., p.227; although attacked over German-held Cagnicourt, this aircraft came down about 7km further south, within British lines at Lagnicourt.

49   Jones, op.cit., ff.

50   Duiven and Sands, op.cit.; 2/Lt F.L. Carter and Cpl A. Morgan (both KiA).

51   *Kofl 6. Armee Wochenbericht Nr 50570, Teil 11*, 28 April 1917

52   *Nachrichtenblatt Nr. 10*, 3 May 1917, p.3.

53   *Nachrichtenblatt Nr 12*, 17 May 1917, p.11; Manfred von Richthofen most likely accounted for B.E.2e A3168, 2/Lt E.A. Welch and Sgt Alfred G. Tollervey (both KiA); Lothar von Richthofen probably shot down .B.E.2g A2876, 2/Lts C.M. Crow (KiA) and E.T. Turner (WiA).

54   *Kofl 6. Armee Wochenbericht Nr 50790, Teil 14*, 4 May 1917.

55   Bruce, *British Aeroplanes 1914-1918*, (1969), p.566.

56   *RFC Communiqué No. 85*, 29 April 1917, p.3.

57   *Kofl 6. Armee Wochenbericht Nr 50570*, op.cit., *Teil 3*.

58   Quoted in Gibbons, op.cit., p.234; B.E.2e 7221 of No.13 Squadron, Lt Reginald W. Follit (DoW) and 2/Lt F.J. Kirkham (WiA/PoW).

59   *Der rote Kampfflieger*, op.cit., p.147; the 1917 edition of this book clearly gives the date 29 April 1917, while the 1933 edition omits the date.

60   Ibid., p.144; again there is a confusion of dates, with the 1917 edition giving 25 April (a date on which Manfred and Lothar scored no victories), the 1933 edition listing no date, and all other German and British records agreeing that *Jasta 11*'s encounter with No.19 Squadron took place on 29 April.

61   Quoted in Gibbons, op.cit., pp.241-242.

62   *Der rote Kampfflieger*, p.145.

63   Jones, op.cit., pp.366-367.

64   Quoted in Gibbons, op.cit., p.248.

65   Jones, op.cit., p.368.

66 Quoted in Gibbons, op.cit., p.250.
67 *Kofl 6. Armee Wochenbericht Nr 50790*, op.cit., *Teil 11*; most likely this was B.E.2e 2738, 2/Lt David E. Davies and Lt George H. Rathbone (both KiA), which took off at 1645 (British time).
68 *Der rote Kampfflieger*, op.cit., p.150.
69 Ibid., p.151.
70 Jones, op.cit., p.368.
71 *Kofl 6. Armee*, op.cit., and *Nachrichtenblatt*, op.cit.
72 Johnstone, *Naval Eight*, (1931), p.33.
73 *Der rote Kampfflieger*, op.cit., p.152.
74 Jones, op.cit., pp.368-369.
75 *Der rote Kampfflieger*, op.cit., pp.154-155.
76 von Richthofen, *Mein Kriegstagebuch*, (1937), pp.75-76, 107-108.

CHAPTER 8
A HERO'S LIFE

Manfred von Richthofen had been ordered to take leave after being credited with his 41st victory. That would have allowed him one victory more than Boelcke, so that he could leave the Front secure in the knowledge that he was the undefeated highest-scoring fighter ace of all the belligerents.

But the war planners and propagandists who wanted to exploit the living legend of German fighter aviation had not reckoned with Richthofen's own needs and iron will. They could not fathom Richthofen's complex image of his mentor. Always in mind, it was the source of an inner conflict between his awe of Boelcke's achievements and his own need to be the best at whatever he did.

Richthofen's mixture of respect and ambition shows in this comment about his victory score at the time: 'In fact, I had been allowed only 41; anyone can guess why the number 41 was set and precisely for that reason I wanted to completely avoid it. I am no record-keeper, [and] in general, records are far from our thoughts in the flying service. One only fulfils one's duty. [By now] Boelcke would have shot down a hundred if the accident had not happened.'[1]

On Tuesday 1 May, 1917, Manfred von Richthofen transferred leadership of *Jasta 11* to his brother Lothar with a simple handshake and a smile. Manfred knew the *Staffel* was in good hands; for, he wrote, Lothar 'has only one thought: [the enemy] must go down. That is of course the proper way ... But if my brother does not get at least one [enemy aircraft] on every flight the whole business is no fun for him.'[2]

Buoyed by success, Manfred must have thought that the aerial killing sprees of April would go on and on. He had not yet encountered such new British aircraft as the fast and rugged S.E.5s then entering front-line service. That pleasure he left to Lothar, who led the morning patrol north of Douai to begin the day's hunting.

When Manfred von Richthofen was ordered to take leave, he was admonished by the *Kaiser*'s aides to travel by train, just as Boelcke had been instructed to avoid flying after Immelmann's death. Richthofen's appointment with the Supreme War Lord had come so late, however, that he would never have reached Bad Kreuznach in time by train. Thus he 'had to' take the faster aerial route.

As a good Prussian officer does not disobey orders, Manfred von Richthofen did not fly his red Albatros, which even he referred to as *le petit rouge*.[3] Rather, he 'flew' as a passenger in a two-seater piloted by his unit's Technical Officer, *Ltn.d.Res* Konstantin Krefft, who was going home on recuperative leave and suddenly found a faster way to get there. A disadvantage of the cramped two-seater was the lack of luggage space for dress uniforms and other refinements; they wore service uniforms under their flight-suits and carried little more than toothbrushes.[4]

Within a short time the speed of the aeroplane took them from the grime of war to a more pastoral setting. 'It was so beautiful to sail through the sea of air without warlike thoughts,' Richthofen later wrote. 'The weather was splendid, such as we had not had for a long time ... Soon even our observation balloons were out of sight. We got ever farther away from the thunder of the battles at Arras. Below us were pictures of peace. Steamers gliding along. There, rushing over the countryside, an express train which we overtook easily. The wind was in our favour.'[5]

The flyers crossed the verdant Meuse River Valley at Namur, then flew over the now quiet devastation of the 1914 battle site at Liège and on past Aachen. They reached Cologne by lunchtime, where a rousing reception awaited them. Richthofen's 52nd victory had been reported in the previous day's newspapers, and local residents gave the young airman a hero's welcome upon his return to German soil. As the hero also had a headache after the three-hour flight from Roucourt, he was shown to a quiet place for a short nap.

By dinner time Manfred von Richthofen was in Bad Kreuznach, following an aerial sightseeing tour of the Rhine Valley. Krefft flew him from Cologne to the Nahe River tributary leading to the quiet little spa city that had been the site of the Supreme Headquarters for the past two months. They landed at an airfield just outside Bad Kreuznach.

'There I was warmly greeted by all of the flyers on the staff of the Commanding General of the Air Force,' wrote Richthofen. 'I knew them all by sight; for the most part they had come from the *BAO* and *BAM* [early air units]. I also got to know the others better. I was greeted with bouquets of flowers and with a thundering cheer.'[6]

With few visitors to the spa because of the war, military guests had their pick of the city's accommodations.[7] The two flyers were put up in a fine hotel within a short walk of the *Kurhaus*, the elegant spa and casino complex that had become the imperial residence. After meeting with *Gen-Ltn* Ernst von Hoeppner, Manfred retired to a level of comfort hardly imaginable in wartime.

CELEBRATING WITH THE *KAISER*

Manfred von Richthofen was in the company of some of the most important people in Germany on his 25th — and last — birthday. In the morning he reported to the luxurious Hotel Oranienhof, which had become the General Staff Headquarters. For an hour he sat outside the office of *Gen.d.Inf* Erich Ludendorff, watching aides enter and depart with great bundles of paperwork. Albert Ballin, *Generaldirektor* of the Hamburg-Amer-ica Shipping Line, sat nearby, completely unaware of Richthofen in his drab service uniform and uninterested in the *Pour le Mérite* at Manfred's collar. Ballin was absorbed in a discussion in hushed tones with a high-ranking member of the General Staff. Then came Foreign Minister Arthur Zimmermann, followed by Chancellor Theobald von Bethmann-Hollweg and then Karl Helferrich, Secretary of the Imperial Treasury.[8]

After several generals had been escorted in, it was Richthofen's turn. With a wave of an adjutant's hand, he was slipped past the other dignitaries and ushered into Ludendorff's office.

The stern-looking Quarter-Master General had no time for pleas-antries, and immediately asked about air operations on the Arras Front. As Richthofen recorded in a reminiscence too candid to have been published during his lifetime: 'I began to tell him and drifted into a little chat that had little military importance. Then he simply cut off my conversation and came [back] to things I had already mentioned. One noted he went all-out. After he elicited from me what he wanted to know about operations on the main battlefront at Arras, I was abruptly dismissed. I must say that I was quite satisfied [with that arrangement], for this serious, professional [and] dispassionate-thinking person was strange to me.'[9]

Richthofen was relieved to leave the Hotel Oranienhof and get out into the sunshine and fresh air of Kaiser-Wilhelmstrasse. It was a short walk to Elisabethenstrasse, at the end of which was the *Kaiser*'s residence, with a commanding view of the Nahe River.

Richthofen found his midday appointment at the *Kurhaus* much more to his liking. He recalled: 'It was my birthday and someone must have divulged that to His Majesty and so he congratulated me. First on my suc-cess, then on my 25th year of life. He also surprised me with a small birth-day present.'[10]

The description of the gift is understated. *Kaiser* Wilhlem II presented a bronze and marble bust of himself in martial splendour; it took two husky servants to carry it into the imperial dining room. It was a rather immodest gift, but Richthofen graciously accepted it as a singular distinction. He had it shipped home to Schweidnitz, where it was displayed proudly for many years when the family residence became the Richthofen Museum.[11]

'The *Kaiser* talked with me for about a half hour after the meal; [but] the conversation was very one-sided. The theme of the dialogue was anti-aircraft guns.'[12]

Then, switching roles from Supreme War Lord to Father of the Nation, *Kaiser* Wilhelm wagged his finger at Manfred von Richthofen and playfully threatened: 'I have heard that you are still flying. You be careful that nothing happens to you!' Turning to his aide-de-camp, *Kapitän zur See* (Naval Captain) Nikolaus *Graf* zu Dohna-Schlodien, the monarch asked: 'How could that be? Have I not forbidden him to fly?' The aide responded: 'Majesty, in the interests of the whole situation, we cannot do that. We need Richthofen as an example and as a *Geschwader-Kommandeur* (Wing Commander), we need him as a combat pilot ...'[13]

The passing reference to Richthofen being named the first *Jagdgeschwader-Kommandeur* indicated that the war planners were not satisfied with the results produced by the fighter units. Clearly, the *Jagdstaffeln* had to be deployed more effectively. Manfred von Richthofen did not question the prospect of an important new appointment. His destiny was linked with the development of the German *Luftstreitkräfte*. He stood ready to accept whatever new challenge was given to him.

Gen von Hoeppner hosted a dinner that evening at which the guests of honour were *Generalfeldmarschall* von Hindenburg and *Rittm* von Richthofen. Sitting side-by-side, the two officers indulged only in inane chit-chat. Richthofen found the experience to be much more pleasant than his earlier meeting with the intense, all-business *Gen* Ludendorff.

'In the course of the conversation,' Richthofen recalled, 'he asked in a good-natured, calm way, which inspired absolute trust: "Now tell me, Richthofen, have you also been a cadet?". I told him that I had begun my military career in the 2nd Company at Wahlstatt and, in fact, in Barracks 6. Then the old gentleman said: "Well, look at this, I also began to play soldier in Barracks 6 and have presented the barracks with my photo as a memento".'[14]

Later in the evening Richthofen struck up a conversation with the *Kaiser*'s aide-de-camp, *Graf* zu Dohna-Schlodien. The 38-year-old Silesian nobleman and one-time commander of the surface raider *SMS Möwe* had been awarded the *Pour le Mérite* and the highest bravery awards of the Kingdoms of Bavaria, Saxony and Württemberg. Richthofen bluntly asked how such a man of action could tolerate the duller pace of court life. '... He gave me a very sly look. But of all of [the other aides] there, this small-statured, inconspicuous-looking man made by far the best impression on me. One could see that he was a front line soldier and no courtier.'[15]

Richthofen, too, was no courtier, but he knew the rôle he had to play. The following day *Ltn* Krefft, who delayed his own leave to enjoy life among the luminaries of the German Empire, flew Richthofen to Bad Homburg vor der Höhe. The old spa city, northeast of Frankfurt am Main, was one of the great playgrounds for Europe's rich and royal families. The most important guests arrived at the *Kaiserbahnhof*, a special wing of the main railway station. It therefore caused a local commotion when Krefft and Richthofen arrived in a great open field in an LVG C.V two-seater.

Lothar von Richthofen recounted what Manfred told him about the reception: 'The *Kaiserin* [Empress Auguste Victoria] had such interest in aviation that she herself appeared at the airfield. During the flight my brother wore the old leather jacket in which he had achieved all of his aerial victories. Right after landing he reported to the Empress. In order to justify to some extent that he had dressed in his old leather jacket for this ceremonious occasion, he told her that he had won 52 aerial combats with it. The

Empress stroked the jacket and said: "The good jacket, you have gone through 52 aerial victories with it".'[16]

Bad Homburg had been spared the wartime deprivation of other German cities and, much to the Empress's liking, was almost devoid of the blur of uniforms seen in Bad Kreuznach. The arrival of the famous flyer became a marvellous diversion. Although forbidden to fly, Richthofen could not resist starting the two-seater's engine and taxiing across the broad lawn, raising a wind at every turn.

Empress Auguste Victoria presented Richthofen with a belated birthday present, 'a gold and white enamelled cigarette case inscribed with her name,'[17] a reminder of his new status as a national hero. With that status came a greater degree of comfort and even affection for his hostess, as he recalled: 'One had a [nice] feeling, as it was with Hindenburg; one was in the presence of a charming old lady, with whom one could compare an old aunt or one's own grandmother, and easily forget that she is the Empress.'[18]

Richthofen concluded his time amongst the high and the mighty that evening. *Generalfeldmarschall* von Hindenburg hosted a formal dinner, an occasion never complete without a major speech. It was a heady experience that made just the right impression on the young hero of the air, who 'would never have dreamed that on my 25th birthday I would sit at Hindenburg's right hand and be mentioned in a speech by the Field-Marshal'.[19]

To keep things in perspective, however, the guest list included Richthofen's peers in other military units. He observed: 'There, sitting together at one table, were no fewer than eight Knights of the *Orden Pour le Mérite*. I would never again see so many in one house unless the war lasted so long that the *Pour le Mérite* became as common as the Iron Cross 2nd Class.'[20]

WAR OF WORDS

In Manfred von Richthofen's absence, *Jasta 11* continued to add to its victory score and to its honours. The day Manfred left, Kurt Wolff shot down his 28th and 29th enemy aircraft, and Lothar von Richthofen shot down his seventeenth. On 4 May Wolff became the eighteenth fighter pilot to receive the *Pour le Mérite*. The award was long overdue by then, but recognized his attaining 29 victories in two months.[21]

On the same day, Manfred von Richthofen was off to hunt wood grouse in the Black Forest. But it was not simply a matter of Konstantin Krefft flying him from Bad Kreuznach along the Rhine Valley to Freiburg im Breisgau, in the southern part of the Grand Duchy of Baden. Freiburg and other Rhine cities had been attacked by British and French bombers — just as British and French cities had been bombed — and area residents were leery of all aircraft. German home front air defences, then being strengthened dramatically, had to be alerted to assure Krefft and Richthofen a quiet aerial tour of the Upper Rhine Region.[22]

Richthofen did not begin a quiet vacation, however, owing to a disquieting story released to German news media. On 4 May the *Wolff'schen Telegraph-Bureau*, a leading German news service, distributed an account of the special British aerial assassination team supposedly bent on his destruction. His mother read the story under the frightening headline 'British Price on the Head of a German Flyer'. Filed under a Berlin dateline, the article stated:

> The British have assembled an aircraft squadron of volunteer flyers that is said to seek exclusively the annihilation of the most successful German combat flyer, *Rittmeister Freiherr* von Richthofen, who has already shot down 52 enemy flyers. The flyer who succeeds in the shooting down or capture of Richthofen will receive the Victoria Cross, a promotion, the gift of his own personal aeroplane, £5,000 and a special prize from the manufacturer of the aircraft he uses. A special motion-picture cameraman is supposed to fly with the British squadron to record the entire event for the purpose of later use in a British Army film.[23]

Manfred von Richthofen read the same account in the *Vossische Zeitung*, a leading national daily newspaper. He had a very clear understanding of his own propaganda value, and his response, dated 6 May 1917, reflects his typical clear thinking in the face of this real or imagined danger:

> I do not want to over-react, but I have the sinister feeling that the gentlemanly British will not be able to settle the matter quite so according to plan as they have imagined. By way of example, what will happen if I pick out and shoot down one of them and am so unlucky as to shoot right at the film cameraman! What then? Then the whole British Army film will be interrupted, the gentlemen will fall into the gravest predicament and put heavy blame on me.
>
> How would [one of them] like it if a number of other gentlemen went up to shoot him down and he was filmed being shot down? I believe that if that were the case, he would first shoot down the cameraman ... I would be contented with that. I want only to shoot down the cameraman who is supposed to film me being shot down. By all means, I would love to do that![24]

LOTHAR vs. ALBERT BALL

Twenty-year-old Capt Albert Ball, DSO, MC, a flight commander with No.56 Squadron, RFC, was a shining example of the Royal Flying Corps' recovery from the devastation of 'Bloody April'. Since returning to France on 7 April, Ball had destroyed twelve enemy aircraft and sent one down out of control. He had a bold, aggressive fighting style and, on 7 May 1917, Capt Ball and other fighter pilots of No.56 Squadron and *Jasta 11* clashed in a rainy-evening fight that continues to be debated by aviation historians. The evening patrol — ten S.E.5s of No.56 Squadron and six SPADs of No.19 Squadron — encountered enemy aircraft north of Lens. At about 2000 hours Capt Ball, his wingman Capt Cyril M. Crowe and a SPAD attacked a lone red fighter aircraft over Loos. Soon, amidst the rain and clouds, the fight developed into a contest between Albert Ball's S.E.5 and the red Albatros of Lothar von Richthofen. Ball, then the highest-scoring RFC fighter ace, and the younger Richthofen, a rising star in his own right, each drew on considerable talents in trying to out-manoeuvre the other.

It was, of course, the sheerest luck that none of the aircraft collided in the haze and gathering darkness. Wilhelm Allmenröder, brother of the ace, witnessed the end of the contest between Albert Ball and Lothar von Richthofen:

> I thought that they wanted to stop the fight because of the darkness, but then both turned and rushed at each other as if they intended to ram. Lothar dipped under the other and then both turned and rushed at each other, only a few shots being fired. At the third frontal attack, Lothar came from the south and his opponent from the north. I waited. The machine-guns peppered again. This time Lothar's opponent did not give way sideways, but dived down to the ground. I had wanted to see where the aircraft crashed ... I became anxious because Lothar also went down in a rather steep turn and disappeared in the mist.[25]

Lothar's aeroplane had been hit in the fight, and he had been forced to land. There can be little doubt that he was Capt Albert Ball's 45th, but uncredited, victory. Lothar was down but uninjured, and resumed flying the following day.

Capt Ball, on the other hand, came down near Annoeullin and was found dead in his crashed aircraft. The wreckage showed no evidence of major combat damage that would have disabled the S.E.5, and a medical examination of Ball's body revealed no combat wounds.[26] That evidence did not deter German authorities from quickly crediting Lothar von Richthofen with bringing down the celebrated British ace. The next issue of the *Luftstreitkräfte*'s weekly news bulletin not only mentioned Lothar's victories in the summary of events for 7 May, but included the unusual addition of the name of one of his victims. The bulletin also added a confusing element to the account, as this translation shows: '*Ltn. Frhr.* von Richthofen [shot down] his 19th and 20th opponents. The 19th ... was a triplane, whose pilot apparently was the British combat flyer Captain Ball. The pilot is dead.'[27]

Albert Ball, who received the Victoria Cross posthumously, was not brought down in a Sopwith Triplane. That contention, repeated in

Lothar's own report,[28] has always cast a shadow over his claim. In any event, Lothar von Richthofen was credited with the victory and presented with souvenirs from Ball's aircraft: 'Vickers machine-gun No. A451, two Very pistols, part of the Vickers ammunition belt, some instruments from the S.E.5's dashboard, and a small section of petrol feed pipe slashed by a bullet scar'.[29] The last-named item strongly hints at the true cause of Albert Ball's demise; it and the other trophies were sent home to Schweidnitz for eventual display in the Richthofen Museum.

To establish the claim firmly, for obvious propaganda reasons, photographs of Albert Ball's grave and a note of disingenuous tribute were dropped over British lines: 'R.F.C. Captain Ball was brought down in a fight in the air on the 7th of May, 1917, by a pilot who was of the same order as himself. He was buried at Annoeullin.'[30]

As previously noted, there are many indications that Manfred von Richthofen felt a strong inner drive to compete with the image and the legend of Oswald Boelcke. He continued to talk and write about Boelcke long after his mentor's death, and could not seem to shake the Master's image alongside his own. Less psychologically complex but every bit as intense was Lothar von Richthofen's drive to prove himself to be as good as his brother.

At first Lothar was considered to be very impulsive; more of a shooter than a hunter who pursued his quarry relentlessly.[31] When *Jasta 11* decimated a flight of R.E.8s on the morning of 13 April, Manfred saw Lothar attack and set fire to one British machine and then immediately go after another two-seater nearby. Manfred noted that Lothar 'turned his machine-gun on the next one and immediately shot at him [even though] the first one had barely fallen. This one ... fell after a short battle.'[32]

Manfred made his point about being sure the enemy aircraft had been destroyed by sending Lothar out to obtain the crewmen's names and other information about his two victories. Late that afternoon Lothar returned and noted he had found only one. The wreckage of the second was located the next day by forward troops. Lothar learned the lesson.

On 10 May Lothar von Richthofen was awarded the Knight's Cross with Swords of the Royal House Order of Hohenzollern.[33] The next step, of course, was the *Pour le Mérite*. Manfred recognized Lothar's achievements and the prospect of this high honour, as indicated in a letter to his mother dated 9 May:

> Surely you are angry that I have been sitting here in Germany for almost eight days without writing to you. I am in Freiburg [hunting] for wood grouse and will stay here until the 14th. Then I must go to Berlin to look at new aeroplanes, which will take about three days, [and] then I will come to Schweidnitz. You must excuse me that it is so long.
>
> From Schweidnitz I will go to [the estate of] *Fürst* von Pless and shoot a bison. Toward the end of the month I will tour the other Fronts in the Balkans, etc. That will take about three to four weeks. Mean-

while, Lothar leads my *Staffel* and will indeed be the next to receive the *Pour le Mérite*. What do you say now about both of your wayward sons?[34]

Lothar surely knew that he had earned the *Pour le Mérite*, but he did not relent in his efforts to catch up with Manfred. On 11 May Lothar led *Jasta 11* against a flight of Bristol F.2Bs of No.48 Squadron. Bristol two-seater crews claimed several victories,[35] but lost three of their own aircraft. Among the confirmed German victories credited was Lothar von Richthofen's 22nd.

Manfred's leave was interrupted by an urgent telegram from the Front. 'Lothar wounded, not life-threatening' was all it said.[36] Further checking revealed that, at about 1130 on Sunday 13 May, Lothar and Karl Allmenröder spotted a pair of two-seaters at low altitude over Arleux Forest, within British territory, and dived after them. They were credited with shooting down both aircraft —Lothar's 24th victory and Allmenröder's 12th[37] — but they became separated during the fight.

Manfred understood all too well what happened next:

> After such a battle, especially at really low altitude, in which one twists and turns so often, flying once around to the right and once around to the left, the normal mortal no longer has an idea where he is. Now on this day it was somewhat misty, [and] therefore especially unfavourable weather. Quickly he oriented himself and noticed that he was quite a way behind the Front. He behind the Vimy Heights ... which are about a hundred metres higher than the rest of the area. My brother had disappeared behind these Vimy Heights —in any case that is what the ground observers contended.
>
> The flight home, until one reaches one's own position, is not among the most pleasant feelings that one can think about. One can do nothing about it when the enemy fires at him. Only seldom do they hit ... [but] at such a low altitude, one can hear every shot; it sounds like chestnuts snapping in a fire when individual infantrymen shoot.[38]

Just as he approached the lines, Lothar's aeroplane was hit. There was a pain in his right hip and he felt blood trickling down his leg. When the shooting stopped he knew he was over German lines, and the first flat meadow he spotted became his landing field. Then Lothar lost consciousness and woke up in a field hospital.

Lothar was subsequently transferred to the Bavarian War Hospital in Douai. His fast-paced streak of aerial victories — 24 in little over six weeks — was interrupted by treatment and convalescence lasting more than five months.

'Had my brother not been wounded on [13] May, I believe that after my return from leave he likewise would have gone on leave with 52 [enemy aircraft] having been dispatched,' Manfred wrote.[39]

After being shot down on 13 May, Lothar von Richthofen always considered the number 13 to be unlucky. In fact, he was shot down twice more — both times on the 13th of the month. Coincidentally, one of the two-seaters downed by Lothar and Allmenröder was B.E.2e 7150 of No.13 Squadron.[40]

TURNABOUT

The major British success on the ground in the Battle of Arras was the capture of Vimy Ridge by the Canadian Corps.[41] The major aerial triumph was the tenacity of British airmen to persevere until more new aircraft and better equipment arrived at the Front.[42]

Further, the failure of the French Aisne offensive and the shake-up in the French High Command freed Field-Marshal Sir Douglas Haig, Commander-in-Chief of the British armies in France, to pursue his earlier plans for a major offensive in Flanders. In May he began to shift ground and air units northward. Haig's move forced his adversaries to do likewise, and to prepare for the Battle of Messines.[43]

Part of the effect of these developments was felt while Manfred von Richthofen pursued smaller aerial game in the Black Forest. On 4 May two telegrams were sent to his home in Schweidnitz. His mother could not resist opening them, and read:

> Today your brother has been awarded the *Orden Pour le Mérite* by His Majesty.
> Your brother is in satisfactory condition at the hospital in Douai, according to a telephone inquiry made today by your Staffel.[44]

Manfred made his own enquiries and, satisfied that his brother was not in any mortal danger, continued his leave. He was flown from Freiburg to Nürnberg, where the ground staff advised against flying on to Berlin until an impending storm had passed. A perverse element in Richthofen's nature occasionally caused him to suspend good judgement, as when he had imprudently flown into a storm on the Verdun Front the previous summer. Having learned nothing from that brush with disaster, Richthofen urged his pilot on.

'We had fun with the clouds and the beastly weather. It poured in buckets. Now and then there was hail. After that the propeller looked grotesque, it had been so beaten up by hailstones that it looked like a saw blade,' Richthofen wrote.[45]

To complicate matters, the two flyers became disoriented and could not find any meaningful reference points on the ground. At length they set down on what appeared to be a flat meadow, only to discover its rough spots when the undercarriage crumpled. They had landed outside Leipzig, southwest of Berlin, and had to continue their journey by train.

Manfred von Richthofen looked like just another war-weary front-line pilot when he stepped off the train in Berlin. His rumpled flight suit was still wet from the two-hour adventure in the storm.

Once he arrived at the Inspectorate of Military Aviation (*Idflieg*) offices, however, Richthofen was transformed into the polished, well-dressed hero that Germany wanted the world to see. Then he was taken to the exclusive studio of C.J. von Dühren to sit for a new formal portrait photograph. To aid the glorification process and its own business, the Sanke souvenir postcard firm was eager to print thousands of copies of the new photo for admirers throughout Germany; Sanke's previous Richthofen card had grown in popularity as the toll of victories rose.

Next, the major publisher Verlag Ullstein wanted Richthofen to begin work on his memoirs. Then there were meetings with various dignitaries until, on 16 May, Richthofen was free to pursue his main purpose in Berlin: a visit to the aeronautical test centre at the Adlershof portion of Johannisthal airfield, outside the capital. He wanted to test-fly the LFG Roland D.III, another sleek, plywood-fuselaged fighter being considered for production.

Richthofen was concerned by the lower wing failures in the Albatros D.IIIs. If the problem could not be corrected, he wanted to know what alternatives were available from other manufacturers. Dutch-born Anthony Fokker, once the darling of German fighter aviation, was still out of favour owing to quality control problems with his earlier aircraft. He, for one, would have welcomed the opportunity to produce a new fighter series.

The Albatros company did not give up. Pilots complained that, in the warmer weather of March and April, the existing radiator could not keep the engine cool during the rigours of a long flight or aerial combat. Albatros engineers assured them that 'new, larger surface radiators with "beehive" cooling louvres were [being] supplied and retrofitted in the field ... to alleviate the overheating problem'.[46] Furthermore, they said, D.III aircraft produced at the Ostdeutsche-Albatroswerke (OAW) in Schneidemühl had reinforced lower wings, which 'did not develop the wing failure syndrome with the frequency of the earlier Albatros-built airframes'.[47]

A HERO'S HOMECOMING

Manfred von Richthofen was a tough soldier and a fierce airfighter. No quarter was asked or given. But away from the parade grounds, the palaces of the mighty and the aerial arenas of France he was a shy, private person. Once the work week ended in Berlin, he was so eager to leave the 'social life' of the German capital behind him that, rather than wait until Saturday morning, he took a night train to Schweidnitz.

If he thought he could slip into his home town as easily and anonymously as he had entered the cavernous railway station in Berlin, Richthofen was mistaken. When his train pulled into Schweidnitz at 0700, his sister Ilse was there to meet him and accompany him on the short walk to their home. But even at that early hour on a Saturday, word of the great air hero's arrival spread quickly.

His mother recalled his homecoming on 19 May: 'Scarcely had the news of his arrival [begun to] spread then a flood of floral bouquets and small presents rained down upon us. The whole city seemed to be mobilized. I knew how very much Manfred opposed being honoured [like this]. But now it could not be helped and he found himself reluctantly in [this] role. There was no lack of tributes, neither from the *Wandervogel* [Bird of Passage youth movement] with the whirring imitation of a whooping crane, nor the day nursery school children with paper helmets and tassels.'[48]

Fine weather the following day brought out a huge crowd of people who filled the street in front of the Richthofen home. All were eager to catch a glimpse of Germany's greatest air warrior. Manfred, his mother and sister spent the day in the garden, but there were frequent interruptions. 'Delegations came and went,' his mother wrote. 'The *Jung-Deutschland* (youth movement), the Youth Defence Corps, the local elementary school, speeches, serenades, the City Council sent an oak sapling decorated with Marshal Niel roses (a regional botanical speciality); military bands resounded — and again I see Manfred as he busies himself with the children; how they are devoted to him, how it gives him such joy to look into so many young faces glowing with enthusiasm.'[49]

By the day's end Manfred was worn out from talking to so many people and shaking so many hands.

Manfred recognized that part of the hero's role was inspiring the people. When his many visitors, young and old alike, asked him to sign their Sanke postcards, he patiently obliged them. But he recognized the difference between inspiration and exploitation.

Freifrau von Richthofen remembered: 'One time, however, when a woman showed up with a hundred postcards and asked him to autograph them, he said gruffly: "I will not sign a single one". Startled by this almost brusque tone of the refusal, I gave him a wounded look. He explained ever more resentfully that in another city someone once asked him to sign 50 photo postcards [and] he did it. Later he watched from his window as the 50 postcards were sold on the street.'[50]

When the 'assault' of visitors did not let up, *Freifrau* von Richthofen took forceful means to ensure that her son secured the rest and privacy he needed. She informed the newspapers that Manfred was 'travelling' and gave no specific destination. In fact, she and Ilse took him by car only a short distance away, to a beautiful old game preserve in Stanowitz. Manfred always found hunting relaxing.

Again, Manfred's new national standing infringed on his need for privacy. As the car drove into Stanowitz the villagers poured into the main street and hung out of the windows for a glimpse of their famous neighbour. A painter took photographs of Manfred in a variety of poses as children provided a stream of musical greetings. *Freifrau* von Richthofen feared that the worst was yet to come as she watched from the sidelines. Manfred tried to accept all of this interest graciously, but he was becoming more and more dismayed by the fuss being made over him.[51]

Then, before the situation became totally unbearable, the day was saved by the appearance of Manfred's long-time friend and fellow hunter, *Herr* Schwanitz. The old woodsman whisked Manfred away from the crowds and into the safety of the forest for the rest of the day. They returned to a quiet hunting lodge that evening with the day's bag, a good-sized ram. That evening Manfred regaled his family and friends with stories about the joys of hunting in the air and the rigours of his visit to the Supreme Headquarters.[52]

'For the most part,' wrote his mother, 'I believe that Manfred was glad that he had the [visit to] the Supreme Headquarters behind him. For him, the totally dedicated front-line soldier ... He longed for the din of the propeller, the laughter of the machine-gun, the strict but refreshing life with his comrades out there in the barracks and tents. He wanted to conquer anew every day, at the risk of his own life. That was his nature.'[53]

THE PRETTY YOUNG WOMAN FROM BERLIN

To facilitate work on Manfred's memoirs, *Der rote Kampfflieger* (The Red Battle-Flyer), his publisher in Berlin sent a stenographer to Schweidnitz. By all accounts the stenographer and Manfred had a perfectly proper, businesslike relationship. She was put up in the Hotel Crown, where Manfred visited her in the mornings to dictate his reminiscences. She typed her notes in the afternoon and then brought them to the house, where Manfred reviewed them with his mother and Ilse in the evening.

It did not take long for these comings and goings of the handsome young air hero to attract attention and fuel speculation about the pretty young woman from Berlin.

His mother wrote:

> Once just when Manfred brought her to the garden gate, a pair of inquisitive ladies passed by. Hesitating, with barely restrained curiosity they came to a standstill and greeted Manfred cordially, while their eyes did not move from the modest, smiling young woman at his side. A gleam came to Manfred's eyes; he was again quite the [mischievous] boy. He gestured toward her with his hand and in all seriousness introduced her as: "My fiancée".
>
> I stood in the garden and watched as the attractive Berliner bit her lips, and I also had to laugh. For their part, with the guarded mistrust that is usually bound up with inquisitiveness, the ladies turned aside somewhat cooly and strode away.
>
> "Yes," asserted Manfred laughing, "at least that settles the situation."[54]

THE TERRIBLE TRIPLANES

Irrespective of the credit accorded for the destruction of Sopwith Triplanes, the plain fact was that German pilots were acquiring too much respect for them to suit the German High Command. Even though three-winged aircraft had been built by such pioneers as A.V. Roe, the Sopwith Triplane's 'phenomenal rate of climb and manoeuvrability apparently suggested to the Germans that there must be some extraordinary quality inherent in the triplane configuration'.[55] Anxious to regain the aerial superiority their pilots had enjoyed in April, the German Inspectorate of Military Aviation (*Idflieg*) set their sights on the triplane as a means to achieve that objective.

No doubt the Inspectorate were spurred on by reports from such skilled pilots as Manfred von Richthofen, who had shot down a Sopwith Triplane as his 52nd and most recent victory. Moreover, Sopwith Triplane N5457 of No.1 Squadron, RNAS, had landed with engine trouble within German lines on 6 April,[56] and offered much to study. In short order, the Inspectorate ordered triplane prototypes from Pfalz, Siemens-Schuckert and Fokker. As noted in other texts,[57] the Fokker Dr.I was ultimately selected as the full-production triplane fighter, and went on to win great fame as an 'acrobatic champion, quite unlike any contemporary fighter'.[58]

THE THRILL OF THE HUNT

While on leave, Manfred von Richthofen truly arrived among the old-line landed nobility of Silesia. The new national hero was welcomed as an honoured guest at the estate of Hans Heinrich XI, *Fürst* (Prince) of Pless, which had hosted the Supreme Headquarters from 1915 until the recent move westward.[59] The Prince, whose family holdings in the Oppeln District of Lower Silesia were established in 1185,[60] invited Richthofen to hunt bison with him. It was a rare treat in many respects.

Richthofen's comments reflect on both his social advancement and his totally omnivorous and amoral hunting appetite:

> The bison is that animal which in the vernacular is referred to as the aurochs. The true aurochs is extinct. The bison is the next best thing to it. On the whole earth there are only two places [where they are found] and that is in Pless and in the game preserve of the former Czar in Bialowicz Forest ...
>
> Therefore, it was through the kindness of His Serene Highness that shooting such a rare animal was allowed. In about a generation there will be no more of these animals, as they will be exterminated.
>
> I arrived at Pless [today Pszczyna, Poland] on the afternoon of 26 May and had to go right from the train station [to the game preserve] in order to bring down a bull the same evening. We travelled along the famous road through the Prince's enormous wildlife preserve, on which to be sure many crowned heads had travelled before me. After about an hour, we got out [of the car] and had to walk for half an hour more to

reach my hunting place ... I stood on the high spot where, the head gamekeeper told me, His Majesty had stood numerous times and had bagged many bisons.[61]

As quoted in the introduction to this book, Richthofen's hunt at the Pless estate was very exciting — indeed, evocative of the feelings he had in aerial combat — and just as successful. Once again, Richthofen had matched the feats of the high and the mighty, and done so with his usual bravery and concentration.

'... Five minutes later the monster was finished. The hunt was ended and *"Hirsch tot"* [dead stag = a successful hunt] was trumpeted. All three shots were right above his heart — a very good sign.'[62]

After the kill, it took the hunting party more than two hours to reach Pless Castle. Along the way they passed the Prince's sumptuous hunting lodge and had a look at a home at Promnitz, a family treasure since 1542 when the *Graf* (Count) of Promnitz married into the princely family.[63] In all, there were over 300,000 acres of fenced game preserve. It was a hunter's paradise for someone with Richthofen's proclivities.

But the vacation ended quickly and Richthofen was back in Schweidnitz a few days later. Early on the morning of 31 May a two-seater and a single-seater landed on the parade ground near the Richthofen home. The latter, a Halberstadt, was provided to enable Manfred to maintain his flying proficiency en route to his further duties in Berlin.

After breakfast, Manfred bade farewell to his family and set off in the Halberstadt. Before take-off, one of the other flyers told him the flight would be so easy that he need not fasten his safety belt. With that, the great hero who laughed at thunderstorms looked the junior man dead in the eye and replied: 'I buckle up for every overland flight'.[64]

Manfred's caution in this instance paid off, as related by Lothar von Richthofen:

> Halfway between Schweidnitz and Breslau he let go of the control column. In the same situation a normal machine flies on. At the Front when nothing is wrong, from time to time ... one puts one's hands on the fuselage sides and admires the view. Then the aeroplane flies by itself, so to speak. My brother forgot that he flew a machine entirely strange to him. Suddenly he was flying ... upside-down. He was held in solely by the seat harness; if by chance he had not fastened it, he would have fallen right out. The [Halberstadt] was so nose-heavy that the moment he let go of the controls, it went over on him and he continued on in a wheels-up position. Fortunately, my brother regained control of the aeroplane and brought it back to the right position. But after he landed he said he was very shaken by the experience.[65]

More bad luck with the Halbertstadt was experienced by Richthofen at his next stopover, Militsch. As he was preparing to take off again, the engine simply quit and could not be restarted. Then a bad storm blew up, bringing hail and gale-force winds.

Richthofen knew better than to tempt fate. The next day he and his orderly, Menzke, went by train to Vienna. There he was to begin a grand tour of Central Powers aviation facilities, first in Austria and then in Turkey. Like Oswald Boelcke before him, Manfred von Richthofen was being sent off, out of harm's way.

SCHÄFER FALLS, RICHTHOFEN RETURNS

The French failure on the Aisne placed the burden of the Western Front offensive on British forces in Flanders. As the British Second Army prepared to drive German troops from the advantageous high ground of the group of hills forming the Messines-Wytschaete ridge, RFC Corps squadrons became more active. There was a proliferation of targets for the German fighter pilots, but they had to go farther to reach them and place themselves at greater risk. Thus, on the afternoon of 5 June, German fighter aviation lost one of its brightest rising stars. *Ltn* Karl-Emil Schäfer, commander of *Jasta 28*, was shot down and killed over Zandvoorde by a seasoned two-seater crew. His body was recovered and sent back to his home town of Krefeld in Westfalia. Upon learning this sad news the following day, Manfred von Richthofen cancelled the remainder of his appointments in Vienna, then went to Berlin and on to Krefeld for the funeral of his friend and one-time pupil.

Richthofen dispatched his orderly, Menzke, in anticipation of a possible visit to Schweidnitz. As *Freifrau* von Richthofen later wrote:

> To my astonished question of why he had come back so early, [Menzke] ventured: "We did not like it amongst the Austrians." ... I inquired further and discovered that ... everything was fine for Manfred. It had been harder and harder for him to be away from his *Staffel* [and] he was homesick for it. I could [only] think that he had been stricken by a feeling of responsibility over the release of ever more severe reports of British numerical superiority in the air and [that] was the real reason for which the restful and interesting journey to Turkey was interrupted in Vienna. He would be granted no rest as long as the German positions were overshadowed by enemy air units.[66]

Manfred was unable to visit Schweidnitz, where, on Friday 8 June, his mother learned that the spectre of death in the air was ominously close to her family. She was informed by telephone that her nephew, *Ltn* Oskar von Schickfuss und Neudorff, a pilot with *Jasta 3*, was reportedly shot down behind enemy lines. Immediately, she went to her sister's home in Rankau to offer hope that Oskar had been brought down and captured, as had some of Manfred's victims. She promised that Manfred would make all possible enquiries.

The importance of Manfred's visit to Berlin was clear. He had to use his position and prestige to goad his contacts in the Inspectorate for Military Aviation into providing a successor to the Albatros fighters. Even the improved D.V series continued to suffer wing failures and were becoming less and less of a match for newer British and French fighters.[67]

Richthofen was physically rested and psychologically ready to return to the Front, where RFC aircrews would feel the sting of his fury. He returned to action with a renewed and even more dedicated sense of purpose.

NOTES

1   von Richthofen, *Der rote Kampfflieger*, (1917), p.154.
2   Ibid., p.163.
3   Ibid., p.155.
4   Ibid., p.155.
5   Ibid., p.156.
6   von Richthofen, *Ein Heldenleben*, (1920), p.141.
7   Schowalter, *Bad Kreuznach als Sitz des Grossen Hauptquartiers im Ersten Weltkrieg*, (1981), pp.8-9.
8   Ibid., p.142.
9   Ibid..
10   *Der rote Kampfflieger*, op.cit., p.159.
11   Gibbons, *The Red Knight of Germany*, (1927), p.259.
12   *Ein Heldenleben*, op.cit., p.143.
13   Quoted in Lampel, *Als Gast beim Rittmeister Frhr. v. Richthofen*, (1923), p.219.
14   *Ein Heldenleben*, op.cit.
15   Ibid., p.146.
16   Quoted in *Ein Heldenleben*, op.cit., p.223.
17   Gibbons, op.cit., p.261.
18   *Ein Heldenleben*. op.cit., p.143.
19   *Der rote Kampfflieger*, op.cit.
20   *Ein Heldenleben*, op.cit.
21   Zuerl, *Pour-le-Mérite-Flieger*, (1938), p.481.
22   Kilduff, *Air War Over Baden*, (1991), p.204.
23   von Richthofen, *Mein Kriegstagebuch*, (1937), p.106.
24   von Richthofen, *Der rote Kampfflieger*, (1933), pp.175-176.
25   Quoted in Nowarra, *Capt Ball's Last Flight*, (1963), p.244.
26   Bowyer, *Albert Ball, VC*, (1977), p.156.
27   *Nachrichtenblatt Nr 11*, 10 May 1917, p.3; the civilian press published a similar story, as seen in the weekly news magazine *Kriegs-Echo Nr 145*, 18 May 1917, p.518.
28   Bowyer, op.cit., p.154; all editions of Manfred von Richthofen's memoir *Der rote Kampfflieger* state in error that Ball was flying a triplane during his fight with Lothar.
29   Ibid., p.155.
30   *RFC Casualty List*, 1917.
31   *Der rote Kampfflieger*, (1917), op.cit., p.174.
32   Ibid.; as noted in Chapter 7, No.59 Squadron, RFC, lost all six R.E.8s of its morning patrol to a combined attack by *Jastas 4* and *11*, making identification of individual victims difficult.
33   O'Connor, *Aviation Awards of Imperial Germany in World War I and the Men Who Earned Them*, vol II, (1990), p.141.
34   *Ein Heldenleben*, op.cit., p.196.
35   *RFC Communiqué No. 87*, op.cit., p.7; there are no matching German losses for these claims.
36   *Der rote Kampfflieger*, op.cit., p.163.

37   *Kofl 6. Armee Wochenbericht Nr 180/1, Teil 11*, 18 May 1917.

38   *Der rote Kampfflieger*, op.cit., p.164.

39   Ibid., p.173. In this text, Manfred von Richthofen mistakenly notes 5 May as the date Lothar was wounded.

40   Rogers, *RFC and RAF Casualties 1917-1918*, (1975), p.185; 2/Lt F. Thompson and Lt. A.C.C. Rawlins (both uninjured).

41   Esposito, *A Concise History of World War I*, (1964), p.95.

42   Jones, *The War in the Air*, vol III, (1931), pp.370-371.

43   Jones, *The War in the Air*, vol IV, (1934), p.113.

44   *Mein Kriegstagebuch*, op.cit., p.108.

45   *Der rote Kampfflieger*, op.cit., p.160.

46   Grosz, *The Agile and Aggressive Albatros*, (1976), pp.41-42.

47   Ibid., p.42.

48   *Mein Kriegstagebuch*. op.cit., pp.108-109.

49   Ibid., p.109.

50   Ibid..

51   Ibid., p.110.

52   Ibid., pp.111-112.

53   Ibid., p.112.

54   Ibid., p.113.

55   Bruce, *The Fokker Dr.I*, (1965), p.3.

56   Grosz and Ferko, *The Fokker Dr.I: A Reappraisal*, (1978), p.10.

57   The latest is *The Fokker Triplane* by Alex Imrie, (1992).

58   Grosz and Ferko, op.cit., p.14.

59   Schowalter, op.cit. p.8.

60   *Meyers Enzyklopädisches Lexikon*, vol XVIII, (9th ed, 1981), p.794.

61   *Der rote Kampfflieger*, op.cit., pp.176-177.

62   Ibid., pp.178-179.

63   *Meyers Konversations-Lexikon*, vol XIII, (9th ed., 1888), p.132.

64   *Mein Kriegstsagebuch*, op.cit., p.113.

65   Quoted in *Ein Heldenleben*, op.cit., pp.223-224.

66   *Mein Kriegstagebuch*, op.cit., p.116.

67   Grosz, *The Agile and Aggressive Albatros*, (1976), pp.46-47.

CHAPTER 9
GATHERING OF EAGLES

When Karl-Emil Schäfer returned to Krefeld from Paris on the eve of the First World War, his mother met him at the railway station.[1] Days later he marched off to war with the local Westphalian rifle company *Bückeburger Reserve-Jägern*. When his body was returned home in a special railway car, Krefelders from all walks of life joined the local, state and national dignitaries who paid tribute to the fallen warrior. War is a great equalizer, and bravery one of its instruments of advancement; both had propelled the son of a silk manufacturer into the first rank of German heroes. The tangible sign of his elevation was the presence of *Rittm* Manfred *Frhr* von Richthofen as head of the guard of honour.

No longer restricted from flying, Richthofen had piloted his *Staffel*'s two-seater from Berlin to Krefeld to perform this last tribute. His previous pilot, *Ltn.d.Res* Konstantin Krefft, was still on leave, so Richthofen was joined by an instructor from Wahlstatt, *Hptmn* Erich von Salzmann,[2] who had not flown previously.[3] The sad flight to one friend's funeral was balanced by the pleasure of seeing another friend enjoy his first flight.

ANOTHER VISIT TO THE *KAISER*

Despite the urgent need to return to the Front, Richthofen was ordered to fly from Krefeld to Bad Kreuznach for another visit with *Kaiser* Wilhelm II and other dignitaries. He knew that the Battle of Messines had begun on 7 June with an all-out assault against German forces in Flanders. And, most likely, he was aware that *Jasta 11*'s overall successes were down — even though they were the best fighter unit on the 6. *Armee* Front. The most recent week's statistics showed:[4]

UNIT	COMBAT FLIGHTS	FLIGHT HOURS	AERIAL COMBATS	AERIAL VICTORIES
Jagdstaffel 3	103	112	13	1
Jagdstaffel 7	63	53	6	–
Jagdstaffel 11	118	106	39	7
Jagdstaffel 12	165	123	52	4
Jagdstaffel 27	92	116	29	1
Jagdstaffel 30	117	130	55	3
Jagdstaffel 33	90	96	14	2

Jasta 11 was too far from the new battle lines and on 9 June, during

Richthofen's absence, the unit moved from Roucourt to Harlebeke, north-east of Courtrai, on the *4. Armee* Front.[5] Between the move and the arrival of new Albatros D.V aircraft, however, *Jasta 11* achieved no further victories until Richthofen's return.

During Richthofen's second visit to Bad Kreuznach he met Czar Ferdinand of Bulgaria, who made a special impression on him: '[The Czar] is a tall, stately gentleman with an angularly hooked eagle-nose and a very intelligent face. Everything that he says is substantive. He spoke with me for quite a while, asked me about this and that in aerial combat and I must say [that] I was astonished at how broad an insight he had gained into my business. Seldom have I found such an awareness among Regular Army officers who are not flyers.'[6]

It was not unusual that the Bulgarian monarch conversed in German. He was born a Prince of the House of Saxe-Coburg-Gotha and was elected to rule by the Bulgarian National Assembly in 1887.[7]

At the *Kaiser*'s official state dinner, Richthofen joined a list of luminaries — including Hindenburg and Ludendorff — who filled two long tables. Richthofen sat at the end of the *Kaiser*'s table, next to *Fürst* von Pless, whom he thanked for the recent hunting invitation. The flyer was surprised, however, when the elderly nobleman hinted that he wanted a favour. Richthofen wrote:

> He told me that he wanted his son to become a flyer. I find this quite a decision for a Prince like him to let his oldest son take up such a dangerous trade as war ... [But] one thing impressed me about the old gentleman: that at the age of 75 he sat in an aeroplane with Fritz Falkenhayn[8] and flew around the area for an hour and a half. He was so thrilled by it [that], after alighting, he pressed 20 Marks into the hand of each mechanic. He would have preferred to take off again. That is a thing that impressed me greatly, for one would find no end of younger gentlemen who are knights without fear or reproach, but who would never be moved to climb into an aeroplane.[9]

The next day Czar Ferdinand made sure he was not outshone by his distant cousin, Duke Carl Eduard of Saxe-Coburg-Gotha, who had awarded Manfred von Richthofen the duchy's Silver Bravery Medal. The Bulgarian monarch presented the pilot with his kingdom's Bravery Order 4th Class 1st Degree.

Manfred wore the new honour when he visited his brother Lothar briefly in a convalescent hospital in Hamburg. Then, after trying to cheer up the injured warbird, whose greatest ache was to climb back into an aeroplane, Manfred was off to the Front.

By the time Manfred von Richthofen returned to *Jasta 11*, *Ltn* Karl Allmenröder had become the fourth *Staffel* member to receive the *Pour le Mérite*. Now Richthofen had to raise other new pilots to Allmenröder's level of effectiveness.

Jasta 11's new airfield was far enough behind the lines for Richthofen and his pilots to spend uninterrupted hours gaining familiarity with their new aircraft before going into battle. Duly prepared, the *Staffelführer* led morning and afternoon patrols on 18 June. During the second patrol Manfred von Richthofen achieved another aerial victory. North of Ypres, Richthofen attacked R.E.8 A4290 of No.9 Squadron. In his combat report he stated: 'Driven by the wind, it fell into Struywes's farm, where it began to burn'.[10]

That evening Manfred von Richthofen wrote a long-overdue letter to his mother and recounted recent events. He noted that he was back at work, having shot down No.53 that day. He also related with pride his latest visit to Supreme Headquarters.

Then, as promised, Manfred reported what he had learned about the fate of his cousin, *Ltn* Oskar von Schickfuss und Neudorff, who had been shot down a few hours after Karl-Emil Schäfer:

> About Oskar I have been able to determine with certainty that he is in fact dead, for he fell or jumped from his aeroplane [during] the last 1,500 metres. He lies near the Front, but on the other side. Through notes dropped to the British I have attempted to determine if they were able to recover [his body]. The Royal Flying Corps are very noble in this regard.
>
> Yesterday, unfortunately, [Georg] Zeumer fell in aerial combat. Perhaps it was best for him, for he knew the end of his life was just ahead of him. This splendid, pleasant fellow! It would have been terrible if he had had to be tormented to death slowly. So this was a beautiful hero's death. The funeral will be held in the next few days.[11]

RICHTHOFEN'S 54TH AND 55TH VICTORIES

Richthofen inflicted the same fate on an adversary during an evening patrol on 23 June, when his formation attacked a flight of British aircraft. According to his combat report it was a brief encounter in the classic attack style, from above and behind: '... I fired some 300 shots into a SPAD from the shortest possible distance. My adversary did not start to turn and did nothing to evade my fire. At first the aeroplane began to smoke and then it fell, turning and turning, three kilometres north of Ypres, where it touched the ground without having caught itself.'[12]

On the strength of his report, Richthofen was credited with his 54th victory. British and French casualty lists show no SPAD losses for that day, or anything similar at 2115 when the victory is supposed to have taken place. There is much speculation,[13] but no conclusive evidence to settle this claim.

The following morning, however, there was no doubt that Manfred von Richthofen shot down a D.H.4 near Becelaere, just over 20km west of his own airfield and still within German lines. He reported: 'With six machines of my *Staffel*, I attacked an enemy formation consisting of two reconnaissance aeroplanes and ten fighter aircraft. Unimpeded by the enemy fighter aircraft, I managed to break one of the reconnaissance aeroplanes in my fire.'[14]

The two-seater shot down on 24 June was logged as Richthofen's 55th victory. He was not distracted by the escorting Sopwith Triplanes of No.10 Squadron, RNAS, as his comrades dealt with them. *Ltn* Karl Allmenröder shot down one, for his 28th victory, and *Ltn* Wilhelm-Gisbert Groos shot down another, his second victory.[15] Richthofen's comrades allowed him to attend to the more important mission of stopping the D.H.4 from returning with the fruits of its photographic and visual reconnaissance.

THE FIRST *JAGDGESCHWADER*

Crown Prince Rupprecht of Bavaria, nominally a senior German military commander on the Western Front, announced on 24 June 1917 the formation of *Jagdgeschwader I* (Fighter Wing 1), comprising the *4. Armee* units *Jagdstaffeln 4, 6, 10* and *11*. The *Geschwader* was to be a self-contained unit, dedicated to achieving aerial supremacy over decisive battle sectors. It was to remain immediately subordinate to the *AOK 4* (High Command of the 4th Army) and, to the greatest degree possible, was to be combined at one airfield.[16]

The formation of a single massive fighting unit, *JG I*, was largely a reaction to the deployment of Royal Flying Corps units in greater strength. As *Gen* von Hoeppner pointed out in his memoirs:

> Due to his number and his sporting spirit, the Englishman was always our most dangerous enemy and the British Front required, as a matter of course, the main force of the German air service.
>
> The ever-increasing number of aircraft which the opposition deployed to reach a target made it seem desirable for us to combine several *Jagdstaffeln* into a *Jagdgeschwader* ... In the personage of *Rittmeister* von Richthofen ... the *Geschwader* received a *Kommandeur* whose steel-hard will in relentlessly pursuing the enemy was infused in every member of the *Geschwader*. His refined lack of pretension, his open, gallant manner [and] his military skill secured for him amongst the Army an unshakeable trust that, despite his young age, was matched with great respect.[17]

As if to show the trust was well placed, on 25 June Richthofen shot down his 56th enemy aircraft. Karl Allmenröder, designated to succeed Richthofen as leader of *Jasta 11*, watched for intruders while his commander dived on R.E.8 A3847 of No.53 Squadron and, at 1735, sent it crashing down into the trenches near Le Bizet.[18]

The next evening, Allmenröder led five of his comrades against an offensive patrol of No.1 Squadron over Becelaere. He was credited with shooting down Nieuport 17 B1649 near Ypres, logged as his 30th victory.[19]

The acting *Staffel* leader had watched out for the newer pilots as carefully as he had been looked after. He wrote to his sister: 'There are always new men arriving at the *Staffel* and I am the only one of the old pupils who Richthofen still has around him. You may well think that he does not want to let me go and that at the moment I do not want to get away. [But] I will take my long leave later. The entire responsibility [of *Staffel* leadership] has been given to me by Richthofen. Hopefully I will remain in his *Staffel* a long time!'[20]

At about 0945 on 27 June 1917, thirteen days after being awarded the coveted *Pour le Mérite*, the 21-year-old Rhinelander was shot down and killed over a front-line area near Klein-Zillebeke. Aviation historians have long thought that Allmenröder was an uncredited victory of Flt-Lt (later Air Vice Marshal) Raymond Collishaw, a flight commander with No.10 Squadron, RNAS. There is little doubt that Sopwith Triplanes of Naval 10 and red Albatroses of *Jasta 11* clashed that day, but the Canadian pilot never sought credit for downing Allmenröder. More recently, publication of a German eyewitness account affirms that the German ace was hit by anti-aircraft fire.[21]

Allmenröder's body was recovered under cover of darkness the following night. There was an elaborate military funeral at St. Joseph's Church in Courtrai, and chief among the mourners was *Gen* Friedrich Sixt von Armin, commander of the *4. Armee*. The flower-bedecked coffin was sent back to Germany for final services at the Lutheran church in Wald, Allmenröder's home town.[22]

At the time, Manfred von Richthofen was back in Hamburg, visiting his brother Lothar in a convalescent hospital. He wrote to Allmenröder's father: 'I myself cannot wish for a more beautiful death than to fall in aerial combat; it is a consolation to know that at his end Karl felt nothing ...'[23] He also wired *Ltn* Otto Brauneck, who was home on leave, designating him to represent the *Staffel* at the funeral. Brauneck carried his friend's *Ordenskissen*; the black velvet pillow was crowned by the *Pour le Mérite* that Allmenröder was wearing when he was killed.[24]

To assure strong leadership continuity at *Jasta 11*, *Ltn* Kurt Wolff was transferred back to to the unit. Wolff had been leader of *Jasta 29*, and was succeeded in that post by the *Pour le Mériter Ltn.d.Res* Werner Voss.[25]

By the time Manfred von Richthofen returned to the Front, the silent machinery of administration had moved forward to assure a smooth establishment of the first *Jagdgeschwader*. At Marcke, on the southwest edge of Courtrai, the estate of Baron Jean de Bethune was being converted for military use. The sprawling green lawns, adjacent castle and other buildings of the area called Marckebeke were ideal for the centralized location needed by *JG I*.

Jasta 11 moved from Harlebeke, northeast of Courtrai, and on Monday 2 July *Jasta 4* came from Cuerne to Marckebeke and *Jasta 6* was at neighbouring Bisseghem, just across the Lys River from the new airfield. *Jasta 10* was at Heule airfield, a short distance away, but soon moved to Marcke to be closer to the other *Staffeln*. On that day of convergence, Richthofen filed this report:

> Deulemont, between the lines, 10:20 a.m.
> I attacked the forward aircraft of an enemy squadron. The observer collapsed under the first shots. The pilot was mortally hit shortly thereafter. The R.E. dropped. I fired some shots at the falling aircraft from 50 metres distance until flames came out of the machine and the opponent crashed in flames.
> /s/ von Richthofen
> *Rittmeister und Kommandeur des Jagdgeschwaders I* [26]

The terse paragraph does not note that Richthofen and a host of his red-coloured eagles had pounced on a photo-reconnaissance flight of slow, lumbering R.E.8s from No.53 Squadron and shot down two of them. The nature of the two-seaters' mission required steady, precise flying to enable the observers to photograph important ground positions. They presented a fairly easy target and *Jasta 11* made quick work of them. Richthofen was credited with his 57th victory.[27]

The new *Geschwader-Kommandeur* set the right example for his new, larger unit. He also staffed it with the best people he could find and transferred those who did not measure up. The two positions closest to him were filled by people with whom he had served. *Ltn* Konstantin Krefft, who had already scored two victories with *Jasta 11* and served as that unit's Technical Officer, was given the same duties for the *Geschwader*.[28] To handle the larger unit's administrative tasks Richthofen selected the best adjutant he knew, *Obltn* Karl Bodenschatz of *Jasta Boelcke*. He accepted Richthofen's telephoned invitation to join *JG I*, and was off to Marcke before all of the paperwork was done.[29]

Bodenschatz arrived just as word of Richthofen's latest aerial victory was circulating amongst the newcomers streaming in. The news added to the excitement of the arrival of aircraft and people at the airfield. There was an enthusiastic spirit that even the confusion of assigning living quarters could not dampen. *Jasta 11* and *JG I* staff officers moved into the elegant Marckebeke Castle, and *Jasta 4* into the nearby convent vacated by sisters of the Order of the Immaculate Conception. A few days later an orderly room was established in a private house at Kortrijkstraat No.74, a short walk from Marckebeke Castle.

Within a short time orderliness was achieved, as described by Karl Bodenschatz:

Once all of the *Staffeln* were assembled at the airfield, twelve machines stood behind each *Staffel* leader ... The assembled *Geschwader* looked extremely colourful. The *Stammstaffel* [core unit], *Jasta 11*, with which Richthofen flew, had the machines painted red; Jasta 10 [used] yellow; *Jasta 6* had zebra stripes; and *Jasta 4* bore a black snake line along the natural wood-finished fuselage ...

On the evening of 2 July, the *Kommandeur* invited all of the leaders of the *Jagdstaffeln* to a meeting in his room on the second floor [of the castle].30 Everything was still barren and unpleasant. Moreover, not all of the rooms in the castle were at our disposal because the [Baron] who was lord of the manor here wanted most of all to blow up this whole flying business and, as this was not possible, at least he exploded every polite contact with his sullen lack of friendliness and locked up as many rooms as possible. The *Rittmeister* watched this inhospitable business patiently for a few days and then it was changed.[31]

Richthofen had more important things in mind, however, than the behaviour of the Belgian nobleman he was dispossessing. He was more concerned about the four *Staffel* leaders who were to help him meld their units into an effective fighting force.

Richthofen's first meeting with the *Staffel* leaders set the tone of his leadership style. His adjutant recorded:

The *Kommandeur* gave his instructions in clear sequential order. First, he no longer wanted to leave to chance [the prospect] that take-off orders would be received by the command positions in a roundabout way. He wanted information about enemy aviation activity communicated precisely. Therefore he ordered that direct connections with the most advanced front lines be established immediately. Also he insisted on a direct telephone line to his four *Staffeln* so that when he picked up the receiver, all four would be on the line at the same time.

That was Number One.

In addition, the *Rittmeister* discussed the ground [war] situation and it was not pleasant to listen to.

The enemy breakthrough attempts were repeated with a tenacity not previously experienced and each new attack was more brutal and bitter than the one before. The [ground] troops who had to endure these beserk assaults suffered immensely under heavy bombardment that never ceased. And when, astonishingly, there was a pause in the shelling, then infantry-strafing aircraft came roaring over just above the trenches and dugouts. And high above the infantry-strafers, clusters of bombing squadrons swung far over [our] rear areas.

That was how it looked on the ground and, as a consequence, the mission in the air for *Jagdgeschwader I* and for each [member] was: annihilation of the infantry-strafers, annihilation of the single-seat fighters, annihilation of the bombing squadrons.[32]

Initially, Richthofen concentrated on having his units respond individually, but in a co-ordinated manner, to interdict enemy aircraft along the *4. Armee* Front. Massed, *Geschwader*-strength operations came after the initial discipline was established. *Geschwaderbefehl Nr 1* (Wing Order No.1), which he issued on 5 July, stated: 'Beginning on 6 July, the sequence of daily take-off readiness (from daybreak on) in rotation is *Jastas 11, 10, 6, 4;* the daily midday take-off sequence (from 1330 to 1500 hours) is *Jastas 10, 6, 4, 11.*'[33]

Before that schedule took effect, however, *Obltn* Edouard Dostler went hunting on the early evening of 5 July and shot down a balloon north of Ypres; it was credited as his thirteenth victory.[34] While Dostler violated the intent of *JG I*'s co-ordinated effort, the Bavarian showed the aggressive spirit that Richthofen liked.

MANFRED VON RICHTHOFEN SHOT DOWN

JG I's operations began on a bright summer day with clear skies. All *Geschwader* aircraft and pilots were on the airfield, waiting for the first alert to be sounded. To ensure that no enemy aircraft slipped undetected into his sector, Richthofen took over a 5m rangefinder and stereotelescope equipment from a nearby observation post and had it set up and manned in front of Marckebeke Castle.[35]

Initially, Richthofen set up a rotation schedule and sent the units out in shifts. Thus, when enemy artillery-spotting aircraft were reported near Ypres at mid-morning, it was *Jasta 4*'s turn to be despatched. They returned a short time later, reporting that the enemy aircraft had quickly withdrawn.

At 1030 *JG I* were detailed to repel low-flying trench-strafers and, as *Jasta 11* pilots were then in readiness, Richthofen led them to the Front. On the way to the Front, and flying at about 4,000m, Richthofen spotted an equally desirable target below him, a flight of F.E.2d pusher biplanes. Immediately he fired a flare to signal his comrades to follow him in manoeuvring behind them to cut off their escape. He later wrote:

> After quite a while I had the rearmost [aircraft] so close to me [that I could] consider all the ways to attack him. Wolff flew beneath me. I recognized by the [distinct] sound of the German machine-gun that he was already engaged in combat. Then my opponent went into a dive and took up the fight with me. But ... it was from such a great distance that one really could not yet call it a true aerial combat. I had not yet cocked [my machine-guns], there was still so much time until I got into combat with my opponent. Then I watched as the observer, in great excitement, fired at me. I calmly let him shoot, for even the best sharpshooter's marksmanship could not help at a distance of 300 metres. One just does not hit!

Then he turned completely toward me and I hoped to get behind him in the next turn and burn his hide. Suddenly there was a blow to my head! I was hit! For a moment I was completely paralyzed ... My hands dropped to the side, my legs dangled inside the fuselage. The worst part was that the blow on the head had affected my optic nerve and I was completely blinded. The machine dived down.[36]

For a moment, Germany's premier fighter pilot thought he was as good as dead, diving out of control and wondering whether the wings would snap off under the strain of the dive before he smashed into the ground.

Richthofen regained enough mobility to switch off the engine and then, as his body began to respond, his vision returned. He looked at the altimeter. It showed 800m. He restarted the engine and headed eastward. As the world came into focus for him, Richthofen looked around and saw that two comrades, *Ltns.d.Res* Otto Brauneck and Alfred Niederhoff,[37] had come down with him. They stayed with their commander as he set down in a field of high grass near Wervicq, Belgium.[38]

Manfred von Richthofen was almost certainly brought down by Capt Douglas C. Cunnell and 2/Lt Albert E. Woodbridge in F.E.2d A6512 of No.20 Squadron.

Woodbridge later recalled that they fought two German aircraft that:

> ... came at us head on, and I think the first one was Richthofen. I recall there wasn't a thing on that machine that wasn't red, and God how he could fly! I opened fire with the front Lewis [machine-gun], and so did Cunnell with the side gun. Cunnell held the F.E. to her course and so did the pilot of the all-red scout. Gad, with our combined speeds we must have been approaching each other at ... 250 miles an hour.
>
> Then something happened. We could hardly have been twenty yards apart when the Albatros pointed her nose down suddenly ... We saw the all-red plane slip into a spin. It turned over and over and round and round. It was no manoeuvre. He was completely out of control ...[39]

The 'Fee' crew were not credited with shooting down Richthofen. And, such is the luck of war that, six days later, while flying F.E.2d B1863, Capt Cunnell was killed by anti-aircraft fire. His observer, Lt A.G. Bill, took control of the aircraft and brought it back to base.[40]

Manfred von Richthofen was luckier than his opponent. He and his escorts had landed near a road, where local troops recognized his red aircraft and summoned help immediately. By noon he was in Courtrai at St Nicholas' Hospital, which had been caring for the sick and wounded since 1362. The hospital, which the Germans called *Feldlazarett 76*, was a short ride from Marckebeke. 'I had quite a respectable hole in my head, a wound of about ten centimetres across which could be drawn together later; but in one place clear white bone as big as a *Taler* [large-size coin] remained exposed,' he wrote. 'My thick Richthofen head had once again proved itself. The skull had not been penetrated. With some imagination, in the X-ray photos one could notice a slight swelling. It was a skull fracture that I was not rid of for days, [and] was not very comfortable.'[41]

News of Richthofen's absence from the Front spread quickly among German forces. His opponents obtained somewhat exaggerated information, as noted in a British intelligence report: 'According to statements of prisoners of 29th I.R. [Infantry Regiment] captured in La Bassée Ville on 26th/27th July, this Officer is reported to have received two bullet wounds in the head, in combat with an Allied machine over Wervicq on 7th July, 1917.'[42]

Irrespective of what his opponents believed, Manfred von Richthofen seemed more concerned about getting back into the air before Lothar. 'I am curious as to who can climb into the crate first, my brother or I,' he wrote. 'My brother is afraid it will be me and I am afraid it will be my brother.'[43]

He would have almost three weeks to think about it. In the interim, *Obltn* Kurt von Döring, who had been slightly injured that day, became acting *Geschwader-Kommandeur*.[44]

HEADACHES

Manfred von Richthofen awoke in the hospital with the top of his head shaved and swathed in a thick snow-white bandage. As the anaesthetic wore off, he began to experience throbbing head wound pains[45] that would trouble him to the end of his life. The administrative headaches were yet to come.

A few hours later he was visited by *Obltn* Bodenschatz and the leaders of *Jastas 4, 6* and *11*.[46] They wanted first-hand knowledge of the *Kommandeur*'s condition, and were not put off by nurse Kätie Otersdorf's iron will and zealous protection of her patient. They wore down her resistance and, finally, were taken to the room where their leader was resting.

Richthofen looked pale and uncharacteristically weak in the antiseptic setting of the darkened room. He was aware enough to anticipate their questions, and managed a word of encouragement to his *Staffel* leaders: 'I am very sorry to be away right in the middle of things, but I will be back again, very soon.'[47]

When the four officers returned to Marckebeke they were mobbed by their comrades, clamouring for news. Bodenschatz wrote: 'They wanted to know precisely how he looked, what he said, how he felt, whether he had to lie in bed or could sit on a chair, and whether he had a good doctor or at least a pretty nurse, how long [his convalescence] was likely to last, etc., etc.'.[48]

The pilots were relieved to learn that their *Kommandeur* and idol was out of mortal danger, but then another mood set in. The following day, 7

July, dawned with clear skies and favourable weather, and the pilots of *JG I* went looking for their opponents with vengeance clearly in mind. Acting *Kommandeur* von Döring sent twelve aircraft of *Jastas 4, 6* and *11* on a morning patrol that came upon three Albatroses from *Jasta 24* attacking a larger British formation over Dadizele. Two Sopwith 1½ Strutters of No.45 Squadron on a photo-reconnaissance, escorted by six Sopwith Triplanes, were darting about, easily fending off the German trio. The arrival of *JG I* changed the scenario dramatically.

Jasta 11 leader *Ltn* Kurt Wolff went after a Triplane, chased it southward and, at 1100, shot it down over Comines; he was credited with his 33rd victory.[49] Five minutes later, *Ltn.d.Res* Richard Krüger of *Jasta 4* scored his first (and only) aerial victory, a Triplane brought down west of Wervicq.[50] And, five minutes after that success, *Ltn.d.Res* Alfred Niederhoff of *Jasta 11* sent down a Triplane near Bousbecque, recorded as his fourth victory.[51]

The two Sopwith two-seaters also went down, one credited at 1200 north of Warneton to *Obltn* Eduard Dostler, leader of *Jasta 6*, as his fourteenth victory,[52] the other possibly hit by *Ltn* Krüger, but not attributed to him. *Vzfw* Fritz Krebs' sixth victory was recorded as an R.E.8 downed in flames near Zillebeke at 1135,[53] but there is no matching loss,[54] so this *Jasta 6* pilot's claim of a two-seater may have been the other 1½ Strutter.

During the afternoon and evening patrols, *JG I* Albatroses brought down four more enemy aircraft: three credited to *Jasta 4* and one to *Jasta 11*. The total of nine enemy aircraft shot down, with no losses of their own, was a day's work the new *Geschwader* could reflect on with pride.

KURT WOLFF WOUNDED

Jasta 11 claimed two enemy aircraft and three balloons on 11 July,[55] but suffered a serious loss when acting leader *Ltn* Kurt Wolff was wounded over Ypres during a fight with twelve Sopwith Triplanes. One of the Triplanes bore down on Wolff and fired a stream of bullets that hit him in the left shoulder and hand, and knocked out his machine gun. He made a safe landing and was taken to the same hospital in Courtrai where Manfred von Richthofen was convalescing.[56]

Command of *Jasta 11* passed to 26-year-old *Obltn* Wilhelm Reinhard. A Regular Army officer, Reinhard began his aviation career as an observer with *Fl.-Abt. (A) 205* in 1915, later became a pilot and flew with *Feldfl.-Abt. 28*. After completing fighter pilot training, he was assigned to *Jasta 11*.[57] Reinhard had no aerial victories to his credit at the time, but, as a career officer with a breadth of experience, he was eligible for command. He did not disappoint his superiors.

According to a British source, more fighting took place in the air on 12 July than on any day since the beginning of the war. The activity was greatest over the British Fifth Army Front.[58] That was in *JG I*'s operational area, and the *Geschwader* logged eight victories, six for *Jasta 6* and two for *Jasta 4.*

JG I losses also increased, especially during evening encounters. Acting *Kommandeur* von Döring recognized that night-time combat against enemy fighter aircraft was not a productive use of his resources. For one thing, flying in the late afternoon or evening, British aircraft had the advantage of advancing with the sun against their backs, making them hard to see by German attackers. Even sending up only one *Staffel* at a time would simply result in the piecemeal loss of German aircraft, with little achieved for the overall effort. As noted in his report of 17 July, von Döring focused on the original purpose of the *Geschwader*'s foundation:

> After the experiences of the last few days it has been proven that single flying *Staffeln* are in no position to do battle successfully with British *Geschwaders*, which appear chiefly in the evening. For this reason, a simultaneous deployment of *Staffeln* is required and will happen from now on every time the *Geschwader* is ordered [to fly]. The *Staffeln* must appear together over the Front at great height (4,000 to 5,000 metres) and, as much as possible, carry out their attacks together against the strong British *Geschwaders*. The *Staffeln* must make every effort to fly in such a way that they support each other. For the present the mission of the entire *Geschwader* must be limited during the evening hours.
>
> During the course of the day it is recommended that the flights of the individual *Staffeln* attack principally the artillery-ranging and reconnaissance aircraft that fly at the lowest altitudes, as the activity of these aircraft is tactically most important and most troublesome for the ground troops.[59]

In his hospital bed in Courtrai, Manfred von Richthofen read this and other reports. He expected impressive performance from *Jagdgeschwader I* even during his absence and, when the results did not meet his expectations, he proved to be as tenacious at political air service battling as he was at fighting in the air.

The day after Döring's report, Richthofen used his unique access to the office of the Commanding General of the Air Force (*Kogenluft*), and wrote a scathing letter to his friend *Obltn* Fritz von Falkenhayn, the *Kogenluft* staff's technical officer. He complained that his tactical dicta had been subverted by *Hptmn* Otto Bufe, the Air Officer in Charge of Aviation (*Kofl*) on the *4. Armee* staff. Richthofen favoured aggressive attacks on both sides of the lines, while Bufe wanted to hinder British aircraft from crossing German lines. It became a contest of wills that Richthofen was determined to win. Richthofen also complained that *Kogenluft* had not done enough to develop more improved aircraft. He wrote:

> We have 16 *Jagdstaffeln* in the [4.] *Armee*. These must really suffice. When an [enemy aircraft] has been shot down recently, it was

[done] only by the *Jagdgeschwader.60* What are the other 12 *Staffeln* doing?

This [situation], of course, is not due to individual pilots or *Staffel* leaders; rather, the blame lies elsewhere.

When I came to this *Armee*, the following was told to me by Bufe: "It does not matter to me that [enemy aircraft] are shot down in my *Armee*; rather, that you with your *Jagdstaffel* [and] by your presence at the Front at a certain time will barricade the air!" This is such an insanely great mistake that one could not make a bigger one in fighter aviation [*Jagdfliegerei*]. I explained to Bufe that this was not at all my view of fighter aviation and also gave him a copy [of a report] about what I think about the use of *Jagdstaffeln* (*Geschwader*) and have accomplished so far. At the same time I sent it to [*Hptmn* Hermann] Kastner. When you peruse it then you must know it is really a reply to Bufe's remarks.

Bufe has arranged all of the *Jagdstaffeln* on a timetable whereby each *Staffel* has a set time, a set area, [and] a prescribed altitude to barricade for an hour and a quarter. It is indeed quite clear, of course, that this will never be a fighter sortie [*Jagdflug*], but rather maintains the character of a barricade flight [*Sperreflug*]. But in Bufe's view there should indeed be no fighter sorties; rather, he wants to have barricade flights.

The other *Jagdstaffeln* are ... unhappy about it. The *Jagdgeschwader* is a thorn in [Bufe's] side, as from the beginning I have not engaged in routine barricade flights. So now he uses the opportunity of my being sick and issues the idiotic orders [regarding] how the *Geschwader* should fly, how the take-off preparations should go, etc., as if he were the *Kommandeur* of the *Geschwader*.

I can assure you it is no fun these days to be leader of a *Jagdstaffel* or in this *Armee*. In the 6. *Armee*, after all, I had the good [*Hptmn* Max] Sorg, who had no grasp at all of the fighter sortie and the mission of a *Jagdstaffel*. This Bufe is prejudiced in such a way that it is absolutely impossible to deal with him. The [lack of] success is also strikingly clear. For [the past] three days the British have done what they want. They come over, fly wherever they want and absolutely dominate the air [and], not just over their lines, oh no, they dominate the air far over the countryside. Almost none at all are shot down, in any case [few] in proportion to the masses [of aircraft deployed] ...

Now comes a matter that I want to discuss with you: Our aircraft, quite frankly, are ridiculously inferior to British [aircraft]. The [Sopwith] Triplane and 200hp SPAD, as well as the Sopwith [Camel] single-seater, play with our [Albatros] D.V. In addition to having better-quality aircraft, they have far more [of them]. Our really good fighter pilots are lost in this manner. The D.V is so far surpassed by and so ridiculously inferior to the British single-seaters that one cannot begin to do anything with [the D.V]. But the people at home have brought out no new machines for almost a year, [only] these lousy Albatroses, and have remained stuck with the Albatros D.III [types], in which I fought in the autumn of last year.[61]

Richthofen complained that the Albatros company was so firmly entrenched as a supplier of fighter aircraft that it was no longer competitive. He was well-informed enough to know that Anthony Fokker's designers had produced a fighter biplane which, although faster and more manoeuvrable than the Albatros D.V, still had not gone into production. Promising reports about a Fokker triplane only confirmed Richthofen's fears of a lethargic Albatros monopoly. A contract for 20 Fokker triplanes had been signed on 14 July 1917,[62] but such a small order hardly signalled the re-emergence of Fokker fighters. *JG I*'s success with the Fokker triplane would do that.

Manfred von Richthofen was making good progress in his convalescence, but he was impatient to return to the Front. He tried not to be influenced by his own condition, exacerbated by night-time British, French and Belgian air raids and daytime traffic noises, but perhaps unconsciously hinted at that possibility in the conclusion of his letter to Fritz von Falkenhayn: 'This letter is not something from overwrought nerves or the boredom that torments me amply [as I lie] here in bed. Also it is no momentary irritation or personal antipathy against certain people; rather, I want only to bring to your attention the conditions in this *Armee*.'[63]

A FANCIFUL TALE

Rittm Manfred *Frhr* von Richthofen finally returned to Marckebeke and resumed command of *Jagdgeschwader I* on Wednesday 25 July, 1917. Before that he had made only brief visits to his comrades to break the boredom of hospital life.

On one occasion *Obltn* Bodenschatz brought Manfred from the hospital to *JG I*'s airfield accompanied by old *Maj* von Richthofen, *Ltn* Kurt Wolff and nurse Kätie Otersdorf. The *Kommandeur* was a 20th-century man with 19th-century ideals, as demonstrated by his visible displeasure at having to expose a woman to the dangers of the Front. Bodenschatz recalled that, for her part, 'the nurse ... paid little notice that the *Rittmeister* grimaced. Showing up at an aviation facility with a nurse was not at all to his liking. But he was up against a brick wall. The nurse declared sternly that if the *Rittmeister* should try to make any mischief with his head still not completely healed, she would be there.'[64]

Richthofen's bruised sense of chivalry was assuaged during the 15-minute ride to the airfield when he was spotted by a long column of infantrymen heading back to Courtrai. As soon as one soldier recognized the officer in the uhlan jacket with the white head bandage and *Pour le Mérite*, he cried out: 'Richthofen!' The word spread faster than Bodenschatz could drive, and the great fighter ace was the object of waves, smiles and hurrahs from marching soldiers and lorry drivers alike.[65]

The *Kommandeur* welcomed all forms of adulation and, even though he was in no condition to fly at the time of the alleged incident, Richthofen liked to tell how he earned the gratitude of the people of Courtrai by shooting down one of the night marauders that interrupted their sleep and damaged their city.

According to Richthofen, one evening in 'about mid-July' he saw a local home take a direct hit, killing at least fifteen Belgian inhabitants. Despite the public outcry against the night raiders, Richthofen wrote: 'A lot of people still had faith in these impudent bomb-flingers and so early one morning I shot down one such ugly customer. He came down just outside of Courtrai and once again caused considerable devastation among the residents of that area. One crewman was dead, the other had been slightly wounded; he was brought to a hospital in Courtrai.'[66]

Possibly the wounded flyer had been brought to St Nicholas' Hospital, where Richthofen witnessed the following day's event. Area residents were outraged when they learned that this prisoner was not only a Belgian, but a Courtrai native, using his familiarity with his home town to select his targets. A large group of men marched on the hospital and demanded that the culprit be handed over to them.

'Of course, when that was denied them, the anger of the residents only rose,' Richthofen wrote. 'Then they asked permission to at least give a standing ovation to their saviour, namely myself, because I had shot down this fellow.'[67]

JG I HOLDS ITS OWN

Manfred von Richthofen returned to *JG I* bearing good news. He told his assembled pilots: 'You will receive new Fokker triplanes, [which] climb like apes and are as manoeuvrable as the devil'.[68] He received good news in return. Among reports that elicited the warm smile that Richthofen's men treasured was one of an encounter with Sopwith Triplanes of No.10 Squadron, RNAS, on 22 July in which *Ltn* Otto Brauneck scored his tenth victory.[69] In the same fight *Obltn* Wilhelm Reinhard also tangled with the Triplanes, but was credited only with shooting down a Sopwith two-seater, his first victory.[70] And the evening before Richthofen's return, *Jasta 4* leader *Obltn* Ernst *Frhr* von Althaus achieved his ninth aerial victory. The *Pour le Mérite* ace shot down one of the new Sopwith F.1 Camels of No.70 Squadron southeast of Moorslede.[71] Althaus' opposite number, Capt Noel W.W. Webb (also an eight-victory ace), tried to protect the new man, but was himself attacked by an Albatros.[72]

The day after Richthofen's return, Capt Webb evened the score. He was part of a large formation of S.E.5s, Sopwith Pups, Sopwith Camels and SPADs of the 9th Wing, RFC, that fought with a big German fighter formation over Polygon Wood.[73] Webb dived on an Albatros and sent it down south of Zonnebeke, just inside the German forward lines. Webb's ninth aerial victory was an Albatros flown by *Ltn.d.Res* Otto Brauneck, who was killed.[74] His body was recovered by his mechanic, *Gefr* Schaeffler, and an assistant and sent back to his home town in the Saarland for burial.[75]

Manfred von Richthofen could only watch from the ground as wave after wave of his Albatroses headed for the Front. In some cases he watched old comrades depart for the last time, as on the morning of 28 July, when 22-year-old *Ltn.d.Res* Alfred Niederhoff of *Jasta 11* took off in search of his eighth victory and was, instead, shot down and killed east of Ypres at noon.[76]

Later the same day, however, Richthofen exulted in triumph as reports came in that *Obltn* Eduard Dostler and his *Jasta 6* flight had shot down six British aircraft attacking Ingelmünster, north of Courtrai.[77]

Almost three years of war had hardened Manfred von Richthofen to such events as the loss of Niederhoff; hence, on balance, the 28 July victory log exemplified what the *Geschwader-Kommandeur* expected of his units.

Richthofen was also pleased with the recognition his men were receiving. The day before, *Obltn* Dostler had been awarded the Knight's Cross of the Royal House Order of Hohenzollern with Swords, the *de facto* prerequisite for receiving Prussia's premier award for bravery, the *Pour le Mérite*. And, as was learned subsequently, on that date another participant in the fight with No.57 Squadron, *Ltn der Landwehr* Hans Adam, became the third aviator to be awarded the Kingdom of Bavaria's highest bravery honour, the *Ritterkreuz des Militär-Max-Joseph-Ordens* (Knight's Cross of the Military Order of Max Joseph).[78] That high distinction was presented primarily to Bavarians, and was thereby denied to Silesian-born Manfred von Richthofen.[79]

The festive occasion at *JG I* was disrupted shortly after midnight when F.E.2bs of No.100 Squadron bombed Marcke airfield. They reported: 'von Richthofen's hangars are believed to have been hit'[80]; actual damage recorded was roofs blown off some neighbouring houses and windows smashed in others.[81] But the message was clear: the RFC knew where Richthofen was and they were out to get him, his men and his equipment.

WERNER VOSS JOINS *JG I*

The following morning a quiet change of command took place. *Obltn* Ernst *Frhr* von Althaus was transferred to *Jastaschule II* (Fighter Pilot School No.2) in Valenciennes. Even though he had scored one more aerial victory while commanding *Jasta 10*, Althaus was not the inspirational leader that Richthofen wanted. Further, his tendency to fly alone[82] — harking back to the earlier successes that had earned him the *Pour le Mérite* — contradicted the mass aerial attack tactics that Richthofen instilled in his pilots. Richthofen could not condone having his tactics disregarded, even by a famous pioneer fighter pilot. Unbeknownst to Richthofen, at the young age of 27 Althaus' eyesight had already begun to fail; subsequently, he was reassigned from the air service to the ground forces and eventually became completely blind. Being posted out of *Jasta 10* probably saved Althaus' life.

Althaus was succeeded by 20-year-old *Ltn* Werner Voss, by now a 34-victory ace, recipient of the *Pour le Mérite*, and clearly Manfred von Richthofen's keenest competitor for the title of highest-scoring German fighter pilot.

Richthofen knew from their days together in *Jasta Boelcke* that Voss' aggressive fighting style and sense of purpose matched his own. Moreover, despite his youth, Voss had command experience, albeit fast-paced. On 20 May 1917 he became acting leader of *Jasta 5* following the death of 38-year-old *Hptmn* Hans von Hünerbein; on 28 June Voss was placed in charge of *Jasta 29*; five days later he was switched to *Jasta 14*, from whence he moved to *Jasta 10*. Voss was so highly regarded by the Inspectorate of Military Aviation that he was recalled from the Front in 'late June/early July 1917' to test-fly the Fokker V 4 prototype triplane.[83] His reports of the new fighter convinced Richthofen that the triplane would help *JG I* regain aerial superiority.

Werner Voss hailed from Krefeld, the home town of Manfred von Richthofen's late friend and protegé Karl-Emil Schäfer. Indeed, Richthofen had been a guest at the Voss home while Werner was still temporarily in charge of *Jasta 5*. Richthofen enjoyed the hospitality and the Voss family friends he met. His thank-you note of 19 June 1917 to Max Voss was a peculiar jumble of cordiality, business and the less-than-adroit way Richthofen fell into in matters pertaining to women:

> I would be grateful if I could learn the addresses of both of the charming young ladies.
>
> I think that within eight to fourteen days Werner will also become leader of a *Jagdstaffel*.
>
> I have again taken command of my *Staffel* and feel very happy. Yesterday [I shot down] Number 53.
>
> With best greetings and a kiss on the hand to your good wife...[84]

Manfred von Richthofen enjoyed mixing social life and the business of air combat. In this case, it was as if he sensed that the day would come when he would be able to draw Werner Voss into his own circle of war-birds. The need to replace Ernst von Althaus with a pilot of equal stature was the perfect excuse, and Werner Voss arrived just in time.

At 0350 the following day the great conflict that came to be known as the Third Battle of Ypres began. A massive combined British-French operation, supported by large formations of aircraft flying under a dull cloud cover, made great advances against German positions along the Flanders Front.[85] Many low-flying two-seat trench-strafers and close-reconnaissance aircraft were precisely the targets that Manfred von Richthofen felt his combined *Staffeln* could annihilate.

He needed only the opportunity to prove it.

NOTES

1   Schäfer, *Vom Jäger zum Flieger*, (1918), p.16.

2   von Richthofen, *Mein Kriegstagebuch*, (1937), p.141.

3   von Richthofen, *Ein Heldenleben*, (1920), p.333.

4   *Kofl 6. Armee Wochenbericht Nr 469 I, Teil 4*, 8 June 1917.

5   Ibid., *Teil 1*.

6   *Ein Heldenleben*, op.cit., p.144.

7   *Kriegs-Echo Nr 60*, 30 September 1915, p.12.

8   *Obltn* Fritz von Falkenhayn, son of the previous Chief of the General Staff and a military pilot since May 1914, went on to become the Technical Officer on the staff of the Commanding General of the Air Force (*Kogenluft*); he became a close personal friend of Manfred von Richthofen.

9   *Ein Heldenleben*, op.cit., pp.145-146.

10   Quoted in Gibbons, *The Red Knight of Germany*, (1927), p.278; Lts R.W. Ellis and H.C. Barlow (KiA).

11   *Ein Heldenleben*, op.cit., pp.196-187.

12   Quoted in Gibbons, op.cit., p.281.

13   Evans, *Manfred Freiherr von Richthofen Victory List*, (1992), pp.137-138; a Belgian SPAD of the *5ème Escadrille* and a SPAD of No.23 Squadron are mentioned as remote possibilities, but time and dates do not coincide with Richthofen's report.

14   Quoted in Gibbons, op.cit., p.282, which places the encounter at 2110 on 26 June 1917; *Nachrichtenblatt der Luftstreitkräfte Nr 21*, 19 July 1917, p. 95, and *Kofl 4. Armee* list this victory as occurring twelve hours earlier on 24 June; *RFC Casualty List* offers a match with D.H.4 A7473 of No.57 Squadron, which was witnessed in combat at 0830 British time (0930 German time) over Becelaere; Capt Norman G. McNaughton and Capt Angus H. Mearns (both KiA).

15   Respectively, Sopwith Triplane N5348, Fl-Sub-Lt R.G. Saunders (KiA); Sopwith Triplane N6306, Fl-Sub-Lt A.B. Holcroft (WiA/PoW) [Ref: Collishaw, *Air Command*, (1973), p.100].

16   Quoted in Bodenschatz, *Jagd in Flanderns Himmel* (1935), p.147.

17   von Hoeppner, *Deutschlands Krieg in der Luft*, (1921), p.115.

18   *Nachrichtenblatt*, op.cit.; Lt Leslie S. Bowman and 2/Lt James E. Power-Clutterbuck (both KiA).

19   *Nachrichtenblatt*, op.cit.; Lt Cyril C. Street (KiA).

20   Quoted in Schnitzler, *Carl Allmenröder der Bergische Kampfflieger*, (1927), p.9.

21   O'Connor, *Aviation Awards of Imperial Germany in World War I and the Men Who Earned Them*, vol II, (1990), Appendix XIX.

22   Schnitzler, op.cit.

23   Quoted in *Mein Kriegstagebuch*, op.cit., pp.124-125.

24   Schmeelke, *Leutnant der Reserve Otto Brauneck Part II*, (1986), p.197.

25   Duiven, *German Jasta and Jagdgeschwader Commanding Officers 1916-1918*, (1988), p.152.

26   Quoted in Bodenschatz, op.cit., p.15.

27   *Nachrichtenblatt Nr 24*, 9 August 1917, p.140; R.E.8 A3538, Sgt Hubert A. Whatley and 2/Lt Frank G.B. Pascoe (KiA).

28   Bodenschatz, op.cit., p.147.

29   Ibid., pp.11-13.

30   The meeting must have taken place the evening of 5 July 1917, as the *JG I* war diary in Bodenschatz's book notes (p.148) that *Obltn* von Althaus, newly-appointed leader of *Jasta 10*, was among the new arrivals at Marckebeke on that date; in fact, Althaus was still at *Jasta 14* on 2 July.

31   Ibid., p.16.

32   Ibid., pp.17-18.

33   Ibid., p.147.

34   *Nachrichtenblatt Nr 22*, 26 July 1917, p.142.

35   Ibid..

36   *Ein Heldenleben*, op.cit., pp.147-148.
37   Bodenschatz, op.cit., p.22.
38   Ferko and Grosz, *The Circus Master Falls: Comments on a Newly Discovered Photograph*, (1968), pp.287-288, contend that the aircraft was Albatros D.V 4693/17 (vs. D.V 1177/17, which had a headrest); Grosz revised the opinion (*Over the Front*, Summer 1988, p.183), noting that D.V 4693/17 did not reach the Front until September 1917.
39   Quoted in Gibbons, op.cit., p.292.
40   Shores, et al, *Above the Trenches*, (1990), pp.128-129.
41   *Ein Heldenleben*, op.cit., p.150.
42   *RFC Periodical Summary of Aeronautical Information No 11*, 1 August 1917, p.6.
43   *Ein Heldenleben*, op.cit., p.151.
44   Bodenschatz, op.cit., pp.23, 148.
45   Ibid., p.30.
46   It is likely that *Obltn* Ernst *Freiherr* von Althaus, leader of *Jasta 10*, remained at the airfield to provide command-level leadership in the event *JG I* was called into action again.
47   Ibid., p.23.
48   Ibid.
49   *Nachrichtenblatt Nr 24*, 9 August 1917, p.141.
50   Ibid.
51   Ibid.
52   Ibid.
53   Ibid., which gives 'north of Warneton' as the location.
54   Rogers, *RFC and RAF Casualties 1917-1918*, (1977), p.74.
55   Ibid.
56   Zuerl, *Pour-le-Mérite-Flieger*, (1938), p.482.
57   O'Connor, op.cit., p.93.
58   *RFC Communiqué No. 96*, 15 July 1917, p.4.
59   Ibid., pp.28-29.
60   Richthofen's contention is incorrect. In the days immediately preceding this letter, *Nachrichtenblatt Nr 25*, 16 August 1917, p.157 shows activity on the *4. Armee* Front as follows: one *JG I* victory on 16 July (Adam's sixth) vs two for *Jasta 27* (*Ltn* Hermann Göring's ninth and *Vzfw* Max Krauss' second); two *JG I* victories on 17 July (Tüxen's first and Niederhoff's fifth) vs two for *Jasta 8* (*Vzfw* Rudolf Francke's fourth and *Ltn* Walter Goettsch's thirteenth), one for *Jasta 17* (*Vzfw* Julius Buckler's tenth) and one for *Jasta 20* (*Vzfw* Gustav Beerendonk's first).
61   Letter from the Falkenhayn family via a private source.
62   Ibid.
63   von Falkenhayn, op.cit.
64   Bodenschatz, op.cit., p.32.
65   Ibid.
66   *Ein Heldenleben*, op. cit., pp.151-152.
67   Ibid., p.152.
68   Bodenschatz, op.cit., p.33.
69   Schmeelke, op.cit., p.198 and Shores, op.cit., p.296, indicate that Brauneck most likely shot down Sopwith Triplane N5478, Fl-Lt John A. Page (KiA).
70   *Nachrichtenblatt*, op.cit.; Shores, op.cit., pp.111-112 suggest Reinhard shot down Sopwith 1½ Strutter B2576, Capt Geoffrey Hornblower Cock, M.C., and 2/Lt W.C. Moore (both PoW); Cock had at least thirteen victories to his credit.
71   *Nachrichtenblatt*, op.cit.; Sopwith F.1 Camel B3825, 2/Lt Harlan D. Tapp (KiA).
72   Puglisi, *Enemy Aircraft in German Hands July 1917*, (1976), p.233.
73   *RFC Communiqué No. 98*, 29 July 1917, p.7.
74   Shores, op.cit.
75   Schmeelke, op.cit., p.198.
76   Bodenschatz, op.cit., pp.35, 151; Shores, op.cit., p.127.
77   *Nachrichtenblatt Nr 26*, 23 August 1917, p.173 lists the aircraft types and locations; an eyewitness account from the ground is in the article *Vernichtung eines Bombengeschwaders*

by *Hptmn Ritter* von Mann in Zeidelhack, *Bayerische Flieger im Weltkrieg*, (1919), pp.134-138.

78   O'Connor, *Aviation Awards of Imperial Germany in World War I*, vol I, (1988), p.18.
79   O'Connor, ibid., p.13.
80   *RFC Communiqué*, op.cit., p.4.
81   Bodenschatz, op.cit.
82   Nowarra, *Ernst Freiherr von Althaus*, (1961), p.116.
83   Imrie, *The Fokker Triplane*, (1992), p.16.
84   Letter from the Voss family via a private source.
85   Jones, *The War in the Air*, vol IV, (1934), pp.160-169.

CHAPTER 10

BRITAIN PRESSES THE ATTACK

The Royal Flying Corps owned the skies of Flanders on the morning of 31 July 1917. Undeterred by bad weather, wave after wave of RFC fighters and two-seaters, augmented by Royal Naval Air Service fighters, flew over the front lines, beat back the opposition and inflicted severe damage on German troops, transport and bases.

Inexplicably, *JG I* was not called into action until 1100. Then a report was received: 'an enemy attack is in progress at [Army] *Gruppe Wytschaete*. Infantry lines being penetrated at numerous positions. Troops request air cover. Clouds at 200 to 300 metres.'[1]

Despite the massive British air incursion, Richthofen directed only 'small *Ketten* [flights]' of fighters to respond, instead of a full *Geschwader* flight to sweep the skies. His confidence in the Albatros D.V was probably so low that he chose not to risk too many of his pilots in the face of staggering numbers of enemy aircraft. Yet, of the six aerial victories confirmed for German Army air units that day (all on the *4. Armee* Front), five were credited to *JG I* units.[2]

Manfred von Richthofen was fiercely devoted to the successful men under his command, and encouraged them in every way that he could. He was invited to *Jasta 6*'s mess on the evening of 6 August to celebrate the news that *Obltn* Eduard Dostler had been awarded the *Pour le Mérite* and, when he learned that the decoration itself had not yet reached the 21-victory ace, Richthofen took off his own medal and let Dostler wear it for the occasion.[3]

On 7 August *Ltn* Kurt Wolff was discharged from the hospital in Courtrai[4] and returned to Marckebeke. But, like Richthofen, he was not yet allowed to fly; indeed, Wolff did not return to even nominal command of *Jasta 11*. His old *Staffel* remained under the capable and promising leadership of *Obltn* Wilhelm Reinhard. Richthofen's carefully directed complaints had succeeded in getting *Hptmn* Otto Bufe transferred out of the *4. Armee*, and he could not risk entrusting the prestigious *Jasta 11* to anyone other than a fully qualified commanding officer. The new Officer in Charge of Aviation (*Kofl*) for the *4. Armee*, *Hptmn* Helmuth Wilberg, was a prewar flyer[5] and great admirer of Manfred von Richthofen — a sentiment the *Kommandeur* wanted to preserve.

Richthofen had ways to make his points, however, as demonstrated on 10 August. At 1015 *JG I* was alerted that an F.E.2 formation had crossed the lines. Before his units could take off, however, Richthofen abruptly cancelled the mission. He had to explain this decision, and used his report as another means of expediting the shipment of more and newer aircraft to his *Staffeln*:

> Once again it has been demonstrated that it is pointless to take off against a group that has already broken through.
>
> The reason: The British bombing and reconnaissance aircraft groups now fly over our lines at very high altitudes (4,500 to 5,000 metres). Our machines do not have the climbing ability to reach the enemy in time. It is possible to approach such a group only when the ground observers report them forming up on the other side of the Front.[6]

RICHTHOFEN BACK IN ACTION

On 16 August 1917, 40 days after he was shot down, Manfred von Richthofen climbed into his all-red Albatros D.V 2059/17 and led *JG I* on the morning patrol. The *Kommandeur* was still weak, and his constant headaches were exacerbated by the steady roar of his engine, but he seemed to have lost none of his combat skills, as his combat report shows:

> At about 7:55 a.m., accompanied by four aircraft of *Staffel 11*, I went after a small flight of Nieuports. After a long chase, I attacked an opponent and after a short fight I shot up his engine and fuel tank. The aeroplane went into a spin, [and] I followed right after it until just above the ground, [and] gave it one more shot, so that the aeroplane crashed southwest of Houthulst Forest and went right into the ground. As I was about 50 metres behind him, I passed through a cloud of gas from the explosion that made it hard to see for a brief moment.[7]

Richthofen was credited with his 58th victory.[8] But he was so exhausted from the experience that, upon returning to Marckebeke, he went straight to bed. He was too tired to celebrate his own success or the *Geschwader*'s other three victories, including Werner Voss' 37th. At 2100 Voss shot down a Sopwith single-seater over St Julien, northeast of Ypres. Voss' victim was probably an old adversary of *JG I*, the 14-victory ace Capt Noel W.W. Webb, MC, who was credited with wounding *Ltn* Karl Meyer of *Jasta 11* on 17 July and killing *Ltn.d.Res* Otto Brauneck of the same unit on 26 July.[9]

On the 17th four combat successes were recorded, and the last — a Bristol F.2B brought down near Staden at 2055 by *Jasta 11* newcomer *Ltn* Georg von der Osten as his first kill[10] — became the occasion for some festivities later that evening. *Ltn* von der Osten was, like Richthofen, a Silesian-born former Uhlan; a fortuitous meeting with Richthofen in Breslau two months earlier led to von der Osten's being requested by *Jasta 11*.

Georg von der Osten later recalled: 'On the evening of the same 17 August, *Rittm* von Richthofen suddenly ordered a bottle of champagne and announced that this, my first victory, had been the 200th victory of *Jasta 11*. I would like to add that it was very rarely that we did any drinking in *Jasta 11*, as we always had to keep ourselves ready for action.'[11]

Surely, *JG I*'s less-than-satisfactory performance in recent days made the occasion all the more noteworthy. After ensuring that the good news was sent to the higher commands, Richthofen invited the leaders of the other *Staffeln* to the officers' mess in Marckebeke Castle. He used the occasion to motivate his leaders by sharing the congratulatory messages that he expected to flow in.

Gen von Hoeppner, the *Kogenluft*, was the first to cable: 'After seven months in action, *Jasta 11* today annihilated its 200th opponent. In so doing they captured [a total of] 121 aeroplanes and 196 machine guns.'[12]

Buoyed by support from the top, Richthofen took the opportunity to complain to the officer in charge of aviation for the *4. Armee*:

> The *Geschwader* is being split into individual *Staffeln* for its operations. On days of major combat it is necessary to have several *Staffeln* at the same time in the same place. The *Staffeln* that must provide escorts for the *Kampfstaffeln* [attack units] are drawn away from the *Geschwader* formations for the greater part of the day. A pilot who has already been deployed for protective flights, long-range missions and bombing flights can no longer completely and undividedly fulfil his duty as a fighter pilot on the same day, as he must be completely unfatigued and alert for successful performance in an aerial combat.[13]

His tactic worked. The following day, *JG I* was not ordered to provide escorts for bombers or trench-strafers. Further reinforcement appeared to come when Manfred von Richthofen received another telegram from *Gen* von Hoeppner. At first there was a glow of pride at the old cavalryman's praise of *JG I* and Richthofen's 58th victory. The smile faded with the conclusion: 'I expect that *Rittmeister Freiherr* von Richthofen ... is conscious of the responsibility of the deployment of his person and, until the last traces of his wound are gone, he will fly only when absolute necessity justifies it.'[14]

THE FOKKER TRIPLANES ARRIVE

Gen Erich Ludendorff and his Staff arrived at Marckebeke on 19 August 'to inspect the most audacious pilots in the German Army and to shake their hands'.[15] The only disappointment was that the new Fokker triplanes had not yet arrived at Marcke. They had been promised for over a month, and their development was already known to Germany's enemies. Six weeks earlier, a British intelligence report had contained a very accurate description of the aircraft that Richthofen hoped would turn the tide.[16]

In fact, Fokker triplane development had been progressing as fast as possible. On 16 August the first two prototype V 4 triplanes — designated

F.I 102/17 and 103/17 — had been flown and accepted into service at the Fokker factory in Schwerin. Shortly thereafter the two aircraft were sent to *Armee-Flugpark 4* at Ghent, earmarked for shipment to *JG I*.[17]

When providing air cover for *Kaiser* Wilhelm II's review of the troops at Courtrai on 20 August, however, *JG I* mustered only its Albatroses. Fortunately for the German monarch, enemy air activity around Courtrai was low that day.[18]

Tuesday 21 August was a day of such intense activity that *Jasta 4* was sent to patrol a sector of the adjacent *6. Armee* Front. That development came following the disquieting report that *Obltn* Eduard Dostler, the leader of *Jasta 6*, had failed to return from the morning's operations over Ypres.[19]

Richthofen dispatched several flights to sweep low over the battlefront in hopes of finding some sign of Dostler. Although a later report raised false hopes that Dostler had been taken prisoner, the initial *Kofl 4. Armee* report proved to be correct: 'It is known only that on 21.8.1917 at 11 o'clock British Time (12 o'clock German Time) a British pilot in the vicinity of Frezenberg [northeast of Ypres] brought down a German aeroplane and in all likelihood it lies in the forward-most German lines.'[20]

Although Dostler's Albatros D.Va was not salvaged,[21] it was given the British identification number G64 in the series ordinarily allotted to captured enemy aircraft. Dostler's remains were later recovered and accorded hasty honours disproportionate to the *Jasta 6* leader's ranking as one of the leading German fighter aces of the time. The Kingdom of Bavaria recognized its native son's achievements by posthumously awarding him its highest award for bravery, the Knight's Cross of the Military Max-Joseph Order; the day of Dostler's last aerial combat was listed as the date of his admission to the order.[22]

While *JG I* pilots waited for news in the officers' mess — the same room in which, fifteen days earlier, they had celebrated Dostler's being awarded the *Pour le Mérite* — an important *Kofl 4. Armee* message arrived for Richthofen. It reminded him of his own mortality and high value to the German war effort:

> The opposition is obviously looking after its aviation forces. Similarly, whenever possible, we must do the same during the lull in the fighting.
>
> I refer to the Army Order of 12 August, subparagraph II and, if necessary, request notification in case this aspect is not being sufficiently taken into account.[23]

Cutting through the bureaucratic verbiage, Richthofen understood that 'subparagraph II' virtually prohibited him from flying in combat. He could administer the *Geschwader* and appoint the (then) twelve-victory ace *Ltn* Hans Adam to succeed to the leadership of *Jasta 6* on 22 August. He could graciously accept the Austro-Hungarian Empire's *Eiserne Kronen-Orden III. Klasse mit Kriegsdekoration* (Order of the Iron Crown 3rd Class with War Decoration) and be on hand to congratulate *Ltn* Werner Voss on the occasion of his 38th aerial victory on 23 August. But he was not supposed to fly in combat unless it was absolutely necessary.

RICHTHOFEN'S 59TH VICTORY

JG I was aroused by an early morning raid on 26 August. At 0545 (British Time) a flight of SPAD S.7s of No.19 Squadron, RFC, came in at low altitude over Heule, Bisseghem and Marcke airfields.[24]

Manfred von Richthofen the Prussian soldier would never be insubordinate and disobey a direct order. But Richthofen the air warrior could use this direct assault to justify ignoring the despised 'subparagraph II' and going after his attackers. Thus, after two days of rain and mist had curtailed flying, *Jasta 11* was off in hot pursuit, led by the familiar all-red Albatros.

It was Richthofen's last combat flight in Albatros D.V 2059/17, as the new Fokker triplanes arrived a short time later. In his combat report, he described what happened after he caught up with one of the SPADs at about 0730 over the German advance lines between Poelkapelle and Langemarck, north of Ypres:

> During a fighter sortie with four gentlemen of *Staffel 11* flying at 3,000 metres altitude, I saw beneath me a single SPAD over a solid cloud cover. The opponent was apparently hunting for low-flying artillery-ranging aircraft. I attacked him coming from out of the sun. He tried to escape by diving away, whereby I got a good shot at him and he disappeared into a thin cloud cover. Following behind, I saw him below the cloud cover, diving straight down, [and] then at about 500 metres altitude he exploded in the air. As a result of [my own] new, very bad *Flugzeug-Brand-Munition* [incendiary ammunition], my pressure line, intake-manifold, exhaust manifold, etc. were so badly damaged that I could not pursue even a slightly wounded adversary ... and I knew I had to go into a glide as far from the Front as possible.[25]

Malfunctions often affected aerial combats. Richthofen was lucky that he was able to hit his opponent before his Albatros caught fire owing to the instability of his own incendiary ammunition. His opponent, 2/Lt Collingsby P. Williams of No.19 Squadron, may well have been as much a victim of malfunction as Richthofen's marksmanship and luck. Williams' aircraft, B3492, had been used the day before by Lt R.I. Van Der Byl, who had been forced to return to his airfield at Bailleul moments after take-off because of a leaking oil pipe.[26]

In any event, once again luck had smiled on Manfred von Richthofen and he was credited with his 59th victory. But it was not like the old days, when he flew home in exultation. He was still feeling the effects of his wound, as he described in a letter home two days later: 'I have made only two combat flights [since returning to the Front] and both were successful, but after each flight I was completely exhausted. During the first one I almost got sick in the stomach. My wound is healing frightfully slowly; it is still as big as a five-Mark piece. Yesterday they removed another splinter of bone; I believe it will be the last.'[27]

More bad weather at the end of August gave Richthofen the respite he needed, but seemed to avoid. The arrival, at long last, of the first two Fokker triplanes on 28 August made him all the more eager to get back in the air. During a break in the weather early that evening, *Ltn* Werner Voss flew one of the new aircraft in the vicinity of Marcke so that his comrades in other *Staffeln* could see the triplane put through its paces. *Jasta 11* pilots had already begun the transition from stationary-engined Albatroses to the different flying and handling characteristics of the rotary-engined triplanes by logging time in similarly-engined Fokker D.V biplanes. By all accounts Fokker D.Vs were easy to fly and well suited to this training task.[28]

FIRST FOKKER TRIPLANE VICTORY

Despite generally unfavourable weather, British night bombers attacked German airfields west of Courtrai on the evening of 31 August/1 September. Manfred von Richthofen again used a night-time incursion as an excuse to overlook 'subparagraph II' and to lead his pilots into battle, this time at the controls of Fokker F.I 102/17, one of the two prototype V 4 triplanes assigned to *JG I*. *Ltn* Werner Voss used the other aircraft, F.I 103/17.[29]

Richthofen scored *JG I*'s first victory that day and, as he noted, his adversary may have mistaken him for an RNAS pilot:

> Flying the triplane for the first time [in combat], I and four gentlemen of *Staffel 11* attacked a very courageously flown British artillery-spotting aircraft. I approached [until] it was 50 metres below me and fired twenty shots, whereupon the adversary went down out of control and crashed on this side [of the lines] near Zonnebeke.
>
> Apparently the adversary had taken me for a British triplane, as the observer stood up in his machine without making a move to attack me with his machine gun.[30]

The two-seater was logged as Richthofen's 60th victory.[31]

TRIUMPH AND FORCED LEAVE

Two days later Manfred von Richthofen and Werner Voss flew their Fokker triplanes. They each added a victory to *JG I*'s overall score that day: ten enemy aircraft down and only one of their own number wounded.

The action began about 5km from their own airfield, when *JG I*'s morning patrol jumped a flight of Sopwith Pups of No.46 Squadron over

Menin. The effect was described in a letter written by Lt (later Air Vice-Marshal) Arthur Gould Lee:

> The news is not good. The squadron has taken a hammering ... The first patrol ran quickly into trouble, five of "A" Flight ... met Richthofen's Circus and had a hectic scrap. The Pups were completely outclassed by the [Albatros] D.Vs and most of their share of the fighting consisted of trying to avoid being riddled. Mac [K.W. McDonald] and Bird were seen to go down in Hunland. [Richard] Asher might have reached the Lines. The two chaps who got away, badly shot about, said that one of the Huns was flying a triplane, coloured red. It must be a captured naval Tripe, I suppose.[32]

Ltn Eberhardt Mohnicke shot down the first Pup south of Tenbrielen at 0730 for his sixth victory.[33] A few minutes later *Rittm* von Richthofen concluded a long-running battle with another Pup and forced it to land south of Bousbecque.

In this instance, Richthofen's usual grim determination was tempered by respect for an adversary who put up a good fight, as he observed in his report:

> I was absolutely convinced that in front of me I had a very skilful pilot, who even at 50 metres altitude did not give up, [but] continued to fire and, even when flattening out [before landing] fired at an infantry column, [and] then deliberately steered his machine into a tree. The Fokker triplane F.I 102/17 is absolutely superior to the British Sopwith.[34]

The downed Pup was recorded as Richthofen's 61st victory,[35] and the uninjured pilot, Lt Algernon F. Bird, was taken prisoner. Richthofen hastened to the scene of Bird's crash to gather souvenirs and to be photographed with one of his few unharmed opponents. Aircraft constructor Anthony Fokker, who was at Marcke looking for opportunities to promote his products (and himself), arrived at the site shortly thereafter. Fokker brought along his ciné camera to record the confident, easy-smiling Richthofen with his latest victim. Lt Bird's slightly nervous but self-satisfied smile made it clear to the viewer of those scenes that the young Briton knew he had done his duty in firing to the last and rendering his aircraft useless to his enemy, and had survived an encounter with 'the bloody red baron', as Richthofen had become known.

Anthony Fokker's filmed record of events in late August and early September 1917 shows Manfred von Richthofen in his rôle as national hero and proponent of progress in the *Luftstreitkräfte*. He is seen preparing for a flight in Fokker F.I 102/17, even stoically pulling down a leather flying helmet over the bandage on his head. In other scenes Richthofen confidently shows the new aircraft to *Gen-Maj* Friedrich Karl von Lossberg, Chief of Staff for the *4. Armee*.[36]

Unseen by the camera, but not unnoticed by Richthofen, was the mounting score of his chief competitor, *Ltn* Werner Voss. Victories 40 and 41 were scored with the new triplane on 5 September. The opportunity for young Voss to match — and perhaps exceed — his mentor's score came closer a day later. Voss recorded his 42nd victory on the late afternoon of 6 September, after Richthofen had been *sent* home on recuperative leave. As *JG I's* adjutant noted: '... on this day, noncompliance with that subparagraph II in the Army Order of 12 July had rather strong consequences: The *Rittmeister* "voluntarily" began a strongly required four-week leave that had been vigorously pushed by everyone in high positions.'[37]

THE PRICE OF GLORY

Manfred von Richthofen went on leave secure in the knowledge that a smooth transition in the command structure placed capable and promising men in charge of *Jagdgeschwader I* and its *Staffeln*. Once again, *Oblt* Kurt von Döring was assigned to leadership, with the title of *stellvertretender Geschwaderführer* (Acting Wing Leader), leaving Richthofen as sole possessor of the mantle of *Kommandeur*. *Oblt* Oskar von Boenigk was named acting leader of *Jasta 4* while Döring served in the higher post. The recent hospitalization of *Oblt* Wilhelm Reinhard resulted in a temporary command shift at *Jasta 11*; six-victory ace *Ltn* Gisbert-Wilhelm Groos was named acting *Staffel* leader until *Ltn* Kurt Wolff returned to active flying.

Bad weather kept *JG I* on the ground for the following two days. By that time *Rittm* von Richthofen had arrived at his destination in the Saxon Duchy of Thuringia. He had been invited by Carl Eduard, the young Duke of Saxe-Coburg-Gotha, to relax at his hunting lodge in Friedrichroda, southwest of Gotha. Even though *Freifrau* von Richthofen awaited her son in Schweidnitz, Manfred simply could not decline this invitation from the first royal house to bestow a high award upon him. Furthermore, of course, hunting was a pleasure never to be missed. For three weeks he left the cares of the Western Front behind him and stalked his prey in the grounds of Reinhardsbrunn Castle.[38]

KURT WOLFF AND THE SECOND TRIPLANE

The second triplane reported by No.70 Squadron on the previous day had been flown by 22-year-old *Ltn* Kurt Wolff, who resumed command of *Jasta 11* on 11 September. He had shared Fokker F.I 102/17 with Manfred von Richthofen[39] and, upon the *Kommandeur's* departure for Germany, had the aircraft to himself.

Wolff, known as '*Wölfchen*' (wolfcub) or the '*zarte Blümlein*' (gentle little flower) owing to his slender, boyish demeanour and mild-mannered good humour, was immensely popular. Despite his youthful, almost frail appearance, Wolff had been the victor in 33 combats. His comrades shared his joy on 12 September when a telegram arrived with the news that *Kaiser* Wilhelm II had had Wolff promoted to *Oberleutnant* in recognition of his outstanding achievements as a fighter pilot. Not overlooking the other star pilot, the Supreme Warlord sent a personally signed photograph to *Ltn* Werner Voss of *Jasta 10*.[40]

These gifts served a purpose. Kurt Wolff was grateful for the promotion and, of course, felt pressured to perform, as he had not scored a victory since 7 July. He wrote to his fiancée: 'I am depressed [about it] only because I receive this honour without having shot down one [more than before]. For until now I have already had the bad luck of scuffling with about twenty Englishmen and have not brought down one of them ...'[41]

On 15 September *Obltn* Kurt Wolff congratulated *Ltn* Georg von der Osten on attaining his third victory, a Sopwith two-seater that had been seen to crash within British lines near Frezenberg.[42] It was their last conversation. Later that afternoon von der Osten followed Wolff, who was again in Fokker triplane F.I 102/17, into an encounter with a flight of Sopwith F.1 Camels over Moorslede, where von der Osten witnessed the death of his *Staffel* leader during a fierce fight.[43]

Wolff's body was recovered from the triplane's wreckage and given a military funeral with full honours befitting a knight of the order *Pour le Mérite*. Following services in St Joseph's Church in Courtrai, Wolff's remains were sent to his parents' home in what was then the German Baltic territory of Memel (today Klaipåda, Lithuania).

WERNER VOSS' LAST FIGHT

Manfred von Richthofen was still hunting in Thuringia when a terse telegram from *JG I* arrived at his home in Schweidnitz on 24 September. It was opened to reveal the news: '*Leutnant* Voss has not returned from a flight, [and he has] probably been killed'.[44]

Later, Richthofen would learn only sketchy details of his chief rival's last fight. The morning before, Werner Voss had led *Jasta 10* against a flight of de Havilland D.H.4s that were bombing German positions in Hooglede, northwest of Roulers. Voss got behind one of the two-seaters and sent it down south of Roulers, thereby scoring his 48th and last aerial victory.[45]

At 1805 Voss again led his *Staffel* into battle. About 90 minutes later he encountered a superior force and was shot down. Although a red-nosed Albatros was seen with Voss initially, there are no *Jasta 10* accounts of their leader's final combat. Only *Ltn.d.Res* Rudolf Wendelmuth of *Jasta 8* reported seeing Voss' Fokker triplane shot down from behind by a 'Sopwith' and then smash into the ground behind British lines, north of Frezenberg.[46]

The story of Werner Voss' demise — nearly legendary for the mixture of recklessness and courage in the face of insurmountable odds — has been told and analyzed before. After a bold ten-minute effort against five S.E.5s of No.56 Squadron, Voss's triplane was hit by 2/Lt Arthur P.F. Rhys-Davids of the same squadron, who had previously driven down a two-seater.[47]

Voss came down on to Plum Farm, about 700m north of Frezenberg. As fighting was still going on in the area, his body was buried near the crash site.[48] The wreckage of Voss' Fokker F.I 103/17 was allotted the captured German aircraft number G72, and provided British intelligence with its first, somewhat imperfect, look at the new aircraft series.

On 25 September *JG I*'s morale was boosted by the return of *Ltn* Lothar von Richthofen. He assumed command of *Jasta 11*,[49] succeeding *Ltn* Gisbert-Wilhelm Groos, who had been wounded in a fight on 14 September. Sense of duty had prompted Groos to remain at Marcke, even though he needed hospital treatment for his wounds. Thus, he was free to depart as *Jasta 11* gloried in the return of one of the Richthofens — 'models of comradeship and gallantry, models of audacity [and] fearlessness, models in every sense of the word,' to quote the *Geschwader* adjutant.[50]

RICHTHOFEN PUBLICLY AND PRIVATELY

Manfred von Richthofen concluded his hunting vacation on 30 September with a hurried note to his mother from the Schloss Hotel in Gotha. Refreshed and too full of life to dwell on the recent bad news, he wrote:

> I am immensely pleased about Lothar's sudden recovery. After my leave, together we can again make it hot for the Englishmen, [as] I am in the same *Staffel* with Lothar.
>
> My bag in the last fourteen days is not bad. A big elk, three very good stags and a ram. I am very proud of this, [as] Papa has shot only three really fit stags in his whole life. I leave for Berlin today and will be with you in a week at the latest.[51]

Emil August Glogau, a passenger on the train from Frankfurt to Berlin, had purchased a copy of *Der rote Kampfflieger* that morning. He never dreamed he would share a first class compartment with the famous flyer. Glogau recorded his brief encounter with Richthofen:

> ... in Gotha a young uhlan officer of acrobatic agility jumped on to the train as it was pulling out, dropped his hunting rifle from his shoulder into the luggage rack of my compartment, pulled the collar of his overcoat up over his chin, settled into the thick seat cushions and in the next moment was fast asleep ... Who could train himself so that in an instant he could transcend the borders of consciousness at will? The

young man must possess strong resolve, I said to myself, but his smooth youthful face seemed to contradict [that notion].

When he got on, did the blonde young man not have good-natured, youthful blue eyes? Was he not deliberate and determined in his movements, [and] vigorous in the way he handled his gun? The squared-off skull and the firmly-set jaw belonged to an eastern German *Junker* [country squire]. But how did worry lines get into this motionless face from cheekbone to chin? Had the war etched these wrinkles into this young officer? Just then I saw the two pips on his shoulder boards. A *Rittmeister*? At 20, at the most 24 years old, a *Rittmeister*? That's it — he got on in Gotha, a Thuringian duchy — [there was] a high award under the collar of his overcoat — therefore, he must be a prince.

Suddenly the eyes popped open ... focused on my luggage rack and sparkled with happiness ... Then he laughed like a rascal who had just been turned loose, turned red like an author who had been published for the first time ... and said: "Oh no, there is the book. It amuses me very much, of course, that all of the travellers buy such a thing ..."

I turned on the overhead light, grabbed the book, opened it to the title page and knew then that I was sitting across from the red battleflier in person, Manfred *Freiherr* von Richthofen.[52]

For the rest of the trip Richthofen entertained his cabin partner with a stream of warm and friendly reminiscences, much to *Herr* Glogau's delight. Glogau did not remember all of them, but he did record one sombre point made by Richthofen:

"'I am after all only a combat pilot," he said, "but Boelcke, he was a hero." With that [Richthofen] tucked the *Pour le Mérite* under his tunic so that the people would not stare at him.'[53]

Later, inside Berlin's cavernous Anhalt Station and back in public view, Richthofen was again a proper and courteous German officer. He offered a formal handshake, bowed slightly and clicked his heels. Then, with a boyish cheery wave, the *Rittmeister* disappeared into the crowd.

Manfred von Richthofen had many contacts in the German capital and never lacked for things to do. Any of the aircraft companies would have gladly entertained him in grand style. But he felt most comfortable with the people he knew before he had achieved his celebrity status. One old friend who hosted him many times in Berlin, *Hptmn* Erich von Salzmann, recalled the private Richthofen:

We sat together during regimental dinners complete with exquisite music. On those occasions, of course, there were drinks. Following the good old Silesian tradition we clinked our goblets together and had a fine time ... Later, Richthofen was with ladies repeatedly at my home in Berlin. There, too, [he showed] the flawless manner, the naturalness that women liked so much. He was not a ladies' man in the well-known sense of the word. He was anything but that. He was almost the personification of modern manliness, [and] the ladies liked him, even though he did not court them in every way as did many of the young cavaliers who had become famous.

Once we were together at the races in [the Berlin section] Grunewald and for a while he remained unnoticed. That morning he had been at Johannisthal, had test flown some new aircraft and his "dress" was not really very elegant racecourse attire. In general, Richthofen was little inclined toward superficial appearances, although he did not seek to neglect the way he looked. Suddenly people recognized him. Then the photographers came. I have seen other young celebrities in such moments, as they put on airs and posed. None of that for Richthofen. His complete self-confidence was obvious. The young girls rushed toward him. He was asked to sign their programs as souvenirs.

Richthofen shrugged his shoulders and said to me: "What else should I do?". Anyone else would have gone off. Richthofen signed calmly, patiently, always with the same friendly smile ...[54]

Recognition also came in other forms, as various entities linked themselves to Manfred von Richthofen by presenting him with awards normally reserved for their own fighting men. Thus, while he was in Berlin, he was notified that, on 22 September, the city-state of Lübeck had conferred its Hanseatic Cross on him. Two days later, Duke Ernst August of Braunschweig and Lüneburg awarded Richthofen his court's *Kriegsverdienstkreuz* (War Merit Cross). And, ever mindful of Richthofen's value as an example of Prussian soldiery, *Kaiser* Wilhelm II sent a bronze bust of himself with the engraved inscription: 'To the praiseworthy combat flyer *Rittmeister Freiherr* von Richthofen [from] his grateful king. 10.9.17.'[55]

RETURN TO SCHWEIDNITZ

Richthofen's stay in Berlin was brief, and on Monday 9 October[56] he was spared the long train ride to Schweidnitz, as the two-seat reconnaissance aircraft he had used in the past was placed at his disposal. Now painted red, the aircraft was instantly recognizable. As he circled Schweidnitz at about 1800 hours, townspeople waved to him and then headed for the parade ground, which had been cleared for his landing. The noise of the crowd drowned out the sound of his engine.

Cheers and good wishes were not enough to settle *Freifrau* von Richthofen's concerns about her eldest son's health. Manfred's wound was deeper than she had thought, and she was distressed to notice that the hair on his head was thinner. She wrote: '... To my horror I have ascertained that Manfred's head injury has not yet healed. The bone is still exposed. Day after day he goes to a local medical aid station to have his bandage changed. He does not look good and is irritable. Previously, it seemed to me that he was like young Siegfried, the invulnerable.'[57]

Later, *Freifrau* von Richthofen asked him to give up flying. He responded: 'Who would fight the war if we all thought like that? Only the soldier in the trenches? When the professional fails at leadership, it will soon be as it is in Russia.'

'But the soldier is relieved of duty from time to time and goes to a rest area, while every day you repeatedly endure the most dangerous duels at 5,000 metres altitude,' his mother responded.

Impatient with this line of questioning, Manfred snapped: 'Would it please you if I were in some safe place and resting on my laurels?'[58]

Obviously, no one knows what Manfred von Richthofen's inner thoughts were. He was a very private person and kept his deepest introspections to himself. But there are enough clues from those around him — particularly his mother — to see a pattern of emotional depression; he seemed locked in the inner turmoil of a need to recuperate versus a guilt-driven compulsion to return to the Front, where he felt his presence could bring some relief to the beleaguered men in the trenches.

Freifrau von Richthofen recalled that one evening after dinner Manfred had such a severe headache that he went to bed. A short time later the members of a local club appeared on Striegauer Strasse, in front of the house, to praise the great hero.

His mother wrote:

> ... my husband had to go upstairs and wake him. A few minutes later he appeared — with a [dour] expression — at the doorway. He was almost unfriendly. He didn't care to accept the ovation. He could hardly conceal his foul mood, even though all eyes were on him [as if] spellbound.
>
> I felt sorry for the people and asked if he would be a little friendlier the next time. Manfred bolted up with an almost brusque movement, his eyes narrowed and hard [and said]: "When I fly out over the fortified trenches and the soldiers shout joyfully at me and I look into their grey faces, worn from hunger, sleeplessness and battle — then I am glad, then something rejoices within me. You should see it; often they forget all danger, jump out on to the roofing, swing their rifles and wave to me. That is my reward, Mother, my nicest reward!"[59]

An invitation to visit the War College in Danzig came as a blessed relief. Richthofen could relax during the long ride north to the port city, where he would again be amongst the uniformed people with whom he was most comfortable. From Danzig it was an easy ride along the Baltic coast, past Königsberg, to Labiau in East Prussia (now Polessk in the Kaliningrad Oblast of Russia). He had been invited to the Neu-Sternberg game preserve in the vast forest and swampland along the Deime River.

After tramping through the marshes and woods for six days, Richthofen finally obtained a clear shot at an enormous elk. The first shot hit the animal, but he did not fall. Richthofen quickly reloaded and fired again. With two bullets in it, the elk charged off into the underbrush. Richthofen was right behind him. 'The stag had both bullets in him, so someone had to administer the *coup de grâce*,' the hunter later recalled.[60] Richthofen caught up with the magnificent beast and put an end to him.

RICHTHOFEN AND THE WEDDING

Fresh from that triumph, Manfred von Richthofen headed back to Reinhardsbrunn Castle in Thuringia. Not for more hunting, but this time to attend the wedding of his friend *Hptmn* Fritz Prestien on 18 October. At 30, Prestien was of a proper age to marry; he had joined the army at seventeen, attained his current rank at 28, and showed great promise as a career officer.[61] He was a native of Gotha, and his marriage to Wally von Minckwitz, daughter of Hans Friedrich August von Minckwitz, Chief Property Manager of the Court of Saxe-Coburg-Gotha, would have been favourably received in local society.

Richthofen had known Prestien since their days together in *Kampfgeschwader 2* on the Verdun Front in 1916, and was acquainted with his friend's prospective father-in-law from visits to Reinhardsbrunn Castle. And it was Manfred von Richthofen's good fortune that Fritz Prestien was then on the staff of the Inspectorate of Military Aviation (*Idflieg*) in Berlin.

An article in the Silesian newspaper *Schlesische Zeitung* reported: 'The ceremony was performed by Chief Court Pastor [Gustav] Scholz from Gotha. At the ceremony were about 30 persons, among others the Duke of Saxe-Coburg-Gotha together with his consort [Duchess Viktoria Adelheid], State Secretary [Hans Barthold] von Bassewitz and several aviation officers.'[62]

Richthofen's attendance at Prestien's wedding excited — and confused — a journalist for the *Gothaisches Tageblatt*, who reported that it was Manfred von Richthofen who had married *Fräulein* von Minckwitz. The story made headlines all over Germany. In Schweidnitz, *Freifrau* von Richthofen had to assure relatives and friends that Manfred had not done something rash,[63] quite out of keeping with his newly-gained station in life. In Berlin, when Richthofen returned to his room at the Hotel Continental, he was greeted by many well-wishers and congratulatory telegrams.

News of the supposed wedding spread even to the rear areas of the battlefield. Hence, *Maj* Albrecht *Frhr* von Richthofen received so many comments that he thought the story was true. Later he said that, with Manfred's eager acceptance of modern ways, it would not be surprising to learn that the young man had married without consulting his father.

Manfred later wrote: 'But, finally, he completely agreed that I was in no position to get married, for he was of the conviction that it would have been somewhat premature. I, myself, could imagine quite well enjoying my life as a carefree bachelor right up to the blessed end.'[64]

Despite that contention, there is a tantalizing clue that he had a serious romantic interest. He confided much to his mother, apparently including the secret in his heart. *Freifrau* von Richthofen has been quoted as saying: 'Manfred loved this one girl. He had for her the love of an honourable man for the woman he wanted to be the mother of his children. I know that she loved him.'[65]

Manfred could be happy for his friend Fritz Prestien, then holding a relatively safe job in Berlin. But what if he were to be recalled to the Front (as Prestien later was)? No, that was not for Manfred, whose total self-control kept him sharply focused on his military mission. 'I cannot indulge myself in the right of marriage as long as I am liable to die any day,' he said.[66]

BACK TO THE FRONT

The fuss and rumours made the *Rittmeister* all the more eager to return to his command. The first batch of Fokker Dr.Is was then en route to *Jasta 11*[67] and, as the only combat leader with triplane experience, Richthofen wanted to help prepare his pilots for their first operational flights in the new fighters.

The comforts of Berlin did not appeal to him. Nor was Richthofen greatly moved when the Principality of Schaumburg-Lippe presented him with its *Kreuz für treue Dienst* (Cross for Faithful Service) on 10 October. The neighbouring Principality of Lippe-Detmold awarded its *Kriegsehrenkreuz für Heldenmütigkeit* (War Honour Cross for Valour) three days later.[68] Both were received graciously, but Manfred von Richthofen's place was not at elegant award ceremonies and social gatherings. It was at the Front.

Geschwader-Kommandeur von Richthofen was a happier man on 23 October, when he arrived at Marckebeke and found that a brand new aircraft, Fokker Dr.I 114/17, was being prepared for him.

NOTES

1   Bodenschatz, *Jagd in Flanderns Himmel*, (1935), p.152.
2   *Nachrichtenblatt der Luftstreitkräfte Nr 26*, 23 August 1917, p.174; the other confirmed victory was attributed to *Jasta 8* and two other claims were noted as 'not yet decided'.
3   O'Connor, *Aviation Awards of Imperial Germany in World War I*, vol I, (1988), p.39.
4   Zuerl, *Pour-le-Mérite-Flieger*, (1938), p.482.
5   Supf, *Das Buch der deutschen Fluggeschichte*, vol I, (1956), p.562; on 15 September 1910 Wilberg qualified for *DLV* licence No.26.
6   Bodenschatz, op.cit., p.153.
7   Quoted in ibid., p.38.
8   *Nachrichtenblatt Nr 30*, 20 September 1917, p.247; Bodenschatz, op.cit., p.153; Nieuport 23 A6611, 2/Lt William H.T. Williams (KiA).
9   Shores, et al, *Above the Trenches*, (1990), p.378; other sources credit Voss with shooting down a D.H.5 of No.32 Squadron, but Voss' claim of a Sopwith is reinforced by the *RFC Casualty List* entry for this date, which records that Capt Webb in Sopwith F.1 Camel B3756 was 'last seen diving on E.A. over Polygon Wood at 4,000ft about 7-45pm [British Time].' Capt Webb was KiA.

10   *Nachrichtenblatt*, op.cit, possibly F.2B A7201 of No 22 Squadron, 2/Lt R.S. Phelan (PoW) and Lt L.J. MacFarlane (DoW); *RFC Casualty List* notes this aircraft 'left aerodrome 6pm and was last seen side-slipping through clouds at 8 pm [British Time; 2100 German Time].'

11   von der Osten, *Memoirs of World War I With Jagdstaffeln 11 and 4*, (1974), p.221.

12   Quoted in Bodenschatz, op.cit., p.39.

13   Ibid., pp.39-40.

14   Ibid., p.40.

15   Bodenschatz, op.cit., pp.41, 154.

16   *Periodical Summary of Aeronautical Information No 7*, 2 July 1917, p.7.

17   Grosz and Ferko, *The Fokker Dr.I: A Reappraisal*, (1978), p.18.

18   Bodenschatz, op.cit.

19   Ibid.

20   Ibid.

21   Robertson, *British Military Aircraft Serials*, (1971), p.86 notes that G64 was 'found to be [with]in enemy lines'.

22   O'Connor, op. cit., p.43; this pilot is often erroneously referred to as Eduard *Ritter* von Dostler, a title he was not able to use in life.

23   Bodenschatz, op.cit., pp.41-42.

24   No.19 Squadron Combat Report, 26 August 1917.

25   Bodenschatz, op.cit., p.42.

26   No.19 Squadron Record Book entry, 25 August 1917.

27   von Richthofen, *Ein Heldenleben*, (1920), p.198.

28   Imrie, *The Fokker Triplane*, (1992), p.15.

29   Ibid., p.37.

30   Bodenschatz, op.cit., p.43.

31   *Nachrichtenblatt Nr 33*, 11 October 1917, p.306; R.E.8 B782 of No.6 Squadron, 2/Lt J.B.C. Madge (PoW) and 2/Lt Walter Kember (KiA).

32   Lee, *No Parachute*, (1970), p.108; the author must have added the triplane's colour to the account later, as Fokker F.I 102/17 was *not* painted red; rather, it was flown in the original factory finish, described as 'greenish grey' upper surfaces and 'greyish blue' under surfaces (Ref: Leaman and Gerrard, *Fokker Fabric*, (1975), p.110).

33   *Nachrichtenblatt*, op.cit.; Sopwith Pup B1754, Lt K.W. McDonald, DoW.

34   Bodenschatz, op.cit.

35   *Nachrichtenblatt*, op.cit.; Sopwith Pup B1795.

36   *Kriegs-Echo Nr 105*, 12 October 1917, pp.859-861.

37   Bodenschatz, op.cit., pp.44, 156.

38   *Ein Heldenleben*, op. cit., p.330.

39   Imrie, op.cit., p.37.

40   Bodenschatz, op.cit,

41   Ibid.

42   Bodenschatz, op.cit., p.157; von der Osten, op. cit., p.222.

43   Bodenschatz, ibid.

44   Ibid., pp.47, 159.

45   Ibid., pp.46, 159; D.H.4 A7643 of No.57 Squadron (presentation aircraft 'South Africa' (Ref: Vann and Waugh, *Overseas and United Kingdom Presentation Aircraft 1914-18*, (1983), p.88)), 2/Lts S.L.J. Bramley and J.M. DeLacey (both KiA).

46   Ibid., pp.47-49.

47   *RFC Communiqué*, op.cit., p.9.

48   Revell, *Aftermath*, (1975), p.105.

49   Bodenschatz, op.cit., pp.49, 159.

50   Ibid., p.54.

51   *Ein Heldenleben*, op.cit., p.199.

52   Quoted in Ibid, pp.328-330.

53   Ibid.

54   Quoted in Ibid, pp.333-334.

55   Bodenschatz, op.cit. p.160.

Right: To capitalize on Lothar von Richthofen receiving the *Pour le Mérite*, an artist modified the most recent portrait photo to show the Lothar wearing the medal; the enhanced photo was issued as a Sanke postcard.

C] von Dühren phot.
BERLIN

Below: At funeral services for *Ltn* Karl Allmenröder, his *Ordenskissen* bearing his *Pour le Mérite* and other awards was given a place of honour in front of the coffin.

Left: Richthofen at the wreckage of his 61st victory, accompanied by Anthony Fokker, wearing the helmet and flying coat of the pilot of Sopwith Pup B1795.

Below left: Anthony Fokker explains aspects of the new Dr.I to *Gen-Maj* Friedrich Karl von Lossberg and Manfred von Richthofen while *Obltn* Karl Bodenschatz and *Ltn* Hans Adam listen.

Right: *Ltn* Kurt Wüsthoff poses alongside Sopwith Triplane N5429 of No. 1 Squadron, RNAS, which was forced down by *Ltn* Carl August von Schoenebeck of *Jasta 11* on 3 September. The pilot, Flt-Sub-Lt John R. Wilford, was taken prisoner.

Right: While at Marcke-beke, *JG I* aircraft escorted bombers and ground-support aircraft of Flanders-based *Kampfgesch-wadern*. Even while Manfred von Richthofen was trying to extricate his units from such duties, he visited *Kagohl* airfields. Here he confers with *Obltn* Rudolf Kleine, *KG 3 Kommandeur*, and his adjutant, *Obltn* Gerlich, at Gontrode. Visible behind Richthofen is the tail of his Albatros D.V 2059/17. The apparently unmarked aircraft at the left, Albatros D.V 1177/17, was red all over, with a red 'wash' over the national markings.

Left: During the 19 August visit to *JG I* by *Gen* Erich Ludendorff and his staff, Manfred von Richthofen's Albatros D.V 2059/17 was prominently displayed at Marcke airfield. Richthofen is seen here saluting the General.

Below left: On 20 August *Kaiser* Wilhelm II inspected the *Geschwader*. The monarch spoke with Richthofen, who still wore bandages from his injuries of more than seven weeks earlier. In the background is *Gen* Friedrich Sixt von Armin, Commander of the *4. Armee*.

Right: Aircraft constructor Anthony Fokker, always interested in maintaining his public presence, was on hand when German Chancellor *Dr* Georg Michaelis visited *JG I* on 25 August 1917. *Gen* Sixt von Armin stands to the Chancellor's left, and over Richthofen's right shoulder is his friend, *Obltn* Fritz von Falkenhayn.

Right: Among the staff officers accompanying *Gen* Sixt von Armin was the Officer in Charge of Aviation, *Hptmn* Helmuth Wilberg, who made his own inspection of *JG I* accompanied by Richthofen and Bodenschatz.

Above: Before returning to the Front, *Rittm* von Richthofen visited the family of Werner Voss (lower left) in Krefeld. The young woman seated above him to his left seems to have been a bit playful and the famed airfighter does not appear to mind. *Frau* Voss (far right), however, casts an enquiring glance.

Below: On 6 July 1917 Manfred von Richthofen is said to have been forced down in Albatros D.V 1177/17, which had an all-red fuselage and wings, with the national markings virtually obliterated by a red 'wash' over them. This view at the crash site, however, shows that the aircraft had the all-red top wing and tail associated with Albatros D.V 4693/17, which is supposed to have arrived later.

Right: When Manfred von Richthofen was first allowed out of St. Nicholas' Hospital in Courtrai, he was accompanied by nurse Kätie Otersdorf. She was as strong-willed as he, and followed strict orders not to let Richthofen do anything to imperil his recovery.

Below: When word was received that *Obltn* Eduard Dostler had been awarded the *Pour le Mérite*, Richthofen made it 'official' by lending the *Jasta 6* leader his own award to wear for the celebration.

Left: Faint national markings visible on the aircraft at left confirm that it is Albatros D.V 1177/17. *KG 3* Gotha G.IV bombers flown over England were housed in the former airship hangar at Gontrode.

Below left: Fokker F.I 103/17, in which *Ltn* Werner Voss was flying as leader of *Jasta 10* when he was killed on Sunday, 23 September 1917.

Below: Lt Arthur P.F. Rhys-Davids alongside S.E.5a B4863 at No. 56 Squadron's aerodrome. He was flying B525 when he shot down and killed *Ltn* Werner Voss.

Left: 2/Lt Wilfred R. May of No. 209 Squadron, RAF, in the Sopwith F.1 Camel (D3326) in which he almost became Richthofen's 81st victim.

Below: Manfred von Richthofen's simple black wood-en coffin is borne with dignity by officers of No. 3 Squadron, AFC, past a guard of honour to Bertan-gles cemetery for the first of its four burials.

Above: *Ltn* Ernst Udet, who emerged as the highest-scoring surviving German ace of the First World War, maintained the Richthofen tradition by flying a succession of red aircraft, such as the Fokker D.VII seen behind him.

Below: The last wartime *Kommandeur* of *JG I*, *Obltn* Hermann Göring (holding Richthofen's *Geschwader* cane), and *Jasta 11* comrades watch practice flights over their airfield. From left are: *Ltn.d.Res* Erich Just, *Ltn.d.Res* Siegfried Gussmann, Wolfram von Richthofen, *Obltn* Erich-Rüdiger von Wedel, Göring, unidentified and *Ltn.d.Res* Julius Schulte-Frohlinde.

Left: Manfred von Richthofen and his dog, Moritz, which he acquired early in his flying career and kept with him up to the time of his death.

Below: 2/Lt David G. ('Tommy') Lewis added the name of his colonial homeland to Sopwith F.1 Camel B7393, which he flew with No. 3 Squadron, RAF. Lewis was in this machine on 20 April 1918, when he was shot down and became Manfred von Richthofen's 80th —and last — aerial victory.

Above: In his final air combat, *Rittm* von Richthofen flew Fokker Dr.I 425/17. He achieved his last two victories in this aircraft, which was dark red on all upper surfaces and had a white rudder. The original *Balkenkreuz* national emblem was subsequently overpainted in a white-bordered Greek Cross design that was specified just before the aircraft was used in combat.

Below: Capt Arthur Roy Brown, DSC of No. 209 Squadron, RAF, and Sopwith F.1 Camel B7270, which he flew when pursuing Manfred von Richthofen on 21 April 1918.

Left: After Fokker triplane problems surfaced, Manfred von Richthofen flew Albatros D.V 4693/17, with red cowling and tail. He is seen here during a refuelling stop at *Marine Feldfl.-Abt 2.*

Centre left: Posing in front of a Pfalz triplane are, from left: *Ltn* Auer, Pfalz construction chief and firm co-owner Ernst Everbusch, *Hptmn* Willy Meyer of *Kogenluft* staff, *Hptmn* Albert Mühlig-Hofmann, *Ltn* Krefft, *Rittm* von Richthofen, *Obltn* Fritz von Falkenhayn of the *Kogenluft* staff, *Jasta 12* leader (and later *JG III Kommandeur*) *Obltn* Adolf *Ritter* von Tutschek, *Dipl-Ing* Ernst Schlegel of the Pfalz testing staff, company founder and co-owner Alfred Everbusch, *Obltn* Rist, an unknown person, and Pfalz test pilot Stuckmann.

Bottom left: Lothar and Manfred von Richthofen (third and fourth from left) attend the aircraft type tests at Adlershof in January 1918. At Manfred's left is *Hptmn* Wagenführ, commander of the *P.u.W.* Next is *Obltn* Fritz von Falkenhayn, who ensured that the noted combat pilot flew the Fokker V 11, which was later put into production as the Fokker D.VII, one of Germany's most successful fighter aircraft of the period.

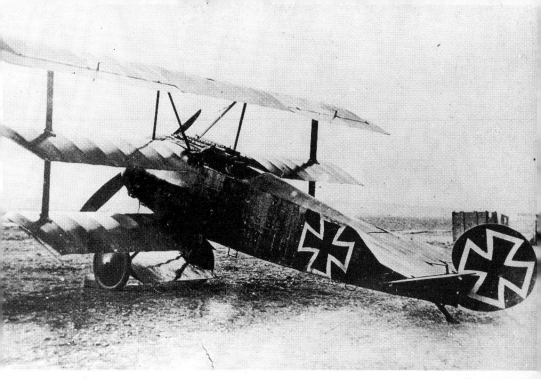

Above: Even though the type was past its prime, Fokker Dr.I 152/17 was supplied to Manfred von Richthofen in advance of the Spring Offensive. The top wing, cowl, tail (from the national marking aft), rudder and wheel covers were painted in Richthofen's favourite shade of red. Other top surfaces had the green-brown 'streak' finish applied at the factory; the undersurfaces were a medium matt blue-green.

Right: As this hospital photo shows, *Ltn* Lothar von Richthofen sustained serious head injuries during his crash of 13 March 1918.

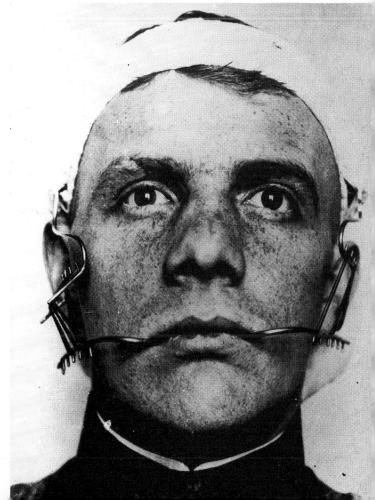

Above: Kunigunde *Freifrau* von Richthofen, centre, accompanied the procession into Berlin's Gnadenkirche for her son Manfred's formal state funeral on 20 November 1925. *Reichspräsident* von Hindenburg wore his Marshal's uniform and dress helmet for the occasion.

Below: The honour guard inside the Gnadenkirche was rotated among *Pour le Mérite* fighter pilots and members of Manfred von Richthofen's old Uhlan regiment. The pilots seen here are former *JG II Kommandeur* Josef Veltjens (37 victories), left, and former *JG I* comrade Kurt Wüsthoff (27 victories). The brown oak casket containing the zinc coffin with the *Kommandeur's* remains was directly behind the *Ordenskissen* bearing all of Richthofen's military awards. The plain wooden cross atop the casket had been the grave marker in Fricourt; it bore only his name and the Graves Commission Registration number 53091.

56   von Richthofen, *Mein Kriegstagebuch*, (1937), p.140; the same text (p.127) gives the date of Manfred von Richthofen's return to Schweidnitz as 17 September, which is not likely, as all other sources indicate he was at *Schloss* Reinhardsbrunn at that time; it is more likely that the events on pp.127 and 140-141 took place during the same period of his leave.

57   Ibid., pp.127-128.

58   Ibid., pp.128-129.

59   Ibid., pp.129-130.

60   *Ein Heldenleben*, op.cit., pp.155-156.

61   Prestien *Personal-Bogen*, (1920), pp.2-3.

62   Quoted in *Mein Kriegstagebuch*, op.cit., p.141.

63   Ibid, p.142.

64   *Ein Heldenleben*, op.cit., p.154.

65   Quoted in Gibbons, *The Red Knight of Germany*, (1927), p.108.

66   Ibid.

67   Imrie, op.cit., p.39.

68   Bodenschatz, op.cit., pp.160, 161.

CHAPTER 11

AIRCRAFT PROBLEMS

T he long-awaited Fokker Dr.I triplanes did not prove to be the 'wonder weapons' that German fighter pilots hoped they would be. Soon after Richthofen's return to the Front, a series of incidents raised questions about the new fighters and their producer, Fokker Aeroplanbau.

First was the sheer bad luck of *Vzfw* Josef Lautenschlager of *Jasta 11*, who was killed while flying Fokker Dr.I 113/17 north of Houthulst Forest on 29 October. His aircraft was apparently mistaken for a Sopwith Triplane and was shot down by an unidentified German fighter aircraft.[1]

Then came an unsettling incident the following day. In their first flight together in over five months, Manfred and Lothar von Richthofen went up in a pair of the new triplanes at the head of *Jasta 11*'s morning flight. Heavy clouds and rain made the flight difficult enough, but then Manfred noticed that his brother's triplane was behaving erratically. He could not tell whether it was just dipping down or beginning to fall apart.

When it became clear that Lothar was going down in a glide with the engine off, Manfred turned back to cover him. Lothar found a flat spot near Zilverberg, just south of Roeselare, and made a smooth, perfect landing. Manfred followed moments later, but was 'the victim of some kind of damned treachery',[2] as his new machine, Fokker Dr.I 114/17, touched down and then crashed. The aircraft was a total wreck, but he emerged unharmed.

Manfred von Richthofen was shocked at the destruction caused by a seemingly minor incident.

A day later, *Ltn.d.Res* Günther Pastor, a veteran of five weeks' service with *Jasta 11*, crashed. He was flying Fokker Dr.I 121/17 when, at about 1520, the top wing structure collapsed and he crashed about a kilometre north of Moorsele, Belgium.[3] Pastor died instantly.

On Friday 2 November, 1917, all Fokker triplanes were grounded pending a complete investigation by the Inspectorate of Aviation Troops. The Inspectorate's *Zentral-Abnahme-Kommission* (Central Acceptance Commission) established a special crash committee under the direction of *Prof Dr.-Ing* Wilhelm Hoff,[4] a distinguished prewar flyer and head of the German Research Institute for Aviation.[5] The committee considered everything from basic design to the quality of construction materials.

On the day the investigation began, the operational loss of the triplanes was minimized by heavy fog and occasional rain, which combined to keep *JG I*'s aircraft within their protective wooden sheds on the airfields around Marcke. When flight operations were resumed the next day, only the *Geschwader*'s Albatroses and new Pfalz D.III biplanes were used.[6]

Manfred von Richthofen was assigned a new aircraft — Albatros D.V 4693/17 — which was distinctive in that it was *not* all red. Photographs of this machine clearly show that only the wings and tail were painted in the deep red associated with the *Kommandeur*. In any event, when Richthofen was able to use the new Albatros, his comrades recognized it easily.

Often, Richthofen was kept out of the air by bad weather, visiting dignitaries or administrative chores. On 4 November, for example, he hosted Turkish General Izet Pasha and *Oberst* Egli of Switzerland. General Izet presented the *Kommandeur* with the Iron Crescent (War Medal) award.[7] Even though Richthofen had not been to Turkey, as had his mentor Oswald Boelcke and his colleague Hans Joachim Buddecke, an appropriate celebration was staged at Castle Marckebeke to place him within the ranks of great German warriors fighting on Turkey's behalf.

Another problem revisited the *Kommandeur* when *Ltn* Erich Loewenhardt, a seven-victory ace with *Jasta 10*, suffered a wing failure on his Albatros D.V on the morning of 6 November. The 20-year-old Silesian-born officer emerged unharmed from the wreckage of an emergency landing at Winkel St Eloi, about 8km from Marcke, but the aircraft was written off. It was bad enough that *JG I*'s aerial victory score was comparatively low; now Richthofen faced the potential problem of having his best available fighter withdrawn, or at least suffering a loss of pilot confidence. That would make him rely on the Pfalz D.III, a sleekly elegant-looking fighter that was reportedly inferior to the Albatros line.[8]

Richthofen's only recourse was to protect his resources. That evening he wrote to Fritz von Falkenhayn in Berlin, asking for help in obtaining 80 flat-roofed wooden sheds, each to house a *Geschwader* aircraft at their new location. He had already identified the construction administration centre in Ghent as having sheds that would protect his aircraft from the weather better than tents. 'Please see what you can do', he implored.[9]

MORE LOSSES

The harsher weather made flying more difficult. Yet, on 9 November, *Ltn* Lothar von Richthofen was credited with shooting down a Bristol F.2B northwest of Zonnebeke; it was his first success as a full-time *Staffel* leader, and his 25th victory.[10]

A thick blanket of fog covered much of the Flanders Front throughout the day on 14 November. When the weather lifted a day later, reconnaissance aircraft from both sides were out in force to gain information. Likewise, fighter aircraft were over the Front to interdict opposing intelligence gatherers. Hence, when *Jasta 6* leader *Ltn* Hans *Ritter* von Adam saw a Rumpler two-seater under attack over Houthulst Forest, he and his six comrades charged into the fray.

They were too late to prevent a Sopwith F.1 Camel of No.45 Squadron from sending the Rumpler down in flames.[11] The Albatroses then went after the five Camels, which were soon joined by a flight of Nieuport 17s from No.29 Squadron. In the mêlée that followed, Albatros D.V 5222/17 went down in flames.[12] Its pilot, 31-year-old *Ritter* von Adam, had been the victor in 21 combats and was the only fighter pilot recipient of Bavaria's *Militär-Max-Joseph-Orden* who did not also receive Prussia's *Pour le Mérite*.[13]

Even though he had lost one of his best *Staffel* leaders, Manfred von Richthofen had no time for grief; a major British land and air attack was a few days away.

THE BATTLE OF CAMBRAI

At 0620 on 20 November, a line of British Mark IV tanks set out to breach German lines from Gonnelieu to Havrincourt. In the absence of a British artillery barrage to signal an offensive, German forces were caught unaware of the enormity of the attack.

The tactic of using tanks followed by infantry was supported by extensive use of air units of the British First and Third Armies, south and southwest of Cambrai.[14] There was little to stop the British aerial onslaught, as the III Brigade 'reinforced for the battle ... possessed a total of 289 aeroplanes, whereas the whole German Second Army, whose right flank only was in the Cambrai area, could count on no more than 78 aeroplanes, of which twelve were fighters [of *Jasta 5* at Estourmel].'[15]

Ground fog that morning freed *JG I* members to attend funeral services for *Ltn* Hans *Ritter* von Adam at the Carmelite Chapel in Courtrai. After the cortège departed and the train was en route to Adam's home in Eisenstein, Bavaria, a lone D.H.4 appeared over the train station at Courtrai and dropped two 112lb bombs. Ironically, the two-seat bomber was from No.57 Squadron,[16] which had been so badly decimated by Adam and his comrades on 7 July.

Two more days of bad weather offered protection to *JG I* during their next change of airfield assignments: *Jasta 11* and the *Geschwader* staff were based at Avesnes le Sec, *Jastas 4* and 6 at Lieu St Amand, and *Jasta 10* at Iwuy — all airfields within 5km of each other. Support equipment was delayed owing to the scarcity of trains and recent air attacks on railway stations in the *4. Armee* sector.[17]

Despite the weather and lack of equipment, *Rittm* von Richthofen led all *2. Armee* fighter squadrons into battle on Friday 23 November. That morning British ground forces, supported by tanks, attacked the village of Fontaine-Notre Dame, just west of the city of Cambrai. The British advance was stalled mainly by German lorries with anti-aircraft guns mounted horizontally as effective anti-tank weapons. Meanwhile, another British division, supported by low-flying fighters from Nos.3, 46 and 64

Squadrons, RFC, and No.68 (Australian) Squadron, had taken Bourlon Wood. *JG I*, joined by *Jastas 5* and *15*, were ordered to clear the skies over Bourlon Wood.[18]

Above Fontaine-Notre Dame, Manfred von Richthofen attacked a D.H.5 fighter and pursued it back over the British lines. According to his combat report: 'After the first shots, the Englishman started to glide downward, but then fell into the south-east corner of Bourlon Wood. I could not observe the aeroplane touching the ground.' Nonetheless, Richthofen was credited with his 62nd victory,[19] which has been documented by official RAF historian H.A. Jones.[20]

Four days of rain provided an ideal cover for *JG I* to complete the move to the new airfields near Cambrai. The lorries had a difficult time of it, threading their way along shell-holed, slippery roads, but bad weather minimized the danger of being strafed by enemy fighters or low-flying two-seaters looking for targets of opportunity.

FINAL HONOURS FOR ERWIN BÖHME

Indications of a German counterattack also included evidence that the *Kommandeur* and his units were in the thick of the fighting. On 29 November near Vendhuille (some 20km south of Cambrai), British ground units were concerned 'by the appearance of many low-flying German aircraft, among which the coloured aeroplanes of the Richthofen "Circus" were said to be conspicuous'.[21]

Also on that day, a package containing a newly-awarded *Pour le Mérite* awaited the return of Manfred von Richthofen's old friend *Ltn.d.Res* Erwin Böhme at *Jasta 2*'s airfield at Bavichove, north of Courtrai. But Böhme, remembered as the pilot who collided with Oswald Boelcke and survived, never lived to wear the coveted 'Blue Max'; he was shot down and killed over Zillebeke while attacking an Armstrong Whitworth F.K.8 photo-reconnaissance two-seater.[22]

Böhme's body was recovered by British ground forces and buried with military honours at a cemetery in Keerselaarhoek.[23] The wreckage of his Albatros D.Va was assigned the British identification number G92, even though it was so badly damaged that the serial number could not be read.[24]

A few days later Richthofen allowed a rare glimpse of emotion — wrapped in the modern Teutonic mythology of which he felt himself to be a part — in his condolence letter to Gerhard Böhme:

> I have just received the painful news of the death of your brother. One becomes firm and hard in war, but this blow hits me right in the heart. You know yourself how close in friendship your brother stood to me.
>
> On the last afternoon before his death, he visited me here at Avesnes le Sec, my new airfield — full of joy about the development of

our dear old *Jagdstaffel Boelcke*, which had been led back to its old heights, singularly and alone due to him.

Now both are united in Valhalla: your splendid brother and his great master, to whom, of all of us, he was closest.

Come and visit me soon, dear *Herr* Böhme, so that we can reflect together on the lost brother and friend.[25]

RICHTHOFEN'S 63RD VICTORY

The German counteroffensive at Cambrai began at 0700 on 30 November. Initially, German fighter aircraft were held back and flights of low-flying two-seaters from *Schutzstaffeln* (Protection Squadrons) came in to bomb and strafe British positions. Later, *Jasta* aircraft were called in to repel RFC fighters.

German troop concentrations on the northern flank between Bourlon and Moeuvres attracted large numbers of British aircraft,[26] five of which were brought down that day by *JG I*. Manfred von Richthofen led the *Geschwader* into battle just after noon and, upon encountering a flight of D.H.5 fighters of No.24 Squadron, stayed above the fray and watched as his young hawks went to work. One of the backstaggered de Havillands was brought down at 1345 by *Ltn* Georg von der Osten of *Jasta 11*, who later recalled of his fourth victory: 'It crashed into the shell-torn ground south of Bourlon Wood. Immediately after the landing, Richthofen congratulated me, but at the same time rebuked me because after my first attack I had not followed the crippled aeroplane into the first turn. I had had to turn away because of the attack by another Englishman who, as we used to say in front-line German, "was spitting into my crate from behind". I mention this to show how closely Richthofen kept watch over the whole battle scene.'[27]

Just west of Bourlon, over Moeuvres, the Germans clashed with a formation of S.E.5a fighters. The fight was concluded quickly, as Richthofen noted:

> With *Ltn* [Lothar] von Richthofen and *Ltn* [Siegfried] Gussmann, at 2:30pm we attacked an enemy single-seater squadron of ten Englishmen, just over the front lines. After I fired at various Englishmen, I came close behind a single-seater, which after [I had fired] 100 rounds crashed in flames in the area of the little wooded quarry.[28]

That encounter was credited as Manfred von Richthofen's 63rd air combat success and his last victory for 1917; he did not score again until March 1918. Some sources have listed Richthofen's victim in that fight as Capt Ronald T. Townsend of No.56 Squadron in S.E.5a B40; however, according to the *RFC Casualty List*, Townsend did not depart Baizieux aerodrome until 1415 (British Time), some 45 minutes *after* Richthofen's adversary fell. It is more likely that Richthofen shot down S.E.5a B644 of

No.41 Squadron, piloted by Lt Donald A.D.I. MacGregor (KiA), who took off from Lealvillers at 1300 (British Time) and was last seen half an hour later, going down in flames near Moeuvres.[29]

The talk in the Mess that evening centered on Richthofen's great score — far exceeding any other fighter pilot's tally —and, at last, 'the telegram' that had arrived for *Ltn* Hans Klein. The 26-year-old Pommeranian had become the 29th fighter pilot and the seventh Richthofen protégé to receive Prussia's highest bravery award, the *Pour le Mérite*.[30]

NEW BLOOD

The example of Hans Klein was further motivation to other young German pilots to seek billets in the *Jagdstaffeln* — and, with luck, a posting to a unit of the *Richthofen-Geschwader*. That good fortune was achieved by *Ltn* Friedrich-Wilhelm Lübbert, who was transferred from *Fl.-Abt. 18* to *Jasta 11* in early December. A successful combat pilot in his own right, Lübbert benefited from further air combat training under Richthofen.

The new pilot had links with *Jasta 11*. His brother, *Ltn* Eduard Lübbert, had been an early *Staffel* member (given the nickname 'bullet catcher'), and had been killed in combat on 30 March 1917. But sentiment alone was no reason for a posting to a *JG I* unit. *Ltn* Friedrich-Wilhelm Lübbert had the additional credentials of having shot down an enemy aircraft as a pilot with *Fl.-Abt. 18*. Further, Lübbert and his observer had been cited for bravery in the weekly *Armee* report.[31] That former observer, *Obltn* Hans-Helmut von Boddien, had been flying with *Jasta 11* since July.

Lübbert recalled of his new leader:

> ... One would think that a man so preoccupied with one of the most strenuous activities there is and who enjoyed the great popularity he did, would have no room within himself for friendship and comradeship. The opposite was the case. Richthofen was just as good a superior officer as a comrade for the officers of his *Staffel* and his *Geschwader*. He associated with us off duty as any other comrade [would]. When we could not fly, he played hockey with us and, in the evenings, often joined in card games. One could go to him with any question and any trouble, and find sympathy and help when they were needed.
>
> Richthofen was unequalled as an instructor. I had been to different flight training facilities and ... I never met an instructor who could make the theory of air fighting technique so clear to me as Richthofen. On every occasion he was ready to answer every question put to him. He especially liked it when his pilots were inquisitive. He never became impatient when our questions were inclined to be elementary or silly. He responded to every one with the greatest patience. Every young pilot who came to his *Staffel* had to fly a few times to the Front alone with Richthofen. After the flight the details of what the beginner had seen and experienced were discussed thoroughly.

Richthofen was very firm on one point: He kept in the *Staffel* only such pilots who really accomplished something. He observed each beginner for a time [and] then if he became convinced that the person concerned was not up to the requirements that Richthofen placed on a fighter pilot —whether due to his moral character or due to his technical ability — that person would surely be sent away ...[32]

Although *Ltn* Friedrich-Wilhelm Lübbert scored no victories with *Jasta 11*, he remained with the unit until he was wounded in an air combat over Rumilly on 17 February 1918. After his convalescence Lübbert did not return to *Jasta 11*.

THE BATTLE ENDS, THE STRUGGLE CONTINUES

The Battle of Cambrai ended with the British withdrawal from hard-won positions in Bourlon on 7 December. In their counteroffensive, German forces used tactics similar to those employed by British troops at the outset of the battle; in both cases low-flying aircraft played a significant rôle.[33]

Further structural problems with the Fokker Dr.I triplane created an opportunity for the Pfalz Flugzeugwerke in Speyer am Rhein, which had also developed a triplane. Thus, Manfred von Richthofen was invited to test-fly the Pfalz Dr.I, which boasted a more powerful engine and a better climb rate than its Fokker counterpart.[34] Richthofen departed Avesnes le Sec on 12 December and returned ten days later, only to report that the more attractive-looking Pfalz Dr.I was disappointing; it did not handle as well as the Fokker Dr.I and its Siemens-Halske Sh III geared rotary engine did not develop the full 160hp claimed by the manufacturer.[35]

The *Kommandeur* could report only that the *Geschwader* would have to make do with its current complement of Albatros and Pfalz biplanes. The new Fokker Dr.Is with modified wings would not arrive until the year's end.[36]

Manfred, Lothar and *Maj* Albrecht von Richthofen spent Christmas together at the Front.[37] Wartime comradeship had given *JG I* a familial quality and, on occasions such as this, *Maj* von Richthofen showed why he was affectionately called the *Fliegervater* (Father of the Flyers) by the men who served under his sons.

Hptmn Wilhelm Reinhard, who subsequently succeeded Manfred von Richthofen as *Geschwader-Kommandeur*, described the old cavalry officer and the points that endeared him to one and all:

> ... Father Richthofen loved his sons equally in an open and sincere manner. In Silesian fashion, he was a bit stand-offish with strangers. He took an especially active interest in aviation and [flying] officers. He never tried to stop his sons [from flying] or warned them to be cautious ... Our *Fliegervater* often sat for hours on end amidst the circle of comrades in the Officers' Mess and let them tell about their air fights. He

enjoyed every daring tid-bit about flying and, as he often was an eyewitness to many fights from the ground, he showed great appreciation of us. He understood our flyers' talk and shared with us the joys and sorrows of fighter pilots.[38]

MISSION TO RUSSIA

Just after Christmas, Manfred and Lothar von Richthofen were on their way to Russia. They had quietly slipped away from Avesnes le Sec to go to Brest-Litovsk at the invitation of *Prinz* Leopold of Bavaria, Commander in Chief of German Forces in the East. The war with Russia was over — following the abdication and subsequent murder of Czar Nikolai II, as well as the failure of the Kerenski government's military actions — and the Central Powers were dictating harsh peace terms to the revolutionary government of V.I. Lenin. The Richthofen brothers were among the celebrities brought to the peace conference in a fruitless attempt to impress the Russian delegation.

Manfred and Lothar spent three-and-a-half days in an unheated railway coach, only to arrive at Brest-Litovsk just as the Russians were returning to Petrograd for consultations with Lenin and his advisors. With little to do in *Prinz* Leopold's headquarters, the brothers eagerly accepted an invitation to go to the virgin forest at Bialowicz, once a crown property of the Romanovs. There they lived in the late Czar's palatial hunting lodge and stalked their choice of a variety of rare species in Europe's last remnant of its former primeval forest.

Manfred von Richthofen lamented the fate of the once large herds of European bison, which had been shot even by German soldiers in the area. He wrote: 'Unfortunately, our hearty troop columns and others have very energetically diminished a stock some 700 head strong and many a bison has ended up in a rifleman's stew pot. Now the herd is estimated at about 150 head. It is a very great pity that this animal has been almost completely exterminated by the war.'[39] As a true hunter, and sharing the German affinity for the forest, Richthofen avoided the few bison he saw and contented himself with bagging a stag.

The Richthofen brothers went back to Brest-Litovsk on 5 January 1918, the day after the Russian delegation returned. They attended some of the plenary sessions of the peace conference, which proved to be boring exchanges of diplomatic formality. The Germans wanted a swift conclusion to the proceedings so that they could begin transferring army and air units to the Western Front in preparation for a massive spring offensive. The Russians were playing for time in the hope that Bolshevism would take root in Germany and they would not have to submit to onerous peace terms.[40]

Attempts to intimidate the Russians by the presence of such German war heroes as the Richthofen brothers failed. Indeed, the Bolshevik delegation to Brest-Litovsk included such formidable revolutionary figures as

Anastasia Bitsenko. Manfred von Richthofen and others were well aware of her rôle in the murder of a Russian general during peasant revolts in 1905, which led to her being characterized as 'a quiet and reserved little grey-haired assassin'.[41] Now, showing the signs of ten years of forced labour in Siberia like a badge of honour, she was a tough-talking member of the Presidium of the Moscow Soviet.

Politics aside, Richthofen would have considered the Bolshevik a worthy adversary in a verbal encounter, as evidenced by his comments about one of the many peace conference dinner parties: 'I almost got *Frau* Bitsenko as a table companion. It would have been a grand, amusing conversation. I would have enjoyed it, for she had also hunted down some of her enemies. Although they were ministers and grand dukes and the like, whom she had had banned to the penal colonies in Siberia, nevertheless, there would have been a common point of conversation [for us].'[42]

THE PUBLIC FIGURE AT WORK

When it became clear that the peace conference would drag on and there was no publicity or propaganda value in keeping Manfred von Richthofen in Brest-Litovsk, he was sent back to Germany. There, he made appearances where his prestige was needed. He performed these tasks gladly, but still felt compelled to explain to his mother why he was not able to spend more free time at home, as noted in his letter of 15 January:

> You will surely wonder why you have been so long without news from me; but that is always a sign that I am well. In this case, to be sure, I have experienced very much. As Lothar has already written to you, we were in Brest-Litovsk. There we saw and met all of the prominent diplomats. I should like so very much to tell you about it myself, [but] in writing only that the peace will be concluded absolutely as Ludendorff intends.
>
> ... Now I am very often in Berlin. From the 20th on, I will be there for fourteen days and then I hope to see you often.[43]

In Germany, Manfred von Richthofen saw signs of the social unrest that the Bolsheviks at Brest-Litovsk had predicted would eventually bring down the German Empire. One recollection of the tight-lipped smile of Anastasia Bitsenko, so pleased at having 'dealt with' former Russian nobility, was enough to make Richthofen keenly aware of the danger to him and the social order he had been fighting to maintain.

He went with a will to munitions factories where workers were on strike to protest against working conditions, food shortages and other problems caused by the long and costly war. Manfred von Richthofen's popularity and personal manner were such that he was a credible representative of the régime. From her conversations with Manfred, his mother recalled:

When he arrived [at the factories] they all rushed up to him and he had to speak to them. Then he made it clear to them just how important their work was and so on. For the most part, they went back to their work. But perhaps they would not do it for long. He was very gloomy on that point. The *Kaiserin* [Empress Auguste Victoria] often went to the striking munitions workers and spoke with the people.

I had the feeling that [Manfred] did not like to talk about such things. I understood that he was a person of duty and discipline, whose whole life was a commitment to self-sacrifice [and] who complied with the government-sponsored tactic of "persuasion" with reluctance.[44]

WITH THE EAGLES IN BERLIN

The *JG I* war diary notes that, on 19 January 1918, Manfred von Richthofen was ordered to Adlershof airfield outside Berlin. Kurt von Döring, meanwhile promoted to *Rittmeister*, assumed command of the *Geschwader*.[45] Adlershof, literally 'eagles court', was home to the former *Prüfanstalt und Werft der Fliegertruppe* (*P.u.W.*, Test Establishment and Workshop of the Aviation Troops). Renamed the *Flugzeugmeisterei* (Aircraft Test Establishment) on 1 January 1917,[46] the Adlershof establishment hosted keen competitions between aircraft manufacturers vying for lucrative production contracts.

Manfred von Richthofen had a hand in having combat-proven frontline pilots evaluate the new aircraft. According to former *JG I* member Richard Wenzl:

These *Typenprüfungen* [aircraft type tests] were an achievement of Richthofen, who was of the viewpoint that not just any old home-front pilot, most of all [not] one working for one of the aircraft companies, should be the man who determines what will be flown at the Front. Thus, representatives from all of the *Jagdstaffeln* at the Front came to these tests. The individual types were test-flown, [and] then the gentlemen agreed amongst themselves on which types were best suited at the moment ...[47]

The January type tests of some 28 aircraft from five different firms[48] were especially important, as they would produce one or more major fighter aircraft to be used during the decisive battles of the spring offensive and beyond.

Former *Jasta 11* member Georg von der Osten also took part in the type tests at Adlershof, flew the Fokker V 11 biplane (later produced as the Fokker D.VII) and recalled one of the lighter moments of the time:

On a rainy day we drove back from Adlershof to Berlin by car. Not much had been accomplished at the tests owing to the rain. On the way Richthofen said, "Well, I will get out here at Schulte's [art gallery] and have a look at the pictures that Reusing has painted!"

Richthofen wore an overcoat with a big collar, typical of the officers' coat that we used to have before the war. As it was raining, it acted like a disguise. He went in [the gallery] and came to the painting that showed him in his plane, captioned *"Rittmeister Freiherr von Richthofen"*.

An elderly gentleman came up and stood beside him. Richthofen said to him: "I beg your pardon, but I am told I have some likeness to this painting!" The gentleman put on his spectacles, took a look at the picture, took a look at Richthofen, and finally said: "I think you can forget that notion."

Ten minutes later, Richthofen joined us at the hotel, beaming with joy, and related the incident to me.[49]

FINAL VISIT TO SCHWEIDNITZ

At the end of January Manfred von Richthofen made what would be his last visit to his home in Silesia. It was almost 1600 when the red aeroplane came into view against the ice-blue winter sky. *Freifrau* von Richthofen, waiting at the edge of the parade ground, was soon joined by Schweidnitz residents who knew from the engine sound that their famous neighbour had come home again.

Richthofen's appearances had become so routine that townspeople seemed to gather out of habit. They waved and cheered, but made no attempt to keep the national hero from his family. Moments after the landing, Manfred von Richthofen and his mother were past the crowds and into their home across the street from the landing field.

Out of the public eye, the great fighter pilot was just a respectful son. And, as he did when he was a boy, he responded quickly to his mother's admonition: 'Come over here, Manfred, and tell me [what you have been doing]'.

His narrative began with the highlight of his two-hour flight from Berlin to Schweidnitz: flying over the Cadet Academy at Wahlstatt, where his youngest brother, Bolko, was following the family tradition. There, the master air tactician violated one of his own rules. Seeing the cadets gathered on the parade ground, Richthofen swooped down and then pulled up into a great loop before continuing on. He told his mother that he could well imagine the boys roaring their approval — and Bolko shouting loudest of all.

Freifrau von Richthofen chided him, and said that Bolko was very disappointed that his famous oldest brother only flew over Wahlstatt and never landed there. In a recent letter Bolko had written: 'Tell Manfred that if he really loves his old Cadet Corps and his brother, then he must land here. If he does not, he is just being mean. Period!'[50]

Bolko would never understand that even famous flyers cannot simply set down wherever they wish. Manfred could only wince in mock anguish.

Later that evening his pain became all too real when he sorted through some photographs he had brought with him from the Front.

One picture showed Manfred and some of his comrades from *Feldfl.-Abt. 69* in Russia. Looking over his shoulder, his mother pointed to one smiling young flyer and asked: 'What has become of him?'

'Fallen in combat.'

She pointed to a second man, to which Manfred replied: 'Also dead'. Before she could enquire further, he said in a voice suddenly hoarse: 'Do not ask any more — they are all dead'.

Then, realizing what must be going through his mother's mind, he quickly reassured her: 'You don't need to worry. In the air I have nothing to fear. In the air. We are ready for them, even when there are many of them. The worst that could happen to me would be to have to land on the other side.'

He got up and looked out of the window, lost in thought about the perils of his calling. Now it was his mother's turn to reassure him: 'I firmly believe that the British would treat you decently.'

Some moments passed before Manfred answered. The conversation had turned to subjects he did not wish to discuss, and his mother could tell that he wanted to end it. He replied simply: 'I believe that also'.[51]

Freifrau von Richthofen did not pursue the subject further. She knew her son well enough to recognize that he had undergone great changes since assuming the mantle of command and the responsibilities of a public figure. Years of leadership training had prepared him for most of the tasks he now faced, but she felt that certain changes — notably his moroseness and aloofness to the point of being almost unapproachable — could come from only one grim source: 'I believe he has seen death too often'.[52]

She kept her opinions from him, but continued to notice certain new turns in his behaviour during this leave period. A routine visit to the dentist suddenly became to him a 'useless' exercise. When he rested or slept, she noticed a nearly constant look of pain about her son. Manfred von Richthofen no doubt suffered from what would later be diagnosed as battle fatigue or post-traumatic stress disorder, aggravated by headaches caused by the head wound he had suffered the previous July. But in those days heroes were supposed to suffer their physical and emotional injuries in silence and with as much dignity as they could muster.

Finally, the day came for Manfred to return to duty. His aeroplane had been removed to Breslau for maintenance, and he had to take the train there to continue on to Berlin by air. His sister Ilse drove him to the railway station and, as they pulled away from the house, *Freifrau* von Richthofen stood by a window at the top of the stairs and called out: '*Auf Wiedersehen* — Until we meet again, my boy'.

At the station, Ilse reinforced the message in the candid, direct way that siblings employ: 'Please be a bit careful, [as] we do want to see you again'.

'Can you imagine, Ilse, that I could ever die in some wretched bed of straw?', he responded in a like manner.

Later that day, to keep the peace with another family member, Richthofen made a low pass over the Cadet Academy in Wahlstatt. When his brother Bolko and the other cadets ran out on to the parade ground, the pilot of the well-known red two-seater emptied a box of candies on to them. No doubt the cadets survived — and, indeed, enjoyed — their first aerial assault.

After a short time in Berlin the *Kommandeur* returned to the battle-front. He had to begin preparations for the forthcoming spring offensive and, as Lothar had to return home to have a severe inflammation of the inner ear attended to, Manfred von Richthofen's return was even more important for morale purposes.

On 11 February Manfred wrote to his mother:

> It is too bad that my duties in Berlin dragged on so long that I could not come back to Schweidnitz once more. It would have been so nice and I would have enjoyed it very much. Now I think I will not be able to come back to Germany for a long time.
>
> Lothar should stay at home as long as possible; he is very careless with his ears and does nothing at all to take care of them. He is missing nothing here. I want him to know that he should not come back before the 1st of March. Should things start up strongly here, I will notify him by wire.
>
> Bolko will surely be very irritated with me, but I really cannot make a landing in Wahlstatt [right now]. In the fall, when the fields are mowed, I will do it.[53]

PREPARING FOR THE BIG PUSH

Manfred von Richthofen had been back at the Front a very short time when an old problem returned. On 3 February *Jasta 11* pilot *Ltn* Hans Joachim Wolff was flying Fokker Dr.I 155/17 about 25km south of his own airfield when the spar and leading edge of his top wing collapsed. Luckily, Wolff was able to make an emergency landing at Villers Outreaux[54] and save both himself and the aircraft, but the incident raised further doubts about the once highly praised Fokker triplane. As it would be two months before the new Fokker D.VII would appear at the Front, this latest incident simply added to Richthofen's concerns about preparations for the coming offensive.

Several *JG I* pilots had demonstrated a special talent for shooting down tethered observation balloons. From their airborne posts over Allied lines, balloon observers could see far into German territory, range artillery with great accuracy and report on train and troop movements. The 'flying sausages', as they were called, were well protected by anti-aircraft batteries, but could be destroyed by a talented and lucky pilot. For example, five of the ten victories then accredited to *Ltn* Erich Löwenhardt of *Jasta 10* were observation balloons.

Manfred von Richthofen had never attacked a balloon and, while he had brushed with death in single- and two-seat aircraft, he had only wondered about being up in a bulbous 'gas bag'. One slow day in February he decided to see what it was like to ride in the wicker observation basket suspended below a balloon. Richthofen and an unnamed but like-minded *Geschwader* comrade flew over to a balloon unit near Cambrai and asked to go up for a short time.

It is unlikely that they were recognized, bundled up in heavy flight clothing to keep them warm in their aeroplane. Their officers' hats and authoritative bearing would have been enough to qualify them for a brief explanation of the balloon and its telephone equipment before being sent aloft.

Richthofen later wrote about the experience:

... The *Gasnullen* [gasbags] generally do not go especially high. That is not done out of some fear of the nasty enemy; rather, it is because they cannot do otherwise. 1,500 to 1,600 metres [altitude] is about normal. In calm weather the ascension takes place rather simply; I will not say it is not interesting, but there is little thrill to it.

The day I flew it was absolutely calm. In a heavy wind it is very easy for one to become seasick. On command the balloon is released by many men and goes up into the air at a rather fast rate. One stands within a small basket beneath [the balloon] and takes in the whole area. I have always believed that one sees much more from inside the "eye of the army," as these airships are often called. I saw frightfully little. It is about the same as in an aeroplane when I climb to 1,000 metres ...

... The most interesting aspect of all about a captive balloon, of course, is when the thing is attacked and the crewman must jump out: the famous leap into the unknown. The decision is made relatively easily, as the *Gasnulle* above him slowly begins to burn and, if he decides not to jump out, he is surely doomed. Then the "unknown" is preferred to certain death. The situation is not at all so uncertain, however, as there is rarely an accident connected with it.

The young man with whom I went up could not resist [the temptation] and had to jump. He did not do it out of fear for his life; rather, purely out of passion. He said they were among the most beautiful, romantic moments there were and a young man should not let them slip away. Toward that end he climbed up [into the rigging], surveyed the region for a while, and then I saw him through my telescope as he acrobatically swung away from the edge of the balloon basket and, in order to make the most of that romantic moment, he swung by his legs for a while outside the basket; then a quick decision and he jumped. But the jump did not last long, for after a few metres the parachute deployed. As he described it to me, there was only a short time in which he was falling freely, which of course was not very pleasant. Suddenly there was a jerk and he hung, held by belts secured under his arms, in the lines of the parachute; [it was] an absolutely secure feeling.[55]

The enthusiastic and acrobatic young balloon observer must have reminded Manfred von Richthofen of pilots he knew who enjoyed displaying their flying skill. Each in their own way, they were like the knights of old, glorying more in the thrill of the fight than in the overall results. He knew that one of his greatest tasks in the weeks ahead would be to have *JG I* fly and function as an organized fighting force — the same concern his two fellow *Geschwader-Kommandeurs* faced. Individual glory would have to give way to results if the German *Luftstreitkräfte* were to defeat the combined air arms of Britain, France and the United States. He would have to channel individual ambition into the group objective.

Manfred von Richthofen's understanding of the challenge is evident in his writing:

> For many people ambition plays an important rôle. Everyone must have a certain amount of ambition. But it should not become an unhealthy ambition. Aerial combat is always singular combat. ... One can also speak of a *Geschwader* battle ... I have, for example, [flown] with my *Staffel* against entire enemy *Geschwaders* and annihilated them. This can be achieved only with very well trained comrades, where each individual is an ace and knows the other like his brother. With a poorly prepared *Geschwader* one can not get the better of any Englishman at all. [In that case] one sits mostly alone below a swarm of enemy [aircraft] and must see to it that he comes out of it with his hide intact.[56]

That admonition was fulfilled by *Ltn.d.Res* Hans Klein, leader of *Jasta 10*, who was wounded during a fight on 19 February. Flying in Pfalz D.III 4283/17, Klein received a flesh wound in his right arm; another bullet smashed the index finger of his right hand,[57] which made further flying difficult.

Hans Klein was succeeded in the command of *Jasta 10* by another fast-rising fighter pilot, *Ltn.d.Res* Hans Weiss, who had already shot down twelve enemy aircraft. There was an abundance of talent within *JG I*, as Manfred von Richthofen had spent a considerable time 'driving around to the Fighter Pilot Schools and [other] *Jagdstaffeln* and had observed operations'[58] to identify promising new pilots whom he could develop into skilled fighters. But a 22-victory ace such as Klein was impossible to replace.

NOTES

1   Bodenschatz, *Jagd in Flanderns Himmel*, (1935), pp.54, 161-162; possibly as a way to alert German air units to the potential danger of firing on Fokker triplanes, this incident was candidly reported in the weekly *Nachrichtenblatt der Luftstreitkräfte Nr 36*, 1 November 1917, p.351.

2   Ibid., pp.54-55, 162.

3   Imrie, *The Fokker Triplane* (1992), pp.30, 114, 115.
4   Grosz and Ferko, *The Fokker Dr.I: A Reappraisal*, (1978), p.19.
5   Supf, *Das Buch der deutschen Fluggeschichte*, vol I, (1956), p.352; *Prof* Hoff qualified for *DLV* licence No.41 on 13 December 1910.
6   Bodenschatz, op.cit., p.162.
7   Ibid.
8   Gray, *The Pfalz D.III*, (1965), p.8; the *Profile* monograph quotes a German comparison of the Pfalz D.III: 'It is slower than the Albatros D.III; it is fast in a dive and is then faster than the Albatros D.V. The climbing performance of [the] Pfalz D.III varies greatly, sometimes almost as good as the average Albatros D.V, but never better ...'
9   Letter from the Falkenhayn family via a private source.
10   *Nachrichtenblatt Nr 42*, 13 December 1917, p.455 lists no comparable F.2B loss.
11   No.45 Squadron Record Book entry, 15 November 1917.
12   Bodenschatz, op.cit., p.163.
13   O'Connor, *Aviation Awards of Imperial Germany in World War I*, vol I, (1988), p.34.
14   *RFC Communiqué No. 115*, 29 November 1917, p.1.
15   Jones, *The War in the Air*, vol IV (1934), pp.230-231.
16   *RFC Communiqué*, op.cit.
17   Ibid.
18   Jones, op.cit., pp.244-245.
19   Bodenschatz, op.cit., p.164.
20   Jones, op.cit., p.246; D.H.5 A9299 of No.64 Squadron, Lt J.A.V. Boddy (WiA).
21   Ibid., p.249.
22   *RFC Communiqué No. 116*, 5 December 1917, p.2.
23   Zuerl, *Pour-le-Mérite-Flieger*, (1938), p.81.
24   Puglisi, *German Aircraft Down in British Lines*, Part 1, (1969), p.159.
25   Böhme, *Briefe eines deutschen Kampffliegers an ein junges Mädchen*, (1930), pp.202-203.
26   Jones, op.cit., p.253.
27   von der Osten, *Memoirs of World War I with Jagdstaffeln 11 and 4*, (1974), p.223; D.H.5 A9509, 2/Lt I.D. Campbell (KiA).
28   Bodenschatz, op.cit., p.57.
29   Evans, *Manfred Freiherr von Richthofen Victory List*, (1992), p.139.
30   Bodenschatz, op.cit., pp.58, 165; O'Connor, *Aviation Awards of Imperial Germany and the Men Who Earned Them*, vol II, (1990), p.219 lists the actual date of award as 4 December 1917.
31   *Kofl 6. Armee Wochenbericht Nr 22639, Teil 14*, 30 January 1917.
32   Quoted in von Richthofen, *Ein Heldenleben*, (1920), pp.312-313.
33   Jones, op.cit., pp.256-257.
34   Imrie, op.cit., p.53.
35   Lamberton, *Fighter Aircraft of the 1914-1918 War*, (1960), p.159.
36   Imrie, op.cit., p.57.
37   *Ein Heldenleben*, op.cit., p.199.
38   Quoted in Ibid., pp.318-320.
39   Ibid, pp.157-158.
40   Esposito, *A Concise History of World War I*, (1965), p.158.
41   Wheeler-Bennett, *The Forgotten Peace — Brest-Litovsk*, (1939), p.114.
42   *Ein Heldenleben*, op.cit., pp.159-160.
43   Ibid., pp.199-200.
44   von Richthofen, *Mein Kriegstagebuch*, (1937), pp.148-149.
45   Bodenschatz, op.cit., p.167.
46   Cron, *Organization of the German Luftstreitkräfte*, (1966), p.55.
47   Wenzl, *Richthofen-Flieger*, (ca.1930), pp.46-47.
48   Van Ishoven, *The Fall of an Eagle*, (1979), p.54; Gray, *Fokker D.VII*, (1965), p.3 lists 31 aircraft from nine different firms.
49   von der Osten, op.cit., p.224; *Ein Heldenleben*, op.cit., p.224 has Lothar von Richthofen relating the same anecdote.
50   *Mein Kriegstagebuch*, op.cit., p.148.

51   Ibid., p.149.
52   Ibid., p.151.
53   *Ein Heldenleben*, op.cit., p.200.
54   Bodenschatz, op.cit., p.168.
55   *Ein Heldenleben*, op.cit., pp.160-162.
56   Ibid., pp.168-169.
57   Ibid., p.169; Shores, et al, *Above the Trenches*, (1990),   p.295 credits Lt Robert J. Owen
     of No.43 Squadron with shooting down Klein, but Owen's first victory, an Albatros
     D.V, went down in flames, and there is no report that Klein's Pfalz D.III caught fire.
58   Ibid., p.63.

CHAPTER 12

OPERATION MICHAEL

As part of the race to preclude the much-heralded American effect on their plans for victory, German forces on the Western Front were bolstered by the steady infusion of fresh, little-used and eager troops from the Eastern Front,[1] where peace had been concluded on 3 March 1918. The plan code-named 'Michael', calling for attacks on both sides of St Quentin, was selected by *Gen* Erich Ludendorff,[2] and German units within the broad operational area began preparing for their rôles.

JG I had been preparing for the coming offensive as early as 28 February. A forward airfield was established at Awoingt, almost 15km southwest of Avesnes le Sec and closer to the front lines.

A *Jasta 15* pilot captured on 26 February confirmed that the 'Pfalz [D.III] scout is not popular with pilots owing to its lack of speed and its bad manoeuvrability; an improved type is expected. Richthofen's squadron is being equipped with Fokker triplanes with a much improved aileron control.'[3]

The same source reported: 'Fokker triplanes have recently been received and are to take the place of the Albatros scouts; this accounts for the high number of machines at present with the flight, the normal number being 15-16 machines. The strength of pilots [in a *Jasta*] is never more than 10-12 on an average, either in his flight or in the majority of Pursuit flights, but [the prisoner] believes that special steps are taken to keep the flights in von Richthofen's squadron up to higher establishment.'[4]

MORE TRIPLANE TROUBLES

JG I did indeed have its complement of new Fokker Dr.Is, but, even though Manfred von Richthofen liked them, the triplanes did not live up to expectations. After the wing structure problem was apparently solved, there were technical problems and, once again, operational problems, as Richthofen felt his *Staffeln* were being poorly deployed by *Hptmn* Wilhelm Haehnelt, Officer in Charge of Aviation for the *2. Armee*. Richthofen noted his concerns in his letter of 27 February to Fritz von Falkenhayn:

> A few days ago I sent you a report about the Rizinus *Ersatz* [synthetic lubricant produced from coal tars[5]] relative to rotary engines. I am of the opinion that, owing to the poor [-quality] oil (Rizinus-*Ersatz*) that is available to us, rotary engines are no longer suitable for this war. Therefore, I set no high value on having rotary engines in my *Geschwader*, even when they produce 200 horsepower. As the situation

is now, I would prefer to have the Fokker [D.VII] with the BMW engine or the supercharged Mercedes. Should the Fokkers be issued with un-supercharged engines, I would not refuse them.

Here there is mostly bad weather and extremely scant enemy fly-ing activity in our *Armee* sector. Furthermore, I am [now] the leader of four *Schutzstaffeln* [ground support units] under Haehnelt and no longer *Jagdgeschwader-Kommandeur*, which after a year and a half of fighter avi-ation is a change. I do not want it said that the change is excessively interesting.

The British are much busier in the *17.* and also the *6. Armee* sec-tors than here on our Front. My brother will arrive here tomorrow and is again in good health, as he confirms. He has missed nothing, only some ground support flights, which he would have put up with, but no aerial combat.[6]

Richthofen craved operational independence, but this time he had to endure his subordinate rôle and be circumspect in his criticism of his immediate superior. *Hptmn* Haehnelt was a prewar military pilot with a dis-tinguished record and many connections in high places.[7] He was not as easily outmanoeuvred as *Hptmn* Otto Bufe had been in *4. Armee* air opera-tions.

In any event, the tempo of British air activities soon increased and Richthofen put *JG I*'s new fighter aircraft in the air to prevent RFC recon-naissance machines from gathering more intelligence information. On 1 March, 30 sorties were flown, but with no success. Indeed, two *Jasta 11* pilots were put out of action: *Ltn* Eberhardt Mohnicke was wounded in the left thigh while flying Fokker Dr.I 155/17, and *Ltn.d.Res* Erich Just was wounded in the left hand while at the controls of Fokker Dr.I 110/17. Both pilots landed safely and received medical attention.[8]

Ltn.d.Res Erich Bahr, flying Fokker Dr.I 106/17, was not so lucky. On 6 March the 24-year-old *Jasta 11* pilot was shot down and killed in a fight, and crashed between Nauroy and Etricourt.[9]

The *JG I* war diary notes that, beginning on 10 March, enemy air activity on the *2. Armee* Front increased markedly.[10] As RFC squadrons strived to gain information about the German build-up, the *Jastas* worked hard to keep them from crossing the lines.

Late on the morning of 12 March, ten of No.62 Squadron's F.2Bs[11] were observed just southeast of *JG I*'s airfields, heading for Le Cateau. Manfred and Lothar von Richthofen and *Ltn* Werner Steinhäuser went after the formation and shot down four.

Flying his new, mostly red, Fokker Dr.I 152/17 in combat for the first time, Manfred von Richthofen claimed his 64th victory:

> ... we attacked an enemy squadron between Caudry and Le Cateau at an altitude of 5,500 metres far behind our own lines. The 'plane I attacked immediately dived down to 1,000 metres and tried to escape. The observer had fired only [when] high up in the air, had then

disappeared in his seat and had only begun shooting again shortly before the machine landed.

During the fight, we had drifted off to Le Catelet. There I forced my adversary to land and, after doing this, both crewmen left the aeroplane.[12]

Lothar von Richthofen, criticized by his brother for being more of a 'shooter' than a 'hunter', charged headlong at the Bristol Fighters and shot down two of them, credited as his 28th and 29th victories. Lothar's bold style of fighting, compared with Manfred's more calculating method, may have thrown the F.2B flight into disarray, driving the other aircraft into the guns of the other triplanes.

The *JG I* war diary shows that Lothar's two victims were shot down at about 1100 hours, over Clary and Maretz, just south of Caudry. Of this fight, Lothar von Richthofen recounted: 'A sea of fire in the form of the British [aircraft] whizzed right by me. The observer stood and stared into the flames. The British machine, completely on fire, made yet another turn. Both crewmen jumped out along the way down. The rest of the machine fluttered in the air.'[13]

At the same time, Steinhäuser claimed an F.2B over Beauvois, just northwest of Caudry, which was recorded as his fourth victory.[14] Manfred's victory 15 minutes later, northeast of Nauroy, indicates that the fight was more protracted than he had reported — the work of the experienced hunter stalking his prey.

LOTHAR SHOT DOWN AGAIN

During his early days in aviation, Lothar von Richthofen met a seasoned pilot who never flew without his lucky teddy bear. At first Lothar scoffed at the idea, but eventually he had his own good luck charms in the air. As a two-seater observer he carried his old cavalry riding crop as a means of warding off evil. Manfred was not superstitious, even though Lothar claimed that his brother always wore the same leather jacket when he flew. Indulging Lothar's beliefs, Manfred gave him the old leather gloves he had worn in combat while shooting down his first ten opponents.[15]

Apparently, these talismans had no effect on unlucky numbers. Lothar von Richthofen was shot down on Sunday, 13 May 1917 and then again on Wednesday, 13 March 1918, as he later recorded:

> The 13th of March! At the Front there is no difference between Sunday and a weekday. Many times one does not even know the correct date. So I did not think at all that the 13th would really be my unlucky day. Our *Staffel* flew to the Front this day under the leadership of my brother ... We had scarcely arrived at the Front when we encountered a swarm of Englishmen. Everyone went after one [of them and] I did, too. I attacked my opponent in a dive. Then there was a loud crash within

my machine! It was hit. Only too late I noticed what was wrong. My tri-plane suddenly became a biplane. It was a horrible feeling to be minus a wing at 4,000 metres. I quickly broke away from my Englishman. He was really so stupid that he did not follow me. Nothing would have been easier than to shoot me down in this condition. Thank God, the machine did not go into a dive. With both remaining wings I could still bring it into a normal glide, but only [flying] straight ahead, as the rud-der no longer functioned.[16]

Lothar von Richthofen's triplane was one of 35 *JG I* aircraft which, in a massed formation, attacked eleven Bristol Fighters of No.62 Squadron. The F.2Bs were escorting D.H.4s of Nos.25 and 27 Squadrons, and were joined by two flights of Sopwith F.1 Camels of No.73 Squadron.[17] Capt A.H. Orlebar of No.73 Squadron and F.2B crew Capts G.F. Hughes and H. Claye claimed to have shot down a triplane that lost its top wing[18]; clearly, one or both aircraft hastened Lothar's departure from the fight and the subsequent incident near *Jasta 11*'s advance airfield at Awoingt. Just as he was coming to it, a high-tension wire loomed before him. Unable to turn, Lothar's aircraft hit the wire and then dropped like a stone.[19]

Unaware of Lothar's predicament, Manfred, in Fokker Dr.I 152/17, was firing away at his 65th victim. According to his report:

> I started with *Staffel 11* and fought later on with two *Staffeln* of my *Geschwader* against 20-30 Englishmen (D.H.4, S.E.5 and Sopwith Camels). I forced down a D.H.4 from 4,000 to 2,000 metres. My oppo-nent glided down in [the] direction of Caudry with only [a] very slowly working engine. The fight took place quite a distance behind our lines. The Englishman landed south of La Terrière in quadrant 2256. Har-rassed by Albatroses of other *Staffeln*, I let my doomed adversary off, [and] rose up to 3,200 metres, where I fought with several Sopwith Camels. In this moment, I saw an Englishman attacking one of my *Staffel*'s 'planes. I followed him, approached him [up to] 20 metres and put holes through his fuel tank. Apparently I had hit the pilot, as the machine dived and dashed to the ground. The Englishman tried to land in the [combat area west of Banteaux] near Gonnelieu, but smashed his machine just behind our lines.[20]

Moments later, *Vzfw* Edgar Scholz attacked a Sopwith F.1 Camel and sent it down in flames north of Vaucelles, less than 5km away from his leader's victim.[21]

Manfred von Richthofen's latest triumph was muted by uncertainty about his brother. A participant in that fight, *Ltn* Friedrich Wilhelm Lüb-bert, recalled:

> The *Rittmeister* was among the last to land. Only his brother Lothar was missing. When Richthofen landed, his first question was: "Is

Lothar back?". The answer: "No, but it was observed that the top wing of his triplane fell off at 5,500 metres and that he went down in a glide."

Calmly, Richthofen went with the pilots to the operations hut. No news had come in yet. Suddenly there was a report by telephone: "*Ltn* von Richthofen has crashed near Cambrai and is dead". Shortly thereafter a second report came in: "*Ltn* von Richthofen has made an emergency landing and has badly injured an eye". No one knew which report gave the actual facts. Everyone spoke in depressed tones.

The *Rittmeister*'s facial features did not change in the least. "We must wait," he said, and very calmly went into a critique of the day's flight. "By the way, I have shot down two today," he said in the midst of things and [rather] casually.

When no further news came in after a long time, he got into his crate and flew to the crash site in order to determine for himself more about the fate of his brother, whose injuries turned out to be relatively light, fortunately, despite the hard crash.[22]

The news about Lothar could not be kept from the German public and, in a roundabout way, from Allied intelligence officers, as noted in an American report:

> The *Neuer Goerlitzer Anzeiger*, 22nd March 1918, announces that Lieut. von Richthofen has crashed and is wounded; the nature of his injuries is not known. He had recently gained his 29th victory.[23]

In public, Manfred von Richthofen maintained a certain coolness and distance about his brother. His private feelings are revealed in his correspondence. To reassure his mother, he sent a brief telegram three days after the incident: 'Lothar superfically wounded in the face and legs; overall condition good'.[24]

A week later he wrote:

> You have of course meanwhile received my telegram, notifying you of Lothar's crash. Thank God, he is doing very well. I visit him daily. So, please, don't worry about anything. He is really doing very well.
>
> His nasal bone has already healed, only the jawbone has been cracked, but all of the teeth have been saved. Over the right eye he has a big gash, but the eye itself has not been damaged. On the right knee some blood vessels have burst, [and] on the left leg from the calf down, likewise some haemorrhaging.
>
> The blood that he coughed up did not come from any internal injuries; rather, he swallowed it in the crash. He is in hospital in Cambrai and hopes to be up and about in fourteen days. He regrets very much only that he cannot be with us now.[25]

ERNST UDET JOINS *JASTA 11*

Manfred von Richthofen continually searched for promising pilots for his *Jagdstaffeln*, and for accomplished fighters to succeed or replace *Staffel* leaders. Hence, when he learned that *Jagdstaffel 37* had been transferred from the *4. Armee* Front to the *2. Armee*, he drove through steady rain to Le Cateau on Friday 15 March. Richthofen knew that he would not be encroaching on another army commander's territory by seeking to attract that *Staffel*'s brave and talented leader to *JG I*. The object of Richthofen's attention was 21-year-old *Ltn.d.Res* Ernst Udet, who had shot down his first aeroplane two years earlier and had since scored nineteen more victories. Udet was in line to receive the *Pour le Mérite* and had all the qualifications Richthofen required of a *Staffel* leader.

When approached by Richthofen, Udet accepted the offer of a transfer immediately. He later noted: 'There were many good *Jagdstaffeln* in the [2.] *Armee* and *Jasta 37* was not the worst. But there was only one *Jagdgeschwader Richthofen*.'[26]

Richthofen looked to the future, but he prepared for every eventuality. As part of his preparations for the coming offensive, that evening he handed an envelope with the *Geschwader* seal on it to his adjutant, *Obltn* Karl Bodenschatz. The envelope was to be opened if — or when — the *Kommandeur* failed to return from the Front. It was Richthofen's official testament, designating his successor.[27]

Thus, when *Gen* von Hoeppner inspected *JG I* on 17 March,[28] Richthofen reported a full state of readiness for the offensive. He had taken care of every administrative detail and the *Geschwader* would demonstrate its capabilities the following day.

Under clear blue skies just before 1100 on 18 March, a large formation of British aircraft crossed the *2. Armee* Front. A member of the *238. Infanterie-Division* quartered near the village of Molain reported some 30 to 40 aircraft, judged to be flying at 4,000m to 5,000m altitude, headed for Le Cateau.[29]

JG I had been alerted half an hour earlier and were in the air. *Kommandeur* von Richthofen led 30 aircraft from *Jastas 6, 10* and *11* up to 5,300m, and targeted one of the several formations determined to reconnoitre the German rear area. His combat report describes the ensuing battle:

> ... As we neared the Front, I saw numerous British groups [*Geschwader*] which were just flying over our lines in the direction of Le Cateau. The first group I encountered was at about 5,500 metres altitude. Together with *Ltn* [Siegfried] Gussmann of *Jasta 11*, I fired at the last of the opponents, a Bristol Fighter. He lost his wings and *Ltn* Gussmann brought him crashing down at Joncourt[sic].[30]
>
> After that, I gathered my 30 aircraft, climbed to 5,300 metres and followed two groups that had broken through [and were heading]

toward Le Cateau. When the opponent made the attempt to turn away and head back toward the Front, I attacked. The [enemy] aircraft closest to me, apparently a Bréguet or a Bristol Fighter, was fired at by me and *Ltn* [Erich] Loewenhardt of *Jasta 10*, whereupon the opponent's fuel tank was shot to pieces and I saw that the aircraft went straight down. *Ltn* Loewenhardt brought him crashing down [south of Le Cateau].[31]

Out of two British single-seater groups, I attacked an aircraft with streamers and forced the opponent to land near Molain.[32]

The lore of First World War aviation history contains numerous stories of noted fighter aces who either gave away victories or took credit for the work of their subordinates. Indeed, Richthofen's victim in this encounter, Lt William G. Ivamy of No.54 Squadron, said: 'I have heard from various sources that the number of machines shot down by the entire circus was claimed by [Richthofen] personally ...'[33] The *Kommandeur*'s combat report, in which he clearly deferred to claims made by *Ltns* Gussmann and Loewenhardt, is a good example of an officer quite secure in his position and smart enough to exercise the good leadership quality of encouraging his subordinates.

But, once Richthofen had claimed a victim, he liked to strenghten his claim by obtaining souvenirs. The witness from the *238. Inf-Div* near Molain further reported the end of the air combat:

> Now an Englishman appeared above us and came down in a glide with his engine shut off. A German machine circled over him like a bird of prey. The Englishman set his aeroplane on the ground about 150 metres from us. He climbed out and we brought him into the village. The German flyer landed right near the enemy machine, climbed out and cut the serial number from the [fuselage] of the opponent ... [The German was in] a red machine that had circled over us and that everyone waved at. It was *Rittmeister* Manfred von Richthofen.[34]

THE OFFENSIVE BEGINS

The Front was quiet for the next two days. *JG I*'s equipment was moved quietly at night from Avesnes le Sec and Lieu St Amand and placed in hangar tents at the advance airfield at Awoingt. On the evening of the 20th all aircraft were flown to the new field and quickly housed in the hangars.

At 0445 the following day, German heavy artillery of the *17., 2.* and *18. Armees* opened fire along a 70km battle line.[35] The German spring offensive had begun.

Anticipating massive aerial action, air commander *Hptmn* Haehnelt had divided the *2. Armee* sector into two air fighting areas. Richthofen was in charge of Zone North, a box-shaped area bounded by Marcoing-Ytres-Longavesnes-Vendhuille. In addition to *JG I*, the units of *Jagdgruppe 2* (*Jastas 5* and *46*) were also under his command for this operation.[36]

The *2. Armee* air operations plan called for *Rittm* von Richthofen and *Jasta 11* to lead the air attack, taking off at 0900, 45 minutes before the infantry assault, to protect German reconnaissance aircraft and to suppress Entente aircraft and observation balloons. However, a heavy mist that morning made early flying impossible, and the first *JG I* aircraft were not able to take off until 1230. The call was for *Jasta 10*'s 'balloon busters' to destroy two of the tethered craft. At 1310 *Ltn* Loewenhardt shot down the balloon at Fins, and 45min later *Ltn* Friedrichs claimed the gas bag at Ryaulcourt. Richthofen's great air armada undertook 52 sorties that day, but claimed only the two balloons as victories.

Despite bad weather over the next two days, there was considerable flying activity on both sides of the lines. Indeed, on the 23rd *JG I* flew 80 sorties in nearly full strength, but gained nothing for the effort.

On the 24th, 105 sorties and involvement in fifteen air fights produced a loss and a victory. The day's sole victory — Manfred von Richthofen's 67th — was scored against one of the RFC's top units, No.56 Squadron. Richthofen, looking like the apparition of red death in his first combat in the all-red Fokker Dr.I 477/17, led an overwhelming force against the British fighters. His terse combat report noted: 'During a long single-seater fight between about ten S.E.5s and 25 machines of my *Geschwader*, I attacked an Englishman at 2,500 metres altitude. Both wings of the British aeroplane broke away in the air in [the stream of] my machine gun fire. The remnants were dispersed in the vicinity of Combles.'[37]

Once again, on 25 March, Manfred von Richthofen achieved *JG I*'s only success and his 68th victory: 'With five aeroplanes of *Jagdstaffel 11*, I attacked some low-flying British [Sopwith] single-seaters north-east of Albert. I came up to within 50 metres of one of the Englishmen and fired a few shots [that] set him on fire. The burning aeroplane crashed between Contalmaison and Albert and continued to burn on the ground. The bombs that he was apparently carrying exploded some minutes later.'[38]

Ltn.d.Res Ernst Udet reported for duty at Awoingt that day, and described Richthofen's method of getting to know new pilots: 'I arrived at 10:00 [am] and at 12:00 I took off on my first flight with *Jagdstaffel 11* ... [Richthofen] attached great importance to personally testing every newcomer.'[39]

Udet recalled that Richthofen led the way, followed first by *Ltns.d.Res* Erich Just and Siegfried Gussmann and then by *Vzfw* Edgar Scholtz and himself. It was Udet's first flight in a Fokker Dr.I, and a chance to watch the master at work. He hung back with the others as Richthofen dived down in his blood-red triplane to seal his 69th victory.

Richthofen's own description, including his first reference to the prized pilot he had attracted from *Jasta 37*, noted: 'With five gentlemen of *Jagdstaffel 11* [flying] at low altitude, *Leutnant* Udet and I encountered a Sopwith single-seater. At the beginning the opponent attempted to escape by skilful flying. I fired from an aeroplane's length away and set him on fire. During the fall it broke into pieces, [and] the fuselage fell into the small woods at Contalmaison.'[40]

Some sources list Richthofen's 69th victim as a Sopwith F.1 Camel, although RFC records show no Camel loss at this time and place. Other RFC documents record that two Sopwith 5F.1 Dolphins of No.19 Squadron[41] were in that area at the time of the fight.[42] Richthofen's observation of the characteristic Sopwith rudders and wing shapes makes it likely that he shot down a Dolphin.

There was no mistaking Richthofen's 70th victim, which he dispatched shortly after the Sopwith broke up in the air. He reported: 'A quarter-hour after the first [aircraft of the day] was shot down, I encountered an R.E. two-seater at exactly the same location at about 700 metres. I went into a dive behind it and fired about 100 rounds at close range [and] set it on fire. At first the observer defended the British [aircraft] with his machine-gun. [Then] the aircraft burned until it hit the ground. Half an hour later the aeroplane was still burning on the ground.'[43]

Ironically, that R.E.8 of No.15 Squadron was shot down less than 20km from its former airfield at Lechelle,[44] which, owing to the rapid advance of German forces, had recently been assigned to *JG I*. By 1800 that evening the airfield was occupied by German forces, but could not be used until numerous shell holes in the landing area were filled; hastily departing British infantry had done their best to impede its use.

The Germans had expected to take over somewhat more 'luxurious' accommodations than they had had at Awoingt, and were disappointed to find sturdy but largely unadorned Nissen huts for the pilots and ground crews. Imagining that his adversaries — not greatly restricted by the German submarine threat — maintained great stores of supplies, *Kommandeur* von Richthofen was especially disappointed to find only 1,500lit of aviation fuel; he had hoped for 15,000lit to bolster his meagre and lower-quality supplies. In any event, Lechelle put *JG I* closer to the Front.[45]

The following day, RFC units crossed the lines and 'concentrated on low bombing and machine-gunning enemy infantry in the neighbourhood of Cambrai, Bapaume, Peronne and Chaulnes.'[46] They attacked just as Richthofen anticipated, and he was ready for them. As his Adjutant commented: 'Now he could show the infantry that he was right there when they needed him.'[47]

The date 27 March 1918 marks one of the most successful days in *JG I*'s history: 118 sorties, 39 inconclusive air combats and, as detailed in Chapter 1, thirteen successful combats, including Manfred von Richthofen's 71st, 72nd and 73rd victories.[48]

The next morning *Ltn* Udet led *Jasta 11* over the Front. By virtue of his previous experience, Udet had been named acting *Staffel* leader, replacing *Ltn* Otto von Breiten-Landenberg, a five-victory ace from *Jasta 6*. In the hard days ahead, Richthofen wanted the most capable people leading his *Staffeln*. Udet did not disappoint the *Kommandeur*; he scored his 22nd victory that day.

Richthofen led the afternoon flight and, as reported, shot down his 74th enemy aircraft: 'Flying at very low altitude I saw shell explosions near the scene of victory. Coming closer, I recognized a British aircraft at 500 metres altitude, flying home. I cut him off and approached him. After 100 shots the enemy aeroplane was on fire. Then it went crashing down, hit the ground near the small wood at Méricourt and continued to burn.'[49]

INTERESTING PEOPLE

Manfred von Richthofen drew a diverse mix of people to *JG I*. Sheer tenacity moved Richthofen to invite *Obltn* Walther Karjus to join *Jasta 11*. Karjus, a valiant observer who had been awarded the Knight's Cross of the House Order of Hohenzollern, had been badly wounded and had lost his right arm. He had been fitted with a prosthetic device, but, as it made aerial photography and other 'backseat' duties impossible, he became a pilot and then a flying instructor.

During Richthofen's search for aggressive new pilots, he spotted Karjus flying at *Armee Flugpark 2* and asked how a combat pilot could fly with one hand. 'Very simple,' Karjus replied, 'I have had the control column and the gun firing lever modified [to be worked with one hand]'.[50] After arriving on 30 March, he flew often with Richthofen and was called 'the Götz von Berchlichingen of the air,'[51] an allusion to the medieval poet and knight who also wore a prosthetic device — an iron claw — into battle.

Richthofen also attracted political figures, anxious to be associated in some way with Germany's great heroes. Hence, when success of the German spring offensive seemed assured, a group of *Reichstag* (Parliament) representatives visited Lechelle.

Toward evening a limousine delivered the legislators to the airfield. They reportedly strutted around as if they were at a social event in Berlin. One of them wore a cutaway coat and, during frequent bowing and gesturing, his coat-tails swayed like the tail of a mocking bird — much to the amusement of the pilots.

Not so amusing, however, were the long-winded, wine-fuelled speeches at dinner in the officers' mess. 'When you motor on against the enemy in your flying machine, *Herr Baron* ...,' one speaker began. For his part, Manfred von Richthofen sat and listened in stoney-faced silence.

Later the guests were offered sleeping quarters in the small Nissen huts used by the *Geschwader* members. That way, when they returned home, they could say they had endured front-line hardships. *Ltn.d.Res* Heinrich Maushake of *Jasta 4* suggested subsequently: 'Actually, they must be allowed to experience more of the war before they return home tomorrow'.

With a knowing smile, *Vzfw* Edgar Scholz piped up: 'Air raid!'.

There was complete understanding by all present, and they set off in different directions to activate their mischevious plan. *Ltn* Hans Joachim Wolff already had a flare pistol and some blank ammunition. Ernst Udet recalled the results:

> Inside the barracks there was a clattering, the crackle of gun fire and the dull thud of bombs being detonated. Right after that [there was] an outcry.
>
> It was a night with a full moon. We stood hidden in the dark shadows of the other barracks. Suddenly, across the way, the door flew open and out charged three forms in flapping white nightshirts. The *Rittmeister* laughed so hard that tears ran down his cheeks.
>
> "Air raid! Back into the barracks!" thundered a mighty voice across the airfield and, in a frantic run, the three white forms disappeared back behind the door.
>
> The next morning they got under way hurriedly. They did not even have breakfast with us. We laughed for a long time afterward. The joys out there [at the Front] are very few and whenever there is a chance for some fun, one enjoys it gratefully and for a long time ...[52]

NOTES

1   Esposito, *A Concise History of World War I*, (1965), p.104.
2   Jones, *The War in the Air*, vol IV (1934), p.264ff.
3   *Summary of Air Intelligence No. 17*, 1 March 1918, p.1; the pilot was most likely *Uffz* Hegeler of *Jasta 15*. On 26 February 1918 he was forced to land near Bonneuil in Pfalz D.III 4184/17, which was assigned the captured aircraft number G141 [Ref: Puglisi, *German Aircraft Down in British Lines*, (1969), p.162].
4   *Summary of Air Intelligence No. 18*, 2 March 1918, p.1.
5   Winans, *World War I Aircraft Fuels and Lubricating Oils*, (1961), p.236.
6   Letter from the Falkenhayn family via a private source.
7   Supf, *Das Buch der deutschen Fluggeschichte*, vol II, (1958), p.272.
8   Bodenschatz, *Jagd in Flanderns Himmel*, (1935), p.169.
9   Ibid., p.170.
10 Ibid., p.64.
11 Bailey, et al, *A Short History of No. 62 Squadron, RFC/RAF*, (1976), p.291.
12 Gibbons, *The Red Knight of Germany*, (1927), pp.318-319; Public Record Office Air 1/686/21/13/2250 XC15183, p.36; F.2B B1251, 2/Lts L.C.F. Clutterbuck and Henry J. Sparks (both PoW).
13 Quoted in von Richthofen, *Ein Heldenleben*, (1920), pp.232-233.
14 *RFC Casualty List* records three additional losses for No.62 Squadron; of them, F.2B B1247, Capt Douglas S. Kennedy, MC, and Lt Hugh G. Gill (both KiA), was probably brought down by Lothar von Richthofen; the crew were buried in Maretz Cemetery.
15 *Ein Heldenleben*, op.cit., pp.221-222.
16 Quoted in von Richthofen, *Der rote Kampfflieger*, (1933), pp.219-220.
17 Jones, op.cit., pp.288-290.
18 *RFC War Diary*, 13 March 1918.
19 Bodenschatz, op.cit., p.65.
20 Public Record Office, op. cit., pp.36-37.
21 Bodenschatz, op.cit., p.170; No.73 Squadron recorded two losses from that fight: Sopwith Camel B5590, 2/Lt J.N.L. Millet (KiA), reported 'brought down in flames by

Fokker triplane', which was most likely by *Vzfw* Scholz for his third victory; the other Camel, B2523, Lt E.E. Heath (WiA/PoW), was probably the 65th victim of *Rittm* von Richthofen.

22   Quoted in *Ein Heldenleben*, op.cit., pp.313-314.

23   *Summary of Air Information, Air Intelligence Bulletin*, 15 April 1918, p.22.

24   Quoted in von Richthofen, *Mein Kriegstagebuch*, (1937), p.158.

25   *Ein Heldenleben*, op.cit., pp.200-201.

26   Udet, *Mein Fliegerleben*, (1935), p.66.

27   Bodenschatz, op.cit., p.70.

28   Ibid., pp.65, 171.

29   Quoted in Ibid., p.68.

30   *Ltn* Gussmann probably shot down F.2B C4844 of No.11 Squadron, Capt A.P. Maclean (KiA) and Lt F.H. Cantlon, reported down 'between Fresnoy le Grand and Bohain', where there is a village called Jonnecourt.

31   There is no corresponding RFC loss.

32   Quoted in Ibid., p.171.

33   Quoted in Gibbons, op.cit., p.328.

34   Quoted in Ibid., p.69; Richthofen recorded the serial number as 'B5243', while the *RFC Casualty List* has it as B5423, one of five aircraft lost by No.54 Squadron in this fight.

35   Ibid., p.71; Jones, op.cit., pp.292-293.

36   Bodenschatz, ibid., pp.72-73, 172; Bodenschatz, *Das Jagdgeschwader Frhr. v. Richthofen Nr. 1 im Verbande der 2. Armee*, (1923), pp.227-228.

37   Public Record Office, op.cit., p.38; Ibid., p.74; S.E.5a C5389, 2/Lt Wilson Porter, Jr. (KiA).

38   Ibid., pp.74-75; very probably Sopwith Camel C1562 of No.3 Squadron, 2/Lt Donald Cameron (KiA).

39   Udet, op.cit., p.67.

40   Ibid., p.75.

41   Sopwith Dolphin C3793, 2/Lt Edward J. Blyth (MiA) 'last seen going down in flames', according to the *RFC Casualty List*; and Sopwith Dolphin C3790, 2/Lt Fernley W. Hainsby (KiA).

42   No.19 Squadron Combat Report, 26 March 1918, of Capt M.R.N. Jennings described a patrol between Albert and Bapaume just over half an hour later.

43   Bodenschatz, op.cit., p.75; R.E.8 B742 of No.15 Squadron, 2/Lts Vernon J. Reading and Matthew Leggat (KiA).

44   Vann and Bowyer, *15 Squadron RFC/RAF 1915-1919*, (1973), p.66.

45   Ibid., pp.75-76, 173.

46   *RFC Communiqué No. 133*, 10 April 1918, p.2.

47   Bodenschatz, op.cit., p.76.

48   Ibid., pp.76-77, 174.

49   Public Record Office, op.cit., p.41; Armstrong Whitworth F.K.8 C8444 of No.82 Squadron, 2/Lts Joseph B. Taylor and Eric Betley (KiA).

50   Quoted in Lampel, *Als Gast beim Rittmeister Frhr. v. Richthofen*, (1923), p.215.

51   Zuerl, op.cit., p.546; Götz von Berchlichingen is also legendary for his scatological contributions to German literature, a point that would not have been lost on *Obltn* Karjus' contemporaries.

52   Udet, op.cit., pp.71-73.

CHAPTER 13

ANOTHER BLOODY APRIL

O n Monday 1 April, 1918, the Royal Flying Corps and the Royal Naval Air Service were amalgamated into the Royal Air Force.[1] There was, however, no formal ceremony for Western Front squadrons, who were fighting furiously against the German advance. Indeed, ground fighting that day was light compared with the pace of air operations and, especially, aerial combat.[2]

Those commanding the new RAF were determined that April 1918 would not be a repetition of the devastation of a year earlier — at least not on the British side. During its first day of operation the RAF claimed nineteen enemy aircraft shot down or driven down out of control, compared with five deaths in its own ranks (two in combat, one owing to an accident and two in a bombing raid) and fourteen airmen listed as missing.[3]

JG I aircraft flew 106 sorties that day, and accounted for the confirmed loss of five enemy aircraft; the *Geschwader* suffered no losses of its own. Richthofen's only complaint was that Awoingt was no longer close enough to the Front; he wanted his *Staffeln* to be close to the front lines, even as those lines continued to move. He was not satisfied until an advance airfield was prepared at Harbonnières,[4] about 8km from the battlefront.

VICTORIES 75, 76, 77 AND 78

Rittm von Richthofen scored the first of *JG I*'s five victories of 2 April. It was described in the usual dispassionate manner in his combat report:

> About 12:30pm I attacked a British R.E. [aircraft] at an altitude of 800 metres above the woods at Moreuil, [and] just below the clouds. As the adversary did not see me until very late, I managed to approach within 50 metres of him. I fired from ten metres' distance until it began to burn. When the flames shot out, I was only five metres away from him. I could see the pilot and observer twisting out of their aeroplane [seats] to escape the flames. The machine did not burn in the air, but gradually burned [on the way] down. It fell out of control to the ground, where it exploded and burned to ashes.[5]

Richthofen was not as emotionally detached from these struggles as the combat reports suggest. One rare unguarded twinge of guilt about his rôle in aerial combat and his view of the value of awards presented to him surfaced in his conversation that day with *Obltn* Lampel, whose postwar recollections — unfettered by propaganda — included this account:

The *Rittmeister* had ... shot down his 75th. He told me that it had been a bitter battle; he had got right up to five metres away from the enemy, who then went down burning.

"It is a strange feeling," he said. "There, once again a pair of men shot dead; they lie somewhere [out] there all burned up and I myself sit here every day at the table and the food tastes as good as ever. I once said that to His Majesty ... [who] said to me only: 'My soldiers do not shoot men dead; my soldiers annihilate the opposition!'"

... Then the door opened and *Oberleutnant* Bodenschatz, the Adjutant, brought a telegram [reporting that] His Majesty had awarded the Order of the Red Eagle Third Class with Crown and Swords to the *Rittmeister*. That is a regimental commander's award. We congratulated him [and] he got all red-faced. He was such a modest, open, sincere person and a candid comrade.

"I know," he told us frankly, "that on my 70th victory, *Exzellenz* Ludendorff himself forwarded a nomination for me to be awarded the Oak Leaves to the *Pour le Mérite*. But the Cabinet Council members proved quite clearly that I could not receive this award because it was [to be presented] only for winning a battle. *General* Ludendorff, of course, said: 'Richthofen has won more than a battle.'"

A lively debate erupted. I maintained that during his [air] fights he had fought a real battle ...

"No," said Richthofen. "[There was] never a strategic victory. Every air battle, no matter how big it is, always ends up in individual combats."

But now it was time for him to go; he had to go out in a car to find a new [advance] airfield closer to the Front ...

"Who will lead the *Staffel* today?" the *Rittmeister* asked. At the time [*Obltn*] Karjus could not, [as] he was newly arrived and flew the triplane for the first time — with a steel claw instead of his right hand! An example of what energy and stubborn willpower could do.

Leutnant [Hans] Weiss was the oldest pilot there. The *Rittmeister* showed him on a map the sector he had to fly that day. Then, in the doorway, [Richthofen] glanced back: "I will watch," he said, "to see if you are brave".[6]

The *Kommandeur* was joking, of course. Hans Weiss, a year older than Richthofen himself, had been selected on the basis of his strong record as a fighter pilot. The aggressive spirit that led Weiss out of two-seaters and into fighters was evident that day. At about 1700 Weiss scored Victory No.14, a Bristol F.2B shot down along the old Roman Road between Morcourt and Harbonnières.[7]

Such short-term successes can be attributed to the momentum that German forces enjoyed at the time, and to numerical superiority: On 2 April 1918 on the battlefront south of Arras, German units had 822 aircraft against the RAF's 645. The balance was different on other Fronts[8] and, overall, the Germans could not easily match the numbers of *new* aircraft arriving at Entente squadrons. Now more than ever, Manfred von Richthofen and the other *Jagdgeschwader* commanders needed new and improved aircraft.

That evening, Richthofen wrote to his old friend *Obltn* Fritz Falkenhayn at the *Kogenluft* office in Berlin:

> After a long time I come once again with a question. When can I count on [receiving] Fokker biplanes and with the super-compressed engines?
>
> The superiority of British single-seater and reconnaissance aircraft makes it even more perceptibly unpleasant here. The single-seaters fight coming over [at high altitude] and stay up there. One cannot even shoot at them. The two-seaters drop their bombs without our being able to reach them. Speed is the most important point. One could shoot down five to ten times as many [enemy aircraft] if he were faster. During the offensive we liked the low cloud ceiling (100 metres), because at low altitude the triplane has its advantages. We could not fly at all with the super-compressed Siemens[-Schuckert] engine, for, as we discussed, [it took] two hours to get from 50 up to 700 metres. So please give me news soon about when when we can count on [receiving] new machines.
>
> The need has become very great now, as every emergency landing in the old bombarded area of the Somme wasteland leads without fail to a total wreck. After aerial combat, frequently one must land urgently; consequently, [there are] very many wrecks.[9]

To make matters worse, Richthofen's new star, Ernst Udet, had begun experiencing severe pain in his ears. A doctor at the military hospital in Valenciennes confirmed that Udet's ears were suppurating[10] and that he needed treatment. Udet stayed on for a few days and even shot down his 23rd enemy aircraft on 6 April, but the pain became so unbearable that he could not continue flying. When Richthofen learned of the condition, he insisted that Udet go on convalescent leave. 'Out here [at the Front] one must be healthy,' Richthofen told him.

'It was very hard for me to give up my new *Staffel* now, to break off my success in the middle,' Udet later wrote. 'He knew that, more or less, we all believed in the old rule of not breaking a lucky streak.

'Then next morning he brought me himself to the old two-seater that we flew in the rear areas. He stayed at the airfield [during the take-off] and waved at me with his cap. His blonde hair glistened in the sun.'[11]

There was still an abundance of talent in *JG I*. That point was proved when another favourite of Richthofen's, *Ltn* Hans Weiss, succeeded Udet in command of *Jasta 11*. And Manfred von Richthofen would not consider any change in his own status, even when his father suggested that, with 75 victories to his credit, Manfred could retire honourably from the field of combat. The *Rittmeister* replied that he felt obligated to serve as an example, to spur his men on to the boldness needed to succeed in aerial combat.[12]

Moreover, yet another Richthofen had joined *JG I*, and he would need instruction in aerial combat. *Ltn* Wolfram *Frhr* von Richthofen, a 22-year-old cousin[13] who had fought on the Eastern and Western Fronts with *Husaren-Regiment 'von Schill'* (*1. schlesisches*) *Nr 4* until he transferred to the *Luftstreitkräfte* in 1917, arrived on 4 April and was assigned to *Jasta 11*. From this beginning, Wolfram von Richthofen went on to enjoy a distinguished *Luftwaffe* career that was capped on 16 February 1943, when he was promoted to *Generalfeldmarschall*.[14]

Manfred von Richthofen shot down an enemy aircraft on 6 April, and two more the following day. As *Geschwader-Kommandeur* he was entitled to his pick of aircraft, and at this time he had three triplanes at his disposal. This arrangement ensured that at least one aircraft would be mechanically ready, fully armed and fuelled whenever he needed a 'fresh' triplane. As noted in chapter 1, on 27 March he achieved three victories with two different aircraft, Fokker Dr.Is 127/17 and 477/17.

Richthofen flew Fokker Dr.I 127/17, which bore his red colouring on the top wing, cowling, tail, and wheel covers, during an extended combat on 6 April. Sopwith F.1 Camels of Nos.43 and 46 Squadrons and Bristol F.2Bs of No.48 Squadron[15] were bombing and strafing German troops and vehicles at Lamotte en Santerrre when Richthofen and his comrades arrived on the scene.

Richthofen reported: 'With five aeroplanes of *Staffel 11* we attacked enemy single-seaters at low altitude flying near Villers Bretonneux. The British aircraft which I attacked began to burn after only a few shots from my gun. Then it crashed burning to the ground in the small woods northeast of Villers Bretonneux, where it continued to burn.'[16]

The Camel pilot, considered by some researchers to have been Capt Sydney P. Smith of No.43 Squadron, was an accomplished fighter pilot whose first victory had been recorded while flying a B.E.2 two-seater with No.6 Squadron. Having scored four more victories,[17] Smith may have become No.76 on the grim tally of Manfred von Richthofen. It is difficult to say with certainty that Smith was Richthofen's victim, however, as *JG I* claimed ten enemy aircraft on that busy day.[18]

The late W/Cdr Ronald Adam, OBE, was one of the Camel pilots of No.73 Squadron who experienced the next encounter with *JG I*. He recalled: 'We were told that the famous von Richthofen "Circus" was expected to be in the sky over the German lines at midday and that our object was to give the "Circus" the biggest dusting possible. This meant that I should have to fly the new Sopwith Camel which I had fetched in the twilight of the previous evening. The plan called for us to fly at 17,000 feet and an S.E.5 screen would be over us at 19,000 feet.'[19]

The 'dusting' began at about 1130, when *Rittm* von Richthofen, flying all-red Fokker Dr.I 477/17, led the way against a flight of S.E.5s over

Hangard, 5km south of Villers Bretonneux. He reported: 'With four machines of *Staffel 11*, I attacked several "S.E.5s" near Hangard. I fired at an enemy aeroplane some 200 metres away. After I had fired 100 rounds, the enemy aeroplane broke apart. The remnants came down near Hangard.'[20]

Several sources list Richthofen's 77th victim as Capt Guy B. Moore in S.E.5a C1083 of No.1 Squadron. However, records show that the ten-victory Canadian ace[21] took off at 1252 and was patrolling Hollebeke,[22] about 100km northeast of Hangard. Possibly, Richthofen shot down Lt Philip J.N. Nolan, DFC, in S.E.5a B63 of No.24 Squadron,[23] the unit assigned to cover No.73 Squadron's Camels. There is a time discrepancy, however, as Lt Nolan is recorded as having taken off at 1500. He was shot down over Moreuil Wood, which *is* in the area of Richthofen's claim. There was no opportunity for pilots to gather victory souvenirs, as there had been a year earlier, so this claim is not resolved.

Just over half an hour later Richthofen shot down his 78th opponent. He described the encounter: 'I observed that a *Kette* [three-aeroplane flight] of German aeroplanes pursuing a British aeroplane was being attacked from the rear. I dashed to their aid and attacked a British aeroplane. After I got behind him several times, the adversary fell. The aeroplane smashed into the ground and I saw that it crashed to splinters. This [encounter] occurred 500 metres east of Hill 104.'[24]

Lt Ronald Adam, who had been reported shot down at 1145 in Sopwith F.1 Camel D6554, crashed into the railway line at the intersection of the old Roman Road and the road from Proyart to Harbonnières. He was taken prisoner and visited in Proyart that evening by a German orderly, who informed him: '*Freiherr* von Richthofen's compliments. You are his 79th [*sic*] victory.'[25]

Most probably, Ronald Adam was the sixth of the 27 victories achieved by *Ltn* Hans Kirschstein of *Jasta 6*. Richthofen claimed to have shot down a SPAD, but there is no matching RAF casualty. Possibly he shot down Adam's squadron companion, 2/Lt A.V. Gallie, who crashed *west* of Villers Bretonneux in Sopwith F.1 Camel D6550 and returned uninjured to his own lines. Richthofen said his victim came down *east* of the city; thus, if a 'directional error' on his part is assumed, Gallie was probably his 78th victim.[26]

April showers beginning on the 8th led to reduced flying on both sides of the lines. The rain provided ideal cover for *JG I* to move to a more suitable field just southeast of Cappy, 6km from the Front. The new airfield was only a fresh, grass-covered open spot along the road to Bray. Barracks had to be brought in from Rosières and erected, while the landing and take-off area was prepared by British prisoners of war and members of a German machine-gun company.[27] Captured British tents provided protection from the rain for personnel and aircraft.

When the German offensive on the Somme became bogged down on 28 March, Ludendorff turned his sights northward. The opening of the Lys Offensive by the *6. Armee* on 9 April diverted British attention to Flanders, thereby adding to the respite given to units on the *2. Armee* Front.

A LAST REFLECTION

Because of the weather, it was a time of little activity in the air. It was a time of reflection, as noted in the 1933 edition of *Der rote Kampfflieger*, which contained a brief essay that reads as if it were Manfred von Richthofen's final comment on his life and career. Entitled 'Thoughts in a Dug-Out', it expresses a sombre mood not evident in earlier writings. Even though he had not lived in a dugout since the spring of 1915, this piece reveals that he had an emotional link with the ground troops right to the end:

> In my dug-out there hangs from the ceiling a lamp that I had made from a [rotary] aircraft engine. It came from an aeroplane that I had shot down. I mounted light bulbs in the cylinders and at night, when I lie awake and let the light burn, Lord knows, this chandelier on the ceiling looks fantastic and weird enough. When I lie like that I have much to think about.
>
> I write this down without knowing whether anyone other than my closest relatives will ever see [it]. I am thinking about doing a continuation of *Der rote Kampfflieger* and, indeed, for quite a good reason. The battle now taking place on all Fronts has become dreadfully serious; there is nothing left of the "lively, merry war," as our deeds were called in the begining. Now we must arm ourselves against despair so that the enemy will not violate our country.
>
> I now have the deepest impression that from [the image of] the "red battle flier", people have been exposed to quite another Richthofen than I truly am deep inside of myself. When I read [my] book, I smile at my own insolence. I no longer so insolent in spirit. Not because I can imagine how it would be one day when death is breathing down my neck; surely not for that reason, although I have thought about it often enough that it can happen. I have been told by [people in] high places that I should give up flying, for one day it will catch up with me. I would be miserable with myself if now, burdened with glory and decorations, I were to become a pensioner of my own dignity in order to save my precious life for the nation, while every poor fellow in the trenches endures his duty as I do mine.
>
> I am in wretched spirits after every aerial combat. But that is surely one of the consequences of my head wound. When I put my foot on the ground again at the airfield, I go [directly] to my four walls, I do not want to see anyone or hear anything. I believe that [the war] is not as the people at home imagine it, with a hurrah and a roar; it is very serious, very grim ...[28]

FINAL VICTORIES

Amid indications that German forces would renew their offensive on the *2. Armee* Front, the Royal Air Force stepped up air activity in the third week of April. Bad weather on 16, 17, 18 and 19 April kept *JG I* on the ground most of the time, but clear skies on the 20th offered Manfred von Richthofen the opportunity to lead his men into battle. Flying his all-red Fokker Dr.I 425/17, he shot down two Sopwith F.1 Camels within a few minutes of each other.

Richthofen's claim for his 79th victory reported: 'With six aeroplanes of *Staffel 11*, I attacked a large enemy *Geschwader*. During the fight I observed that a triplane was [being] attacked and shot at from below by a Camel. I positioned myself behind the adversary and brought him down, burning, with only a few shots. The enemy aeroplane crashed near Hamel Wood, where it burned on the ground.'[29]

At 1843, according to the claim for Richthofen's 80th victory: 'Three minutes after I had shot down the first one in flames, I attacked a second Camel from the same *Geschwader*. The opponent went into a dive, pulled out and repeated this manoeuvre several times. As he did that, I came up to the closest fighting distance and fired about 50 rounds at him [until his machine] caught fire. The fuselage burned in the air, the rest of the aeroplane crashed northeast of Villers-Bretonneux.'[30]

Ltn Hans Joachim Wolff recalled that, on the way back to Cappy, Richthofen 'went down very low so that everyone could recognize his red machine and waved to the infantrymen [in the trenches] and the columns of men [on the roads]. Everyone knew who was in the machine and all of them had seen the burning Englishmen shortly before. Enthusiastically, they all waved and flung their caps into the air.

'After *Herr Rittmeister* landed, he smacked his hands together as he said: "*Donnerwetter* [Heavens above]! Eighty is a respectable number!" And we were all happy for him and thrilled about [his success].'[31]

Rittm Manfred *Frhr* von Richthofen had returned to Cappy in utter triumph. He had scattered the intruders and raised his own victory score to 80 — exactly twice that of his model and mentor *Hptmn* Oswald Boelcke, and higher than that of any flyer of any of the belligerents. Headaches, moroseness and other signs of combat fatigue notwithstanding, Richthofen was *the best*, and he knew it. Now less than two weeks from his 26th birthday, he had spent half of his life in uniform and had become a greater success at the arts of war than any other member of his already illustrious family.

Richthofen was at the zenith of his success.

THE RED EAGLE'S FALL

Cappy airfield was blanketed with heavy grey fog the next morning, Sunday 21 April. Although the ground haze ruled out flying, the pilots of *JG I* were in high spirits, suited up and ready for take-off as soon as the fog lifted. Everyone was cheerful as they continued to enjoy sharing the *Rittmeister*'s success of the afternoon before and the praise that flowed in.

Despite any grim feelings he might harbour, Richthofen recognized that his men needed to let off steam and he let them go, even at his own expense, as *Obltn* Karl Bodenschatz recorded:

> ... [Richthofen] accidentally tripped over a stretcher that *Leutnant* Wenzl had laid out for a good snooze and when another unsuspecting tired mortal lay down on the stretcher for a good snooze, the *Rittmeister* tipped this youngster over into the spring mud. So, some [of the men] who wanted to avenge this private intrusion on the sleeping privilege of their comrades got together and tied a wheelchock to the tail of Moritz, Richthofen's big dog, so that the poor creature, now so encumbered, would seek solace from his comforter.[32]

Under other circumstances, Richthofen was too much a man of the fields and forests to allow even mild abuse of his dog. But, as the animal was not really harmed, Richthofen laughed along with the others at the sight of the big Great Dane, with the chock bouncing along behind him as he ran across the ground.

'Again and again, the *Freiherr*'s laughter rang across the airfield,' Bodenschatz recalled. '[The men] had seldom seen him in such obviously good spirits. And they knew that, fundamentally, this hunter was happy about the very substantial 80th 'head' he had bagged the day before, even if he had few words about it.'[33]

Richthofen's latest triumph increased the pressure on him to retire undefeated. Eighty seemed to possess the same numerical magic that 40, 50 and, most recently, 75 had. The higher echelons knew that Manfred von Richthofen had more symbolic and propaganda value alive than dead. When their direct appeals to him failed, they tried to use his faithful adjutant to persuade him.

Obltn Bodenschatz raised the matter again while Richthofen waited for the fog to lift. He suggested that a very good position for the *Rittmeister* would be as Inspector of Fighter Aviation, drawing on his wealth of experience. Richthofen laughed in response, as Bodenschatz grasped his hand lightly as if seeking a favour, and said: 'A paper-shuffler? No! I am staying at the Front!'[34]

Manfred von Richthofen was too much the Teutonic warrior to step down now. The only German pilot whose score came close was his old competitor Werner Voss, now dead after attaining 48 victories. Being very goal-oriented, Manfred von Richthofen may well have thought that, with 90 or 100 aeroplanes to his credit, the elusive Oak Leaves to the *Pour le Mérite* would be his at last. Or perhaps the Supreme War Lord would find some other unique distinction for the world's most successful fighter pilot.

In any event, a strong wind out of the east was blowing away the fog, the mist and dreams of glory. Then at about 1030 came a telephoned report that British aircraft were approaching their Front.[35] Within minutes, two *Ketten* (flights) of Fokker triplanes thundered into life, one led by *Rittm* von Richthofen in his all-dark-red Fokker Dr.I, 425/17, the other by *Ltn* Hans Weiss in his well-known white-winged Dr.I, 545/17.

Ltn Hans Joachim Wolff, by now a seven-victory ace and hungry for more triumphs, described the flight in a letter to Lothar von Richthofen:

> [In the] first *Kette* were *Herr Rittmeister*, *Ltn* [Wolfram] *Frhr* von Richthofen, *Obltn* Karjus, *Vzfw* Scholtz and I. Scarcely had we arrived at the Front, when from this side [and] below us, in the area around Hamel, we saw about seven Sopwith Camels. In addition to the five of us, *Jasta* 5 [aircraft] were still in the vicinity, but much farther away, in the vicinity of Sailly le Sec. Above us were seven more Sopwith Camels, some of which attacked *Jasta* 5, some of which remained above.
>
> One or two came at us. We began to fight. In the course of the fight I saw that *Herr Rittmeister* was often near me, but he had not yet shot at anything. Of our *Kette* only *Obltn* Karjus was next to me. *Vzfw* Scholtz was fighting in the vicinity of Sailly le Sec [along] with the Albatroses [of *Jasta* 5]. *Ltn* [Wolfram] von Richthofen was apparently not yet completely ready, as this was perhaps his first aerial combat.
>
> While *Obltn* Karjus and I fought against two or three Camels, suddenly I saw the red machine near me, as he fired at a Camel that first went into a spin, [and] then slipped away in a steep dive toward the west. This fight took place on the other side over the heights of Hamelet.
>
> We had a rather strong east wind and *Herr Rittmeister* had not taken that into account. As I now had clear air around me, I got closer to a Camel and shot it down.[36] As the Camel went down, I looked over at *Herr Rittmeister* and saw that he was at extremely low altitude over the Somme [River] near Corbie, right behind an Englishman. I shook my head instinctively and wondered why *Herr Rittmeister* was following an opponent so far on the other side.
>
> While I was looking to see where my [opponent] had fallen, suddenly I heard a machine-gun behind me and [saw that] I was being attacked by another Camel ... [which] had already put 20 holes in my machine. When I luckily got free of that one, I looked around for *Herr Rittmeister*, [but] saw no one else except *Obltn* Karjus, who was close to me, but also not yet completely ready [for combat]. Then I became a bit uneasy, as I certainly should have seen *Herr Rittmeister*. We circled the area for a time, [and] were again attacked by an Englishman who followed us to about 900 metres over Corbie —but of *Herr Rittmeister* there was no trace.
>
> With a sense of foreboding I came home. Reports had already come in. A red triplane had landed smoothly north-west of Corbie. That another Englishman could have shot him down from behind was out of the question — that I would vouch for.

That would also have been the most terrible thing for me, as I considered myself to be the personal shield of *Herr Rittmeister*. And, indeed, should *Herr Rittmeister* have shot down the Englishman, then he would have pulled up, but he suddenly went into a steep dive and landed smoothly. Now there were two possibilities. The machine was overstressed, some sort of a valve let go, and the engine quit. The other possibility [was] that shots fired from the ground hit the engine ...[37]

A member of *Ltn* Weiss' flight, *Ltn.d.Res* Richard Wenzl, later recalled:

> ... Over the lines we attacked seven Sopwith Camels with red noses. The Anti-Richthofen people! ...
> We went through the paces ... but due to the rather strong east wind we [drifted] farther and farther over the other side. Accordingly, Weiss broke off combat and we went back over the lines. With that, suddenly I saw that one of our machines was in trouble. Afterwards someone told me that he was sure it was *Wölffchen*. In the air I thought I had recognized Richthofen's machine. One after another the other machines came back. We landed [and] everyone was there; only Richthofen was missing ...
> Now I voiced my fear. I had a numb inner feeling that something had happened to Richthofen. As I flew back, east of Corbie, I had seen a small machine on the ground on the other side of the lines that had not been there previously. This machine appeared to be red. As I knew the position, *Hptmn* Reinhard asked me to reconnoitre [the area] with some comrades. I took off with Karjus and [Wolfram] von Richthofen ...[38]

Wenzl, Karjus and Wolfram von Richthofen returned with no further information about their leader. Manfred von Richthofen's comrades waited for positive news. Although they had grown accustomed to death and destruction, they hoped that their leader would be spared the fate of so many of his victims.

The following day, newly-promoted *Maj* Wilhelm Haehnelt, Officer in Charge of Aviation for the *2. Armee*, arrived at Cappy airfield. He told the members of *JG I* that it was now certain that their *Geschwader-Kommandeur* had gone down within British lines.[39]

By all accounts, *Rittm* Manfred *Frhr* von Richthofen was killed at about 1145 (German Time) while hotly pursuing Sopwith F.1 Camel D3326 of No.209 Squadron, RAF, along the Somme River from Sailly le Sec to Vaux sur Somme. Richthofen had intended to make the stubby British fighter and its pilot, 2/Lt Wilfred R. May, his 81st victim. The master fighter pilot was halted by one bullet, which entered his chest, passed through his heart and killed him.[40]

The 'credit' for killing Manfred von Richthofen has been the source of long and no doubt endless debate. Capt A. Roy Brown, DSC, leader of No.209 Squadron's 'A' Flight,[41] filed a combat report in which he recounted: 'Dived on large formation of 15-20 Albatros Scouts D 5's and Fokker triplanes, two of which got on my tail and [then] I came out.

'Went back again and dived on pure red triplane which was firing on Lieut. May. I got a long burst into him and he went down vertical and was observed to crash by Lieut [later Sir Francis] Mellersh and Lieut May. I fired on two more, but did not get them.'[42]

May's combat report stated in typically terse fashion that he '... was attacked by a Red Triplane which chased me over the lines low to the ground. While he was on my tail Captain A.R. Brown attacked and shot it down. I observed it crash into the ground.'[43]

May's letter of 9 March 1950 offered a more detailed account of his harrowing encounter with Manfred von Richthofen:

> ... Through lack of experience I held my guns open too long, one jammed and then the other. I could not clear them, so I spun out of the mess and headed west into the sun for home.
>
> After I levelled off, I looked around but nobody was following me ... This wasn't to last long, and the first thing I knew I was being fired on from the rear ... [and] all I could do was try to dodge my attacker. I noticed it was a red tri-plane, but if I realized it was Richthofen, I would have probably passed out on the spot. I kept on dodging and spinning, I imagine from about 12,000 feet until I ran out of sky and had to hedge hop over the ground. Richthofen was firing at me continually, [and] the only thing that saved me was my poor flying. I didn't know what I was doing myself and I do not suppose that Richthofen could figure out what I was going to do.
>
> We came over the German lines, troops fired at us as we went over, this was also the case coming over the British lines. I got on the Somme River and started up the valley at a very low altitude. Richthofen was very close on my tail. I went around a curve in the river just near Corbie, [but] Richthofen beat me to it and came over the hill. At that point I was a sitting duck, [as] I was too low down between the banks to make a turn away from him.
>
> I felt that he had me cold, and I was in such a state of mind at this time that I had to restrain myself from pushing my stick forward [and nosing over] into the river, as I knew I had had it. I looked around again and saw Richthofen do a spin and a half and hit the ground. I looked up and saw one of our machines directly behind. I joined up with him and returned to our [aerodrome].[44]

While Richthofen pursued his quarry at ever lower altitude along the Somme River valley, and was himself followed by Capt Brown, Australian gun batteries also opened fire. The aircraft must have appeared as blurred images, but the gunners knew that a khaki-coloured blur was friendly and a red-coloured blur was the enemy. Consequently, the 53rd Australian Field Artillery Battery, 5th Division, and the 24th Machine-gun Company claimed credit for downing the red triplane.[45]

As the medical examination of Manfred von Richthofen's body revealed, the trajectory of the fatal bullet — entering at about the ninth rib on the right side, just behind the arm, and exiting near the left nipple[46] — was such that proponents of either argument could use it to strengthen their arguments. As the triplane twisted and turned in those final moments, it *could have been on a plane* with ground gunners; and, during Brown's pursuit, he *could have fired from off-centre* and caused such a fatal wound.

Despite strong claims that ground fire had brought down the red triplane — a belief held even by *Gen* Ernst von Hoeppner,[47] the *Kogenluft* — No.209 Squadron, RAF, took credit for bringing down 'the Red Baron'; indeed, when squadron heraldry was later created, it showed a red hawk falling.

The simple fact was that Manfred von Richthofen had violated a point of his own 'Air Combat Operations Manual' and suffered the consequences: 'One should never obstinately stay with an opponent which, through bad shooting or skilful turning, he has been unable to shoot down when the battle lasts until it is ... on the other side and one alone is faced by a greater number of opponents.'[48]

Obviously, had Richthofen broken off his long and hazardously low-level pursuit of May, he would have been out of the ground gunners' range and would have had a chance to elude or shoot down Brown. But he had not and, 25 years and 352 days after his birth, the highest-scoring fighter ace of the First World War was dead.

Richthofen's aeroplane ploughed into a mangel (fertilizer beet) field alongside the road from Corbie to Bray. Australian ground troops subsequently removed the dead pilot's body from the crumpled triplane, which soon became the object of attention of countless souvenir hunters.[49] Ultimately, the wreckage was retrieved and listed as G/5th Brigade/2, which indicated it was the second enemy aircraft captured within the 5th Brigade area.[50]

Richthofen's corpse was taken about 15km from the crash site to Poulainville aerodrome, home to No.3 Squadron, Australian Flying Corps. That R.E.8 unit had another connection with the day's events, as some of its two-seaters had also engaged *JG I* Fokker triplanes at about the time of Richthofen's death.[51] At Poulainville, Richthofen's clothing was removed (and pilfered) so that his body could undergo a 'surface examination'[52] by British and Australian medical officers. The corpse was also photographed fully dressed, so that there could be no doubt that Germany's leading air fighter had, indeed, fallen within British territory.

Later, Richthofen's body was laid out on a makeshift bier in a hangar at Poulainville, and officers of No.3 Squadron, AFC, paid their last respects. At about 1600 the following day, 22 April, a guard of honour consisting of squadron officers accompanied the Crossley tender that bore Richthofen's coffin to the cemetery in nearby Bertangles. This town was also home to No.209 Squadron. The funeral attracted other airmen, including *Capitaine* Moreau and *Lieut* Olphe-Gaillard of *Escadrille Spa 93*, a French fighter squadron then based southwest of Amiens.[53]

Manfred von Richthofen was buried with full military honours in a service that was captured on still and motion-picture film. Shortly after the services, French residents of the area desecrated the grave in the mistaken belief that Richthofen had carried out the night-time bombing of the area.[54]

AFTERSHOCK

Until a British aircraft dropped a message canister containing an official confirmation of Manfred von Richthofen's death and a photograph of the grave, several days later,[55] members of *JG I* nurtured a glimmer of hope that their *Kommandeur* had survived. According to Richthofen's official testament, entrusted to *Obltn* Bodenschatz, in the event the *Kommandeur* did not return, command of *JG I* was to be assumed by *Hptmn* Wilhelm Reinhard. On 22 April the 27-year-old officer's first task was to despatch Bodenschatz to Courtrai, personally to inform *Maj* Albrecht von Richthofen that his son was missing. While he remained hopeful, the pilot's father began to prepare the family for the worst. He sent a brief telegram to his wife:

> Manfred alive in British captivity.
>
> *Major* Richthofen.[56]

After the funeral, however, information was given to the Reuters News Service, which, on 23 April, gave the story international dissemination. Within Germany, the *Wolff'schen Telegraph-Bureau* cited the Reuters report, as did other news media and even the German Air Force's weekly *Nachrichtenblatt*.

The official publication noted: 'As a British war correspondent reported, *Rittmeister Freiherr* von Richthofen was shot down as he flew behind the Australian Front at the lowest altitude. To all appearances, he fell [as] the victim of fire from an Australian battery that had directed a Lewis machine gun at him. [The body of] *Rittmeister Freiherr* von Richthofen showed only one wound: a bullet had hit him in the heart.'[57]

The *Nachrichtenblatt* also published *Gen* von Hoeppner's note of condolence to *JG I* and, in particular, to Manfred von Richthofen's own *Jasta 11*. The old cavalryman *cum* aviation general concluded with an appeal meant to inspire the spirit of Richthofen in all of his subordinates: 'Stronger than [Richthofen's] words were his deeds. It was granted to him to be confirmed and honoured to live as a leader, [and] to be cherished as a comrade. We will not direct our gaze on what he could have been; rather, from what he was we will derive [a] living force, [a] force that stays alert in permanent memorial to his deeds.'[58]

As if anticipating such a call to arms, on the day of Manfred von Richthofen's funeral *Jasta 11* returned to the scene of the previous day's fight. At about the same time of day (just before noon) they shot down three Sopwith F.1 Camels between Hamelet and Moreuil Wood. *Staffel* leader Hans Weiss was credited with his eighteenth victory and *Ltn* Hans Joachim Wolff claimed two.[59]

No doubt survivors of the previous day's encounter were overjoyed at the sight of Sopwith Camels in the combat zone; surely they savoured the thought of destroying more of the red-nosed biplanes that had led to the loss of their leader. However, No.209 Squadron experienced no losses on 22 April. The *RAF Casualty List* records only two fighter aircraft of No.201 Squadron last seen in combat over Hangard at that time; they were probably the Camels that felt *Jasta 11*'s vengeful wrath.[60]

And there was more wrath to come as Manfred von Richthofen was transmogrified into a martyred warrior hero. In the minds of other *Jagdflieger*, the great Richthofen, like the Siegfried of legend, could have been vanquished in battle only because of some secret vulnerability or murky treachery. The source of such sinister feelings was never clearly focused, but legends have never needed much substance to expand to epic proportions.

NOTES

1   Cole, *Royal Air Force 1918*, (1968), p.9.
2   Jones, *The War in the Air*, vol IV, (1934), p.345.
3   *RAF War Diary*, 1 April 1918, pp.5-6.
4   Bodenschatz, *Jagd in Flanderns Himmel*, (1935), pp.78-79.
5   Public Record Office, Air 1/686/21/13/2250 XC15183, p.42; R.E.8 A3868 of No.52 Squadron, 2/Lts Ernest D. Jones and Robert F. Newton (both KiA).
6   Lampel, *Als Gast beim Rittmeister Frhr.v.Richthofen Nr 1*, (1923), pp.215-216.
7   Bodenschatz, op.cit., p.175.
8   Jones, op.cit., pp.349-350.
9   Letter from the Falkenhayn family via a private source.
10 Van Ishoven, *The Fall of an Eagle*, (1979), p.59.
11 Udet, *Mein Fliegerleben*, (1935), pp.78-79.
12 von Richthofen, *Ein Heldenleben*, (1920), p.319.
13 Not to be confused with Manfred's first cousin of the same name, a Dragoons officer, who was killed on 12 August 1914.
14 Obermaier, *Die Ritterkreuzträger der Luftwaffe*, vol II, (1976), pp.53-54.
15 Combat Reports and Squadron Record Book entries from Nos.43, 46 and 48 Squadrons, 6 April 1918.
16 Public Record Office, op.cit.; possibly Sopwith Camel D6491 of No.46 Squadron, Capt Sydney P. Smith (KiA).
17 Shores, et al, *Above the Trenches*, (1990), pp.343-344.
18 Bodenschatz, op.cit., p.176; Evans, *Manfred Freiherr von Richthofen Victory List*, (1992), p.143 notes that, in addition to Smith's aircraft, one Sopwith Camel of No.3 Squadron, another of No.70 Squadron and three Camels of No.43 Squadron were brought down during this fight.
19 Comment in a letter to the author.
20 Public Record Office, op.cit., p.43.
21 Shores, op.cit., p.285.
22 No.1 Squadron Record Book entry, 7 April 1918.

23   Evans, op.cit., pp.143-144.
24   Public Record Office, op.cit..
25   Adam letter, op.cit.
26   Evans, op.cit., pp.144-145.
27   Bodenschatz, op.cit, pp.79, 177.
28   von Richthofen, *Der rote Kampfflieger*, (1933), pp.203-204.
29   Public Record Office, op.cit., p.44; Sopwith Camel D6439 of No.3 Squadron, Maj Richard Raymond-Barker, MC (KiA).
30   Quoted in Bodenschatz, op.cit., p.179; Sopwith Camel B7393 of No.3 Squadron, 2/Lt David G. Lewis (PoW).
31   Quoted in *Ein Heldenleben*, op.cit., pp.260.
32   Bodenschatz, op.cit., p.80.
33   Ibid.
34   Ibid., p.81.
35   Ibid.
36   Probably Sopwith F.1 Camel B7245 of No.209 Squadron, Lt W.J. Mackenzie (WiA).
37   Quoted in *Ein Heldenleben*, op.cit., pp.261-262.
38   Wenzl, *Richthofen-Flieger*, (ca.1930), pp.23-24.
39   *Ein Heldenleben*, op.cit., p.262.
40   O'Dwyer, *Post-Mortem: Richthofen*, (1969), pp.302-304.
41   Wise, *Canadian Airmen and the First World War*, (1980), p.514.
42   No.209 Squadron Combat Report, 21 April 1918.
43   No. 209 Squadron Combat Report, 21 April 1918.
44   Flanagan (ed.), *Lieut. Wilfred 'Wop' May's Account*, (1982), p.112; the red triplane's purported 'spin and a half' into the ground *at low altitude* and other differences in Wilfred May's various accounts of the encounter have only fuelled the controversy concerning Manfred von Richthofen's demise.
45   Jones, op.cit., p.393; Cutlack, *The Official History of Australia in the War of 1914-1918*, vol VIII, (1933), p.231.
46   O'Dwyer, op.cit., p.301.
47   von Hoeppner, *Deutschlands Krieg in der Luft*, (1921), p.157.
48   Full text appears as Appendix II.
49   Carisella and Ryan, *Who Killed the Red Baron?*, (1969), pp.133-149; this work chronicles in considerable detail items 'souvenired' from Richthofen's clothing and aircraft.
50   Puglisi, *German Aircraft Down in British Lines*, Part 2, (1969), p.278.
51   Cutlack, op.cit., pp.249-250.
52   McGuire (Ed), *Documents Relating to Richthofen's Last Battle*, (1987), p.172.
53   Chamberlain and Bailey, *History of Escadrille Spa 93*, (1978), p.70.
54   Carisella and Ryan, op.cit., p.179.
55   Bodenschatz, *Das Jagdgeschwader Frhr. v. Richthofen Nr. 1 im Verbande der 2. Armee*, (1923), pp.232-233.
56   von Richthofen, *Mein Kriegstagebuch*, (1937), p.162.
57   *Nachrichtenblatt der Luftstreitkräfte, 2. Jahrgang, Nr 9*, 25 April 1918, p.128-A.
58   Ibid.
59   Bodenschatz, op.cit., p.178.
60   Sopwith Camels B6428, Capt G.A. Magor, and B6377, 2/Lt W.H. Easty.

CHAPTER 14

RED BIRDS, GREY SKIES

I n the flurry of activity, Lothar von Richthofen was overlooked in the first round of announcements of his brother's death. He was still convalescing in the Aaper Wald Clinic in Düsseldorf, and a telegram and a letter from Schweidnitz arrived after he had already heard the news. 'At first I did not believe it,' he later recalled, 'but the reports in the newspapers were so detailed — it must be true. I lay in a military hospital in Düsseldorf and had not helped my brother! How often had we both saved each other's lives —[and] on his last flight I let him down.'[1]

In this depressed and guilt-ridden state, Lothar answered his mother's letter:

> ... I should have written to you before, but I could find no words for this pain. Since I had to learn the news from the newspapers, a frightful apathy has come over me. Outwardly, I am quite prepared for it, and I am glad that Papa was also. But I know that I will miss Manfred at every step for the rest of my life. We have lost much with him, but we can be proud of him.
>
> I am glad that Papa is with all of you and I hope that you will get used to the unalterable [rôle] as a hero's mother. From the newspapers and from Papa you will have learned everything about Manfred's last flight; for the present I don't know any more, as I am so far still without news from the *Staffel*.[2]

MANFRED VON RICHTHOFEN'S SUCCESSORS

To mollify him, Lothar was returned to command of *Jagdstaffel 11* as of 24 April — on paper, at least.[3] Since he had been obliged to relinquish the post, in March, three acting *Staffel* leaders had filled in for him. The latest, *Ltn.d.Res* Hans Weiss, had been doing a splendid job and had been awarded the Royal House Order of Hohenzollern's Knight's Cross with Swords on the day Manfred von Richthofen died.[4] Lothar knew that Weiss, a seventeen-victory ace, would serve well until he could return to the Front.

Hptmn Wilhelm Reinhard, now officially confirmed as the new *Geschwader-Kommandeur*, had the fighting talent and leadership qualities that Manfred von Richthofen appreciated. Reinhard also had the same directness and clearsightedness as his predecessor, as indicated by his letter of 30 April to his mother:

> ... The death of the *Rittmeister* has affected me very much; for, as you know, he was a dear comrade and a pleasant superior. I cannot

really comprehend that such an outstanding man is no longer with us ... It seems now to have been proved definitely that he has fallen due to ground machine gun [fire], a lucky hit in the heart area. For a flyer that is no beautiful death. One prefers it to fall in aerial combat.

Three days ago I was appointed *Kommandeur* of the *Geschwader*, therefore as his successor. A hard task. It is good only that he spoke with me often, when he thought about [leadership] succession. I will carry out [all] that he instilled in me, [even] at the risk that my subordinates will not agree and that it [might] cost me my position. I owe that to his memory ...

My goal will now be to influence the *Geschwader* by personal example, i.e., to shoot down more than anyone else. When [I was] with *Jasta 6*, I could shoot down [opponents] calmly and take my time. I intended to relax after my sixteenth victory.[5] That [thought] has been dropped. For two to three months long my hands and my feet have been bandaged [from severe wounds received in a fight on 4 September 1917] and when I get up every morning I wish for good weather so that we can [engage in] air fights. Unfortunately, that has not been the case in the last eight days and then we had Frenchmen against us and they are lukewarm [in terms of fighting spirit] ...

Now to share a small joy with you: Yesterday I received the Hohenzollern [House Order], for which I was nominated by the *Rittmeister* after my eighth [victory]. It is so sad that he could not have presented it to me personally, [as] then the award would have given me more pleasure.[6]

EIN DEUTSCHES REQUIEM

Reinhard had to remain at Cappy to motivate the *Staffel* leaders and their subordinates. Thus, when he received word of arrangements being made in the German Empire's capital for a memorial service for his predecessor, he assigned *Hptmn* Kurt Lischke, *Jasta 6*'s chief administrative officer, and the distraught *Ltn* Hans Joachim Wolff of *Jasta 11* to go to Düsseldorf and escort Lothar von Richthofen to the service.[7]

The three flyers, Manfred's parents, his sister Ilse and brother Bolko met at a comfortable hotel in the centre of Berlin. Wartime shortages of food and fuel did not keep the Adlon, the Bristol and other elegant hotels from providing accommodations for dignitaries. *Gen* von Hoeppner, Commanding General of the Air Force, paid a visit to the mourners at 1:00pm on 2 May 1918 — the day that would have been Manfred's 26th birthday and the first anniversary of his first meeting with the *Kaiser*. He tried to answer *Freifrau* von Richthofen's questions about her son's death, and pointed out that Manfred had not fallen because of any lack of flying or fighting skill on his part. She recalled that the general believed 'that he could definitely assure me that Manfred had taken a chance hit from the ground. [Then] he said: "We have no replacement for your son in the whole Air Force."'[8]

Three hours later they proceeded in two official limousines along the Unter den Linden, Berlin's historic victory route, past the Imperial Palace and a short way down Kaiser Wilhelm-Strasse and the tall dark elegant buildings of Rosenstrasse to the old *Garnisonkirche* (Garrison Church), where many Prussian generals are entombed.[9] Throngs of Berliners lined the Neue Friedrichstrasse as the cortège pulled up in front of the historic edifice. Amid a solemn tolling of the bells, the mourners were greeted on the church steps by the *Kaiser*'s representatives, Cavalry *Gen* Manfred von Richthofen, namesake of the fallen flyer, and *Gen* von Hoeppner. They were escorted to reserved pews.

Inside, the altar was entirely draped in black, except for the image of Jesus Christ, symbolizing the Christian hope for redemption and the promise of heaven's glory. Before the altar were symbols of war and the promise of Teutonic glory: four crepe-covered pedestals holding bronze founts with blazing flames licking up. In a modern touch, four machine-gun barrels protruded from beneath the catafalque bearing the black velvet *Ordenskissen* which displayed Manfred von Richthofen's medals. He had not lived long enough to wear some of them, including his final honour, aptly named the Order of the Red Eagle. Below the *Ordenskissen* was a huge black-leaved funeral wreath through which protruded a splintered propeller.

The altar display was flanked by a rotating honour guard of eight young enlisted combat pilots in black leather jackets and helmets; each man wore the Iron Cross and Pilot's Badge. Officers were posted to either side of the catafalque. During the hour-long memorial service the flyers remained at attention.

Just before the service began, *Kaiserin* Auguste Victoria, her nephew *Prinz* Sigismund of Prussia and his consort were seated next to the Richthofen family. This was the final touch, the highest tribute the German Empire could accord to its most successful fighter pilot.

Freifrau von Richthofen recalled that the pastor said: '... the achievements and the work of the deceased must console us. Not that he has been touched by the death of ordinary life; but, rather, [by] death in all of its heroic beauty. When the glow of the spectrum of colour was at its brightest, when the force of the action was at its most powerful, then the curtain came thundering down over this life. Only a poet could do justice to him.'[10]

What words could not say was rendered with the music of Brahms' Mass '*Ein deutsches Requiem*' — brooding, defiant and, ultimately, celebrating the victory of life over death. The service concluded with the 'Retreat', the mournful old cavalry signal so often heard at sunset, echoing across a battlefield littered with the corpses of those who had fallen at their posts.[11]

The Empress and her entourage accompanied the family out of the church. To the Empress's expression of condolence, *Freifrau* von

Richthofen replied: 'I had wished that Manfred could have served his Fatherland longer'.[12]

Back at the hotel, many family and military friends lingered a while with the family. Wakes and memorial services seem to encourage imagination and wishful thinking as balms to emotional wounds, and this occasion was no different. One military participant was certain that *Kaiser* Wilhelm II planned to award Manfred the coveted Oak Leaves to the *Pour le Mérite* after his 80th victory — and then expressly forbid him to fly. Another story had it that Manfred wanted to be able to go off and fly with other *Staffeln* as he wished, encouraging them by his example to raise their victory scores. Even *Gen* von Hoeppner is said to have contributed to the growing legend by noting that, following his 63rd victory, Manfred requested that credit for his victories be assigned to the *Staffel*, rather than to him as an individual; the Commanding General said he had flatly rejected the proposal.[13]

MORE LOSSES OVER THE SOMME

Richthofen family members travelled back to Schweidnitz the next day, unaware that, at the same time they were preparing for the memorial service in Berlin, *Jasta 11* was suffering a harsh fate in France. At about 1400 (German Time) over that portion of the Somme Valley that *JG I* members had come to hate, *Ltn.d.Res* Hans Weiss and seven comrades were battling with five Sopwith F.1 Camels. According to a British report: 'Lieut. M.S. Taylor, No.209 Squadron, with his patrol dived on eight E.A. triplanes and fired a burst at about 20 yards' range into one E.A., which went down on its back out of control and was seen to crash by another pilot of the patrol and also by No.65 Squadron'.[14]

Ltn Weiss was flying his white-winged Fokker Dr.I 545/17 when he was attacked by Lt Taylor and became his fifth victim.[15] With Taylor during the fight was fellow Canadian 2/Lt Wilfred May, flying the same Sopwith Camel (B3326) in which he had survived the encounter with Manfred von Richthofen.[16] Weiss crashed near Etachern, south of Cérisy, just within German lines. His body was retrieved and returned to Cappy for burial. It was later learned that Weiss was to be awarded the *Pour le Mérite*,[17] an unusual circumstance at that time for a flyer with fewer than 20 victories.[18] In any case, Prussia's highest bravery award was not usually presented posthumously,[19] so the velvet *Ordenskissen* at Hans Weiss' funeral showed the Knight's Cross with Swords of the Royal House Order of Hohenzollern as his highest military honour.

That loss notwithstanding, *Jagdgeschwader I*'s victory score continued to rise, as seen in a telegram from *Gen* von Hoeppner:

'I heartily congratulate the *Geschwader* for its successes of 10 May, among which was the 300th aerial victory of the *Geschwader*. To *Ltn* Loewenhardt I express my appreciation for [his] 20th and 21st victories.'[20]

Continuing this progress required bringing in talented new pilots and transferring out 'non-productive' pilots — even when they had been hand-picked by Richthofen. Thus, on 11 May the colourful *Obltn* Walther Karjus was sent to *Armee-Flugpark 2* for reassignment.[21] The one-handed pilot's departure was no reflection on his courage and tenacity; rather, it acknowledged that in six weeks with *Jasta 11* he had scored no victories.

On 16 May *JG I* lost three Fokker triplanes. The first was shot down at about 0820 over the front lines by the Roman Road. German troops found the wreckage near Lamotte Ferme, about 10km from where Richthofen was brought down. In it was *Ltn* Hans Joachim Wolff, dead from two shots just below the heart.[22]

Two days later, *Ltn* Richard Wenzl flew to the *2. Armee* Air Park to exchange his Fokker Dr.I triplane for an aeroplane that was the great German hope for air superiority: the Fokker D.VII. After flying the new fighter, Wenzl recalled:

> This biplane was equipped with the 160hp Mercedes engine, a stationary engine [vs. the rotary engine in the Dr.I]. We were astonished by what Fokker, the *Geschwader*'s favourite [aircraft] builder, had once again squeezed out of the long-antiquated Mercedes [engine].
>
> Although the new biplane was not as manoeuvrable as the triplane, it was still a bit faster; it climbed slower at lower altitude, [but] better at higher altitude; above all, as we had to work at higher altitudes, it was fitted with a super-compressed engine. In recent times we had had such bad experiences with the rotary engine that we were quite happy to receive stationary engines again. The inferior Rizinus [synthetic lubricating] oil, the elixir of life for rotary engines, made it so apparent that on hot days there would be no end to the forced landings.[23]

The return of *Ltn* Ernst Udet, who had received the *Pour le Mérite* on 9 April[24] while on recuperative leave, was as positive a sign as the arrival of the new fighters. After a brief meeting with *Hptmn* Reinhard, Udet was given command of *Jasta 4*.

JAGDGESCHWADER RICHTHOFEN ON THE MOVE

During *JG I*'s last day at Cappy, 20 May 1918, *Gen* von Hoeppner announced that, at the direction of the *Kaiser*, the unit had been designated *Jagdgeschwader Freiherr von Richthofen Nr I*.[25] This news arrived as the *Geschwader* was preparing to move to the *7. Armee* Front to help support the forthcoming third German drive, the Aisne Offensive. That evening, when it was safest to move matériel, the unit's lorries headed south, away from the killing fields of the Somme, leaving behind only their honoured dead.

The offensive began at 0200 on Monday 27 May. The German *7.* and *1. Armees* stormed the Front held by the French *6ème* and *5ème Armées*;

three days later German forces were at Château Thierry on the Marne River, within 40 miles of Paris. The arrival of fresh troops — the American 1st, 2nd and 3rd Divisions — finally stopped the German advance.[26] Throughout these battles air activity was relatively light, so the *Geschwader* moved to Guise and then to Puisieux Ferme, northeast of Laon, and enjoyed modest success.

Like Richthofen before him, *Hptmn* Reinhard wanted *JG I* as close to the Front as possible and, on 30 May, he sent *Obltn* Bodenschatz up in a two-seater to find a suitable location. The Adjutant returned with good news: German troops had just taken Beugneux airfield, north of Château Thierry, and left useable hangars among various destroyed aircraft.

There was more good news after *JG I* settled into Beugneux. *Ltn* Erich Loewenhardt, successor to Hans Weiss in command of *Jasta 10*, received a telegram, informing him that he had been awarded the *Pour le Mérite*. The telegram arrived on the day Loewenhardt scored his 25th victory.

On 12 June *Geschwader-Kommandeur* Wilhelm Reinhard was credited with his 20th victory, a SPAD two-seater. The claim had been contested, however, by *Vzfw* Willi Gabriel, who was persuaded by *Adjutant* Bodenschatz to withdraw his claim so that the *Kommandeur* would be eligible for the *Pour le Mérite*.[27] The enlisted pilot acquiesced and *Hptmn* Reinhard departed for the latest fighter aircraft competition at Adlershof as a ranking ace and potential recipient of Prussia's highest bravery award. The latest German advance was also stalling and, as more new fighters were needed desperately, Reinhard was anxious to see what the aircraft companies proposed to supply for the short term and, possibly, for a spring 1919 offensive.

Hptmn Reinhard went to Berlin accompanied by *Ltn* Hans Kirschstein, acting commanding officer of *Jasta 6*, who was also in line to receive the *Pour le Mérite*. The following day, *Ltn* Erich Loewenhardt was given temporary command of *JG I*.[28]

Three weeks later, on 3 July 1918, Wilhelm Reinhard was killed while testing the metal-skinned Zeppelin-Lindau D.I 2085/18 designed by *Prof Dr* Claudius Dornier. The aircraft had been flown initially by *Obltn* Hermann Göring, a *Pour le Mérite* recipient, 21-victory ace and leader of *Jasta 27*. Reinhard took up the new fighter and, when he made a steep dive, the top wing came off and the aeroplane smashed into the ground.[29] Coincidentally, he was succeeded as *Geschwader-Kommandeur* by Göring. Reinhard's death precluded his receiving the *Pour le Mérite*.[30]

As part of *JG I*'s tradition-building process, Manfred von Richthofen had had a walking stick fashioned from the broken propeller of one of his adversaries. Called the *Geschwader-Stock*, the cane became the *Kommandeur*'s symbol of office. Upon Richthofen's death, *Obltn* Bodenschatz took charge of it and then turned it over to *Hptmn* Reinhard. After his death, on 14 July, Bodenschatz handed it to Hermann Göring.

The fifth German drive, the Champagne-Marne offensive, began on 15 July and ended two days later, adding further losses that culminated in 800,000 German casualties during the first five drives of 1918.[31]

LOTHAR VON RICHTHOFEN RETURNS

The activities, and especially the losses, were all too much for Lothar von Richthofen to bear back in Germany. He felt his convalescence was being extended to keep him from becoming *the second* Richthofen to fall in combat, and the thought of special treatment drove him to desperation, as he later recalled:

> My parents, all my relatives and friends pestered me about not going back. Yet I had taken an oath of revenge and I had to fulfil it no matter what the cost.
>
> Everyone conspired against me. The Commanding General of the Air Force offered me a very nice adjutant's billet at Headquarters [in Berlin]. My doctors did not want to let me go; they wrote I was not "fit for duty". But before that became known, I had to get back to the Front, otherwise I would not be allowed to go back to my *Jagdstaffel*. The normal course to get back to the Front took from [two] to four weeks. In a few days my medical records would be reviewed at the assignment office in Hannover [and] then it would be too late. Terrible! I was not completely sure that my right eye, which was injured the last time I was wounded, would be satisfactory for aerial combat; no one could judge that, [as] I had to try it myself at the Front.
>
> I knew the officer at Corps Headquarters who handled personnel matters. Therefore, I telephoned him [and] declared that I was healthy again and wanted to take command of my *Staffel* again.
>
> "We will do it!" was the answer. In an instant I was on a train bound for the General Headquarters in the Field. There I reported to the Commanding General that I was passing through on the way to the Front, completely restored to health. These lies were necessary, for I could have been stopped at the last moment.
>
> In Verviers I was treated very sympathetically. At lunch I sat between *Gen* von Hoeppner and *Feldflugchef* [*Oberst* Hermann von der Lieth-] Thomsen. That evening I was brought by a staff car to the train, and ... I was berthed in a fabulous sleeping car.
>
> The next morning I was in Maubeuge. There, in pouring rain, I was met by an aeroplane [and was crammed into it] along with my luggage. An hour and a half later we landed at Braisne, near Laon.[32]

Lothar wanted to get back into action immediately, but first he had to familiarise himself with the Fokker D.VII and the new area of military operations. The *Geschwader* completed another move — this time briefly to Monthussart Ferme, near Soissons — on 19 July, when Lothar was officially designated leader of *Jasta 11*.[33] He realized his limitations on his first flight; he nearly became lost and his vision was so blurred that he 'could scarcely tell friend from foe.'[34] But, with typical Richthofen tenacity, Lothar continued to fly and to practise his aerial marksmanship.

On 25 July *Jagdgeschwader Freiherr von Richthofen Nr I* celebrated its 500th aerial victory: a Sopwith F.1 Camel shot down at 1950 by Lothar von Richthofen. It was his first successful combat since returning to active duty, and was logged as his own 30th victory.[35] The unit's top scorer, *Ltn* Erich Loewenhardt, recorded his 44th air combat success.

Despite the critical point in the fighting and the *Geschwader*'s impending withdrawal to Puisieux Ferme, on 26 July *Obltn* Hermann Göring went on leave and transferred acting command of *JG I* to Lothar von Richthofen.

Shortly after arriving at *JG I*, Göring flew Fokker D.VII 294/18 decorated with the red engine cowl, struts and wheel covers symbolic of the *Geschwader* progenitor. In that aircraft he added one more victory to his score — a SPAD shot down over St Bandry on 18 July[36] — but he achieved no further air combat successes to make himself the example that Richthofen and Reinhard had been.

Relinquishing command at this time was a move that perhaps revealed an element of Göring's nature; 22 years later, as *Reichsmarschal* of the *Luftwaffe*, he went on leave after the failure of the Battle of Britain and turned over command to more capable hands (in the latter case, *Generalfeldmarschal* Erhard Milch).[37]

In 1918, Lothar von Richthofen not only presided over an orderly transfer back beyond Laon, but led the destruction of eleven enemy aircraft — 'a *Staffel*'s worth,' according to the Adjutant[38] — and logged his own 31st and 32nd victories.

Erich Loewenhardt's achievement brought with it promotion to *Oberleutnant* and a certain seniority that made him a 'big brother' figure to Lothar von Richthofen. A fellow Silesian but actually two years younger than Lothar, Loewenhardt exuded the confidence based on skill that Manfred had displayed in abundance. The two worked well together, as they proved when *JG I* was ordered to patrol the *2. Armee* sector when the Allied Amiens Offensive began on 8 August. They each scored triple victories — Lothar's 33rd, 34th and 35th victories and Loewenhardt's 49th, 50th and 51st — in a day of heavy fighting over the ominous area of the Somme where the *Rittmeister* had met his end.

Lothar did not give voice to such thoughts. Rather, he recalled: '... It was nice to fly with Loewenhardt, almost the way it had been with Manfred, if only to compare a little. We had got to know each other well in a short time and we had a splendid understanding of each other in the air. Since Manfred [was gone], I was happy to have again found someone on whom I could rely. Loewenhardt expressed a similar view about me.'[39]

During morning and evening patrols on 9 August, Lothar von Richthofen in his 'red bird'[40] shot down a de Havilland D.H.9 bomber in flames on each sortie for victories 36 and 37. Matching him, Erich

Loewenhardt in his yellow Fokker D.VII sent down a Sopwith F.1 Camel escort on each flight for his 52nd and then his 53rd (and last) triumph.[41]

JG I's move the next day from Puisieux Ferme on the *7. Armee* Front to Ennemain, west of St Quentin on the *2. Armee* Front, put the Richthofen-Loewenhardt team close to the activity over the Somme. While the new airfield was still being prepared, at about 11 the two seasoned leaders took beginners from *Jastas 10* and *11* over the Front for a taste of combat. The twelve Fokkers crossed the lines at 3,000m to 4,000m and then avoided a formation of S.E.5s. When a lone Sopwith F.1 Camel came into view, Loewenhardt took his flight into a dive to demonstrate the art of killing and to achieve his anticipated 54th victory.[42]

Then, in horror, Lothar von Richthofen witnessed a scene of destruction he had not expected. He saw Loewenhardt line up behind the Camel for the kill and then, as he recalled:

> ... I saw immediately that one of the other [Fokkers] was unnecessarily close [to Loewenhardt]. But four or five of them did not see that; instead they flew right behind Loewenhardt, apparently to share in the fight. How often was it said that only one man could do the shooting. One had to be ready to attack in case that man's guns should jam and he had to turn away. Suddenly I see that the Englishman is trailing a ribbon of smoke behind him and diving steeply.
>
> At about the same moment, what's this! Loewenhardt is no longer flying behind the falling Englishman; instead there is a wild confusion of thousands of splinters. Immediately I make a steep dive to see what is really wrong. It is immediately clear — Loewenhardt has been rammed![43]

The intended victim was allowed to slip away. All eyes were on the two Fokkers going down, watching as only one parachute opened. The survivor was *Ltn* Richard Wentz, who Lothar officially cleared of any responsibility in the incident.[44] Loewenhardt came down in a hotly contested area near Chaulnes, and it was a week before his corpse was recovered.[45] This time, however, the body of a German high-scoring fighter pilot was sent home to his birthplace in Lower Silesia for burial with full honours.[46]

The day after Loewenhardt fell, Lothar led the *Geschwader* and was credited with shooting down a de Havilland D.H.12 (*sic*) bomber at 0930 for his 38th victory.[47] That gain was marred, however, by *JG I*'s loss of three aircraft.

Clearly, the German *Luftstreitkräfte* — like other German forces — was losing and being forced to withdraw defensively on the *2. Armee* and other Fronts. As the RAF Historian opined:

> ... In the past the German pilots had been able to suit their tactics to the general conditions. The air forces opposed to them were numerically stronger, and it was sound tactics to seek every advantage, to

choose the moments for intervention, to break off an action when the advantages ... had disappeared. It had never been possible for the German air service to prevent the Royal Air Force squadrons from working. All it could hope to do was make those squadrons pay as dearly as possible, and this could best be done by seeking out the weaker elements and avoiding the stronger ...[48]

On 12 August *JG I* recorded five victories, including Lothar von Richthofen's 39th and 40th, and showed no losses. One of Lothar's victims, 23-year-old Capt John K. Summers, MC, was captured and taken to *JG I*'s airfield, where he was a guest at dinner. Capt Summers was the leader of 'B' Flight of No.209 Squadron, the unit that claimed to have shot down Manfred, but Lothar bore no grudges. He had settled the score with No.209 Squadron; indeed, his other victory that day may have been Lt K.M. Walker, a member of Summers' flight.[49] Lothar did not know, however, that Lt Wilfred May of the same squadron had claimed his seventh victory that day. After a few glasses of wine, when Lothar asked eight-victory Canadian ace Summers how long he thought the war would last, the answer was a plucky: 'Well, until we have won!'.[50]

UNLUCKY 13 AGAIN

After promising not to try to escape before 0900 the following day, Capt Summers spent the night with *Jasta 11*. The next morning, Tuesday 13 August, he was safely packed off to St Quentin, but Lothar von Richthofen still had an uneasy feeling. He had been shot down twice before on the 13th, and was apprehensive about this day. He was not much comforted when a congratulatory telegram from Crown Prince Wilhelm, the *Kaiser*'s heir apparent, mentioned: '... With special joy, I took note that on the day the *Geschwader* changed airfields it energetically engaged [and] shot down thirteen opponents over the new battlefront ...'[51]

There was that number 13 again. Lothar knew that on 10 August, the day of the move, *JG I* had scored only four victories and, indeed, had suffered the loss of Loewenhardt. What sort of devilry caused the number 13 to show up in the telegram?

It did not matter. Nothing would stop Lothar. As he later wrote: '... One should not be superstitious. I just wanted to fly, to dispel the last misgivings. If it were another day, perhaps I would not have taken off at all, for I had three different pressing car trips that had to be made. But, no, today the spell of the 13th had to be broken. There were a lot of Englishmen at the Front ...'[52]

Over the lines Lothar spotted a two-seater and went after it. He fired away, and was about to finish off his opponent when he saw that six British fighters were hot in pursuit of him. He broke off his pursuit and headed for his own lines, managing to shake off all of the fighters except one, about 100m behind him.

Lothar dived at full speed, putting distance between him and his pursuer so he would have room to turn and manoeuvre to fire a killing shot. 'Suddenly there was a terrible pain in my right leg,' he later wrote. 'I almost got away. It was the only shot [to hit] the whole machine.. Then I had such pain that I was unable to work the rudder. My right leg was stuck on the rudder bar and I couldn't move it. I had to pull it free with both hands ...'[53]

Lothar plunged toward the ground. He was unable to climb out of his Fokker to use the parachute. He had to ride it down to a small flat area in the lunar-like landscape of the Somme Front.

Lothar survived, but it was his last combat flight. He was probably shot down by Capt Field E. Kindley of the 148th Aero Squadron; the USAS pilot's fourth victory occurred at a time and place that directly corresponds to where the red Fokker D.VII went down.[54]

DAS ENDE

Lothar von Richthofen was sent back to Germany for treatment and convalescence. He was forced into retirement with 40 confirmed victories — the same number as the legendary Oswald Boelcke, but half as many as his brother. Likewise, Lothar was entitled to wear nine awards, compared with the 24 that had graced Manfred's black velvet *Ordenskissen*.[55]

Lothar would always live in Manfred's shadow, as would everyone connected with *Jagdgeschwader Freiherr von Richthofen Nr I*. *Obltn* Hermann Göring, who returned from leave and resumed his post as *Kommandeur* on 22 August, broke with the tradition of red-coloured aircraft and tried to establish his own identity with the all-white Fokker D.VII 5125/18.[56] He finished the war with 22 victories, but gloried in being known as the 'successor' to Manfred von Richthofen.

The real successor, in terms of air combat successes, was *Ltn* Ernst Udet, whose final tally was 62 confirmed victories. But Udet and the few leading aces who emerged in *JG I* survived because of their fighting skills and — despite Manfred von Richthofen's contention to the contrary — their flying ability. The rate of aircraft attrition was high and the brief appearance of the Fokker E.V/D.VIII monoplane interceptor revealed development problems that were overcome too late. Shortages of quality fuel, lubricants, high-compression engines and tyres crippled many a German air unit in the final weeks of the war. The Allies' successful series of offensives pushed German units farther and farther eastward, which took its toll of men and machines.

Jagdgeschwader Freiherr von Richthofen Nr I's last day in combat was Wednesday 6 November, 1918. Operating from an airfield at Marville, on the *5. Armee* Front north of Verdun, the final aerial victories were recorded. Three American SPAD S.XIIIs were brought down near Woevre Wood as *Jasta 6* leader *Ltn.d.Res* Ulrich Neckel's 30th victory, *Jasta 10* pilot

Ltn.d.Res Justus Grassmann's tenth, and his *Staffel* comrade *Ltn.d.Res* Alois Heldmann's fifteenth enemy aircraft.[57]

Ltn Neckel became the final *JG I* recipient of the *Pour le Mérite*, which was awarded to him on 8 November. The next day *Kaiser* Wilhelm II abdicated and further awards from him ceased, as he and his entourage departed for exile in Holland.

Obltn Hermann Göring had the task of organizing *JG I*'s withdrawal from the field of battle. Starting two days before the Armistice, on 9 November, he led the four *Staffeln* on an odyssey from France to several locations in Germany until final demobilization of the *Geschwader* came at Aschaffenburg on 17 November.

JG I's final armed confrontation came not with enemy airmen, but with German communists who held the city of Darmstadt in the abortive Bolshevik-type revolution that followed the collapse of the Hohenzollern monarchy. When advance elements of *JG I* arrived in the Rhineland city, they were seized by the local Soldiers' and Workers' Council and their weapons were confiscated. *Geschwader-Kommandeur* Hermann Göring sent word that, if the men and weapons were not released immediately, he would lead the four *Staffeln* in a full-scale aerial assault on the Reds' stronghold. His demands were met, and the future Nazi deputy leader scored his first triumph against domestic enemies.

Göring and other former comrades went on to other deeds and other places in history.

Just after the First World War, Manfred von Richthofen's grave at Bertangles was disinterred and his remains were transferred to a large German military cemetery at Fricourt, a few kilometres east of the once hotly-contested city of Albert. At the Richthofen family's request, in mid-1925 the body was exhumed again and brought back to Germany on a special train for a formal state funeral in Berlin. The fighter pilot's mother wanted him buried at home in Schweidnitz, alongside his father, who died in 1920, and his brother Lothar, who died in a civilian aeroplane crash in 1922. But the nation that revered him in life now needed to honour his mortal remains properly in its own way.

There was an elaborate state funeral, presided over by *Reichspräsident* Paul von Hindenburg. Police barricades had to be set up to contain the crowds. Finally, Manfred von Richthofen's remains were interred with some of Germany's greatest heroes in the *Invalidenfriedhof* in Berlin.

In 1976, officials of the former East German government announced plans to 'consolidate' its border near the infamous Berlin Wall, and said that the Richthofen grave site in [then] East Berlin was among those that had to be vacated. At the family's request the coffin was delivered to western Germany for burial in a family plot in Mainz. Consequently, Manfred von Richthofen's remains now rest near those of his mother, who died in 1962; his sister Ilse, who died in 1963; and his brother Bolko, who died in 1971.

But the name and legend of Manfred von Richthofen may never rest. Many aspects of his life and career continue to be the focus of extensive research. Within the span of his relatively short life, Richthofen earned a reputation of unquestioned bravery, and ability to inspire total loyalty from his comrades and respect from his adversaries. Add to those qualities the colourful personal style and combat success of 'the red baron', and the product is a larger-than-life figure who inspires interest to the point of fascination.

Another chapter of the Manfred von Richthofen story remains to be written. It concerns the wealth of historical material removed from the family home in Silesia by Soviet occupation forces at the end of the Second World War. With the hoped-for return of these items to a competent authority, researchers and historians may yet learn more about the First World War's most successful fighter pilot.

NOTES

1   von Richthofen, *Das letzte Mal an der Front, Juli-August 1918*, (1921), p.278.
2   Quoted in von Richthofen, *Mein Kriegstagebuch*, (1937), p.168.
3   Bodenschatz, *Jagd in Flanderns Himmel*, (1935), p.180.
4   O'Connor, *Aviation Awards of Imperial Germany in World War I and the Men Who Earned Them*, vol II, (1990), p.265.
5   This comment must refer to a future date, as *Hptmn* Reinhard did not achieve his sixteenth victory until 2 June 1918.
6   Quoted in Zuerl, *Pour-le-Mérite-Flieger*, (1938), pp.535-536.
7   Bodenschatz, op.cit., p.180; Bodenschatz contends (p.97) that *Ltn* Wolfram *Frhr* von Richthofen was among the *JG I* members sent to Berlin, yet *Freifrau* von Richthofen makes no mention of this cousin being at the memorial service — which would have been an odd omission for someone with such a good sense of family history.
8   *Mein Kriegstagebuch*, op.cit., p.169.
9   Baedecker, *Berlin*, (1927), p.145.
10 Ibid., pp.169-170.
11 Ibid., p.170.
12 Ibid.
13 Ibid., p.172.
14 *RAF Communiqué No. 5*, 8 May 1918, p.3.
15 Shores, et al, *Above the Trenches*, (1990), p.359; according to No.209 Squadron Record Book, Lt Taylor was flying Sopwith Camel B3329 that day; he was killed in the same aircraft on 7 July 1918.
16 No.209 Squadron Record Book entry for 2 May 1918.
17 Zuerl, op.cit., p.546.
18 O'Connor, op.cit., pp.64-65, 95.
19 Ibid., p.91.
20 *Nachrichtenblatt der Luftstreitkräfte, 2. Jahrgang, Nr 12*, 16 May 1918, p.169.
21 Bodenschatz, op.cit., pp.97, 182, 185.
22 Shores, et al, op.cit., p.66, contend that Wolff was the fourth victory of Lt [later Capt] Horace D. Barton, DFC and Bar, of No.24 Squadron; given the twelve-hour difference between the time of Wolff's demise and Barton's claim, the time and location of the downing of *Sergt* Otto Schmutzler's triplane make it more likely that Schmutzler was shot down by Barton.
23 Wenzl, *Richthofen-Flieger*, (ca.1930), p.38.
24 O'Connor, op.cit., p.220.
25 Bodenschatz, op.cit., p.184.

26 Esposito, *A Concise History of World War I*, (1964), p.113.

27 Imrie, *Die Gebrüder Gabriel*, (1962), p.342.

28 Bodenschatz, op.cit., p.188.

29 Terry, *The Development of Dornier Landplanes 1914-1918*, (1981), p.112.

30 O'Connor, op.cit., p.93.

31 Esposito, op.cit., p.115.

32 *Das letzte Mal an der Front*, op.cit., pp.278-279.

33 Bodenschatz, op.cit., pp.121, 193.

34 *Das letzte Mal an der Front*, op.cit., p.279.

35 *Kofl 7. Armee Fliegertagesmeldung Nr 211*, 26 July 1918 credits Lothar von Richthofen with achieving *JG I*'s 500th victory, as do other sources.

36 Bodenschatz, op.cit., p.192.

37 Irving, *The Rise and Fall of the Luftwaffe*, (1973), p.110.

38 Bodenschatz, op.cit., p.123.

39 Ibid., p.288.

40 Ibid., p.287.

41 Ibid., pp.125, 196.

42 Ibid. is the only source document that credits Loewenhardt with this aerial victory.

43 Ibid., p.289.

44 Zuerl, op.cit., p.322.

45 *Das letzte Mal an der Front*, op.cit., p.290.

46 Haehnelt, *Ehrentafel der im Flugdienst während des Weltkrieges gefallenen Offiziere der Deutschen Fliegerverbände*, (1920), p.50; Bodenschatz, op.cit., p.132.

47 Bodenschatz, op.cit., p.198; there was no D.H.12 aircraft (Ref: Bruce, *British Aeroplanes*, (1969), pp.157-215); *Ltn* Ernst Udet of *Jasta 4* also claimed a 'D.H.12' that day, as his 55th victory (Ref: Udet, *Mein Fliegerleben*, (1935), p.183); these two-seaters might have been D.H.9s, of which the *RAF Casualty List* notes four were lost that day — but all in the German *4. Armee* area; they remain 'mystery victories'.

48 Ibid.

49 Shores, op.cit., p.373.

50 *Das letzte Mal an der Front*, op.cit., p.291.

51 Quoted in Bodenschatz, op.cit., p.130.

52 *Das letzte Mal an der Front*, op.cit., p.292.

53 Ibid.

54 Shores, op.cit., p.223.

55 O'Connor, op.cit. pp.238-239.

56 Nowarra, *Eisernes Kreuz und Balkenkreuz*, (1968), p.114.

57 Bodenschatz, op.cit., pp.139, 209.

APPENDIX 1

AERIAL VICTORY LIST OF MANFRED VON RICHTHOFEN

Information for the following victory list was compiled from Manfred von Richthofen's combat reports, *Nachrichtenblatt der Luftstreitkräfte* listings, *Kommandeur der Flieger* and other German reports, as well as the *RFC/RAF Casualty Lists* and the *RFC/RAF War Diary*. Dates are rendered in the German style and military time is used, according to the German clock; generally, German time was one hour ahead of Allied time, but relative timeframes are included to obviate any question. Aircraft types preceded by an asterisk (*) indicate actual serial number patches that were acquired by *Freiherr* von Richthofen from the vanquished aircraft and displayed at his home in Schweidnitz, as confirmed by pre-Second World War photographs of the exhibits. Types preceded by (+) indicate serial number was reported in the *Nachrichtenblatt* or other German documentation. In the case of two-seater crews, the pilot is listed first, the observer second. Condition of the aircrew is indicated by the following abbreviations: DoW = Died of Wounds; KiA = Killed in Action; PoW = Prisoner of War. Lack of abbreviation assumes the man was uninjured and returned to his own lines.

No.	Date	Time	Location	Aircraft	Crew and disposition
1	17.9.16	1100	Villers Plouich	F.E.2b 7018	2/Lt L. B. F. Morris (DoW), Lt T. Rees (DoW), 11 Sqdn, RFC
2	23.9.16	1100	Beugny	Martin-syde G.100 7481	Sgt H. Bellerby (KiA), 27 Sqdn, RFC
3	30.9.16	1150	Frémicourt	F.E.2b 6973	Lt E. C. Lansdale (KiA), Sgt A. Clarkson (KiA), 11 Sqdn, RFC
4	7.10.16	0910	Equanacourt	* B.E.12 6618	2/Lt W. C. Fenwick (KiA), 21 Sqdn, RFC
5	16.10.16	1710	north of Ytres	* B.E.12 6580	2/Lt J. Thompson (KiA), 19 Sqdn, RFC
6	25.10.16	0935	north of Bapaume	B.E.12 6629	2/Lt A. J. Fisher (KiA), 21 Sqdn, RFC

223

No.	Date	Time	Location	Aircraft	Crew and disposition
7	3.11.16	1410	Loupart Wood	F.E.2b 7010	Sgt C. G. Baldwin (KiA), 2/Lt G. A. Bentham (KiA), 18 Sqdn, RFC
8	9.11.16	1030	Beugny	B.E.2c 2506	2/Lt I. G. Cameron (DoW), 12 Sqdn, RFC
9	20.11.16	0940	south of Grandcourt	B.E.2c 2767	2/Lt J. C. Lees (PoW), Lt T. H. Clarke (PoW), 15 Sqdn, RFC
10	20.11.16	1615	Guedecourt	F.E.2b 4848	2/Lt G. S. Hall (DoW), 2/Lt G. Doughty (KiA), 18 Sqdn, RFC
11	23.11.16	1500	Bapaume	D.H.2 5964	Maj L. G. Hawker, VC, DSO (KiA), 24 Sqdn, RFC
12	11.12.16	1155	Mercatel	* D.H.2 5986	Lt P. B. G. Hunt (PoW), 32 Sqdn, RFC
13	20.12.16	1130	Monchy le Preux	D.H.2 7927	Lt A. G. Knight, DSO, MC (KiA), 29 Sqdn, RFC
14	20.12.16	1345	Noreuil	* F.E.2b A5446	Lt L. G. D'Arcy (KiA), Sub/Lt R. C. Whiteside (KiA), 18 Sqdn, RFC
			or	F.E.2b 4884	Lt R. Smith (KiA) 2/Lt H. Fiske (KiA) 18 Sqdn, RFC
15	27.12.16	1625	Ficheux/Arras	F.E.2b 6937	Lt H. J. H. Dicksee (WiA), Capt J. B. Quested, 11 Sqdn, RFC
16	4.1.17	1615	Metz en Couture	* Sopwith Pup N5193	Fl Lt A. S. Todd (KiA), 8 Sqdn, RNAS
17	23.1.17	1610	southwest of Lens	F.E.8 6388	2/Lt J. Hay (KiA), 40 Sqdn, RFC
18	24.1.17	1215	west of Vimy	* F.E.2b 6997	Capt O. Greig (WiA/PoW), 2/Lt J. E. MacLenan (WiA/ PoW), 25 Sqdn, RFC
19	1.2.17	1600	southwest of Thelus	+ B.E.2d 6742	Lt P.W. Murray (DoW), Lt D.J. McRae (DoW), 16 Sqdn, RFC

No.	Date	Time	Location	Aircraft	Crew and disposition
20	14.2.17	1200	Lens-Hulluch road, east of Loos	+ B.E.2d 6231	2/Lt C. D. Bennett (WiA/PoW), 2/Lt H. A. Croft (KiA), 2 Sqdn, RFC
21	14.2.17	1645	Mazingarbe (over British lines)	B.E.2c 2543	Capt G. C. Bailey, DSO (WiA), 2/Lt G. W. B. Hampton, 2 Sqdn, RFC
22	4.3.17	1250	north of Loos	B.E.2d 5785	Lt J. E. B. Crosbee, Fl/Sgt J. E. Prance (WiA), 2 Sqdn, RFC
23	4.3.17	1620	Acheville, south of Vimy	+*Sop-with1½ Strutter A1108	2/Lt H. J. Green (KiA), 2/Lt A. W. Reid (KiA), 43 Sqdn, RFC
24	6.3.17	1700	Souchez	B.E.2e A2785	2/Lt C. M. G. Bibbey (KiA), Lt J. G. O. Brichta (KiA), 16 Sqdn, RFC
25	9.3.17	1200	Roclincourt-Bailleul	D.H.2 A2571	2/Lt A. J. Pearson, MC (KiA), 29 Sqdn, RFC
26	11.3.17	1200	Vimy	+*B.E.2d 6232	2/Lt J. Smyth (KiA), 2/Lt E. Byrne (KiA), 2 Sqdn, RFC
27	17.3.17	1145	Bailleul/Oppy	+ F.E.2b A5439	Lt A. E. Boultbee (KiA), 2/AM F. King (KiA), 25 Sqdn, RFC
28	17.3.17	1700	Souchez	B.E.2c 2814	2/Lt G. M. Watt (KiA), Sgt E. A. Howlett (KiA), 16 Sqdn, RFC
29	21.3.17	1725	north of Neuville	B.E.2f A3154	Fl/Sgt S. H. Quicke (KiA), 2/Lt W. J. Lidsey (KiA), 16 Sqdn, RFC
30	24.3.17	1155	Vimy	+ SPAD S.7 A6706	2/Lt R. P. Baker (WiA/PoW), 19 Sqdn, RFC

(25 March 1917: German time synchronized with Allied time)

| 31 | 25.3.17 | 0820 | Tilloy | Nieuport 17 A6689 | 2/Lt C. G. Gilbert (PoW), 29 Sqdn, RFC |
| 32 | 2.4.17 | 0835 | Farbus, northeast of Arras | +*B.E.2d 5841 | Lt P. J. G. Powell (KiA), 1/AM P. Bonner (KiA), 13 Sqdn, RFC |

No.	Date	Time	Location	Aircraft	Crew and disposition
33	2.4.17	1120	Givenchy	+*Sopwith 1½ Strutter A2401	2/Lt A. P. Warren (PoW), Sgt R. Dunn (KiA), 43 Sqdn, RFC
34	3.4.17	1615	Lens	+*F.E.2d A6382	2/Lt D. P. McDonald (WiA/PoW), 2/Lt J. I. M. O'Beirne (KiA), 25 Sqdn, RFC
35	5.4.17	1100	Cuincy	F.2A A3343	Lt A. T. Adams (PoW), Lt D. J. Stewart (WiA/PoW), 48 Sqdn, RFC
36	5.4.17	1100	Lewaarde, southeast of Douai	+*F.2A A3340	2/Lt A. N. Lechler (WiA/PoW), Lt H. D. K. George (DoW), 48 Sqdn, RFC
37	7.4.17	1745	Mercatel	Nieuport 17 A6645	2/Lt G. O. Smart (KiA), 60 Sqdn, RFC
38	8.4.17	1145	Farbus	Sopwith 1½ Strutter A2406	2/Lt J. S. Hagearty (WiA/PoW), Lt L. Heath-Cantle (KiA), 43 Sqdn, RFC
39	8.4.17	1640	Vimy	+ B.E.2e A2815	2/Lt K. I. Mackenzie (KiA), G. Everingham (KiA), 16 Sqdn, RFC
40	11.4.17	0925	Willerval	B.E.2c 2501	Lt E. C. E. Derwin (WiA), Gnr H. Pierson (WiA), 13 Sqdn, RFC
41	13.4.17	0856	Vitry	R.E.8 A3190	Capt J. Stuart (KiA), Lt M. H. Wood (KiA), 59 Sqdn, RFC
42	13.4.17	1145	west of Monchy, near Feuchy	F.E.2b A827	Lt C. E. Robertson 2/Lt H. D. Duncan, 11 Sqdn, RFC
43	13.4.17	1930	Hénin-Liétard	+*F.E.2b 4997	2/Lt A. H. Bates (KiA), Sgt W. A. Barnes (KiA), 25 Sqdn, RFC
44	14.4.17	0915	Fresnoy	+ Nieuport 17 A6796	Lt W. O. Russell (PoW), 60 Sqdn, RFC
45	16.4.17	1730	Gavrelle	B.E.2c 3156	2/Lt A. Pascoe (WiA), 2/Lt F. S. Andrews (WiA), 13 Sqdn, RFC

No.	Date	Time	Location	Aircraft	Crew and disposition

(17 April 1917: German time one hour ahead of Allied time)

No.	Date	Time	Location	Aircraft	Crew and disposition
46	22.4.17	0510	Lagnicourt	F.E.2b A820	Lt C. A. Parker, Lt J. C. B. Hesketh (KiA), 11 Sqdn, RFC
47	23.4.17	1213	Avion/ Méricourt, east of Vimy	B.E.2f A3168	2/Lt E.A. Welch (KiA), Sgt A. Tollervey (KiA), 16 Sqdn, RFC
48	28.4.17	0930	east of Pelves	B.E.2e 7221	Lt R. W. Follit (DoW), 2/Lt F. J. Kirkham (WiA/PoW), 13 Sqdn, RFC
49	29.4.17	1215	Lecluse	SPAD S.7 A1573	Lt R. Applin (KiA), 19 Sqdn, RFC
50	29.4.17	1644	southwest of Inchy	F.E.2b 4898	Sgt G. Stead (KiA), 1/AM (A/Cpl) A. Beebee (KiA), 18 Sqdn, RFC
51	29.4.17	1925	Roeux	B.E.2e 2738	2/Lt D. E. Davies (KiA), Lt G. H. Rathbone (KiA), 12 Sqdn, RFC
52	29.4.17	1945	Lens/Billy – Montigny/ Sallaumines	Sopwith Triplane N5463	F/S/Lt A. E. Cuzner (KiA), 8 Sqdn, RNAS
53	18.6.17	1315	north of Ypres	R.E.8 A4290	Lt R. W. Ellis (KiA), Lt H. C. Barlow (KiA), 9 Sqdn, RFC
54	23.6.17	2115	north of Ypres (Dickebusch)	SPAD	possibly aircraft from 23 Sqdn, RFC
55	24.6.17	0930	Becelaere	D.H.4 A7473	Capt N. G. McNaughton (KiA), Lt A. H. Mearns (KiA), 57 Sqdn, RFC
56	25.6.17	1735	Le Bizet	R.E.8 A3847	Lt L. S. Bowman (KiA), 2/Lt J. E. Power-Clutter-buck (KiA), 53 Sqdn, RFC
57	2.7.17	1020	Deulemont	R.E.8 A3538	Sgt H. A. Whatley (KiA), 2/Lt F. G.B. Pascoe (KiA), 53 Sqdn, RFC
58	16.8.17	0755	southwest of Houthulst Forest	Nieuport 23 A611	2/Lt W. H. T. Williams (KiA), 29 Sqdn, RFC

No.	Date	Time	Location	Aircraft	Crew and disposition
59	26.8.17	0730	Poelkappelle	SPAD S.7 B3492	2/Lt C. P. Williams (KiA), 19 Sqdn, RFC
60	1.9.17	0750	Zonnebeke	R.E.8 B782	2/Lt J. B. C. Madge (PoW), 2/Lt W. Kember (KiA), 6 Sqdn, RFC
61	3.9.17	0735	south of Bousbecque	Sopwith Pup B1795	Lt A. F. Bird (PoW), 46 Sqdn, RFC
62	23.11.17	1400	Bourlon Wood	D.H.5 A9299	Lt J. A. V. Boddy (WiA), 64 Sqdn, RFC
63	30.11.17	1430	Moeuvres	S.E.5a B644	Lt D. A. D. I. Mac-Gregor (KiA), 41 Sqdn, RFC

(10 March 1918: German time synchronized with Allied time)

No.	Date	Time	Location	Aircraft	Crew and disposition
64	12.3.18	1110	Nauroy	F.2B B1251	2/Lt L. C. F. Clutter-buck (PoW), 2/Lt H. J. Sparks (PoW), 62 Sqdn, RFC
65	13.3.18	1035	Gonnelieu/ Banteaux	Sopwith F.1 Camel B5590	Lt E. E. Heath (WiA/PoW), 73 Sqdn, RFC
66	18.3.18	1115	Andigny	Sopwith F.1 Camel B5243	Lt W. G. Ivamy (PoW), 54 Sqdn, RFC
67	24.3.18	1445	Combles	S.E.5a C5389	2/Lt W. Porter (KiA), 56 Sqdn, RFC
68	25.3.18	1555	Contalmaison	Sopwith F.1 Camel C1562	2/Lt D. Cameron (KiA), 3 Sqdn, RFC
69	26.3.18	1645	south of Contalmaison	Sopwith 5F.1 Dolphin	Possibly aircraft of 19 Sqdn, RFC
70	26.3.18	1700	northeast of Albert	R.E.8 B742	2/Lt V. J. Reading (KiA), 2/Lt M. Leggatt (KiA), 15 Sqdn, RFC
71	27.3.18	0900	Aveluy	Sopwith F.1 Camel C6733	Capt T. S. Sharpe (WiA/PoW), 73 Sqdn, RFC
72	27.3.18	1630	Foucaucourt	F.2B	Possibly aircraft of 11 Sqdn, RFC

No. Date	Time	Location	Aircraft	Crew and disposition
73 27.3.18	1635	northeast of Chuignolles	F.2B B1332	Capt H. R. Child (KiA), Lt A Reeve (KiA), 11 Sqdn, RFC
74 28.3.18	1230	east of Méricourt	A.W. F.K.8. C8444	2/Lt J. B. Taylor (KiA), 2/Lt E. Betley (KiA), 82 Sqdn, RFC
75 2.4.18	1235	east of Moreuil	R.E.8 A3868	2/Lt E. D. Jones (KiA), 2/Lt R. F. Newton (KiA), 52 Sqdn, RAF
76 6.4.18	1545	Villers-Brettoneux	Sopwith F.1 Camel D6491	Capt S. P. Smith (KiA), 46 Sqdn, RAF
77 7.4.18	1130	Hangard	S.E.5a	Possibly aircraft of 24 Sqdn, RAF
78 7.4.18	1205	east of Hill 104, north of Villers-Brettoneux	Sopwith F.1 Camel D6550	2/Lt A. V. Gallie 73 Sqdn, RAF

(16 April 1918: German time one hour ahead of Allied time)

No. Date	Time	Location	Aircraft	Crew and disposition
79 20.4.18	1840	south of Bois de Hamel	Sopwith F.1 Camel D6439	Maj R. R. Raymond-Barker, MC (KiA), 3 Sqdn, RAF
80 20.4.18	1843	Villers-Brettoneux	Sopwith F.1 Camel B7393	2/Lt D. G. Lewis (WiA/PoW), 3 Sqdn, RAF

RICHTHOFEN'S AIR COMBAT OPERATIONS MANUAL

Kogenluft cover message
Nr. 42360. Fl. II.

Supreme Headquarters, 19 April 1918

In the enclosure I bring to your attention a report submitted to me by the *Kommandeur* of *Jagdgeschwader I, Rittmeister Frhr* von Richthofen, in his original draft to the fighter units in the course of an exchange of experiences.

/s/ v. Hoeppner

GESCHWADER FLIGHTS

Boelcke divided his twelve pilots into two *Ketten* [flights] in autumn 1916. He made each five to six aeroplanes strong. Six to seven aeroplanes are best led, watched over and manoeuvred by one leader. In general this combat strength is sufficient even today. Regarding *Geschwader* flights, the British have the greatest experience and and are likewise mostly formed up this way.

During very strong British flight operations, however, one is forced to work with stronger *Geschwadern*; I take off with 30 to 40 machines [in a] *Geschwader* flight. (Reason for this: inferior German fighter aircraft or strong [enemy] *Geschwader* activity.)

The formation of such a large *Geschwader* is as follows:

The *Geschwader-Kommandeur* is the farthest out and lowest.

Staffel 1 to the left

Staffel 2 to the right

Staffel 3 [is] 100 metres above the *Kommandeur*

Staffel 4 at the [same] altitude as *Staffel* 3 [and] as the last behind the *Kommandeur*. The *Staffeln* form up a distance of 150 metres behind their *Staffel* leaders, [and] the *Staffel* leaders are behind their *Kommandeur*.

Before every take-off, without fail, one must discuss what one wants to do (e.g., the direction in which I will fly first). The discussion before take-off is at least just as important as the one after the flight.

It takes greater preparation for a *Geschwader* flight than for a *Staffel* flight. Accordingly, it is necessary to give notice prior to a *Geschwader* flight. Therefore I announce in the evening, for example, that beginning at 7 o'clock the next morning the *Geschwader* should keep itself ready for take-off. In this case I understand 'ready for take-off' to be: completely dressed for a flight, each pilot near or in his machine and not perchance in a ready room without being dressed in flightsuits. The mechanics are standing by their machines. The machines are fully ready for take-off. As I cannot know whether the enemy operation is set for 7 o'clock, it is possible that the entire *Geschwader*, fully suited-up, has to wait one or several hours at the airfield.

Take-off is ordered by telephone calls (when [the units] are at different airfields), or by ringing a bell (when they are are at one field). Each *Staffel* takes off, the last person being the *Staffel* leader, [and] the *Staffel* assembles at the lowest altitude (100 metres) over a point right or left of the flight direction previously designated by the *Kommandeur*. Then the *Kommandeur* takes off and sets out in the direction he ordered previously. The *Kommandeur* flies to where the assembled *Staffel* leaders have taken up their prescribed places, all on low throttle. So that the *Staffeln* do not come together in disorder, it is advisable that each *Staffel* has its own emblem marking. The *Kommandeur*'s aircraft must be very conspicuously painted. During the assembling [of units in the air] the *Kommandeur* may make no turns. He flies, therefore, as slowly as possible [and] mostly toward the Front. When the *Kommandeur* is satisfied that the *Geschwader* is closed up and no machines are straggling, then he can begin gradually to make good use of his machine's capability.

The altitude at which the *Kommandeur* flies is the altitude at which the *Geschwader* has to fly. It is absolutely false that a pilot flies 200 metres higher or 50 metres lower. In such a large formation (30 to 40 machines) the position of the *Staffel* leader must be maintained during the entire flight. It is recommended that, especially for beginners, there be an order of position within the *Staffel*. The order of position within a *Staffel* can be so diverse that it would be hard to give firm direction. In a well-organized flight there is usually a precise arrangement of individuals. I prefer to lead *Jagdstaffel 11* as if hunting on horseback across a field, then it is of no consequence if I turn, push ahead or pull back. If, however, the *Staffel* is not so well organized, an order of position is appropriate. If the *Geschwader* flight is not successful, in 99 cases it is the fault of the leading aircraft. He has to adjust his pace to that of the slowest [member] of his *Geschwader*. The *Staffel* leader flying next to the *Kommandeur* should not fly so close [to him] that it is impossible for him to make a sudden turn about. This hinders him very badly during an attack and in some circumstances ruins the success of the entire *Geschwader* flight. When an enemy formation is sighted, the leading aircraft has to increase its pace. This moment must be recognized immediately by every individual in the *Geschwader* in order that the very strong *Geschwader* does not disintegrate. When the *Kommandeur* makes a dive, at the same time the entire *Geschwader* must do the same with him. In doing this, tight spirals are to be avoided and turning in long, wide lines downward is to be sought. Unnecessary turns about are to be avoided. In every 180° turn the *Ketten* have to change their positions. By doing that, great confusion arises and it takes a long time under these circumstances before the formation is reassembled as ordered.

If the *Kommandeur* is out of action owing to unforeseen circumstances, his deputy will have been previously designated. A flare pistol signal signifies the transfer of leadership to his deputy.

Turning back by pilots whose engines are misfiring or the like is inappropriate.

The purpose of such a strong *Geschwader* flight is to destroy enemy formations. Attacks on individual aircraft by the *Kommandeur* are inappropriate in this case. Accordingly, these kinds of strong *Geschwader* flights are warranted in good weather only when brisk [enemy] flight operations are expected. The most favourable [situation] is when one can get between an intruding enemy formation and the Front. One cuts off its escape, gets above it and forces it to fight.

The continuous attack assures success. When the *Kommandeur* has decided to attack the opponent, then he flies toward the main body of the enemy formation. Shortly before the attack he slows his pace so that the *Geschwader*, which through fast flying or turning has become dispersed, is all assembled. Every individual counts the number of opponents at the moment he sights them. At the moment when the offensive begins, everyone must ascertain where all of the enemy aeroplanes are.

The *Kommandeur* should not focus his attention on aircraft pulling away; rather, he should always follow the main body; those that are falling away will be destroyed by the [friendly] aircraft following behind. By that time none [of the enemy] will have flown past the *Kommandeur*'s field of vision. Speed is regulated by throttling back and not by turning.

But at the moment the *Kommandeur* goes into a dive to swoop down on the enemy formation, under any circumstances it must be the aim of each and every [pilot] to be the first to engage the opposition.

Through the brunt of the first attack and through the absolute will of one of each of us to do battle, the enemy formation will be torn apart. When this is successful, then shooting down an enemy is only a matter of individual combat. Moreover, there is a danger that one could spoil the [surprise] effect of the attack and thereby give many British the opportunity to escape from the turmoil of battle. Therefore it must be rigorously noted that the one who is closest to an opponent is the one who alone shall fire at him. If two or more are within firing range (100 metres) of the same enemy, then the others must wait either to see if the first attacker has a gun jam and likewise further battle is hindered and he turns away, or [they must] seek a new opponent. I have seen scenes in which about ten to fifteen craft were involved in a fight and followed one Englishman down to the ground, while up above the enemy formation flew on undisturbed. One does not help [a comrade] by firing with him, rather than holding back in reserve. If, in the course of such a fight with a formation, individuals lose altitude, they should not wait until one of the opponents comes spinning down or is sent down in aerial combat and go after this already conquered opponent; rather, they should climb, flying toward the lines and attack one of the enemy craft escaping to the Front.

When such a large-formation battle succeeds and splits up into individual combats, the *Geschwader* is scattered about. Now it is not easy to regroup the *Geschwader*. In most cases, it is only by luck that scattered individuals are found, as the *Kommandeur* circles over the main battle scene or over previously determined, well-marked points. At this position, individuals join up directly with him. If he gathers sufficient strength the fighter mission will continue.

If the individual members of the *Staffel* no longer find the contact point, they may not loiter at the Front separately, but must fly home in order to avoid unnecessary casualties.

It is not absolutely necessary to get above an enemy formation. There could be a case when one can no longer climb above a very high flying enemy formation. Then one holds back with his aeroplanes in the proximity of the frontline positions, where one assumes the enemy will cross over the Front on the return flight. When the enemy formation comes, one follows along below it, [and] by diving at full speed and attempting to get up there by pulling up vertically, draw the enemy into battle. Very often the enemy takes up the fight. Especially an Englishman. It usually occurs to the last one to go down and then pull up his machine again. When an aeroplane [of ours] is attacked in this way, he evades the attack by going into a turn at full speed, while every other [comrade] tries to get above the opponent at this moment. In this way, usually one individual in the *Geschwader* succeeds in getting to the same altitude as the opponent and can try by pulling above him in aerial combat to gain superior altitude, engage him and send him crashing down. Such battles often tend to be minutes long. At the same time the *Kommandeur* must continually turn, the *Geschwader* is thrown into confusion and the formation that has been ordered no longer needs to be maintained; rather, everyone heads for the *Kommandeur* and tries by turning with his machine to gain altitude. Flying straight ahead at this moment is very dangerous, as the opponent waits at every instant to attack unnoticed from out of the sun.

Immediately after every *Geschwader* flight a discussion is the most important instructive activity. At that time, everything that happened during the flight from take-off to landing must be discussed. The questioning of individuals can be very useful for clarification.

Practice flights in *Geschwader* strength are not necessary when each individual *Staffel* flies well. *Geschwader* flights within the *Staffeln* for practice purposes in a forward area give no real practice. They can be used only by the enemy for instruction.

What I do with a *Jagdgeschwader* can be carried out likewise by a *Jagdgruppe*.

THE LEADER

From *Ketten-*, *Staffel-*, or *Geschwader* leaders I require the following: He knows his pilots thoroughly. The way the *Staffel* [functions] on the ground is the way it will be in the air.

Therefore, these are the prerequisites:

1. Comradeship
2. Strict discipline.

Everyone must show absolute trust in the leader in the air. If this trust is lacking, success is impossible from the outset. The *Staffel* gains trust by [the leader's] exemplary daring and the conviction that [he] sees everything and is able to cope with every situation.

The *Staffel* must develop diversity, i.e., not become accustomed to one position or the like; rather, individuals must learn to work together, so that each recognizes from the movement of the [next] aeroplane what the man at the joystick wants to do, especially when the leader proceeds to attack or a tight turn indicates an enemy attack from above to his fellow flyers.

Consequently, I consider a separation of such very compatible pilots to be very dangerous.

Within the *Staffel*, each [pilot] has a special distinguishing emblem on his machine, best [applied] on the rear part of the tail above and below. The leader takes off last, gathers his *Kette* at low altitude, [and] makes allowance for the worst machine. At the approach to the Front he becomes oriented to the overall flight operation, the enemy's and his own. At this time he may never let his *Staffel* go unobserved. There will always be this one or that one turning off course. They must be guided back by turning and throttling down.

The flight to the Front is no fighter mission. Rather, the leader flies to the Front preferably up the centre of his sector and satisfies himself about the enemy flight operations. Then, flying away from the Front, he seeks to attain the altitude of his opponents and tries, this time from out of the sun and over the Front, to attack the enemy. Thus, the fighter mission consists of thrusts over the lines and back again. When there is no enemy to be seen over there, then these thrusts over the lines have no purpose.

THE ATTACK

I distinguish between attacks on a formation and on a single aeroplane. The latter is the simplest. I am on the lookout for artillery-spotting aircraft, which mainly fly around on the other side of the lines and not at any great altitude. I keep in view five, six or ten of the single-seat aircraft at a time, observe their altitude and [course] changes, and whether or not they have high-flying escort aircraft. [Then I] fly away from the Front a bit and come back to the enemy lines at somewhat higher altitude than the enemy aircraft which I want to attack. As I distance myself from the Front, I must constantly keep them somewhat in view. The most favourable moment for attack against such an artillery-spotting aircraft is when the opponent flies toward the Front from the other side [of the lines]. Then, allowing for the wind factor (east to west), I drop down on him in a steep dive from out of the sun. Whoever is first in position against the enemy has the right to fire. The entire *Staffel* goes down with him. A so-called 'cover' at a higher altitude is a cover for cowardice. If the first [aircraft] has a gun jam, then the second one moves up, then the third, etc. Never do two fire at the same time. If the artillery-spotting aircraft is attentive and a surprise is not successful, in most cases he will go into a dive or make turns at the lowest altitude. Then, in most cases, pursuit is not accompanied by success, as I can never hit an opponent who is turning. Also there is no practical value in driving him away; [for,] in no more than five minutes he can resume his activity. In this case I consider it better to let him go, fly back to the Front again and repeat the manoeuvre. I have often bagged a British artillery-spotter during the third attack.

A *Geschwader* battle on this side of the lines is usually most successful, as I can force an opponent to land. A *Geschwader* battle on the other side is the most difficult, especially if there is an east wind. Then the leader may only clench his teeth, as he must usually count on heavy casualties. As long as I can be on the offensive, I can also carry out a *Geschwader* flight far on the other side. With an especially well-co-ordinated *Staffel* I can also attack a [numerically] superior enemy from above and on the other side. When a single-seater is put on the defensive, and if his guns jam, if he is separated from the *Staffel*, if his engine is shot up [or] is defective, if he has to come down low or something like that, [or] if far on the other side he faces a superior opponent who attacks him energetically, he is defenseless.

The leader may not pursue an intruding [enemy] formation; rather, he bores high up between the Front and the opponent until he has climbed above him and then cuts off the opponent's retreat. If the enemy formation intrudes far [into our territory] there is the danger that he will be lost from sight. It is the *Staffel* leader's concern that this does not occur. As I approach the enemy, I count the individual enemy flyers. In that way I avoid being surprised at the moment of attack. During the battle the leader should not lose the overall view of his *Kette* and the enemy formation. This [state of perfection] is achieved only after numerous *Geschwader* battles. This vision is a basic necessity and the most important point for a *Kette* leader.

HOW DO I TRAIN BEGINNERS?

Under my leadership six *Pour le Mérite* knights shot down their first to 20th [victims]. Before I let a beginner fly in combat, he must prepare the interior of his aeroplane so that it is best suited for him.

The main thing for a fighter pilot is the machine gun. He has to master it so that he recognizes the cause of a gun jam. When I come back home with a jammed gun, usually I can tell the mechanics precisely what is the matter with it. The machine guns will be practice fired on the ground until they are parallel to a target 150 metres out. The gunsight looks like so: (+)

When the pilot personally fires his machine gun(s) at the testing station, he will [also] practise on targets from the air until he has great proficiency at it.

The pilot, not the armourer or the mechanic, is responsible for having his machine gun fire faultlessly. There is no such thing as a gun jam! When it occurs, I blame only the pilot. A well-firing machine gun is better than a smooth-running engine.

While loading the ammunition belts he has to make sure that every single bullet is re-measured precisely with a special jig. The time to do this must be found (during bad weather or good weather at night).

I place little significant value on the skill of flying itself. I shot down my first 20 [victims] when I still had the greatest difficulties with flying itself. It does not matter whether [or not] one is an aerobatic artist. Furthermore, I prefer the one who can fly only in left-hand turns, but who goes after the enemy, to the diving and turning specialist from [the training centre at] Johannisthal, who attacks too cautiously.

I forbid the following being practised over the airfield: Looping, tailspins and turns at low altitude.

We need no aerial acrobats; rather, [we need] daredevils.

I insist on target practice in flight and at high altitude in tight turns and at full throttle.

If a pilot satisfies me in all of the points [just] discussed, then he will make the very image of the available types who can be trusted at the Front.

He knows the terrain without a map and the course to and from the Front by heart.

He must have practised many times long orientation flights at home, even during bad weather.

If he meets these requirements, then he flies the first few times 50 metres behind and to the left of me and pays attention to his leader.

For a beginner it is at least just as important to know what he has to do to keep from being shot down. The greatest danger for a single-seater is the surprise attack from behind. A very large number of our best and most experienced fighter pilots were surprised and shot down from behind. The opponent looks for the most favourable moment to attack the rearmost aircraft of a *Kette*. He dives on him from out of the sun and can cause him to go down with a few shots. Without fail, everyone must give the highest consideration [to the air space] behind him. One is almost never surprised from the front. Also during a battle one must especially bear in mind that one should not [let oneself] be attacked from behind. If a beginner is attacked from behind, however, under no circumstances should he try to escape by [just] slipping away. The best, and in my view the only correct method, is a sudden, very tight turn and then as quickly as possible take the offensive.

INDIVIDUAL COMBAT

Every *Geschwader* battle breaks up into individual combats. With one sentence one can cover the theme 'Air Combat Tactics', and that is: 'I approach the enemy until about 50 metres behind him, take aim at him carefully, [and] then the opponent falls'. Those are the words with which Boelcke brushed me off when I asked about his trick. Now I know that is the whole secret to shooting down [another aeroplane].

One does not need to be an aerobatic artist or a trick shooter; rather, [one has] to have the courage to fly right up to the opponent.

I make only one distinction between single-seaters and two-seaters. Whether the two-seater is an R.E.8 or a Bristol Fighter, the single-seater an S.E.5 or a Nieuport, it is all the same to me.

One attacks the two-seater from behind at great speed, in the same direction he is going. The only way to avoid the adroit observer's field of machine-gun fire is to stay calm and put the observer out of action with the first shots. If the opponent goes into a turn, I must be careful to not fly above the enemy aeroplane. A long aerial combat with a completely combat-ready, manoeuvrable two-seater is the most difficult. I fire only when the opponent flies straight ahead or, better yet, when he starts into a turn. But never right from the side or when the aeroplane is tilted on one wing. It is then that I try to harrass him by firing warning (streaks of phosphorous ammunition). I consider it to be very dangerous to attack a two-seater from the front. In the first place, one seldom encounters the opponent [this way]. One almost never makes him incapable of fighting [this way]. On the contrary, first of all I am within the field of fire of his fixed [forward-firing] machine gun, and then in the observer's [wider field of fire]. If I squeeze through below the two-seater and then want to make a turn, while in the turns I offer the observer the best target.

If one is attacked from the front by a two-seater, that is no reason for one to have to pull away; rather, in the moment when the opponent flies over and away, one can try to make a sudden sharp turn below the enemy aeroplane. If the observer has not been careful, one can pull up and easily shoot down the opponent. But if he has been careful and, while making the sharp turn, one lies well within his field of fire, it is often advisable not to fly further into the observer's range; rather, to turn away and make a new attack.

Individual combat against a single-seater is by far the easiest. If I am alone with an opponent and on this side [of the lines], I can shoot down the opponent unless I am hampered by a gun jam or an engine defect.

The simplest thing is to surprise a single-seater from behind, which very often succeeds. Then the main point is to make tighter turns and to stay above the opponent.

Whether the battle is on this side or the other, with a favourable wind an aerial combat like that will end with the opponent on this side until he is brought down to the ground. Then the opponent must decide whether he wants to land or risk flying straight ahead in order to make it to his own Front. If he does the latter, I sit behind the enemy and can easily shoot him down.

If I am attacked by a single-seater from above, I make it a point to never let up on the throttle; rather, to make all turns and dive at full speed. I turn toward the opponent and try by pulling up in each turn to attain the enemy's altitude and get the better of him. At the same time I never let the enemy get at my back. When I get the better of him, then the course of the battle is as it was during the first one. One can attack a single-seater calmly from the front. In spite of that, I believe that shooting down from in front, even a single-seater, is rare, as the moment at which one is at the right distance for combat is only a fraction of a second.

GENERAL PRINCIPLES

1. During an attack from behind at three-quarter speed, I must be careful that I never 'jump' past my slower opponent. If I do that, I make the greatest mistake. At the last moment I must adjust the speed of my own craft to that of the opponent.

2. One should never obstinately stay with an opponent who, through bad shooting or skilful turning, one has been unable to shoot down, when the battle lasts until it is far on the other side and one is alone and faced by a greater number of opponents.

THE MISSION

The mission, in my view, can be determined only by a fellow fighter pilot. For that reason we need older, experienced officers in fighter aviation.

During a defensive battle, I maintain that it is best that each *Gruppe* [army group] is assigned a *Jagdgruppe* [fighter group]. This *Jagdgruppe* is not bound strictly to the *Gruppe* sector, but its main purpose is to enable the working aircrews to perform their function and, in exceptional cases, to provide them with immediate protection.

Moreover, the *AOK* [Army High Command] has at its disposal a large number of *Jagdstaffeln* (*Geschwadern*), which by all means must be allowed to hunt freely and whose mission throughout is dedicated to [stopping] the enemy flight operations. With the help of Air Defence Officers and a large telephone reporting network and radio-telegraphy they will catch the enemy air operations in progress.

These *AOK* forces should not be dispersed for protection flights, escort flights or defensive patrols. Their mission is determined by the *Geschwader-Kommandeur* according to the instructions of the *Kofl* [individual Armies' Officers in Charge of Aviation].

DURING BREAKTHROUGH BATTLES AND MOBILE WARFARE

At the breakthrough itself, the collective fighter pilots of an Armee must be placed under one command and have precise orders, places and times, but not [specified] altitudes, and with that the time of the assault and the preparation of the troops will be supported immediately by the *Luftstreitkräfte*.

If the breakthrough battle turns into mobile warfare, then a mission that follows a timetable would be discarded completely. Also, the Englishmen will not be brought down by [our] being ready to take off from the fields; rather, only by frequent flying.

When a change of airfields is undertaken, from the very first moment each *Jagdgruppe* or *Geschwader* must work independently, as every telephone connection will be next to impossible. From the *General-Kommando* [Corps Headquarters] in the area they will learn about the situation hourly in the course of events. If a fighter pilot does not know the precise developments at the Front, then it is impossible for him to fight against the low-flying [enemy] infantry attack aircrews.

He will get his orientation of the air situation from the Air Defence Officer, who follows the movements of the troops and is in contact with the *Geschwader-Kommandeur* through radio messages. The *Jagdgeschwadern* and *Jagdgruppen* must take action independently with regard to allowing the missions [to proceed].

The only thing that must be ordered a day in advance in the *Armee* is:

I. The first [unit's] take-off is at dawn. The reason: In that way the other *Staffeln* have the opportunity to sleep-in.

II. The mid-day take-off of one to two [aircraft at a time]. The reason: If I call for a continous series of take-offs against the enemy by my *Jagdstaffeln*, they need an hour's break during the day to take a rest.

III. The third take-off ordered is the last one before the onset of darkness. This is necessary, as late in the evening it is not practical to fly any longer; rather, one has to get his machine ready for take-off on the coming day. Meanwhile, the only possibility is to hunt freely in order to make life easier for the infantry.

It is understood that hunting freely does not include scouting [for targets] in the areas of neighbouring *Armees* or in the support area behind the Front; rather, a destruction of the enemy within the closest area over the infantry battlefield and to fly as frequently as it can be done only with one's own *Staffeln*.

/s/ *Freiherr* v. Richthofen.

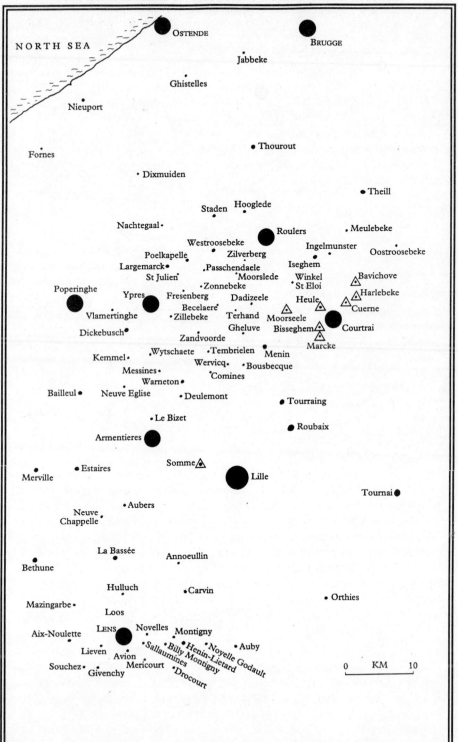

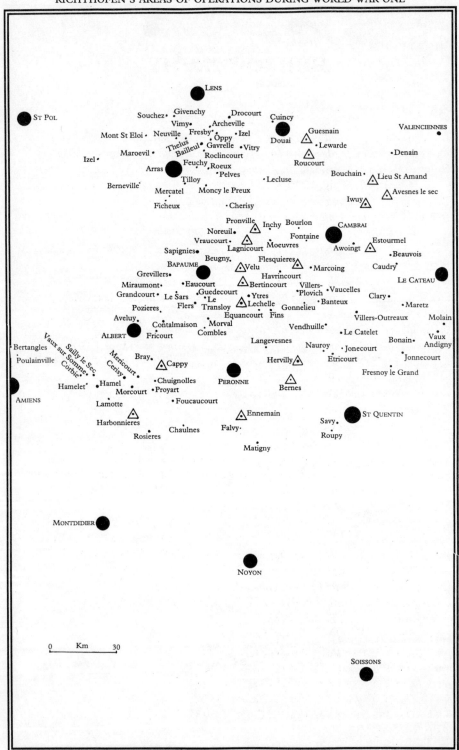

BIBLIOGRAPHY

BOOKS:

Bodenschatz, K., *Jagd in Flanderns Himmel - Aus den sechzehn Kampf-monaten des Jagdgeschwaders Freiherr von Richthofen*, Munich, 1935.

Böhme, E. (ed J. Werner), *Briefe eines deutschen Kampffliegers an ein junges Mädchen*, Leipzig, 1930.

Boelcke, O., *Hauptmann Boelckes Feldberichte*, Gotha, 1916.

Bowyer, C., *Albert Ball, VC*, London, 1977.

—— *For Valour - The Air VCs*, London, 1978.

—— *The Flying Elephants - A History of No. 27 Squadron*, London, 1972.

Bruce, J., *British Aeroplanes 1914-1918*, London, 1969.

Burge, C., *The Annals of 100 Squadron*, London, ca.1919.

Carisella, P. and Ryan, J., *Who Killed the Red Baron?*, Wakefield, Mass., 1969.

Cole, C. (ed), *Royal Air Force 1918*, London, 1968.

Collishaw, R., *Air Command - A Fighter Pilot's Story*, London, 1973.

Cutlack, F., *The Official History of Australia in the War of 1914-1918*, Vol VIII, Sydney, 1933.

Dickhuth-Harrach, G. (ed), *Im Felde unbesiegt*, Vol I, Munich, 1921.

Eberhardt, W. von (ed), *Unsere Luftstreitkräfte 1914-1918*, Berlin, 1930.

Esposito, V. (ed), *A Concise History of World War I*, New York, 1965.

Fipts, A., Faillie, M. & R., *Marke Wereledoorlog I*, Marke, 1984.

Gibbons, F., *The Red Knight of Germany*, New York, 1927.

Haehnelt, W., *Ehrentafel der im Flugdienst während des Weltkrieges gefallenen Offiziere der Deutschen Fliegerverbände*, Berlin, 1920.

Hartney, H., *Up and At 'Em*, Harrisburg, Pa., 1940.

von Hindenburg, P. [transl. F. Holt], *Out of My Life*, New York, 1921.

von Hoeppner, E., *Deutschlands Krieg in der Luft*, Leipzig, 1921.

Imrie, A., *Pictorial History of the German Army Air Service*, London, 1971.

—— *The Fokker Triplane*, London, 1992

Irving, D., *The Rise and Fall of the Luftwaffe*, New York, 1973

Italiaander, R., *Manfred Freiherr von Richthofen - Der beste Jagdflieger des grossen Krieges*, Berlin, 1938.

Johnstone, E. (ed), *Naval Eight*, London, 1931.

Jones, H., *The War in the Air*, Vol II, Oxford, 1928.

—— *The War in the Air*, Vol III, Oxford, 1931.

—— *The War in the Air*, Vol IV, Oxford, 1934.

—— *The War in the Air*, Vol V, Oxford, 1935.

—— *The War in the Air*, Vol VI, Oxford, 1937.

Kilduff, P., *Germany's First Air Force 1914-1918*, London, 1991.
Lamberton, W., *Fighter Aircraft of the 1914-1918 War*, Letchworth, 1960.
Lee, A. G., *No Parachute*, New York, 1970.
Louda, J., *Heraldry of the Royal Families of Europe*, New York, 1981.
Mittler, E., *Ehren-Rangliste des ehemaligen Deutschen Heeres*, Berlin, 1926.
Morris, A., *Bloody April*, London, 1967.
Nelson, W., *The Soldier Kings: The House of Hohenzollern*, New York, 1970.
Neumann, G. (ed), *Die deutschen Luftstreitkräfte im Weltkriege*, Berlin, 1920.
—— *In der Luft unbesiegt*, Munich, 1923.
Nowarra, H. and Brown, K., *von Richthofen and the Flying Circus*, Letchworth, 1964.
Nowarra, H., *Eisernes Kreuz und Balkenkreuz*, Mainz, 1968.
Obermaier, E., *Die Ritterkreuzträger der Luftwaffe* Vol I: *Jagdflieger*, Mainz, 1966.
—— *Die Rittenkreuzeträger der Luftwaffe*, Vol II: *Stuka- und Schlachtflieger*, Mainz, 1976.
O'Connor, N., *Aviation Awards of Imperial Germany in World War I*, Vol I - *The Aviation Awards of the Kingdom of Bavaria*, Princeton, 1988.
—— *Aviation Awards of Imperial Germany in World War I and the Men Who Earned Them*, Vol II - *The Aviation Awards of the Kingdom of Prussia*, Princeton, 1990.
Richthofen, K. von, *Mein Kriegstagebuch*, Berlin, 1937
Richthofen, M. von, *Ein Heldenleben*, Berlin, 1920.
—— *Der rote Kampfflieger*, Berlin, 1917.
—— *Der rote Kampfflieger*, Berlin, 1933.
—— [transl. P. Kilduff], *The Red Baron*, New York, 1969.
Ritter, H., *Der Luftkrieg*, Berlin, 1926.
Robertson, B., *Air Aces of the 1914-1918 War*, Letchworth, 1959.
—— *British Military Aircraft Serials 1911-1971*, London, 1971.
Schäfer, K., *Vom Jäger zum Flieger*, Berlin, 1918.
Schnitzler, E., *Carl Allmenröder der Bergische Kampfflieger*, Wald, 1927.
Schowalter, E., *Bad Kreuznach als Sitz des Grossen Hauptquartiers im Ersten Weltkrieg*, Bad Kreuznach, 1981.
Shores, C., Franks, N. and Guest, R., *Above the Trenches*, London, 1990.
Supf, P., *Das Buch der deutschen Fluggeschichte*, Vol. I, Stuttgart, 1958.
—— *Das Buch der deutschen Fluggeschichte*, Vol. II, Stuttgart, 1958.
Thüringen im Weltkrieg, Vol I, Leipig, 1921.
Udet, E., *Mein Fliegerleben*, Berlin, 1935.
Van Ishoven, A. (ed C. Bowyer), *The Fall of an Eagle*, London, 1977.
"Vigilant" [C. Sykes], *Richthofen - The Red Knight of the Air*, London, (n.d.).
—— *German War Birds*, London, 1931.
Wenzl, R., *Richthofen-Flieger*, Freiburg im Breisgau, (ca 1930).
Wheeler-Bennett, J., *The Forgotten Peace - Brest-Litovsk*, New York, 1939.
Winter, P. *Gotha als Fliegerstadt in der Vergangenheit*, Gotha, (ca. 1935).

Wise, S., *Canadian Airmen and the First World War*, Toronto, 1980.

Wolff'schen Telegr.-Bureaus, *Amtliche Kriegs-Depeschen nach Berichten des*, Vol 6, Berlin, (n.d.).

Woodman, H., *Early Aircraft Armament - The Aeroplane and the Gun up to 1918*, London, 1989.

Zeidelhack, M. (ed), *Bayerische Flieger im Weltkrieg*, Munich, 1919.

Zuerl, W., *Pour le Mérite-Flieger*, Munich, 1938.

DOCUMENTS:

AOK 1. Armee Berichte, published in the field, 1916.

AOK 2. Armee Berichte, 1916.

AOK 3. Armee Berichte, 1915.

AOK 5. Armee Berichte, 1916.

Jagdstaffel 11 Berichte, 1917, 1918.

Jagdstaffel 12 Berichte, 1916.

Kampfgeschwader 2 OHL Berichte, 1916.

Kommandeur der Flieger der 1. Armee Berichte, 1916.

Kommandeur der Flieger der 4. Armee Wochenberichte, 1917.

Kommandeur der Flieger der 6. Armee Wochenberichte, 1917.

Kommandeur der Flieger der 7. Armee Fliegertagesmeldungen, 1918.

Kogenluft. *Chef des Feldflugwesens Berichte*, Berlin, 1916.

—— *Nachrichtenblatt der Luftstreitkräfte* Vol I, Berlin, 1917.

—— *Nachrichtenblatt der Luftstreitkräfte* Vol II, Berlin, 1918.

Kriegsministerium (organisational manual), *Teil 10 Abschnitt B, Flieger-Formationen*, Berlin, 1918.

Kriegsministerium Berichte, Berlin, 1917.

Richthofen Combat Reports (Translations), Public Record Office, London, (n.d.) (PRO File Air 1/686/21/13/2250 XC15183).

Royal Air Force, *Communiqués*, in the field, 1918, (PRO Air 1/2097/207/14/1).

—— *No. 3 Squadron Combat Reports*, 1918, (PRO Air 1/1216/204/5/2634/3 Sqdn).

—— *No. 73 Squadron Combat Reports*, 1918, (PRO Air 1/1226/204/5/2634/73 Sqdn).

—— *No. 209 Squadron Combat Reports*, 1918, (PRO Air 1/1228/204/5/2634/209 Sqdn).

—— *No. 209 Squadron Record Book*, 1918, (PRO Air 1/1858/204/214/6).

Royal Flying Corps, *Communiqués*, in the field, 1916, 1917, 1918.

—— *No. 1 Squadron Combat Reports*, in the field, 1917, (PRO Air 1/1216/204/5/2634/1 Sqdn).

—— *No. 2 Squadron Combat Reports*, 1917, (PRO Air 1/1216/204/5/2634/2 Sqdn).

—— *No. 19 Squadron Combat Reports*, 1916, 1917, (PRO Air 1/1220/204/5/2634/19 Sqdn).

—— *No. 19 Squadron Record Book*, 1917,
(PRO Air 1/1486/204/37/1 - 7).
—— *No. 29 Squadron Combat Reports*, 1917,
(PRO Air 1/1221/204/5/2634/29 Sqdn).
—— *No. 40 Squadron Combat Reports*, 1917,
(PRO Air 1/1222/204/5/2634/40 Sqdn).
—— *No. 45 Squadron Record Book*, 1917.
(PRO Air 1/1565/204/80/47).
—— *Periodical Summary of Aeronautical Information*, in the field, 1917.
—— *Summary of Air Intelligence*, 1918.
—— *War Diary*, in the field, 1917, 1918,
(PRO Air 1/1185 - 1188/204/5/2595).
—— *Western Front Casualty List*, in the field, 1916, 1917, 1918,
(PRO Air 1/967/204/5/1097 - 969/204/5/1102).
Royal Naval Air Service, *No. 1 Squadron Combat Reports*, in the field, 1917,
(PRO Air 1/1216/204/5/2634/1 Naval Sqdn).
—— *No. 10 Squadron Combat Reports*, 1917,
(PRO Air 1/1219/204/5/2634/10 Naval Sqdn).
Stabsoffizier der Fliegertruppen der 1. Armee Berichte, 1916.
Stabsoffizier der Fliegertruppen der 6. Armee Berichte, 1916.

ARTICLES, MONOGRAPHS AND PERIODICALS:

Aeronautics, New York, 1916.
Bailey, F. and Chamberlain, P., "L'Escadrille de Chasse Spa 57," *Cross & Cockade Journal*, 1985.
——, Duiven, R. and Manning, R., "A Short History of No. 62 Squadron, RFC/RAF," *Cross & Cockade Journal*, 1976.
Bodenschatz, K., "Das Jagdgeschwader Frhr v.Richthofen Nr 1 im Verbande der 2. Armee," *In der Luft unbesiegt*, Munich, 1923.
Bruce, J., "The Fokker Monoplanes," *Aircraft Profiles*, 1965.
—— "The Fokker Dr.I," *Aircraft Profiles*, 1965.
Chamberlain, P. and Bailey, F. "An Analysis of German Balloon Claims on the Western Front During 1917," *Cross & Cockade Journal*, 1975.
—— "History of Escadrille Spa 93," *Cross & Cockade (Great Britain) Journal*, 1978.
Chionchio, J., "Defeat by Design," *Air Enthusiast*, 1989.
Cron, H. (ed. P. Grosz), "Organization of the German Luftstreitkräfte," *Cross & Cockade Journal*, 1966.
Duiven, R. and Sands, J., "The Original Flying Circus: The Combat Log of Royal Prussian Jagdstaffel 11," *Over the Front*, 1987.
Duiven, R., "German Jasta and Jagdgeschwader C.O.s 1916-1918," *Over the Front*, 1988.
Evans, W., "Manfred Freiherr von Richthofen Victory List," *Over the Front*, 1992.
Ferko, A., *Fliegertruppe 1914-1918*, Salem, Ohio, 1980.

—— "The Origin of the First Jagdstaffeln," *Cross & Cockade Journal*, 1965.

—— "Guynemer's Last Patrol," *Cross & Cockade Journal*, 1974.

—— and Grosz, P., "The Circus Master Falls: Comments on a Newly Discovered Photograph," *Cross & Cockade Journal*, 1968.

Flanagan, B. (ed), "Lieut. Wilfred 'Wop' May's Account," *Cross & Cockade Journal*, 1982.

Gray, P., "The Albatros D.I-D.III," *Aircraft Profiles*, 1966.

—— "The Pfalz D.III," *Aircraft Profiles*, 1965.

Grosz, P. and Ferko, A., "The Fokker Dr.I - A Reappraisal," *Air Enthusiast*, 1978.

Grosz, P., "The Agile and Aggressive Albatros," *Air Enthusiast*, 1976.

Hayes, S., "Schweidnitz Revisited," *Over the Front*, 1991.

Hitchins, F., "Enemy Aircraft in German Hands, June 1916-September 1918," *Cross & Cockade Journal*, 1969.

Imrie, A., "Die Gebrüder Gabriel," *Cross & Cockade Journal*, 1962.

Joly, P. (transl. S.A. Wiliams), "Victory List of Capitaine Georges Guynemer," *Cross & Cockade Journal*, 1971.

Kilduff, P., "Albert Dossenbach Baden's *Pour le Mérite* Ace," *Over the Front*, 1989.

—— "Combat Fliers of Baden," *Over the Front*, 1989.

Kriegs-Echo, Berlin, 1916, 1917, 1918.

Lampel, P., "Als Gast beim Rittmeister Frhr. v.Richthofen," *In der Luft unbesiegt*, Munich, 1923.

McGuire, R. (ed.), "Documents Relating to Richthofen's Last Battle," *Over the Front*, 1987.

Miller, T. and Puglisi, W., "Jasta B," *Cross & Cockade Journal*, 1968.

Nowarra, H., "Ernst Freiherr von Althaus," *Cross & Cockade Journal*, 1961.

—— "Capt Ball's Last Flight," *Cross & Cockade Journal*, 1963.

O'Dwyer, W., "Post-Mortem: Richthofen," *Cross & Cockade Journal*, 1969.

Osten, G. von der (ed L. Zacharias), "Memoirs of World War I With Jagdstaffeln 11 and 4," *Cross & Cockade Journal*, 1974.

Pearce, M., "Aéronautique Militaire," *Cross & Cockade International Journal*, 1991.

Puglisi, W., "German Aircraft Down in British Lines," Parts 1 and 2, *Cross & Cockade Journal*, 1969.

Revell, A., "Aftermath," *Cross & Cockade (Great Britain) Journal*, 1975.

Richthofen, L. von, "Das letzte Mal an der Front, Juli-August 1918," *Im Felde unbesiegt*, Vol I, Munich, 1921.

Rogers, L., "RFC and RAF Casualties, 1917-1918," *Cross & Cockade (Great Britain) Journal*, 1974, 1975, 1977.

—— "RFC and RAF Casualties, 1917-1918," *Cross & Cockade (Great Britain) Journal*, 1975.

Schmeelke, M., "Leutnant der Reserve Otto Brauneck," *Cross & Cockade*

Journal, 1983.

—— "Leutnant der Reserve Otto Brauneck - Part II," *Over the Front,* 1986.

Skelton, M., "Jagdgeschwader Nr. 1 Pilots," *Cross & Cockade Journal,* 1977.

Terry, G., "The Development of Dornier Landplanes 1914-1918," *Cross & Cockade (Great Britain) Journal,* 1981.

Vann, R. and Bowyer, R., "XV Squadron 1915-1919," *Cross & Cockade (Great Britain) Journal,* 1973.

Vann, R. and Waugh, C., "Overseas and United Kingdom Presentation Aircraft 1914-1918," *Cross & Cockade (Great Britain) Journal,* 1983.

Warne, J., "60 Squadron - A Detailed History," *Cross & Cockade (Great Britain) Journal,* 1980.

Waugh, C., "A Longer History of No. 21 Squadron," *Cross & Cockade Journal,* 1983.

Winans, D., "World War I Aircraft Fuels and Lubricating Oils," *Cross & Cockade Journal,* 1961.

Wright, P., "Richthofen's 23rd - Or Was It?" *Cross & Cockade (Great Britain) Journal,* 1983.

Wynne, H., "The Richthofen Museum," *Over the Front,* 1991.

Zickerick, W., "Verlustliste der deutschen Luftstreitkräfte im Weltkriege," *Unsere Luftstreitkräfte 1914-1918,* Berlin, 1930.

OTHER SOURCES:

Adam, R. Correspondence.

Baur, H. Correspondence.

Delang, K. Correspondence.

Falkenhayn, F. von. Correspondence.

INDEX

II.Personnel

37; first airfight, 37-38; unofficial aerial victory, 39; meeting Oswald Boelcke, 39-40; combat pilot training, 40-41; assigned to *Kagohl 2*, first successful aerial combat, 44; first crash, 46; bombing missions over Russia, 47-48; selected by Boelcke for *Jasta 2*, 49; first confirmed aerial victory, 51-52; participation in Boelcke's funeral, 56; decorated by the Duke of Saxe-Coburg-Gotha, 60-61; aerial combat with Major L.G. Hawker, VC, 62-63; named to command *Jasta 11*, 67; awarded *Orden Pour le Mérite*, 67-68; shot down, uninjured, 79-80; promoted to *Oberleutnant*, 83; promoted to *Rittmeister*, 91; Boelcke's victory score equalled, 92; *Jasta 11* renamed *Jagdstaffel Richthofen*, 98; four victories in one day, 99-102; first visit with the *Kaiser*, 108-111; hero's welcome in Schweidnitz, 117-118; initial work on *Der rote Kampfflieger*, 119; hunting at the Pless estate, 7, 120-121; second visit with the *Kaiser*, 125-126; appointed commander of *Jagdgeschwader I*, 128; shot down, hospitalized, 132-133; complaints about *Hptmn* Bufe, 136-137; returned to active duty, 138; prohibited from flying in combat, 148; forced landing, 149; on leave in Thuringia, 152, 154-155; on leave in Schweidnitz, 156-157; at Prestien's wedding, 158-159; back at the Front, Fokker Triplane troubles, 159, 163-164; last Christmas at the Front, 169-170; attending Brest-Litovsk peace talks, 170-171; at aircraft type tests in Berlin, 172-173; final visit to Schweidnitz, 173-175; making a balloon ascension, 176-177; more Triplane troubles, 181-182; selects Udet to join *Jasta 11*, 186; Spring 1918 offensive, 187-190; *Reichstag* visitors, 190-191; awarded Order of the Red Eagle, 194; evidence of combat fatigue, 198; shot down and killed, 201-203; funeral, 204-205; memorial service in Berlin, 210-212; postwar official state funeral, 220; reburial in western Germany, 220

Richthofen's aerial victories: *No 1*, 51-52; *No 2*, 53; *No 3*, 54; *No 4*, 54; *No 5*, 55; *No 6*, 55; *No 7*, 59, 75; *No 8*, 60, 75; *No 9*, 62, 75; *No 10*, 62, 75; *No 11*, 62-63; *No 12*, 64, 76; *No 13*, 65; *No 14*, 65; *No 15*, 66; *No 16*, 66; *No 17*, 69-70; *No 18*, 70; *No 19*, 72; *No 20*, 74; *No 21*, 74; *No 22*, 78; *No 23*, 78; *No 24*, 78-79; *No 25*, 80; *No 26*, 81; *No 27*, 82; *No 28*, 82; *No 29*, 82-83; *No 30*, 83, 85; *No 31*, 83, 85; *No 32*, 87-88; *No 33*, 88; *No 34*, 88, 103; *No 35*, 89, 103; *No 36*, 89, 103; *No 37*, 91, 103; *No 38*, 91-92, 103; *No 39*, 92, 104; *No 40*, 92, 104; *No 41*, 94, 104; *No 42*, 95, 104; *No 43*, 95, 104; *No 44*, 95, 104; *No 45*, 96; *No 46*, 97; *No 47*, 98, 104; *No 48*, 99, 104; *No 49*, 100; *No 50*, 100; *No 51*, 100, 105; *No 52*, 101; *No 53*, 127, 142; *No 54*, 127, 142; *No 55*, 127-128; *No 56*, 128, 142; *No 57*, 130; *No 58*, 146, 159; *No 59*, 149; *No 60*, 150, 160; *No 61*, 151; *No 62*, 166, 178; *No 63*, 167-168; *No 64*, 182-183, 191; *No 65*, 184, 192; *No 66*, 186-187; *No 67*, 188, 192; *No 68*, 188, 192; *No 69*, 188-189, 192; *No 70*, 189, 192; *No 71*, 14; *No 72*, 17; *No 73*, 17, 18; *No 74*, 190, 192; *No 75*, 193, 206; *No 76*, 196, 206; *No 77*, 197; *No 78*, 197; *No 79*, 199, 207; *No 80*, 199, 207

Richthofen, *Gen* Manfred *Frhr* von, 23, 24, 211

Richthofen, Siegfried *Frhr* von, 32, 35

Richthofen, Wolfram *Frhr* von (1st cousin), 27, 206

Richthofen, *Ltn (Gen-Feldmrsl)* Wolfram *Frhr* von, 196, 201, 202, 206, 221

Riehl, *Ltn.d.Res* Wilhelm, 76

Riezenstein, *Oberst* von, 82

Robertson, Lt C.E., 104, 226

Robinson, VC, Capt W.L., 89

Roe, A.V., 120

Rothenbiller, *Prof.Dr* Franz J., 12

Rudorffer, *Maj* Erich, 10

Rupprecht, Crown Prince of Bavaria, 128

Russell, Lt W.O., 104, 226

Salzmann, *Hptmn* Erich von, 125, 155-156

Saundby, MC, Lt (Air Vice Mrsl Sir) Robert, 62

Saunders, Fl-Sub-Lt R.G., 142

Schack, *Rittm*, 60

Schäfer, *Ltn* Karl-Emil, 69, 71, 72, 73, 74, 80, 81, 87, 88, 91, 92, 95, 122, 125, 127, 141

Schaeffler, *Gefr*, 140

Scheele, *Ltn* Franz Christian von, 47

Schickfuss und Neudorff, *Rittm.d.Res* Alexander von, 34